LEAGUE
Publications Ltd

RUGBY LEAGUE '99-2000
Days of Thunder

Tim Butcher
Martyn Sadler
Tony Hannan
Daniel Spencer
Terry Liberopoulos

Malcolm Andrews
Vicky Matthers
Gareth Walker
Harry Edgar

League Publications Ltd

First published in Great Britain in 1999 by
League Publications Limited
Wellington House
Briggate
Brighouse
West Yorkshire HD6 1DN

A CIP catalogue record for this book is available from the British Library
ISBN 1 901347 06 0

Designed and Typeset by League Publications Limited
Printed by Redwood Books, Trowbridge, Wiltshire

Contributing Editor	Tim Butcher
Contributors	Tony Hannan
	Malcolm Andrews
	Martyn Sadler
	Terry Liberopoulos
	Gareth Walker
	Harry Edgar
Stats Editor/Design	Daniel Spencer
Picture Editor	Vicky Matthers
Photographers	Andrew Varley
	Gareth Copley
	Vicky Matthers
	Andy Howard
	Col Whelan
	Simon Wilkinson

CONTENTS

ACKNOWLEDGMENTS

Rugby League '99-2000, is the fourth in League Pubications Ltd's annual series of Rugby League Yearbooks, and again would not have been possible without the hard work and inspiration of a number of people.

As ever, we are indebted to all our Rugby League Express, Total Rugby League and Rugby League World writers and contributors who regularly provide us - and our growing band of readers - with the liveliest and most accurate match reports and news stories all through the year. Their continued efforts are much appreciated.

In particular, we would like to thank Mike Latham, Trevor Hunt, Mike Rylance, Raymond Fletcher, Tony Beattie, Phil Caplan, Andy Donnelly, Neil Fissler, Andy Wilson, Dave Hadfield, Nathan Ashurst, Dave Fleming, Mike Sterriker, Michael Bennison, Richard Newlove and Steve Kilgallon.

The statistical review section was once again painstakingly put together by Daniel Spencer, and thanks also to that other "statto", Rob Lowe at Atlantis Communications, for his invaluable help throughout 1999. Ray Fletcher's added assistance in this area is also a regular boon, as is Terry "The Libber" Liberopoulos's global expertise.

The majority of the pictures are again from the files of League Publications Ltd and Varley Picture Agency (Leeds). Additional photography is by Andy Howard and Simon Wilkinson. Col Whelan looked after things splendidly in Australia, and we apologise for frequently waking him in the early hours of the morning.

Help from the Rugby Football League, Super League (Europe), the Association of Premiership Clubs, BARLA and the Rugby League Conference has again been greatly appreciated at many times throughout the season.

And thanks again go to all the players and coaching staff at all our clubs and their fans for providing another season of top drawer entertainment. We can't wait for more in the new millennium.

Oh, and our long-suffering other halves deserve a mention too. We'll be home soon. Honest.

FOREWORD

Professional Rugby League has now completed its fourth season as a summer sport, and it is no coincidence that we at League Publications Limited, the country's leading publisher of Rugby League newspapers, magazines and books, are producing our fourth yearbook to chart the progress of this wonderful sport as it goes forward into the new Millennium.

As always, the game has enjoyed a turbulent year in 1999, both on and off the field.

While the action on the field was spectacular in 1999, the game's key decision makers seem unable to match the excellence that players serve up week by week on the pitch.

While we were watching wonderful matches almost every week, whether in the JJB Super League, the Northern Ford Premiership, the Silk Cut Challenge Cup, the various amateur competitions, the Australian National Rugby League Championship, or in the international arena, Rugby League's governing bodies seemed to be enveloped in a permanent state of chaos.

Sadly, in 1999 the game was beset by division, mistrust, outdated parochial thinking, and financial mismanagement, all of which grabbed the headlines, at the expense of some more enlightened work being done behind the scenes, not least on the Lincoln World Cup 2000.

It all climaxed shortly before the deadline for publishing this yearbook, when the Super League clubs agreed to the proposed merger of Hull Sharks and Gateshead Thunder, with the merged club set to move to the Boulevard, Hull's home ground, and Gateshead fans being left high and dry in the north-east, without a team to support in the 2000 season.

The RFL has invested in junior development in the north-east for roughly ten years. And with the Thunder having attracted a hard core fan-base in its first year of more than 3,000, the sight of the Super League clubs pulling the plug on Gateshead was shameful. Gateshead may have lost, as the club claimed, £700,000 during 1999, but that figure should have surely been regarded as the start-up costs of the operation, and as an investment in goodwill, the benefits of which would have been reaped in future years. Surely Super League should have been ready for losses, and should have kept its nerve in the north-east.

The Gateshead fiasco showed up the game for its lack of long-term planning, and its lack of any coherent strategy for expanding its audience. Tragically, with the demise of Sheffield Eagles as a Super League club, only London Broncos survive outside the M62 corridor.

It isn't just in Super League, however, that the game seems unable to govern itself properly. The Northern Ford Premiership clubs, in a paroxysm of self-doubt, have panicked and moved their competition back to winter, starting their 2000 season on Boxing Day, with their Grand Final scheduled for late July. And we had the sight of Hunslet Hawks winning the NFP Grand Final in a thrilling match against Dewsbury Rams, then being turned down for Super League by an Independent Franchise Panel which had been set up to consider their application.

That was followed by legal action by the Hawks against the RFL, as the joy of winning their competition quickly dissipated in frustration.

And it isn't just in Great Britain that chaos reigns supreme.

In Australia there was also a wonderful season on the field, which climaxed with Melbourne Storm's historic and compelling late win against St George-Illawarra Dragons in the NRL Grand Final. But the NRL refused to compromise in its determination to reduce its 17-team competition to 14 teams for the year 2000. Manly and North Sydney, long time bitter enemies, found themselves forced into a merger, as did the historic Balmain and Western Suburbs clubs.

The one club left out in the cold was South Sydney, Australia's most historic club, who have not been included in the 2000 competiton, but who have promised to pursue legal action to get back in the competition. The club has many sympathisers in Sydney, and the saga of their unnecessary dismissal is set once more to put money into the pockets of the lawyers.

Rugby League has always had to survive incompetent, dim-witted and parochial rulers, and no doubt it will continue to do so in future.

Martyn Sadler
Chairman, League Publications Limited

INTRODUCTION

This was the year St Helens, Leeds Rhinos, Hunslet Hawks, Melbourne Storm and Australia won the big trophies in 1999.

But the real winners were Rugby League fans the world over, as the game served up another year of wonderful action-packed drama, with outstanding performances, momentous achievements, and heartstopping triumph and tragedy in equal measure.

It was the year when Ellery Hanley returned to British Rugby League as a rookie club coach. Hanley started with a winning streak, then fell out with the St Helens directors, was suspended, then reinstated, before walking off with the big prize. Saints took out the JJB Super League Grand Final by surviving an onslaught from the Bradford Bulls and coming back to win the game at Old Trafford by a whisker.

It was the year when Sean Long made his mark on the game, as the young Saints star held his nerve superbly to kick the final conversion from the touchline for that amazing Grand Final win. It was hardly a surprise that Long's Super League colleagues voted him the player of the season.

It was the year when Leeds Rhinos finally satisfied the yearning of their supporters for a major trophy, when they triumphed against London Broncos in the Challenge Cup final. And what a personal triumph for their coach Graham Murray, who would return to Australia at the end of the season.

And what about the game itself, when a young man called Leroy Rivett broke all previous records by scoring four tries at Wembley, enough to win him the Lance Todd Trophy, and Richard Branson broke all the sartorial rules by leading his Broncos team out of the tunnel wearing blue jeans.

And who could forget the two Silk Cut Challenge Cup semi-finals, when the Rhinos and the Bulls collided explosively at Huddersfield's McAlpine Stadium, and the city slickers of London Broncos grabbed a late winner with a try by Steele Retchless against Castleford Tigers at Headingley.

It was the year when Gateshead Thunder came to the Super League party, gained some memorable wins, particularly at home to St Helens and against Wigan at an 'On the Road' game at Edinburgh, before migrating to Hull in controversial circumstances at the end of the season.

It was the year when Wakefield Trinity came back into the big time, as the newly promoted club, now named the Wildcats, started as 2000/1 outsiders, but ended with ten wins from 30 starts, fulfilling their coach Andy Kelly's objective at the start of the season.

It was the year of Castleford Tigers' charge into the top five, and almost

St Helens and Bradford Bulls take the field at Old Trafford as the Grand Final
brings down the curtain on the 1999 domestic season

into the Super League Grand Final, as they fell at the final hurdle at St Helens, but not before their coach Stuart Raper had done a wonderful job to thrill the growing crowds at Wheldon Road. Their skipper Adrian Vowles was a highly deserving winner of the 1999 JJB Man of Steel award.

Several top coaches departed from the scene in 1999, none more significant that 1998 Coach of the Year John Pendlebury, who left Halifax Blue Sox after a mid-season financial crisis. Andy Gregory ended his tenure at Salford; Dan Stains quit the Broncos after leading them to Wembley, and his successor Les Kiss quit at the end of the season; Peter Walsh got the push at Hull Sharks; John Monie surprisingly was pushed out at Wigan, and his successor Andy Goodway followed him at the end of the season; and Malcolm Reilly departed from Huddersfield Giants after the club merged with Sheffield Eagles at the end of the season.

There was some significant transfer activity before, during and after the 1999 season.

Henry Paul moved from Wigan to Bradford Bulls to join his brother Robbie, and won the Harry Sunderland Trophy as the outstanding player in the Grand Final, despite being on the losing side.

St Helens signed Kiwi Test star Kevin Iro from Auckland, and watched him score the winning try for them at Old Trafford. The Rhinos signed Sheffield's Test star Keith Senior in time for the play-offs, but then bombed out with two successive defeats against St Helens and Castleford.

It was the year of Hunslet Hawks in the Northern Ford Premiership, as the south Leeds club finished the season in second place, and went on to defeat Dewsbury Rams in a Grand Final at Headingley that demonstrated that wonderful rugby wasn't restricted to Super League in 1999. Hooker Richard Pachniuk was their outstanding player in 1999, and was linked with several

Super League clubs, although scrum-half Latham Tawhai won the Tom Bergin Trophy as man of the match in the final.

On the international front, Great Britain and Ireland, as they are now called, performed abysmally in the inaugural Tri-Nations tournament in Australia and New Zealand, going down heavily to both home nations, and having to play the New Zealand Maoris in a curtain-raiser to the final of that competition. The Australians won the tournament in a thrilling game that ended with a call by the video referee on the final whistle denying the Kiwis victory.

On a personal level in 1999, Andy Farrell's record breaking run of Super League appearances came to an end at Bradford in May, when he made his 80th successive appearance for Wigan, but then had to pull out of the next game with an injured ankle.

Iestyn Harris set a new Super League record, with 343 points, from 18 tries, 135 goals and a field goal, and against Huddersfield Giants he set another record, with 42 points in the Rhinos' 86-6 slaughter of the Giants.

Perhaps the most thrilling game of all in 1999 was the Grand Final in Australia, when Melbourne won virtually on the final hooter with a penalty try in front of a new world record crowd of 107,558 supporters. The Storm, in only their second season, had an unforgettable year, and one of their Grand Final heroes, Tawera Nikau, will join Aussie legend Alfie Langer at Warrington for the 2000 season.

There's an awful lot to look forward to in the new Millennium.

Tim Butcher
Contributing Editor
Rugby League 1999-2000

1
PERSONALITIES OF '99

Adrian Vowles

Adrian Vowles wears squad number 13 for the Castleford Tigers.

And 13 is anything but an unlucky number down Wheldon Road, as the Tigers fans would be the first to agree. They are indeed lucky to have a captain like Vowles, the 1999 JJB Man of Steel - labelled Mr Indestructible by his coach Stuart Raper - who led from the front for the Tigers' most successful season in Super League.

Vowles demonstrates all the qualities needed by a modern Rugby League captain. The ability to inspire his teammates, to lead from the front, to make sure that his team takes the right options on the field, and to set an example for others to follow, are all traits of Adrian Vowles. Find a good captain, and you'll often find a good team, and in 1999 the Tigers were certainly that.

But things didn't always look that good. Vowles, who hails from Charleville, a remote Queensland outback town some ten hours from Brisbane, joined Castleford in the dark days of 1996, when the club was struggling to come to terms with summer rugby and Super League. He wasn't an instant success, and some sections of the Castleford crowd questioned why the club had brought him half way round the world, although no one would question their skipper's credentials now.

Previously with the Gold Coast and then the North Queenland Cowboys,

Vowles greatest honour in the game is a State of Origin appearance for Queensland in Melbourne in 1994. But this year he very nearly exceeded that achievement on two fronts, leading his team to semi-final defeats in both the Silk Cut Challenge Cup, in that dramatic game against London Broncos, and in the JJB Super League play-offs, against Ellery Hanley's St Helens at Knowsley Road.

Earlier in the season Vowles took over the record from Andy Farrell of having made the longest number of successive appearances in Super League, having turned out on 58 successive occasions, before a groin injury finally caught up with him.

He was a worthy Man of Steel, however, and you can guarantee that, with him at the helm, the Tigers will once again be a highly competitive outfit in 2000.

Leon Pryce

Former England Schoolboys captain Leon Pryce celebrated his 18th birthday on 9 October, the day when Bradford Bulls appeared in the JJB Super League Grand Final at Old Trafford.

Sadly for Pryce, his birthday celebrations never hit top gear, as the Bulls went down in a compelling final to St Helens. Two weeks later, however, he was making his England debut, as John Kear's team beat the French 50-20 in Hull, with Pryce, in for Leeds Rhinos' Paul Sterling, scoring the first try of the game and playing with typical poise and assurance. Other honours will surely follow for the young Bulls star, who is the epitome of the resurgence that has taken place at Odsal in the last few seasons, symbolising the club's new emphasis on youth development.

The son of former York and Hunslet forward Dennis, he is without doubt the most exciting talent to emerge at Odsal since Ellery Hanley. Pryce was the first Bradford-born England schools captain for a generation.

He made his Bulls debut at Salford towards the end of the 1998 season, at the tender age of 16, and in 1999 he became a regular in the Bulls side on the wing, for much of the time replacing the injury troubled Tevita

Vaikona. He made a total of 21 starts, plus another four off the bench, and scored an impressive 13 tries.

An elusive runner with blistering pace, Pryce, despite serving his first team apprenticeship on the wing, in time is expected to mature into a centre or stand-off. And next year he is almost certain to be playing for his country in the World Cup, as England coach John Kear recognised immediately after Pryce's international debut.

"His attitude, his application, his commitment and his Rugby League intelligence have been first class," said Kear.

"He did himself a lot of favours by the way he conducted himself in the England camp, and to come up with a performance like that on his international debut was outstanding."

Sean Long

The ability to carve up even the strongest defences with a quick turn of pace, a terrific partnership with his halfback partner Tommy Martyn, and a Rugby League brain that seems to work at lightning speed, are the factors that make Sean Long such an outstanding player.

Judged the Super League Player of the Year by his fellow professionals at the RLPA Awards Night at the Royal Armouries Museum in Leeds, Long has enjoyed his best ever season in 1999, scoring 326 points.

The sight of Long and Martyn working in tandem in midfield, and providing the space for Saints' sizzling backs, was one of the lasting memories of the 1999 season in the top flight. No wonder Saints supporters cheered long and hard when Saints announced, before their play-off game against Castleford Tigers at Knowsley Road, that Long had committed himself to the club by signing a new contract.

In that game Long returned to the Saints ranks from a shoulder injury, and he came off the bench to play a blinder in just 44 minutes to sink the Tigers' own play-off hopes. Two tries, five goals, and the creation of another try for Martyn, helped his side to a 36-6 win.

And Long, again coming on as a substitute to protect his fragile shoulder, played a vital role in the Grand Final, playing a key part in the move that led to Kevin Iro's decisive try for St Helens, and then landing the conversion from the touchline to secure that pulsating two-point win.

It was a great day for a player who had truly made his mark on Super League, and who will surely do the same next season in the World Cup.

17

Richard Pachniuk

Richard Pachniuk was voted the Northern Ford Premiership Player of the Year in 1999 on two successive evenings. First of all he walked away with the award at the Association of Premiership Clubs dinner at Widnes' Auto Quest Stadium. The following night he won the award at the Rugby League Players' Association dinner at Leeds' Royal Armouries Museum.

So you could say that Pachniuk had impressed a lot of good judges with his performances for Hunslet Hawks. He was certainly a key factor in the Hawks' march to the Northern Ford Premiership title, and no player more thoroughly deserved his awards than the former Rochdale Hornets star.

Earlier in the season he was somewhat bizarrely linked with St Helens at the time of the bust up between that club and its coach Ellery Hanley, when Saints football manager Eric Hughes suggested that Hanley had wanted to swap Keiron Cunningham for Pachniuk. Whether that was true or not, Hunslet fans were grateful to keep their star performer.

The Hawks had invested heavily in a revamped squad for the 1999 campaign, and integral to coach David Plange's Grand Final push was his new hooker. And it wasn't just in winning awards and trophies that Pachniuk had an outstanding year. He also broke Len McIntyre's 40 year record of tries in a season for a hooker. Throughout the season his keen eye for the slightest gap, a deceiving turn of pace, and an intelligent kicking game were key elements in the Hawks' surge to second place in the NFP table.

Opposition coaches had to take special measures to improve their marker defence around the rucks in a bid to thwart Pachniuk's dangerous runs from that area. But Pachniuk's awards at the end of the season showed that very few of them had succeeded.

Darren Holt

Barrow Border Raiders scrum-half Darren Holt produced a series of fine displays in 1999 to help the Raiders to mid-table respectability in the Northern Ford Premiership.

It was an important year for Barrow, once one of the giants of the game, as the club finished a creditable tenth, and opened the new Willie Horne stand, named after the former Barrow captain who is one of the true legends of the game.

Holt may not be in the Horne class, but it wasn't surprising that Super League clubs were sitting up and taking notice of the young Cumbrian star's performances. Neither was it a surprise that he was voted the 'Best Emerging Talent' in the Northern Ford Premiership at the Rugby League Professional Players Association dinner in September.

He set the tone for the season by clinching the Northern Ford Player of the Month award in March; his attacking running, ball distribution and accurate goal kicking taking the Raiders to a lofty position in the early season standings in the league table.

Raiders coach Paul Charlton, who switched Holt into the halfback role from his previous position of hooker, had no doubt about his star player's qualities.

"He's very cocky and confident, like every good scrum-half should be, and he's great when he's running and attacking defences," said Charlton, who added: "He's also a pointscoring machine, and doesn't miss many goal kicks."

His success in 1999 was all the more impressive in view of the fact that he only recently took up the scrum-half berth, having earned the Division Two "Hooker of the Year" accolade in 1998.

Many predicted a difficult season for the Border Raiders, after the previous season's Division Two campaign saw only two clubs finish below them.

But Holt's explosive start to the year, followed by sustained consistency, ensured a comparatively successful season for the Furnessmen, one that they can surely build on for the 2000 season. The great news for Barrow fans is that Darren Holt will once again be with them when the new Millennium begins.

19

2
THE 1999 SEASON

DECEMBER '98
Cup takes the high road

Challenge Cup First Round

Rugby League is set for more change in the new millennium, but the 1999 season again got underway with the first round of the Silk Cut Challenge Cup, when 48 amateur sides fought out the first tentative steps towards the last ever Wembley as we knew and loved it.

The opening salvoes were fired on the weekend of 5th-6th December 1998, as BARLA's finest took a break from their winter league fixtures to soak up their share of the glamour associated with Rugby League's oldest and most nationally prestigious competition.

16-team World Cup announced for Europe in 2000 ● Plans for a World Club Challenge between Brisbane and Wigan are abandoned, while South Africa will host World Nines in 1999 ● Darryl Van de Velde agrees a three-year deal at Warrington Wolves as takeover by local consortium goes through ● Chris Joynt confirmed by Ellery Hanley as Saints skipper for 1999 ● Halifax Blue Sox sign Graham Holroyd from Leeds; Paul Broadbent and Nick Pinkney from Sheffield; and Daryl Cardiss from Wigan Warriors.....Simon Baldwin, Martin Pearson and Daio Powell move to the Eagles ● Featherstone Rovers re-sign Brendon Tuuta...

Tie of the round was at Bus Vale, where Leeds side Queens beat Castleford's Redhill 20-18. Other top clashes saw Wigan Rose Bridge see off Blackbrook 23-16, Moldgreen carve out an injury-time 24-34 win over Eastmoor Dragons and a close 12-15 success for Wigan St Judes at Middleton Marauders.

As well as offering the attraction of seeing the more traditional clubs in action, the first round of the Cup is always an expansionist's delight and this year's competition was no exception.

For a start, it boasted the first ever Challenge Cup tie to be played in Scotland, when the Scottish Border Eagles went down 10-34 to Cumbrian League Champions Wath Brow Hornets in Glasgow.

Northside Saints represented the Ireland league, but were outclassed 90-10 in their match at Siddal. UWIC, Cardiff went down 24-4 at Barrow Island, Midlands League champions Garibaldi were sunk 78-10 by Eccles and Gateshead Panthers finally succumbed 10-58 to Crosfields the week after the matches in Glasgow and Tyneside had been initially frozen off.

1999 SILK CUT CHALLENGE CUP ROUND ONE RESULTS
Saturday 5th December, 1998
Oulton Raiders 42 York Acorn 8; Dudley Hill 66 Leeds University 0; Barrow Island 24 UWI Cardiff 4; Shaw Cross 12 Featherstone Miners 16; Norland 28 Milford 22; Queens 20 Redhill 18; Middleton Marauders 12 Wigan St Judes 15; Eccles 78 Garibaldi 10; Ideal Isberg 39 Millom 4; Dewsbury Moor 6 Ellenborough Rangers 40; Hull Dockers 23 Park Amateurs 6; Keighley Albion 6 Dodworth 12; Eastmoor Dragons 24 Moldgreen 34; Wigan Rose Bridge 23 Blackbrook 16; Leigh East 12 Haydock 18; New Earswick All Blacks 14 Townville 16; Featherstone Lions 34 Queensbury 26; London Skolars 16 Thatto Heath 4; Siddal 90 Northside Saints (Dublin) 10
Saturday 12th December, 1998 - postponed matches
Clayton 10 Normanton Knights 28; Ovenden 22 East Leeds 14; Rochdale Mayfield 36 Leeds Met. University 18
Sunday 13th December, 1998 - postponed matches
Scottish Border Eagles 10 Wath Brow Hornets 34; Gateshead Panthers 10 Crosfields 58

Better luck for National Conference Division Two side London Skolars, however. Their 16-4 home victory over Thatto Heath, one of the amateur game's most illustrious clubs, came in front of the BBC TV Grandstand cameras.

It was only two years ago that North West Counties side Thatto were beating Chorley Borough in the third round to grab the headlines. This time the boot was on the other foot as the Skolars raced in for four tries and showed superb defensive commitment.

In other games, Ellenborough Rangers pushed Dewsbury Moor

Leeds owner Paul Caddick pulls out of Hull KR takeover
● Wendell Sailor arrives at Headingley ● Gateshead complete inaugural squad with signing of Brett Grogan ● Ex-Great Britain forward Roy Powell dies, aged 33 ● Peter Deakin rules out move to Warrington ● Oldham announce groundshare with Rochdale ● Australian clubs Gold Coast Chargers and Adelaide Rams shut down ● Maurice Lindsay confirms he is to quit Rugby League at the end of his contract in September 1999...

aside 6-40, the students of Leeds University found Dudley Hill too strong, going down 66-0, while Leeds Met. did the student game proud before finally succumbing 36-18 in another rearranged match at Rochdale Mayfield.

Challenge Cup Second Round

As ever, the second round of the Cup saw the introduction of the National Conference Premier Division clubs - and this year threw up some mouthwatering clashes.

In the match of the round, White Rose League leaders Queens had set their sights on ending West Hull's cup run early, but a packed Bus Vale saw them fall 26-48 in a match that featured eleven tries, a fantastic Queens fightback from 28-2 to 28-26 and three players sent off.

West Hull now had a chance to repeat their feats of two years ago when professional clubs York and Prescot were dispatched by the amateur giant killers.

Back on Humberside, and there was a local derby to savour as Skirlaugh beat Ideal Isberg 8-2 in a defence-dominated encounter which brought back memories of duels past in the Hull and District League.

Cumbria's finest, Ellenborough Rangers, faced a daunting trip to Oldham St Annes, where their famous cup run of 1998 was firmly consigned to the history books at a full-to-busting Higginshaw Road, 34-6.

In the round's other big matches, a terrific first-half show helped Leigh Miners Rangers beat local rivals Wigan Rose Bridge 6-17, while Wath Brow Hornets ended London Skolars' hopes with a dramatic 16-10 victory in the very last play of the game.

The match looked to be heading for the distinction of being the first Silk

1999 SILK CUT CHALLENGE CUP ROUND TWO RESULTS
Saturday 19th December, 1998
Askam 25 Heworth 22; Beverley East Hull 12 Townville 28; Dodworth 12 Castleford Lock Lane 24; Dudley Hill 29 Wigan St Patricks 8; Eccles 37 Normanton Knights 16; Moldgreen 21 Oulton Raiders 18; Norland 39 Crosfields 0; Oldham St Annes 34 Ellenborough 6; Queens 26 West Hull 48; Rochdale Mayfield 28 Hull Dockers 10; Saddleworth Rangers 10 Walney Central 8; Siddal 24 Featherstone Miners 7; Skirlaugh 8 Ideal Isberg 2; Thornhill 25 Barrow Island 12; Wigan Rose Bridge 6 Leigh Miners Rangers 17; Wigan St Judes 32 Woolston Rovers 8; Wath Brow Hornets 16 London Skolars 10
Saturday 2nd January, 1999 - postponed matches
Egremont Rangers 21 Haydock 0; Featherstone Lions 38 Ovenden 18

Cut Challenge Cup tie to go to extra time when young BARLA international forward Phil Sherwen powered his way through a half gap for the matchwinning try.

Conference first division hopefuls Dudley Hill stormed past relegation threatened premiers Wigan St Patricks 29-8, and the enigmatic Wigan St Judes dumped the elite league's most successful team Woolston Rovers 32-8.

They, and the round's other successful amateur sides, had the reward of a potential tie with a professional club to look forward to in round three.

Away from the Challenge Cup, 1998 came to a sad close with the tragic and sudden death of Rochdale assistant player-coach and ex-Great Britain international Roy Powell.

The immensely popular and experienced player, renowned for his 100 per cent displays and tenacious tackling, collapsed while walking through a Sunday morning training drill and died after suffering a massive cardiac arrest.

Powell's death came less than two months after the passing of fellow Hornets star Karl Marriott, who died in uncannily similar circumstances at the end of October. Powell had recently joined his friend Deryck Fox in a coaching capacity at Spotland, and was just 33 years old.

In an outstanding career that spanned 15 years, Powell was capped 19 times by Great Britain, and spent time at the very top level with Leeds and Bradford, as well as having spells with Featherstone and Batley.

On a happier note, the seasonal transfer merry-go-round was again in full swing.

Bradford Bulls boss Matthew Elliott welcomed a couple of Aussies, Nick Zisti and the unknown Michael Withers to a cold, damp Odsal. Halifax Blue Sox signed Graham Holroyd from Leeds, Daryl Cardiss from Wigan Warriors, and Paul Broadbent and Nick Pinkney from Sheffield. Simon Baldwin, Martin Pearson and Daio Powell went in the opposite direction to the Eagles, who also snapped up giant centre Karl Lovell from Parramatta.

Huddersfield Giants were linked with Auckland Warriors' Test halfback Gene Ngamu and Irish internationals Tommy Martyn and Brian Carney - who eventually found his way to newboys Gateshead Thunder. The injury-plagued Nigel Wright did, however, make it to the McAlpine Stadium, settling an on-going dispute with Wigan in the process.

Former Canterbury Bulldogs captain Simon Gillies arrived at Warrington, Hull's new millionaire owner David Lloyd personally welcomed £100,000 signing Karl Harrison to the Sharks from Halifax, and Alan Hunte played down reports that he was about to quit the Boulevard.

Elsewhere, Castleford snapped up Darren Rogers from Salford Reds, while Brisbane's Wendell Sailor made his first appearance for Leeds Rhinos after a shared-code deal had brought the Kangaroo international to Headingley. Leeds beat their West Yorkshire neighbours Halifax Blue Sox 12-6 in a Boxing Day derby watched by 14,000 people.

In another Christmas fixture, a Castleford side made up largely of under-21s players proved too strong for Featherstone Rovers, the division one club going down 12-25 at their newly christened Lionheart Stadium.

On the coaching front, London Broncos unveiled their new dynamic duo in the shape of Dan Stains and Les Kiss, two of the most promising coaches in the Australian ranks, while the new owners of Doncaster Dragons set their sights on League legend Garry Schofield to revitalise the club's fortunes.

Meanwhile, the on-off saga of a proposed World Club Championship match between Wigan and Brisbane Broncos gathered pace. As December dawned, the £500,000 showdown was still not certain to go ahead, with a dispute over the date of the game reportedly the main stumbling block.

1998 Super League Champions Wigan wanted to play their Aussie counterparts at Bolton's Reebok Stadium in February, a week before they were due to launch their own Wembley Challenge Cup campaign. But the NRL top dogs Brisbane preferred to play a fortnight later, and the match was eventually scrapped.

Just up the road, meanwhile, the Warriors' neighbours St Helens announced plans to play a top Australian side - thought to be Balmain Tigers - in Dubai, as part of the following winter's millennium celebrations.

There was more apparent international good news when a Sydney meeting of the newly-formed Rugby League International Federation announced Johannesburg's Ellis Park as the venue for the 1999 World Nines after the intervention of controversial rugby union boss Louis Luyt. And Sydney's new Olympic Stadium would host the final of the following autumn's inaugural Tri-Nations series.

Hunslet Hawks sign Richard Pachniuk from Rochdale Hornets ● Post Office Road becomes Lionheart Stadium ● Huddersfield Giants sign Nigel Wright and Aussie David Boughton ● Wakefield snap Glen Tomlinson up from Hull Sharks ● Keighley Cougars re-sign Martin Wood from Sheffield, while official Jack Wainwright dies, aged 67 ● Workington Town sign Josh White ● Wakefield Trinity left in dark over financial backing in 2000 ● St Helens confirm match with Balmain in Dubai in January 2000 ● Bradford Bulls complete their overseas signings with David Boyle from Gold Coast Chargers ● Graeme Bradley is reprimanded by RFL for accusing referee Stuart Cummings of lying after the Elimination Play-off at St Helens...

"If you think that it's 1992 since the Lions last toured Australia," said RFL chief executive Neil Tunnicliffe, "you can see why the Aussies want to stage more international games.

"They believe the Australian public is crying out to see more Tests between Australia and Great Britain." Ten months later somebody would be "crying out", but it wouldn't be the Australian public.

The same meeting also gave the go-ahead for one particularly innovative rule change, and one that was to prove extremely popular with fans the world over.

In a move designed to reward tactical kicking, a player finding touch in the opposition 20-metre area from a kick within 40 metres of his own tryline would see his team rewarded with head and ball at the resulting scrum.

'Zero tackles' from kicks downfield would also be scrapped, although they would still apply after errors from opposing sides.

No Rugby League month is complete without politics, and while the chairman of Super League (Europe) Maurice Lindsay was announcing his intention to quit Rugby League when his SLE contract expired in September 1999, the FASDA clubs - as they were then still known - scrapped plans for a five-team second division.

Instead, it was announced, all the 18 professional teams outside Super League would play in one league, with the Championship going to the club that would win an end of season top five play-off.

The FASDA clubs also decided to adjust their News Limited income, with the 13 clubs that would have been in the first division receiving £325,000 each, and the five 'second division' outfits getting £165,000.

Some club's Christmas presents would be bigger than others.

JANUARY
A Thunder-ous new year

The third round of the Silk Cut Challenge Cup was scheduled for the last weekend in January, but as the year turned there was plenty going on to keep Rugby League fans occupied until then.

For a start there were the usual round of so-called festive friendlies. Huddersfield, with new coach Mal Reilly in tow, beat local rivals Halifax Blue Sox 28-10 at the McAlpine Stadium.

"It's good to be back in England again," said Reilly afterwards. "The players are working hard and saw a reward for their efforts today. It's early days yet but the signs are promising."

Over 10,000 people turned up at Headingley to watch Leeds Rhinos just edge it 26-21 over Castleford Tigers in a match packed with skill, verve and breathtaking excitement right to the final hooter. The Tigers were in control for 55 minutes, but a touch of magic from on-loan Wendell Sailor turned the match.

An innocuous kick from Francis Maloney went loose and gave the giant Australian Test winger his only real running chance of his brief two-match stay. Sailor had promised the Rhinos fans a try before the game and he delivered, burning off the Castleford defence on his way to a memorable 60-metre score.

Tigers assistant coach Graham Steadman, meanwhile, was pleased with his side's effort and -

Bobbie Goulding faces GBH court charges ● St Helens re-sign former hero Sonny Nickle from Bradford Bulls, while Joey Hayes finally gets his move to Salford ● the Reds sign Hull's South African winger Mark Johnson and giant Aussie second-rower Hudson Smith ● Barcelona bid to enter French second division in 2000 ● Alex Murphy awarded OBE in New Years Honours Lists ● North Sydney legend Greg Florimo lands in Wigan ● Doncaster sign Garry Schofield ● first batch of Gateshead Thunder's Aussie recruits lands at Newcastle airport ● Hull release Alan Hunte and Warrington Wolves pounce ● Former Australia Test coach Ted Glossop dies ● Wigan claim aborted transfer deal damages from Wendell Sailor...

with three overseas signings still due to fly in - declared that Castleford would have "a competitive squad" in Super League IV.

Unusually, there was no festive fixture for Saints and Wigan this year. Any Lancashire fans looking for New Year action had to head for Spotland, where ground-sharers Rochdale Hornets and Oldham met in the annual AJ Law Cup.

This winter's game had more poignancy than usual, after the recent deaths of Karl Marriott and Roy Powell. But, after observing a minute's silence before the start, the Hornets players paid their own tribute in the best possible way, overpowering the Roughyeds 48-10 in front of a 2,879 crowd.

Elsewhere, Hunslet Hawks warmed up for 1999 with a 22-10 over Bramley, who had Mike Ford in charge for the first time. And a Chico Jackson Select side beat

Hull Sharks 24-30 in his testimonial match, Chico himself scoring the winning try!

With the new, combined division one season set to kick off in February and the Challenge Cup around the corner, there were a plethora of friendlies around as January unfolded. The introduction of the Bosman ruling to Rugby League meant that an unprecedented number of players had changed clubs during the close season, particularly at the level below Super League, raising hopes of a fascinating campaign ahead.

Off the field, motor giants Ford announced that they would be sponsoring the competition through their network of 450 northern dealers - with the first division to be known as the Northern Ford Premiership.

On the field, Oldham again went down - 20-6 to Widnes - and backed that up with a 34-12 defeat at Leigh Centurions. Hunslet had another victory, 18-12 over Keighley Cougars, whose under-21s then lost 6-40 to Doncaster Dragons. Both Keighley and Leigh had earlier fought out a 20-20 draw. Whitehaven Warriors overpowered Warrington Wolves' under-21s, 34-14, at Wilderspool, while Swinton were unsurprisingly beaten 48-4 by St Helens at an expectant Knowsley Road.

● South Africa unilaterally cancels World Nines ● Hull sign Castleford forward Michael Smith and Wigan hooker Martin Hall ● RFL launch "think tank" aimed at improving standards in Britain ● promoted Wakefield Trinity make 12th close season signing in Vince Fawcett ● Kerrod Walters confirmed as first Gateshead captain ● Robbie Paul regains Bradford Bulls captaincy, lost last year to the now retired Graeme Bradley ● Oldham chairman Chris Hamilton denies merger between Roughyeds, Rochdale and Leigh is on cards ● Sheffield Eagles capture ex-Academy international Paul Anderson from St Helens ● Castleford unveil Aaron Raper ● Leeds boss Gary Hetherington blasts Wigan over Terry Newton ● London deny move to Watford ● Hundreds turn out for funeral of Roy Powell ● Northern Ford revealed as first division sponsors ...

Other Super League sides were in action, too, with mixed fortunes. Hull Sharks unveiled their new recruits against York, but the Wasps stole the Boulevard show, fighting hard for a 20-20 draw. Things didn't improve a week later for Peter Walsh's men, as Dewsbury Rams sent them crashing to defeat, 10-14. Salford Reds beat Barrow Border Raiders 36-12, but found newly-relocated Lancashire Lynx a much tougher proposition, a serious injury to promising loose forward Ricky Helliwell overshadowing the Reds' 14-17 win at Chorley's Victory Park.

As January reached its close, Batley Bulldogs handed the Castleford Tiger cubs a valuable lesson; that you have to maintain concentration for the full 80 minutes. A narrow, late 20-22 defeat was the result.

But the following week a match of a much more historic nature took place at Wheldon Road, as the Tigers played host to Gateshead Thunder in the Super League newboys' first ever game of Rugby League.

A foggy night in West Yorkshire had seen Shaun McRae's "geordie Aussies" - as they were already being called in some quarters - slightly delayed due to the vagaries of Friday night traffic on the A1. They eventually went down 18-8, but showed enough defensive commitment, attacking momentum and individual excellence to suggest that they would be a real force in their debut season.

For the record, winger Matt Daylight scored the first Gateshead try on seven minutes, trialist winger Epi Taione had the first touch of the ball, fullback Ben Sammut the first kick, and Tony Grimaldi made the initial Thunder tackle.

In other matches, Warrington Wolves put one over on St Helens, producing a confident 25-14 win at Wilderspool. "The place is buzzing," remarked coach

Darryl Van de Velde later. Bradford Bulls beat Huddersfield Giants 20-8 at Odsal, and anyone under the assumption that Wakefield were cast-iron certainties for relegation were made to think again as Trinity beat last season's Challenge Cup winners Sheffield Eagles 30-26 at Belle Vue.

Challenge Cup Third Round

With the entry of the division one sides, round three of the Cup always has its surprises.

This year's biggest came at Headingley, where Bramley suffered a second successive third round defeat at the hands of an amateur side, Leigh Miners Rangers emerging 12-18 victors in a hard-fought encounter.

Ellenborough did the damage in 1998, and many of the Bramley players must have been suffering from a sense of déja vu when the Miners took the lead as early as the sixth minute. The professional side fought back, but some superb late scrambling defence ensured the National Conference side their glory.

"That has to be up there with my all-time worst defeats," admitted Bramley coach Mike Ford.

There was almost a shock on the cards at Doncaster too, when the Dragons thought they had been pushed to a draw by Oldham St Annes. Over 1600 people, treble last season's average attendance, turned out to witness the home debut of ex-Great Britain international Garry Schofield, but only half were around to witness the final outcome.

At the end of 80 minutes it was 15-15 and the St Annes players were celebrating a famous result, while their first division opponents left for the dressing rooms. At least half the

1999 SILK CUT CHALLENGE CUP ROUND THREE RESULTS
Saturday 30th January, 1999
Barrow Border Raiders 44 Dudley Hill 16; Batley Bulldogs 40 Castleford Lock Lane 10; Bramley 12 Leigh Miners Rangers 18; Dewsbury Rams 38 Siddal 10; Doncaster Dragons 35 Oldham St Annes 21 (AET); Featherstone Rovers 70 Thornhill 6; Hemel Stags 8 Featherstone Lions 29; Hull Kingston Rovers 56 Wath Brow Hornets 4; Hunslet Hawks 66 Townville 6; Keighley Cougars 48 Rochdale Mayfield 2; Lancashire Lynx 50 Askam 3; Leigh Centurions 42 Norland 6; Rochdale Hornets 52 Wigan St Judes 12; Swinton Lions 38 Moldgreen Marauders 4; Whitehaven Warriors 22 Saddleworth Rangers 6; Widnes Vikings 34 West Hull 4; Workington Town 30 Skirlaugh Bulls 4; York Wasps 57 Egremont Rangers 2
Monday 1st February, 1999
Oldham 26 Eccles 7

spectators left with them, but five minutes later there came an announcement that the game would have to go into extra-time.

A further eight minutes passed before referee Russell Smith reappeared to restart the game, by which time the visiting players had clearly lost focus, eventually going down 35-21.

A spirited West Hull gave Widnes a game, before succumbing 34-4, and Eccles gave Oldham a scare in the Monday night match at Spotland despite finally finishing on the end of a 26-7 reverse. Up in Cumbria, Saddleworth Rangers went out 22-6 to Whitehaven, but not before giving the Warriors the fright of their lives with a plucky display at the Recreation Ground.

Featherstone Lions, meanwhile, became only the second amateur team to make round four, courtesy of their 8-29 win away to Hemel Hempstead in Sudbury. Hemel had been given direct passage to the third round stage, but found their more streetwise opposition too hot to handle.

There wasn't much in the way of Challenge Cup romance elsewhere either. Top notch Conference side Skirlaugh fell to Workington Town 30-4, Featherstone ran riot 70-6 over Thornhill, Hull KR cruised past Wath Brow Hornets 56-4 while all the other Premiership outfits had comfortable wins over spirited but ultimately outclassed opponents.

If January was an eventful month on the pitch, it was no less eventful off it.

As well as the continuing transfer merry-go-round which saw ex-Saints star Sonny Nickle head back to Knowsley Road from Bradford Bulls, and Alan Hunte finally make the break from Hull to sign for Warrington, along with new chief executive Peter Deakin, the international scene was again taking centre-stage.

To an almost complete lack of surprise, the South African Rugby League and their new patron Dr Louis Luyt unilaterally scrapped the World Nines due to be held on the first weekend in February in Johannesburg.

It was a hugely embarrassing volte-face for the game, and took administrators on both sides of the world completely by surprise. On the day of the announcement, for example, newspaper offices received two faxes within minutes of each other. One came from the RFL with details of the Great Britain squad, the second from South Africa informing the world that the tournament was cancelled.

● Lancashire Lynx return to Chorley ● RLSA survey reveals summer rugby is "catching on with fans" ● David Boyle arrives at Odsal ● Ex-Wigan chairman Jack Hilton dies, aged 77 ● Huddersfield fullback Ben Barton quits at 24 ● RFL and Scottish RFU agree to stage 2000 Challenge Cup at Murrayfield ● Ex-Bulls marketing guru Peter Deakin takes Warrington chief executive job ● New signing Josh White fails to arrive at Workington Town ● Gateshead lose to Castleford in first ever match ● Saints secure Fereti Tuilagi work permit ● Graham Murray announces Headingley departure at end of season ● young Wigan hooker Jon Clarke jailed for assault ● Treize Tournoi future in doubt...

RFL chairman Sir Rodney Walker admitted that the decision to award the Nines to the fledgling League nation only two months before the event was probably taken in haste, but denied that it had caused the game any lasting damage. "We can all be more precise with hindsight," he said.

"But I am confident that the Nines will go ahead in 2000 and 2001."

The RFL also revealed plans to stage an international Home Nations tournament in 1999, although final details on dates were still to be finally decided, and set up a "think tank" charged with raising standards for the game in Great Britain. An eight-strong panel was made up of Huddersfield boss and ex-GB coach Mal Reilly, Castleford coach Stuart Raper, ex-GB boss Phil Larder - now involved with the England rugby union team - RFL chief executive Neil Tunnicliffe, referees director Greg McCallum, Leeds supremo Gary Hetherington and RFL associate director Tom O'Donovan.

Elsewhere, the Giants' Bobbie Goulding found himself facing court charges for GBH, Hetherington blasted Wigan over their attempts to sign Leeds hooker Terry Newton - "they are an embarrassment to Super League" - and Maurice Lindsay, already retiring from his position at SLE at the end of September, was resisting efforts to push him out of the door sooner.

Leeds coach Graham Murray, meanwhile, announced that he, too, would be going at the season's end - to the North Sydney Bears in Australia's NRL. "Like Norths, Leeds haven't won anything big for a while," he said. "But I really think this could be our year."

FEBRUARY
Rhinos on the charge

Despite the Northern Ford Premiership season kick-off (see separate chapter), the Silk Cut Challenge Cup dominated February profile-wise, and several Super League clubs took the opportunity to warm up with more friendlies.

Last year's Cup-winners Sheffield Eagles, for example, continued Hull's pre-season woes with a 24-6 victory at the Don Valley Stadium. Beaten finalists Wigan, meanwhile, prepared for their tie of the fourth round against Leeds Rhinos with a narrow 16-18 win over Halifax Blue Sox at the New Shay.

Championship hopefuls Bradford Bulls gave the newly renamed Wakefield Trinity Wildcats a taste of what to expect in the top flight with a resounding 62-6 win at Odsal. And Gateshead Thunder - sitting out the Cup in their first season - took advantage of Hunslet's week off to record a convincing 0-50 win over the Hawks at the South Leeds Stadium.

With the game's politicians being uncharacteristically quiet for once, and Edinburgh's Murrayfield officially revealed as the venue for next season's final, all attention could now focus on the last ever road to those famous old Twin Towers.

Challenge Cup Fourth Round

This stage of the Challenge Cup has a knack for throwing up mouth-watering fixtures, and 1999 was no exception.

There was no doubt about the most mouth-watering of all either, as the BBC Sunday Grandstand cameras headed for Headingley where cup kings Wigan had been given the mother of all challenges, drawn away to last season's Grand Final opponents Leeds Rhinos.

But first there were the Friday and Saturday matches to deal with. Batley Bulldogs gave Wakefield a real fright at Belle Vue, before going down 12-2 in a Friday night tie, and the following day Hull Kingston Rovers and Halifax Blue Sox eased past the remainder of the amateur opposition, Leigh Miners Rangers and Featherstone Lions, 0-52 and 6-74 respectively.

1999 SILK CUT CHALLENGE CUP ROUND FOUR RESULTS

Friday 12th February, 1999
Wakefield Trinity Wildcats 12 Batley Bulldogs 2
Saturday 13th February, 1999
Featherstone Lions 6 Halifax Blue Sox 74; Leigh Miners Rangers 0 Hull Kingston Rovers 52; Salford Reds 16 Sheffield Eagles 6
Sunday 14th February, 1999
Barrow Border Raiders 16 Leigh Centurions 33; Bradford Bulls 92 Workington Town 0; Castleford Tigers 36 Hull Sharks 22; Huddersfield Giants 78 Swinton Lions 4; Hunslet Hawks 10 St Helens 40; Leeds Rhinos 28 Wigan Warriors 18; London Broncos 64 Doncaster Dragons 0; Rochdale Hornets 19 York Wasps 22; Warrington Wolves 50 Featherstone Rovers 6; Whitehaven Warriors 24 Lancashire Lynx 6; Widnes Vikings 28 Keighley Cougars 20
Monday 15th February, 1999
Oldham 18 Dewsbury Rams 10

Anthony Farrell burrows under the Wigan defence as Leeds end the Warriors' Challenge Cup hopes

For the nation's TV viewers, meanwhile, 1998 Wembley victors Sheffield Eagles faced a repeat of that year's semi-final, as they met the new-look Salford Reds at the Willows. Expectations were high, and it was always going to be a tricky hurdle for the South Yorkshire side to overcome, with Andy Gregory's men seeking to lay the ghost of last season's disappointment.

In the end it was a hurdle too high and, despite a fine opening half hour, the Eagles crashed to a 16-6 defeat. Salford's new Aussie second row pairing Darren Brown and Hudson Smith were outstanding, as Gregory admitted while also paying tribute to his team's strength of character as a whole. "We've got no big heads in this side," he said. "The victory was down to all the hard work we've put in since last season."

A horror hit on Gary Broadbent earned Eagles forward Darren Turner ten minutes in the sin bin and later a one-month ban after the RFL Executive Committee looked at the offence on video. He also made an immature gesture to the home fans in full view of the TV cameras as he was leaving the field and was fined £1000, half of it suspended for a year.

Apart from that, Sheffield took their defeat well, and coach John Kear copped it on the chin. "The best team won," he admitted. "Last year we were smiling but now we'll just have to concentrate on the start of Super League."

Entertaining or not, all this served as a mere hors d'oeuvre to the main course: Leeds v Wigan. A clash between the two leading clubs of 1998, the game had all the intensity, passion and rivalry we have come to expect, and produced Leeds' first cup win over Wigan in 31 years.

That the Rhinos emerged 28-18 victors in a hothouse atmosphere such as only

Headingley can provide was testament to the resilience, character and dogged determination instilled by coach Graham Murray. Particularly as the home side played for an hour with only twelve men, prop Barrie McDermott dismissed by referee Russell Smith after only 19 minutes for a high tackle on Wigan second-rower Simon Haughton.

"We were entitled to be beaten," beamed Murray afterwards, "but we hung in there and I haven't been as proud of a bunch of blokes either as a player or a coach as I am of these guys."

There was a more than creditable performance in South Leeds, too, where Hunslet Hawks proved sticky opposition for St Helens, the Super League side finally progressing via an unconvincing 10-40 win.

Apart from Hull KR, the only other first division sides to progress were Whitehaven, Widnes, Leigh, York and Oldham who put paid to Lancashire Lynx 24-6, Keighley Cougars 28-20, Barrow Border Raiders 16-33, Rochdale Hornets 19-22 and Dewsbury Rams 18-10 in that order. As ever, Super League clubs had proved too strong. Warrington beat Featherstone Rovers 50-6, London Broncos hammered Doncaster Dragons 64-0, Huddersfield Giants cruised past Swinton Lions 78-4 and Bradford Bulls posted a record 92-0 victory over Workington Town.

In the round's only other all-Super League tie, Castleford Tigers ensured Hull Sharks' misery went on, winning 36-22 at Wheldon Road.

Challenge Cup Fifth Round

If Leeds Rhinos were going to get to Wembley this year, they were obviously going to have to do it the hard way.

Their reward for having dumped Wigan out at the fourth round stage? A fifth round tie with Ellery Hanley's St Helens, and Headingley prepared for its second major cup clash in a fortnight.

This time, though, the game was played on the Saturday, and the BBC cameras were treated to another classic as an absorbing, if not exactly free-flowing, cup-tie provided more evidence that Rugby League was in rude health at the start of the 1999 season.

Saints were fired up alright, and finished the match with Sean Long and Chris Smith on report, but it was Leeds who again coped best with the pressure, seeing off another of the north-west's finest 24-16 on their way to the quarter-finals.

The fact that the Rhinos' win was only assured with Terry Newton's try

1999 SILK CUT CHALLENGE CUP ROUND FIVE RESULTS
Friday 26th February, 1999
Castleford Tigers 28 York Wasps 2
Saturday 27th February, 1999
Leeds Rhinos 24 St Helens 16
Sunday 28th February, 1999
Huddersfield Giants 14 Salford Reds 22; Hull Kingston Rovers 0 London Broncos 6; Wakefield Trinity 8 Bradford Bulls 26; Warrington Wolves 34 Halifax Blue Sox 4; Whitehaven Warriors 18 Oldham 2; Widnes Vikings 20 Leigh Centurions 17

six minutes from time proved how much new coach Hanley had steeled the St Helens defence, and there were already signs that his team were beginning to play in his image; uncompromising, resilient and competitive. On this occasion, though, that wasn't enough as their discipline, or lack of it, proved to be a costly factor.

"We were indisciplined across the paddock and that was our downfall," admitted the one-time Headingley favourite. Murray, for his part, again paid tribute to a great team effort led by veteran stand-off Daryl Powell. "We've earned respect from other teams, and we produced some quality football. Our attitude's right, and we're playing it pretty tough defensively."

As were Warrington Wolves, who swept through to the last eight 34-4 in the weekend's other televised match against Halifax Blue Sox.

Classed as underdogs before the match, the Wolves shoved those predictions back in the pundits' faces with a performance which promised much better things for the season ahead. The Blue Sox contributed to a pulsating cup-tie for an hour of a blood and thunder clash, but they fell away in the last quarter and Jon Roper - playing in the unaccustomed position of loose forward - finally edged the home side clear with an 80-metre solo special.

Shaun Edwards becomes London's first ever English captain ● Graeme Bradley joins Oldham coaching staff ● RFL warns players about "mooning" at crowd ● Wakefield get planning permission for new stadium next to M1 ● Home Internationals dates set for October ● St Helens confirm plans for new stadium in 2001 ● Treize Tournoi in doubt ● outgoing Norths coach Peter Louis linked with Leeds ● Wigan open talks with John Monie over new contract ● RFL and BARLA come together to form united Young Lions team ● Gateshead net huge sponsorship deal with Northern Electric and Gas ● Halifax in ground capacity rows with local council ● Michael Smith sacked, and then re-instated, by Hull after nightclub spotting ● Aussie League players embark on "week of shame" ● Super League unveils website ● Caro Wild appointed Oxford development officer ● Castleford's Brad Davis fronts nude billboard campaign ● SLE chairman Chris Caisley predicts boom year ● London sign Canberra prop Anthony Siebold ● Saints deny Anthony Sullivan move to Cardiff ● RFL look to launch West Cumbria Centre of Excellence...

There was almost a huge surprise at Craven Park, where Northern Ford Premiership side Hull Kingston Rovers trailed London by a mere 0-2 when centre Whetu Taewa was literally inches from grabbing a sensational try on three-quarter time that would probably have dumped the Broncos out of the Cup. Rovers, with a gale force wind and driving rain now at their backs, were pounding the visitors' line.

The conditions which had threatened to turn the tie into a lottery certainly proved a crucial factor in the move, as Stanley Gene's chip to the left corner accelerated in the wind and just beat the diving Taewa to the dead ball line. Ten minutes from time a relieved London booked their passage, 0-6, when Martin Offiah crossed for a simple try out wide.

"We did remarkably well to come through in the circumstances," said London chief executive Tony Rea, while Rovers coach Dave Harrison debunked the "myth" that there is such a big gap in standards between the top two professional levels. "It was hard to tell which was the Super League side today," he said.

York Wasps had added further fuel to that argument on Friday night when they pushed Castleford Tigers all the way before finally going down 28-2, while newly promoted Wakefield improved on their recent friendly performance against Bradford Bulls but still lost 8-26 at Belle Vue. In another all Super League tie Salford Reds, fresh from their win over Sheffield, this time ended Huddersfield Giants' interest 14-22 in a convincing display at the McAlpine Stadium.

In the round's only all-Premiership matches, Widnes Vikings narrowly pipped Leigh Centurions 20-17 at the Auto Quest Stadium, while Whitehaven Warriors made lighter work of Oldham, 18-2.

With the start of the top flight league season now only one week away, all eyes turned towards Super League.

MARCH
Virgin territory

"The 1999 JJB Super League is set to be the best ever," said SLE managing director Maurice Lindsay at the official launch of Super League IV at Mottram Hall in Cheshire. "There have been record season ticket sales, and we expect to break the one million attendance barrier."

Australian fans were already turning out in force. An incredible 104,583 people saw the NRL opening weekend double header at the new Olympic Stadium in Sydney. That broke the previous world record crowd of 102,569 set at Bradford's Odsal Stadium in 1954 for the Challenge Cup Final replay between Halifax and Warrington.

While there weren't quite that many fans at Central Park on the opening Friday night, a slightly disappointing 9,186 to be precise, those who did turn up were treated to pre-match fireworks and a comprehensive 58-6 victory as Wigan put already struggling Hull Sharks to the sword. To be honest, despite those fireworks, as a competitive match the season's opener was a bit of a damp squib. But you can only beat what's put in front of you, and the Warriors did that in resounding style.

This was to be the last ever season at the historic old ground before the cherry and whites upped sticks to the brand spanking new JJB Stadium just up the road at Robin Park. With new signings Mark Reber and Greg Florimo slotting in well at halfback, and young Lee Gilmour having a wow of a game in the second row, hopes were raised for a final season to remember.

Meanwhile, up on Tyneside, history was about to be made as Gateshead Thunder took to their own field for the first time in their Super League debut against Challenge Cup quarter-finalists Leeds Rhinos. Hopes for a big crowd were dashed as incessant rain lashed down on the Gateshead International Stadium or

JJB SUPER LEAGUE
ROUND ONE RESULTS
Friday 5th March, 1999

Wigan Warriors 58 ....Hull Sharks 6

Sunday 7th March, 1999

Bradford Bulls 18 ....Sheffield Eagles 6
Castleford Tigers 12 ....Wakefield Trinity Wildcats 10
Gateshead Thunder 14 ....Leeds Rhinos 24
Halifax Blue Sox 14 ....Warrington Wolves 16
London Broncos 24 ....Huddersfield Giants 18
Salford Reds 12 ....St Helens 30

"Thunderdome" as it was now known. Still, just under 6,000 people were attracted to see an incident-packed encounter which the Rhinos eventually edged 14-24, with a superb performance from last year's Man of Steel, Iestyn Harris, the deciding factor.

It was debatable whether the mudbath of a pitch was playable, but both sets of players got stuck in and produced a splendidly entertaining match in which the Thunder staged a magnificent second-half fightback. Both clubs were

Gateshead skipper Kerrod Walters leads the Thunder out for their Super League debut against Leeds

left with plenty of reasons to be cheerful.

"You've got to give credit to Leeds," said Shaun McRae afterwards, "but I'm really happy with our effort. I'm proud of the way we played as a team tonight, but we're a little underdone in terms of match conditioning."

"Gateshead are certainly going to give sides trouble up here," declared Graham Murray.

Defeat or not, professional Rugby League had arrived in the north east.

The Super League's other newboys, Wakefield Trinity Wildcats, got their season off to an encouraging start too, as only a pair of Danny Orr penalties in the last three minutes robbed them of a sensational opening day victory at Castleford Tigers.

The top flight newcomers led 10-8 going into the closing stages, and had looked anything but 2000-1 outsiders for the title as they tackled like the Wildcats they had recently been named after. "It's a cruel game," sighed Wakefield boss Andy Kelly, "but I'm very proud of my team and they deserve a pat on the back. I think we answered our critics and showed them that we are ready for Super League."

Warrington Wolves completed a quickfire double over Halifax Blue Sox, seven days after dumping them out of the Challenge Cup. This time, though, the setting was the New Shay and a much closer match produced only a slender 14-16 success for Darryl Van de Velde's men.

On a mud bath of a pitch more suited to water polo than Rugby League, it was a game that was always likely to have more than its share of handling errors and so it turned out, Warrington making fewer to earn the two valuable points.

"We made far more than even the conditions warranted and were suitably punished," insisted Blue Sox coach John Pendlebury. "It was a game from which I could take nothing positive whatsoever."

Bradford Bulls kicked off Super League IV by grinding out a solid 18-6 victory over Sheffield Eagles in a cold, wet and blustery throwback to the bad old days of winter rugby at Odsal. With close-season additions such as Henry Paul now in his armoury, however, coach Matthew Elliott looked ahead to the firmer pitches of summer with relish. "I am very excited about this football team," he said.

Over the Pennines at the Willows, Salford coach Andy Gregory was given a worry or two ahead of the Reds' Challenge Cup quarter-final tie at Castleford. Joe Faimalo and influential Aussie playmaker Darren Brown picked up injuries in the 12-30 defeat by St Helens. Saints' newly-found defensive resolve and the match-winning skills of Paul Newlove and hat-trick League Express gamestar Sean Long sent their legions of fans back down the East Lancashire Road happy.

And in the capital, Martin Offiah rewrote the record books at the end of a week he would much rather have forgotten. Offiah, whose father had been gunned down in Nigeria the previous Monday, became the game's leading try-scoring Englishman with a four-pointer seven minutes from time in London's scrappy 24-18 win over Huddersfield Giants.

It was his 447th career try, putting him one score ahead of St Helens legend Alf Ellaby. Only Australian Brian Bevan (796) and Welshman Billy Boston (571) now stand ahead of Offiah in the all-time try charts. "I didn't know whether to be happy or to cry when I scored," he said afterwards.

Challenge Cup Quarter-finals

Only one week in, and already Super League was taking a break as the Silk Cut Challenge Cup again loomed into view.

Martin Offiah broke a Rugby League record for the second week running, when he grabbed London's record for tries-in-a-match - picking up five in the Broncos' comfortable 54-6 win over Northern Ford Premiership side Whitehaven Warriors at the Stoop. "It showed that there is a bigger gap between the first division and Super League than I would like to admit to," said the Cumbrians' feisty coach and former Kiwi prop Kevin Tamati, his valiant team's Challenge Cup heroics now at an end.

With a tied score of 10-10 at half-time, Widnes Vikings may not have agreed with that sentiment when Leeds Rhinos visited the Auto Quest Stadium. But the genius of Great Britain Academy captain Kevin Sinfield swung an entertaining match the Rhinos' way four minutes after he had taken the field as a replacement for the injured Marc Glanville. Two quickfire tries as good as ended the Vikings' brave resistance and the visitors eventually ran out 10-46 winners.

In one of the weekend's two televised clashes, Danny Orr made it a hat-trick of Silk Cut awards with another man of the match performance which helped Castleford Tigers past Salford Reds 30-10 at Wheldon Road. The youngster's try-making pass out of the tackle for ex-Salford man Darren Rogers was probably the pass of the season, and the Reds had no answer to his all-round skills and five goals.

An ordinary game in the first half came alive in the second when Francis Maloney's 85-metre try out of nothing turned the match the Tigers way, leaving the Reds defence in tatters and coach Andy Gregory a very unhappy man indeed.

"Total embarrassment," was his aftermatch verdict. "We've been totally outplayed in every department. I will not tolerate it. I've told the players: don't one of you come up to

**1999 SILK CUT CHALLENGE CUP
QUARTER FINAL RESULTS**
Saturday 13th March, 1999
Castleford Tigers 30 ....Salford Reds 10
Sunday 14th March, 1999
Bradford Bulls 52 ....Warrington Wolves 16
London Broncos 54 ....Whitehaven Warriors 6
Widnes Vikings 10 ....Leeds Rhinos 46

me and say sorry. If in my playing career I had put in a performance like that, I wouldn't even want to face my family, let alone my friends." It wouldn't be the last time that Gregory would publicly blast his players.

Meanwhile, at Odsal, Bradford Bulls were simply superb as they routed Warrington Wolves 52-16. Before the match a close game had been predicted, but it turned out to be anything but. The previously buzzing Wolves had no answer to Bradford's ten-try slaughter, as they were tormented by the Paul brothers at halfback and giant Tongan winger Tevita Vaikona who picked up four tries.

"It was a good, old fashioned hiding," admitted shell-shocked Wolves boss Darryl Van de Velde.

Stuart Spruce, David Boyle, Tevita Vaikona and James Lowes celebrate as the Bulls blast Warrington

Back to Super League action and Friday night's match couldn't have been any bigger as Leeds and Wigan again locked horns after the Challenge Cup spectacular of only a few weeks ago.

This time, however, it was the Warriors who would emerge with the spoils. With perhaps one eye on next week's semi-final, Leeds took to the field without five first-team regulars. As a result they lacked the firepower to break one of the game's most obdurate defences, despite actually being 12-10 in front at the break.

Wigan hooker Mick Cassidy's try on the restart - one of a brace on the night - pushed the Warriors ahead, however, and a further twelve unanswered points gave the Warriors a hard-earned 12-26 win.

The Rhinos' semi-final opponents, Bradford Bulls, also found it tough going at the Boulevard where Hull Sharks almost pinched a remarkable victory. Putting their dreadful pre-season form behind them with an incredible defensive display, Peter Walsh's men began the task of winning over their critical fans in inspirational style.

A penalty and a field goal from Steve Prescott were the only points Hull could muster, but to hold the free-scoring Bulls to one first-half Nathan McAvoy try and two Steve McNamara goals said everything about their commitment. "If you had told me after the Wigan game that we'd play Bradford next and lose by 3-8, I think I'd have been happy," said Walsh.

Castleford Tigers warmed up for their date with destiny with a 19-14 defeat at Wilderspool. Star of an error-ridden match, which nevertheless made for pulsating viewing, was Warrington centre Toa Kohe-Love. The exciting Kiwi bagged two tries and gave opposite number Michael Eagar, returning to Wilderspool for the first time since his winter move to Wheldon Road, headaches all afternoon.

The result apart, Castleford coach Stuart Raper was chiefly concerned with the fact that stand-off Danny Orr had been carried from the field with an apparent medial ligament injury. Orr was now in doubt for next Saturday's Headingley showdown against London Broncos.

The men from the capital compounded injury problems of their own at the Don Valley Stadium a day earlier. 20-8 down with less than half an hour to play, the Broncos produced a great escape that Steve McQueen would have been proud of. A try from Dominic Peters, impressive West London product of the club's youth development scheme, gave kicker Brett Warton the chance to bring the sides level, and when centre Greg Fleming roared in for his second with only 90 seconds remaining the comeback was complete.

Wakefield Trinity Wildcats unveil record sponsorship with Sainsburys supermarket chain ● Martin Offiah becomes game's highest try-scoring Englishman in history ● Gateshead Thunder make first Super League appearance ● Australia celebrates 104,583 world record rugby crowd for NRL opener ● Wigan linked with Alfie Langer ● Hull coach Peter Walsh slams 'inane' critics ● South African bid to snatch World Cup derailed ● John Kear calls for Aussie coaches to count on overseas quota ● Treize Tournoi ditched ● Bob Scott quits as NFP manager ● North Sydney reported to be chasing Iestyn Harris ● Leading BBC official describes Super League as 'dull'...

"We lost the game rather than London won it," cursed Eagles coach John Kear. "We played for 25 minutes of the game at Salford, 40 minutes at Bradford

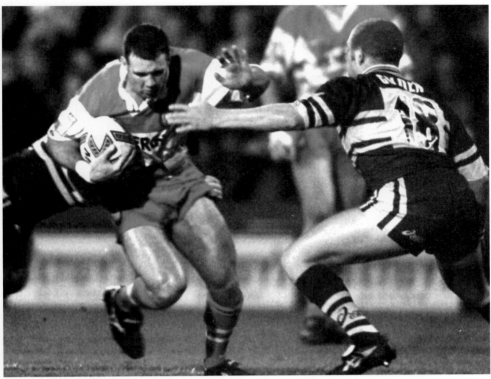

Paul Johnson looks for a way through as Wigan defeat Leeds at Headingley

and 55 minutes today. It's about time we put up or shut up." The Broncos, though, had lost Kiwi Test prop Grant Young for the season with a broken leg, a week after Darren Bradstreet had been ruled out for the season with a dislocated shoulder, and now faced an alarming front row shortage ahead of the biggest day in the club's history.

For those teams with only the end of season JJB Super League Grand Final to aim for, Halifax Blue Sox picked up a 14-17 win over Huddersfield Giants in a tense game at the McAlpine Stadium, but only after referee Robert Connolly had controversially ruled out a late Ian Pickavance "try" for a Bobbie Goulding forward pass.

And Wakefield Trinity Wildcats again confounded the cynics by picking up their first two points of the season, 22-10 over Salford Reds, with young hooker David March having a

JJB SUPER LEAGUE
ROUND TWO RESULTS
Friday 19th March, 1999
Leeds Rhinos 12..Wigan Warriors 26
Saturday 20th March, 1999
Sheffield Eagles 20 ....London Broncos 26
Sunday 21st March, 1999
Huddersfield Giants 14 ....Halifax Blue Sox 17
Hull Sharks 3 ....Bradford Bulls 8
St Helens 34 ....Gateshead Thunder 22
Wakefield Trinity Wildcats 22 ....Salford Reds 10
Warrington Wolves 19 ....Castleford Tigers 14

stormer. The result left Reds boss Andy Gregory on the edge, and looking like the first coach to be on his way out after only two rounds. "I don't think I have ever been so low as I am at the moment," he reflected. "The players might be here next week but I might not."

As for the Wildcats, their smiles told their own story. "Our first target of the

Martin Offiah celebrates scoring his try in the Challenge Cup semi-final with John Timu

season was to get two points and we've achieved that," said their coach Andy Kelly. "The luxury of having that win in the first couple of matches is good for the team. It confirms to the players that they are of the quality to compete at this level."

It was only the individual brilliance of international centres Kevin Iro and Paul Newlove which stood in the way of a dream return to Knowsley Road for former St Helens coach Shaun McRae, currently being linked with the Scotland job.

For 68 minutes - and despite a horrendous error count - his Gateshead Thunder side had every chance of stealing the match, incredibly at that stage only two points behind. But then Thunder winger Ian Herron added to the game's tally of mistakes by knocking on at the play-the-ball, and Saints prop Apollo Perelini charged over from close range to effectively seal the game and cap a much improved second-half display which ensured a final result of 34-22.

Challenge Cup Semi-finals

"London pride!" yelled the front page of Monday morning's League Express, after one of the most nerve-wracking and sensational semi-final finishes ever.

Between them, Castleford Tigers and London Broncos had contrived to produce four separate climaxes in a final ten minutes, but it was to be the Broncos who had the last laugh - making history as the first professional Rugby League side in the capital to get to Wembley in the process.

To say the scenes at the end of their amazing 33-27 Headingley win were joyful is a gross understatement, as League legends Shaun Edwards and Martin Offiah danced a jig of delight in each other's arms. They certainly contrasted sharply with the tears of frustration being openly wept by many of the Castleford contingent in a crowd which had been served up with some of the finest sporting entertainment imaginable.

1999 SILK CUT CHALLENGE CUP SEMI FINAL RESULTS

Saturday 27th March, 1999

Castleford Tigers 27 ....London Broncos 33

Sunday 28th March, 1999

Bradford Bulls 10 ....Leeds Rhinos 23

London were 21-20 in front going into those last ten minutes, when Michael Eagar scorched through for a try off a miraculous over the shoulder pass from his captain Adrian Vowles. When pre-match injury doubt Danny Orr added the goal, it looked like the Broncos had blown their chance. But five minutes later they were back in the lead via veteran Aussie Peter Gill, and Brett Warton held his nerve to land a superb touchline conversion under the severest of pressure.

London were back on Wembley Way. Or were they?

With only one minute left on the clock, that man Orr equalised with a field goal that would surely push the game into extra-time. Er, no actually. The Broncos regained the ball from the restart and worked their way back upfield where, with everybody expecting another field goal, the hugely impressive Steele Retchless took advantage of the Tigers' defensive indecision to stride through for the winning score.

Gary Mercer in neck injury scare ● Cambridge beat Oxford 14-10 in annual Varsity match ● Salford advertise for players in Welsh newspapers ● Ovenden kicked out of National Conference ● Andy Gregory rumoured to be ready to quit Salford ● Grant Young out for season as London suffer prop shortage ● Melbourne boss Chris Anderson named Aussie Test coach ● Saints dismiss Phil Adamson release story ● RFL launch "love this game" logo ● Doncaster release Garry Schofield after only two months, Bramley snap him up ● Wigan sign Phil Jones from Lancashire Lynx ● London beat Castleford to make first ever Wembley ● BBC North to show Super League highlights ● John Kear appointed England coach ● Super League Week' is reborn as 'Total Rugby League'...

Before the game, much had been made of the fact that London's injury-ravaged pack wouldn't be big enough to contain their much larger adversaries. "Big people don't win Rugby League games, good people win Rugby League games," declared the Broncos' openly religious and enigmatic coach Dan Stains. "I just thank God that we got the job done."

Small consolation though it was, Castleford boss Stuart Raper could at least be proud of his side's monumental effort. "People say they don't remember losing semi-finalists," he said, "but I think they'll remember us in this game."

The question now was what would the Broncos' win mean for the national profile of Rugby League, and for the profile of the game in the capital?

At the McAlpine Stadium, one day later, it was to be Leeds Rhinos who emerged with smiles on their faces, as pre-match favourites Bradford Bulls saw their Wembley hopes ended by a Ryan Sheridan-inspired smash and grab raid.

The Bulls were leading 10-2, and had totally dominated the first half hour when the young scrum-half struck, pinching the ball from Bulls centre Danny Peacock before scampering away for a try. Midway through the second half he created another for Marcus St Hilaire, and then calmly edged his side a vital extra point in front with a field goal.

With a revitalised Robbie Paul back from injury, Bradford created plenty of opportunities but couldn't capitalise and Leeds finally ran out 10-23 winners gaining revenge for last season's Challenge Cup knockout by the Bulls at the same stage.

"We didn't start well," admitted Rhinos boss Graham Murray. "But we held them out and clawed our way back." Bradford boss Matthew Elliott insisted he wasn't too despondent: "It's early in the season and it's certainly not the end of the day for us. For a new team there are a lot of real positive things happening in our camp."

Iestyn Harris celebrates reaching Wembley

JJB SUPER LEAGUE - *Monday 29th March, 1999*

	P	W	D	L	F	A	D	PTS
Wigan Warriors	2	2	0	0	84	18	66	4
St Helens	2	2	0	0	64	34	30	4
Bradford Bulls	2	2	0	0	26	9	17	4
London Broncos	2	2	0	0	50	38	12	4
Warrington Wolves	2	2	0	0	35	28	7	4
Wakefield Trinity Wildcats	2	1	0	1	32	22	10	2
Halifax Blue Sox	2	1	0	1	31	30	1	2
Castleford Tigers	2	1	0	1	26	29	-3	2
Leeds Rhinos	2	1	0	1	36	40	-4	2
Huddersfield Giants	2	0	0	2	32	41	-9	0
Sheffield Eagles	2	0	0	2	26	44	-18	0
Gateshead Thunder	2	0	0	2	36	58	-22	0
Salford Reds	2	0	0	2	22	52	-30	0
Hull Sharks	2	0	0	2	9	66	-57	0

APRIL
Unsinkable Saints

As often happens, two sides who had clashed in the Challenge Cup were going to get the chance to re-prove their point within a matter of days.

So it was with the Bulls and the Rhinos, but the Thursday night TV clash on April Fool's Day was no joke. "Revenge mission: Bulls hold out in Odsal bloodbath" was the headline in Rugby League Express the following Monday. Match reporter Raymond Fletcher lost count of the blood-binnings at eight as the two rivals tore into each other with the same ferocity as five days before, the Bulls sneaking through for two invaluable league points by 18-14.

The match marked the start of the Easter weekend, with most teams - the clubs having voted for more fixtures in 1999 - playing two games in four days.

That didn't please coaches or players, with Rhinos boss Graham Murray speaking for both battered teams when he made a plea for a more humane fixture formula.

"It was a huge effort after a tough game on Sunday to come up with not just a game of football, but a performance like that," said Murray.

"I still can't believe we had to back up so quickly. Why can't we have one round every weekend? It's not fair to the players.

"There's more ice being used in the dressing room tonight than there has been since I've been here."

Over 16,000 spectators turned up on the night hoping and expecting an encounter to match the previous Sunday's Cup-tie, and they got it. The Bulls again surged into a 10-2 lead, had a try disallowed for a forward pass, and then Ryan Sheridan came up with a try that put Leeds right back into the game.

But there was to be no Bradford slump this time, and they took a 12-6 lead with an Henry Paul penalty goal after Leeds' Marc Glanville was sent to the sin bin for holding down, just as the half-time hooter sounded. By the time Glanville returned the Bulls had stretched their lead to 18-6 with a try from gamestar Robbie Paul, goaled by brother Henry.

Ryan Sheridan again was in top form for the Rhinos, following up his brilliant semi-final performance with another impressive display until going off injured in the second half. But it was a second defeat in three Super League games for Leeds - not an ideal start when compared to their nine-match winning

JJB SUPER LEAGUE
ROUND THREE RESULTS
Thursday 1st April, 1999
Bradford Bulls 18..Leeds Rhinos 14
Friday 2nd April, 1999
Castleford Tigers 14..Halifax Blue Sox 10
Gateshead Thunder 24 ....Wakefield Trinity Wildcats 6
London Broncos 12..Hull Sharks 10
Salford Reds 22 ....Warrington Wolves 26
Sheffield Eagles 32...Huddersfield Giants 28
Wigan Warriors 12..St Helens 14

Julian O'Neill takes on Neil Cowie as Saints down Wigan on Good Friday

run at the start of 1998.

Besides the Bulls, three clubs - St Helens, London Broncos and Warrington Wolves - maintained their own hundred per cent records on Good Friday.

The Wolves inflicted Salford Reds' third defeat with a 26-22 win at the Willows.

The Reds were still missing influential Aussie second-rowers Hudson Smith and Darren Brown as Lee Briers' landed two crucial touchline conversions to Jason Roach's two second-half tries. "Three wins out of three is a good positive start," said Wolves coach Darryl Van de Velde.

London Broncos, coming off that sensational win against the Tigers at Headingley, were not too impressive as they beat the Hull Sharks at the Stoop. The Sharks could well have grabbed their first two points - had Graeme Hallas not missed three relatively easy goal attempts.

St Helens had the stiffest task of the early pacesetters with the traditional derby with Wigan, this year at Central Park.

And what a mighty battle it proved to be, one befitting the last ever Good Friday derby at the great old ground, due for demolition at the end of the season.

The Warriors looked to have won it when Danny Moore snapped up a Greg

Florimo kick to put Wigan in the lead with only eleven minutes left on the clock, but Kevin Iro stunned Wigan with a trademark try three minutes later to seal a magnificent St Helens win.

"The Wigan game is in the past," said Saints coach Ellery Hanley immediately. "We now have to focus on Bradford."

Something had to give at the Don Valley Stadium and it was Huddersfield Giants as the Eagles picked up their first two league points with a 32-28 win.

"It was an appalling game," said Giants coach Mal Reilly. "Defensively both teams were awful. Ours was awful and until we learn to control it we won't win again."

Ben Sammut scored two tries for the newboys Gateshead Thunder as they registered their historic first win of the season against Wakefield Trinity at the Thunderdome, by 24-6.

The Tigers had every reason to struggle against the Blue Sox at Wheldon Road after their heartbreaking experience at Headingley the Saturday before, but a late try from Michael Eagar - completing his hat-trick - snatched the game for the Tigers by 14-10 and typified the Cas' spirit of '99.

Hardly time to draw breath and onto round four on Easter Monday.

A series of lacklustre games on the day fuelled the growing criticism from coaches of the fixture system for 1999. "Those who voted for it have shown no consideration for the players," Leeds coach Graham Murray told Total Rugby League magazine.

Murray's Rhinos bounced back from the Odsal defeat with a 38-12 win over Wembley opponents London Broncos at Headingley. "It was difficult to feel anything other than short-changed on leaving Headingley after this encounter," wrote TRL reporter Phil Caplan, although over twelve and a half thousand fans turned up for the Challenge Cup final rehearsal.

The Broncos held a 12-10 lead at the break through tries from Shane Millard and Karle Hammond and two Brett Warton goals, but there was to be no repeat of the fairytale finish against the Tigers, as Leeds scored four tries after the break to cruise home.

"Mentally it might steel us," said Broncos coach Dan Stains, one eye on Broncos' date with destiny at Wembley as they lost their unbeaten start to the Super League season, "but I don't think today gives them an advantage."

BBC announce a new 30-minute magazine programme fronted by Harry Gration devoted to Super League ● John Kear is appointed England coach for the end-of-season two-match series against France ● Salford Reds become first League club to get Investors in People award ● Stacey Jones turns down Wigan to extend his contract with Auckland Warriors ● Lord Hoyle becomes chairman of Warrington Wolves ● Hull Sharks rip up Matt Calland's contract because of an injury problem ● RFL announce two French clubs will play in Challenge Cup in 2000...

Two unbeaten sides met head to head at Knowsley Road in what should have been one of the closest matches of the season.

It didn't turn out like that at all as St Helens blasted the Bulls in front of their biggest crowd for almost three years.

Stand-off Tommy Martyn scored a personal best of 26 points with a try and eleven goals (from twelve attempts); Anthony Sullivan scored a hat-trick of tries; and Sean Long and Keiron Cunningham dominated the rucks in a vintage Saints performance.

April

Plenty was made of the Bulls' injury situation and the effects of those titanic two games against the Rhinos the week before, but Saints had hardly had a cakewalk at Wigan on Good Friday, so Bulls coach Matthew Elliott was making no excuses.

"There was an edge missing from our game," he said, "and if you don't compete physically with St Helens you're in trouble."

Just over the M62 motorway, a much closer and controversial game was unfolding as Warrington Wolves clung onto their own unbeaten start to the season with a 23-18 win over the Gateshead Thunder.

Referee Steve Nicholson's performance came under the spotlight as a 17-5 penalty count in favour of the home side was instrumental in deciding the outcome.

"I have to be very careful choosing my words," said an irate Thunder coach Shaun McRae after the match. "Put it this way, if one of my players had shown decision making like that they wouldn't be in first grade next week."

Luke Felsch's try on 56 minutes, converted by Ian Herron, gave the Thunder what looked like a winning 18-8 lead but the Wolves got two tries - courtesy of Jason Roach and Alan Hunte - on the back of a string of penalties and

JJB SUPER LEAGUE ROUND FOUR RESULTS	
Monday 4th April, 1999	
Hull Sharks 21	Sheffield Eagles 23
Leeds Rhinos 38	London Broncos 12
St Helens 58	Bradford Bulls 14
Wakefield Trinity Wildcats 22	Wigan Warriors 52
Warrington Wolves 23	Gateshead Thunder 18
Tuesday 5th April, 1999	
Halifax Blue Sox 30	Salford Reds 14
Wednesday 6th April, 1999	
Huddersfield Giants 14	Castleford Tigers 36

Warrington's Mark Hilton crashes through the Gateshead defence

Lee Briers field goal gave them a single point lead before Mark Forster's try in injury-time wrapped it up.

There was an even closer game at the Boulevard as Aussie Karl Lovell - a close season capture from Parramatta - scored the wining try off a kick from Geordie Chris Thorman with 13 seconds left on the clock, and Mark Aston's conversion secured a 23-21 win Sheffield Eagles .

It was a bitter blow for the Sharks - seemingly on course for their first win when Graeme Hallas handed off Keith Senior for a try ten minutes from time, and then form loose forward Rob Roberts put over a field goal for a four-point lead.

"The players are all mentally injured today," said Sharks coach Peter Walsh, "but the joint's still buzzing."

At Belle Vue, Denis Betts played his first game for eight months after incurring a serious knee injury against the Broncos - and it seemed like he had never been away as he scored his 100th try of his career as Wigan hammered the Wildcats 52-22. Wigan, with Jason Robinson at scrum-half, were 34-0 up at the break as Paul Johnson rattled up a hat-trick and Andy Farrell kicked eight goals from nine attempts.

Trinity came back after the break roared on by a crowd of over 6,000, but Wigan were never in danger.

On the Tuesday night there was little to cheer for the Salford Reds as they went down to defeat number four at the New Shay, the Blue Sox coming up with a 30-14 win, their second of the season.

"Too many players are in the comfort zone," said Andy Gregory. "So we'll be in the gym at 7.00am. Other people in other jobs have to go out early and work hard for a living. It wasn't a Super League performance."

It wasn't a great display from Halifax either, but at least their new halfback partnership of Gavin Clinch and Graham Holroyd showed signs of firing, though their top performer on the night was close-season signing Paul Broadbent.

To add to Salford's woes, they lost form hooker Malcolm Alker with a sprung shoulder.

One the Wednesday night, centre Michael Eagar and Francis Maloney each collected a brace of tries for Castleford Tigers as they accounted for the Giants at the McAlpine Stadium. Skipper Adrian Vowles also got a try. "Adrian has about 15 or 16 injuries," said coach Stuart Raper. "He is hung together by tape and strapping."

Fullback Paul Reilly was the Giants best, prompting coach Mal Reilly to say: "He's a local kid and we need four more of them to emerge quickly", as Huddersfield looked forward to a crucial date that weekend when Hull Sharks were due in town.

And then there was one.

After the weekend of 11 April, Ellery Hanley's Saints sat proud atop the table with the only 100% Super League record intact.

On the Friday night they travelled to the capital for a potentially daunting contest against the Broncos.

Three tries from fullback Paul Atcheson - who played all game wearing a bandage protecting the 15 stitches in a head wound - and two more from Anthony Sullivan eventually took the Saints home in a superb second-half display after London had deservedly led 16-10 at the break.

It was London's first home defeat under coach Dan Stains who could only stand on helpless as his troops fell like nine-pins. Stains had already lost three props in Marty McKenzie, Darren Bradstreet and Grant Young, and now saw winger Brett Warton - whose goal-kicking had been a revelation - break an arm early in the second half, just after he had extended the Broncos lead with a penalty.

Saints' marvellous comeback confirmed their Championship credentials in many people's minds, but Hanley refused to be carried away.

"Nothing changed and nothing will change," he said. "I take one game at a time, it's as simple as that."

April

The Wolves suffered their first loss of the season, at the hands of Wigan at Central Park. The Warriors had Jason Robinson and Andy Farrell starting at halfback in the absence of Tony Smith - struggling to recover from a broken ankle - and Greg Florimo - out with a knee problem - were missing Kris Radlinski, and suffered further blows when Paul Johnson (foot) and Simon Haughton (shoulder) were added to the injury list.

Wigan, at the end of a week in which Kiwi scrum-half Stacey Jones finally turned down the chance of a move to the club - were 18-0 up at the break through tries to Mark Reber, back at hooker, Gary Connolly and Farrell, which was enough to hold off what was looking by now a very competitive Wolves side.

The Eagles moved up to the fringes of the top-five, inflicting the Rhinos' third loss of the season in a fine match at the Don Valley Stadium, by 22-16.

Jeff Hardy slotted in at stand-off in the injury absence of Martin Pearson (ribs) and had a blinder, scoring the winning try with four minutes left on the clock.

JJB SUPER LEAGUE
ROUND FIVE RESULTS
Friday 9th April, 1999

London Broncos 18 ....St Helens 34

Saturday 10th April, 1999

Gateshead Thunder 22..Halifax Blue Sox 14

Sunday 11th April, 1999

Bradford Bulls 26 ....Wakefield Trinity Wildcats 16
Huddersfield Giants 26 ....Hull Sharks 12
Salford Reds 17 ....Castleford Tigers 29
Sheffield Eagles 22..Leeds Rhinos 16
Wigan Warriors 24 ....Warrington Wolves 10

Mark Aston did plenty of damage with some punishing 40/20 kicks in the first half and it was ironic that the team which had suffered Wembleyitis in 1998, took full advantage of another suffering from the same syndrome a year later.

Rhinos boss Graham Murray was at a loss as to why his side should give up a 14-4 half-time lead. "There are no excuses for that performance," he said."

The Bulls had to grind out a 26-16 win against Wakefield at Odsal, Matthew Elliott reflecting that the "game was played at a snail's pace."

"We are getting up to the level of intensity that is required," said Wildcats boss Andy Kelly, seeing it slightly differently.

It was only 10-8 at half-time, but twelve points in as many minutes after the break, via tries from David Boyle and Danny Peacock, both converted by Steve McNamara, proved crucial as tries from Neil Law and Shane Kenward put Trinity within six points with five minutes to go. Fortunately for the Bulls, gamestar James Lowes was on hand to score a trademark try from dummy-half to keep Bradford in the top-five.

Gateshead got their second win of the season on the Saturday against the Blue Sox - lacking Chris Chester, Kelvin Skerrett and Martin Moana - by 22-14, a Willie Peters interception on 50 minutes ending the Blue Sox hopes.

At the McAlpine, the Huddersfield Giants ended their run of 17 consecutive Super League defeats, hanging over the club since 1998, with the Hull Sharks the victims, 26-12.

It was coach Mal Reilly's first win. "I'm sure the win will have helped the guys mentally," he said. "But we could have had three or four wins because we haven't really played badly all season."

Bobbie Goulding kicked five goals and scored a brilliant solo try against a Sharks team missing eight players through injury, and then lost Steve Prescott midway through the second half. Jamie Smith deputised and gifted a try to Basil Richards minutes later, after throwing a wild pass in his own in-goal area, and then three minutes later spilled the ball in a tackle near his own line and from the scrum Andy Cheetham raced in. Peter Walsh refused to blame Smith personally but remarked after the game: "Teams should be queuing up to play Hull because we just give, give, give."

"What a load of rubbish" was the chant from a section of the Salford crowd after the Reds went down to Super League defeat number five at the Willows, losing 29-17 to the Tigers, who moved into third spot in the table.

"People pay their money and they are entitled to shout what they want," said a

Bobbie Goulding races away from Andy Ireland as Huddersfield end their losing sequence against Hull

defiant Andy Gregory. "I'll cop all the flak, it doesn't bother me."

Danny Orr was impressive for the Tigers who raced into an 11-0 lead and never looked like losing, a Jason Flowers try eight minutes from time putting the nail in Salford's coffin.

Halifax Blue Sox had hardly looked like emulating their 1998 third in Super League but on the Friday night of round six they looked the business, putting Wigan to the sword at the New Shay 19-8.

It was Halifax's first win over Wigan in Super League as Chris Chester and Kelvin Skerrett were back and South African Jamie Bloem move into the second row with great effect.

Stories of financial troubles at the Shay were beginning to emerge with coach John Pendlebury saying after the game: "I'm piggy in the middle (between the directors and the players)".

Aussie halfback Gavin Clinch was the gamestar as Wigan boss John Monie conceded. "Gavin Clinch kicked us to death," he said. "I don't like to lose any game but you are going to lose a few in a season." But Wigan's squad was starting to wear a little thin, with local Phil Jones signed from

Warrington Wolves sign St Helens prop Andy Leathem ● Gateshead Thunder sign forward Steve O'Neill from Newcastle rugby union ● Sheffield Eagles announce they are to switch their home game against Bradford Bulls to Chesterfield ● Lincoln Financial Group announced as sponsors of World Cup in 2000 ● Edinburgh and Leicester named as On the Road venues ● Hull Sharks prop Steve Holgate is out for the season with a shoulder injury ● Auckland Warriors announce bid to bring Paul brothers home after they star for New Zealand in the 20-14 ANZAC Day Test ● RFL appoint Jason Harborow...

Lancashire Lynx making his debut, joining other youngsters Wes Davies, Rob Ball and Mark Smith. Mick Cassidy gave Wigan the lead with a try but the Blue Sox comeback included a Carl Gillespie try which featured a classic "Clinch-pinch" - a one-on-one ball-stealing feat on Davies - and three field goals - two from

April

Graham Holroyd and one from Clinch.

Wigan remained in the top three thanks to Gateshead's shock 17-14 win at Castleford on the Sunday night. The Tigers were twice denied tries by the video referee. "If the game hadn't been on TV we would have probably won," opined Cas coach Stuart Raper after the game, while taking a swipe at Gateshead's style of play. "I don't want to copy Gateshead's head down-arse up approach. That sends me to sleep."

Andy Gregory saw his side pipped by the Giants at the Willows, 15-14, thanks to a Bobbie Goulding field goal four minutes from time, after the Reds had come back from 14-2 at half-time.

Giants boss Mal Reilly wasn't too happy though. "It was the worst team performance I have ever been associated with," was his verdict.

Two tries from Leroy Rivett helped Leeds Rhinos to a less than impressive 22-18 win against the Sharks at Headingley.

It was the Sharks' fourth loss of the campaign by just a single score and they played with plenty of heart while fielding three impressive debutant teenagers in 16 year old Richard Horne, Craig Poucher and Richard Fletcher. "The commitment was top shelf and you couldn't ask for anything better than that," said Peter Walsh after the game, reflecting on three sin-binnings and a 13-4 penalty count against his team.

**JJB SUPER LEAGUE
ROUND SIX RESULTS**
Friday 16th April, 1999
Leeds Rhinos 22 ....Hull Sharks 18
Halifax Blue Sox 19.............................Wigan Warriors 8
Sunday 18th April, 1999
Castleford Tigers 14 ....Gateshead Thunder 17
Salford Reds 14 ....Huddersfield Giants 15
St Helens 39.......................................Sheffield Eagles 30
Wakefield Trinity Wildcats 40 ....London Broncos 8
Warrington Wolves 14 ....Bradford Bulls 22

If Leeds still had a touch of the Wembley nerves, London Broncos had them in abundance. They went down 40-8 against the impressive Wildcats at Belle Vue, who were fast making a nonsense of their favoritism for relegation. A try hat-trick and six goals from Adam Hughes stunned the Broncos, who had Robbie Simpson put on report after a high tackle on Wakefield prop Francis Stephenson. Simpson copped a one-match ban.

Warrington Wolves had Andy Leathem on debut as they tried to avenge the Challenge Cup humiliation at the hands of Bradford Bulls. Over seven and half thousand fans packed Wilderspool as the Bulls ended the Wolves' unbeaten home record to leapfrog them into second place in the table. James Lowes was once again outstanding in a bruiser of a game the Bulls won 22-14.

But they were all still chasing St Helens who just held off a series of Sheffield comebacks, 39-30, after the leaders had shot into a 22-6 lead on the half-hour mark. Not for the first time, a coach had grounds for concern at refereeing interpretations with Eagles boss John Kear saying of official Karl Kirkpatrick's policing of the ten metres: "I'm glad he's not measuring my carpets!"

The Tigers had never beaten Wigan in Super League and they were expected to cop a backlash from Wigan's loss at Halifax the week before when they travelled over the Pennines that Sunday.

"I never thought we were going to lose," said captain Adrian Vowles after Castleford's stunning 24-8 win. "That's not being cocky, it's just there is a different feeling about this side this year."

Brad Davis had a brilliant game in an outstanding Castleford team performance, scoring the first try from a Danny Orr grubber. Wigan's first try didn't come until ten minutes before the end, via Mark Reber, and the return from injury of Greg Florimo and Tony Smith couldn't halt the Tigers.

"Some of the senior players look flat and the youngsters are finding out how hard it is to play in Super League," said John Monie.

Wigan were back in fifth now with local rivals St Helens seemingly unstoppable at the top, a 30-10 win at the Boulevard achieved with four long range tries - two from Anthony Sullivan. It

Wakefield's Jamie Field skips through the London ranks

could have been worse for Hull who were 30-0 down early in the second half, but with their youngsters again proving their ability - Paul Cooke was given his debut from the bench - they salvaged some pride.

Thankfully for the Sharks, Salford Reds were also registering defeat number seven on the same afternoon, at the Thunderdome, Gateshead skipper Kerrod Walters at the centre of a 38-14 win that upped the pressure on Reds coach Andy Gregory.

Super League Europe advertise for a replacement for Maurice Lindsay who is set to retire at the end of the season ● Widnes announce they are to apply for Super League franchise ● Australian legend Alfie Langer announces his retirement from Rugby League ● Bulls prop Brian McDermott is fined for causing actual bodily harm ● Ian Tonks signs a new two-year deal at Castleford ● Dale Laughton is banned for two matches after a headbutt on Wakefield's Andy Fisher ● Huddersfield Giants' Bobbie Goulding denies reports he is leaving for Australia ● Wigan chairman Peter Norbury denies a fall out with captain Andy Farrell...

"I have never been a loser or a quitter," said Gregory after the match. "I have a job to do. I shall see my contract through. I will still be here at the end of the season."

The Rhinos, with Wembley only a week away, came back from an early 6-0 deficit at McAlpine to run out 42-20 winners over the Giants.

Coach Graham Murray was happy to see his side hitting some form and not to suffer any injuries, although he had to bring Darren Fleary off the field as the fiery prop was involved in a running feud with Giants' Leeds old boy Nick Fozzard. There was another two tries for Leroy Rivett and one for Francis Cummins - the 100th of his career.

No apparent re-discovery of form for Leeds' Challenge Cup final opponents though as the stuttering Broncos sank to their fourth straight defeat at the hands of the Wolves, 30-18.

"Going to Wembley had nothing to do with this defeat," said Dan Stains. "We were beaten by a better team." With Shaun Edwards still nursing a broken hand and not certain of making Wembley, the Broncos hopes of a Cup

Wigan's Lee Gilmour gets a lift from
Castleford's Dean Sampson

turnaround were looking bleaker by the week, two Jason Roach tries helping the Wolves pull away in the second half after Martin Offiah had given the Broncos the lead on 42 minutes.

And on the Friday night a great performance by Steve McNamara helped the Bulls to a 20-2 victory in the local derby against the Blue Sox, a week after he had been dropped from the side to play at Warrington. McNamara was handed the captaincy in the absence of Robbie Paul - on Test duty down under along with brother Henry.

Another Test player, Dale Laughton, was sent off in a spiteful game between the Eagles and the Wildcats at the Don Valley Stadium, for headbutting Andy Fisher. He copped a two-match ban the following Tuesday. Darren Turner was found to have no case to answer after being put on report for a challenge on Tony Kemp. A late Bright Sodje try finally clinched a 22-12 win for Sheffield.

JJB SUPER LEAGUE
ROUND SEVEN RESULTS
Friday 23rd April, 1999
Bradford Bulls 20...Halifax Blue Sox 2
Saturday 24th April, 1999
London Broncos 18....................................Warrington Wolves 30
Sunday 25th April, 1999
Gateshead Thunder 38 ....Salford Reds 14
Huddersfield Giants 20...Leeds Rhinos 42
Hull Sharks 10 ....St Helens 30
Sheffield Eagles 22 ....Wakefield Trinity Wildcats 12
Wigan Warriors 8 ....Castleford Tigers 24

JJB SUPER LEAGUE - *Monday 26th April, 1999*

	P	W	D	L	F	A	D	PTS
St Helens	7	7	0	0	239	118	121	14
Bradford Bulls	7	6	0	1	126	113	13	12
Castleford Tigers	7	5	0	2	143	95	48	10
Warrington Wolves	7	5	0	2	138	132	6	10
Wigan Warriors	7	4	0	3	188	107	81	8
Leeds Rhinos	7	4	0	3	168	130	38	8
Gateshead Thunder	7	4	0	3	155	129	26	8
Sheffield Eagles	7	4	0	3	155	160	-5	8
Halifax Blue Sox	7	3	0	4	106	108	-2	6
London Broncos	7	3	0	4	118	190	-72	6
Wakefield Trinity Wildcats	7	2	0	5	128	154	-26	4
Huddersfield Giants	7	2	0	5	135	177	-42	4
Salford Reds	7	0	0	7	103	190	-87	0
Hull Sharks	7	0	0	7	80	179	-99	0

CHALLENGE CUP FINAL
Record breakers

1999 was a special year in the history of the Challenge Cup - the last to be staged at the old Empire Stadium before it was knocked down to accommodate a new modern national stadium.

And the great old stadium - home to the Challenge Cup final for the first time in 1929 - bade a fond farewell in rip-roaring style.

Especially for the huge contingent of Leeds Rhinos supporters, who saw their heroes win Leeds' first Challenge Cup since 1978, and shatter some all-time records along the way: the biggest ever win at Wembley, beating the 33-point margin set by Wakefield Trinity in 1960 (Wakefield beat Hull 38-5); the highest score registered in a Challenge Cup final, succeeding the 40 scored by St Helens three years before; and the highest number of tries scored by a winning team at Wembley, as they touched down nine times, equalling Huddersfield's 1915 record, when they beat St Helens 37-3 at Oldham.

The result suggested a totally one-sided match. But for 50 minutes the history-making Broncos - more or less written off before the final because of their horrific run of injuries - gave their bigger and heavier counterparts one heck of a game, before size and possession drained away the last of their resolve.

A 40-point Rhinos blitz in the last half-hour without reply was cruel to the Londoners on their big day out.

"Leeds are a big, strong, powerful team," reflected London coach Dan Stains straight after the game. "They had the possession and the weight, and that ground us down. We had an opportunity to grab history, but we will be back."

Rhinos coach Graham Murray's strategy of patiently wearing down the Broncos couldn't have worked better. And with the heavy work done, Leeds' seven second-half tries left onlookers - and London's lighter pack - totally breathless.

"All the talk is of aggressive defence, but there is a lot of ability in this side," Murray reminded us. "Every one of my blokes deserves what they got, and the bottom line is they have brought credibility back to Leeds."

There were outstanding individuals on both sides. Captain Iestyn Harris had been the pre-match favourite to win the Lance Todd Trophy, and in any other year his 20-point, eight-goal haul - equalling two Wembley records - might have won a fair few people some money. But for the fourth time this decade the Lance Todd Trophy went to a winger - only one player, St Helens South African Len Killeen in 1966, had achieved it before Martin Offiah's first in 1992.

Offiah had scored four Wembley tries in four previous Wembleys, adding a fifth as he opened the scoring in sensational style in only the fifth minute of the Wembley final. But injury, that affected the rest of his season, saw him hobble off at half-time, never to return.

But even Offiah's Wembley scoring feats were overshadowed by the try-scoring performance from Leroy Rivett. The 22 year old scored only the second hat-trick at Wembley in a Challenge Cup final, with a thrilling 90-metre interception try on 67 minutes, before completing Wembley's first ever four-timer three minutes from the end.

There were other contenders. Broncos stand-off Karle Hammond, in his third Wembley final, would have strolled off with it if the result had gone London's way. In the centre, Greg Fleming was chiefly responsible for restricting Harris with some high-pressure hits, as well as scoring the try that put the Broncos back into the lead three minutes into the second half.

In a powerhouse Rhinos pack Darren Fleary, Anthony Farrell, Adrian Morley and Barrie McDermott all got votes from the pressmen. And at their heels Ryan Sheridan did so much to absorb the damage of the early Broncos onslaught. Sheridan had produced the gamebreaker five minutes before the half-time hooter when he got back to cut down Shaun Edwards, who had supported a Steele Retchless break up the middle in classic style. It prevented the Broncos going into a 16-6 lead.

It was Sheridan who made a searing break straight from the back of the scrum on his own '20' on 58 minutes. He was just cut down by Rob Smyth and Robbie Simpson, but two plays later Harris sent out an awesome long ball for Farrell and Richie Blackmore to create the overlap for Rivett's second.

The Rhinos were two scores clear, and the scoring roll had begun.

Leeds' damage limitation exercise of the first half-hour had looked like it might founder. London had got a dream start - after a scare when a magnificent Tulsen Tollett tackle stopped Terry Newton inches short - when John Timu put in a kick down the left centre. He mis-hit it, the ball ricocheted off Blackmore, and Offiah collected and bamboozled Rivett and Blackmore before stepping Harris on his way to the line,

After an interminable delay while the video referee decided whether Offiah had been onside, Rob Smyth put over a mighty conversion and we were sniffing a sensation.

The Rhinos were struggling to find their composure, demonstrated when a mix up at dummy-half ended with a pass bouncing off Marc Glanville's head to gift the Broncos possession. They didn't waste it, as Hammond attacked down the right this time, and a split-second decoy move fooled Brad Godden, who took out the wrong runner in Fleming, and Simpson scythed through for a 10-0 lead.

But the Rhinos gradually started to turn the screw.

Simpson was penalised for a punch in the tackle on the intervention of the touch-judge, Terry Newton was tackled at dummy-half on the line, Offiah could find no way out of his own in-goal after taking a Harris kick, and when Shaun Edwards - who took a heap of punishment in this game while playing with pain-killing injections - was pulled up under his own posts for offside at the play-the-ball, it was a relief for the Broncos when Harris took the two easy points on offer.

Sheridan's scramble to deny Hammond proved crucial as Godden broke for 20 metres from dummy-half and within a minute Leeds had their first try.

It took a clever decoy move, as Daryl Powell twice dummied drop-offs with Farrell and Glanville, sucking in Edwards and haring through a gap in the right centre before lofting a pass via the fingertips of Offiah to Rivett.

The young winger scored try number one, wrong-footing the back-pedalling Offiah and riding John Timu's tackle to pull it back to 10-6.

More Leeds' pressure and, after Jackson had trapped Edwards in-goal with an attacking kick, they thought they had taken the lead when Sheridan put in Fleary, but Powell was pulled back for the shepherd.

Sheridan's backtrack on Edwards proved itself even more important when, in the last act of the half, and with the Broncos beginning to show signs of wear and tear from a pulsating 40 minutes, Fleary went down the middle, handed off Simpson and put a lovely inside ball to the supporting Godden.

Godden's one-two with Lee Jackson - though there looked a forward pass at the end - was just enough to foil the scrambling Simpson, Edwards and Shane Millard,

SILK CUT CHALLENGE CUP FINAL

LEEDS RHINOS 52 ....**LONDON BRONCOS 16**
Wembley Stadium - Saturday 1st May, 1999

RHINOS: Iestyn Harris; Leroy Rivett; Richie Blackmore; Brad Godden; Francis Cummins; Daryl Powell; Ryan Sheridan; Barrie McDermott; Terry Newton; Darren Fleary; Adrian Morley; Anthony Farrell; Marc Glanville.
Subs: Marcus St Hilaire for Powell (ht); Lee Jackson for Newton (22); Andy Hay for Glanville (49); Jamie Mathiou for McDermott (26).
McDermott for Fleary (43); Newton for Farrell (65).
Tries: Rivett (26, 56, 65, 77), Godden (40), McDermott (51), St Hilaire (60), Harris (71), Cummins (73); **Goals:** Harris 8

BRONCOS: Tulsen Tollett; Rob Smyth; Greg Fleming; John Timu; Martin Offiah; Karle Hammond; Shaun Edwards; Steele Retchless; Robbie Beazley; Matt Salter; Shane Millard; Robbie Simpson; Peter Gill. *Subs:* Matt Toshack for Salter (19); Dean Callaway for Beazley (57); Chris Ryan for Offiah (ht); Glen Air for Tollett (78).
Salter for Gill (37bb, reversed 53); Beazley for Simpson (62).
Tries: Offiah (5), Simpson (12), Fleming (43); **Goals:** Smyth 2

League Express Men of the Match -
Rhinos: Ryan Sheridan; **Broncos:** Karle Hammond
Penalties: 7-7; **HT:** 12-10; **Ref:** R Smith (Castleford); **Att:** 73,242

and Godden dropped under the posts to give Leeds, after Harris's second goal, an unlikely lead.

The Broncos were back in the lead within two minutes of the second half.

Hammond looked to have taken a crazy option on the last tackle when he went blind from dummy-half, but as he was tackled he lobbed an inside ball to substitute Matt Toshack. Toshack put a high kick to the right wing and as Francis Cummins hesitated, Fleming took the ball on the run and rounded to the posts.

There was another interminable wait as the BBC tried to find a camera angle to decide if Fleming had been in front of the kicker. After over three minutes, the video referee was able to make a decision in London's favour.

Smyth converted, but a marginal decision opened the floodgates. The Rhinos attacked down the right and Rivett put in a kick down the touchline which just dribbled dead before Lee Jackson, a workhorse substitute for Newton half way through the first half, could get a hand to it.

But Rivett was brought down after he'd kicked by Timu and, from the tap penalty, Barrie McDermott drove in the ball, Matt Salter dashed diagonally out

The victorious Leeds side celebrate their Challenge Cup success

of the line to meet him, but was brushed aside, and the big prop stepped Millard on an unstoppable charge to score.

Harris's conversion gave the Rhinos back the lead they were never going to give up, although London never stopped chipping away, Jackson defusing chips from Edwards and Hammond, and Millard being adjudged to have not grounded the ball over the Leeds line five minutes from the end.

But the tide of the game was coloured blue and amber from the moment that Sheridan scampered past Peter Gill and set up Rivett's second try. Harris's touchline conversion was a hammer blow.

A minute later Andy Hay put Morley through the sweetest of gaps down the right. Tollett cut him down, but from the play-the-ball Hay again linked with Jackson and he fed Marcus St Hilaire for another high-speed try.

Hammond regained possession for the Broncos with the second of his low driving kick-offs to the touchline, and had his chip near the Leeds line collected by the covering Jackson before the Broncos' road back was blocked off for good.

Hammond fired out a long pass to the left, looking for the try that would get the Broncos back into the game. Three inches higher, and Tollett would have scored four points. But Rivett just managed to make the ball stick before racing 90 metres for the clincher.

Four minutes later Harris got his reward for keeping the ball alive, when St Hilaire made the break in the Broncos '20', and supplied him with the try-making pass; two minutes after that a Godden break gave Harris the chance to send Francis Cummins racing down the left for his second try at Wembley; and a minute from normal time Rivett brilliantly brushed off the tackles of subs Dean Callaway and Glen Air to round off 70 years of try-scoring at Wembley Stadium.

MAY
Nuts in May

The furore surrounding the increase in fixtures had started way back at the end of 1998 but the reality really started to hit home in May 1999.

The Challenge Cup final was on Mayday bank holiday weekend so it didn't seem too bad an idea for a round of fixtures to be squeezed in on the Monday. Apart from the Wembley finalists - who were given a couple of days grace to squeeze their games in - Leeds having another tricky tie the following Friday against the Wildcats.

Unfortunately for the Rhinos, their immediate reward for that record win at Wembley was a trip to St Helens on the Tuesday who rattled up a 62-18 win. "A disgrace," blasted coach Graham Murray. "There were a few people robbed here tonight and the spectators were the main ones. A fixture schedule like this devalues the game."

Saints were quite happy to tighten their grip at the top of the table with twelve tries, in front of 11,314 people.

The following night London Broncos put in an heroic performance at the New Shay, denied by two late tries by Martin Moana and Paul Broadbent in a 26-24 loss. "The players showed real ticker and class," said Dan Stains.

The midweek stuff might have been moderate fare but the Monday TV game was an absolute belter as the Tigers and the Bulls fought out an 18-18 draw at Wheldon Road.

Cas looked to have the win in the bag when, with the Tigers leading 18-16, Paul Anderson was sent off by referee Steve Ganson for leading with the elbow. Bulls coach Matthew Elliott claimed after the game that the victim Lee Harland wasn't hurt but Anderson copped a two-match ban. As it was, Steve McNamara levelled with a 40-metre penalty in the most frantic finish of the season.

JJB SUPER LEAGUE
ROUND EIGHT RESULTS
Monday 3rd May, 1999

Castleford Tigers 18 ....Bradford Bulls 18
Gateshead Thunder 36 ....Huddersfield Giants 10
Salford Reds 6 ....Wigan Warriors 46
Wakefield Trinity Wildcats 22 ....Hull Sharks 29
Warrington Wolves 40 ....Sheffield Eagles 4

Tuesday 4th May, 1999

St Helens 62..Leeds Rhinos 18

Wednesday 5th May, 1999

Halifax Blue Sox 26 ....London Broncos 24

Bulls fans will probably remember the match as Danny Peacock's last for the club, the popular Aussie centre having to finally call it a day after another serious knee injury.

Peter Walsh earned himself a reprieve as the Hull Sharks got off the mark at Belle Vue with a 29-22 win, with the local youngsters to the fore once more as the Sharks raced into a 15-0 lead at the break against a Wildcats side lacking invention with both Tony Kemp and Willie Poching absent.

No way through for Jason Flowers as the Tigers and Bulls fight out a bank holiday thriller

"Winning solves a lot of problems," said Walsh.

Which left Salford looking sad at the bottom of the pile after Wigan hammered them 46-6 at the Willows on the Monday night.

It was a cruel outcome for the Reds, who opened with a Carl Briggs try and should have been 12-0 up when Paul Highton went over by the posts. Referee Steve Presley ruled he hadn't grounded the ball without consulting the video referee, although replays proved he had scored.

Jason Robinson took full advantage, scoring a hat-trick from fullback and centre.

Warrington gave Sheffield a real hiding at Wilderspool, after the club paraded their 1974 Cup winning side, in what was the Wolves' best performance of the year. "We got our arses kicked," said a bemused Sheffield coach John Kear.

Meanwhile, stand-off Will Robinson was cementing his reputation at the Thunderdome as Gateshead beat Hudersfield Giants 36-10. "Some of the kids out there are just not up to it," said Mal Reilly.

As stories surfaced that Super League Europe, judged as a moderate performer by many of the clubs, might be about to relocate at Rugby Football League headquarters, Ellery Hanley's St Helens could not stop winning.

They had to survive watersplash conditions in the Friday night TV game to withstand a stiff challenge from Huddersfield Giants at the McAlpine, coming out 11-0 winners.

Form winger Anthony Sullivan dislocated a shoulder as the Saints winning run was stretched to nine games.

Hooker Keiron Cunningham summed the night up: "Those are the worst conditions I have played in in my life," he said.

It wasn't ideal for open Rugby League but it was a terrific game as the Giants' St Helens old boy Bobbie Goulding put in a magnificent display. It had looked like routine stuff for the leaders against an already struggling side when Fereti Tuilagi charged into the corner after only four minutes of the match. But it wasn't until a searing break by young stand-off Scott Barrow sent in skipper Chris Joynt, late in the second half, that the game was won. "If we play like that in coming games we will certainly pick up a lot more points," said Giants' boss Mal Reilly.

The Bulls had little problem staying within three points of St Helens in second place when the Salford Reds were swept aside 46-6 for the second time in a week, this time at Odsal. On the day that Andy Gregory was inducted into the Wigan Hall of Fame, he saw his side later that evening totally overrun by the power of the Bulls.

The Reds had Gary Broadbent, Malcolm Alker and David Hulme back after injury and were just about in it in the first half, trailing 18-6 at the break despite the sin-binnings of Craig Makin and Steve Blakeley. "With a 16-4 penalty count against you, you're not going to win many games," said Gregory after watching Bradford totally dominate the second half. "We've got to plod on and my first priority is to get a team on the field for Wednesday against Leeds."

Stuart Spruce scored two tries in a fabulous individual display that had assistant coach Brian Noble nominate in him as a must for the Great Britain Tri-Series squad.

JJB SUPER LEAGUE
ROUND NINE RESULTS
Friday 7th May, 1999
Huddersfield Giants 0 ....St Helens 11
Leeds Rhinos 22 ....Wakefield Trinity Wildcats 8
Saturday 8th May, 1999
Sheffield Eagles 27 ....Halifax Blue Sox 8
Sunday 9th May, 1999
Bradford Bulls 46 ....Salford Reds 6
Hull Sharks 22 ....Warrington Wolves 33
London Broncos 12 ....Castleford Tigers 12
Wigan Warriors 16 ....Gateshead Thunder 13
Wednesday 12th May, 1999
Salford Reds 30 ....Leeds Rhinos 38

New scheme for the redevelopment of Odsal is announced ● Bulls prop Paul Anderson is banned for two matches for leading with elbow against Cas ● Halifax Blue Sox survive a winding up petition from Inland Revenue, but vow to stay in Super League ● Toa Kohe-Love signs two-year extension to his contract at Wilderspool, Danny Farrar a one-year deal ● Cas sign Brad Hepi on short term contract ● former chairman Roy Waudby ready to buy out David Lloyd at Hull Sharks ● Super League Europe sign broadcast deal with Talk Radio for season 2000 ● World Cup 2000 launched at Savoy Hotel in London ● Gateshead sign Mick Jenkins from Workington Town after Kerrod Walters flies home to be with his wife, victim of a road accident in Thailand ● Andy Gregory and Billy Blan installed in Wigan Hall of Fame as Reds boss calls it quits ● John Harvey named as new Salford boss...

The Friday night rain also marred the Leeds-Wakefield clash at Headingley, where the Wildcats had two men sin-binned either side of half-time, when they led 8-2, before tries to Marvin Golden, Ryan Sheridan and Francis Cummins took Leeds home and into seventh place.

Wildcats coach Andy Kelly's post-match criticism of his side's treatment by referees prompted a meeting between the club and RFL's liaison officer John Holdsworth later that week.

Leeds - with Kiwi national coach Frank Endacott the latest to be tipped as Graham Murray's successor at the end of the season - were level on ten points with Gateshead and Sheffield Eagles at the end of the weekend.

On the Saturday the Eagles played one of their best games of the season beating Halifax Blue Sox 27-8. Three tries in nine minutes in the second half from Keith Senior, Jeff Hardy and Dale Cardoza proved too much for a Blue Sox side who had had a tough game only two and half days before against the Broncos.

The Thunder almost got into the top-five for the first time, a Jason Robinson wonder try proving the difference, when he took a Will Robinson bomb on his foot and hared 70 metres for a crucial try and an eventual 16-13 win for the Warriors. "It's the first bit of luck we have had all year," said coach John Monie. Robinson also prevented Willie Peters

Jason Robinson rips into the Gateshead defence

from taking the league points with a superb cover tackle in the closing stages.

Despite the defeat it was an amazing performance by the Thunder who had been rocked on the morning of the match when skipper Kerrod Walters had left for Thailand to be at the bedside of his wife - involved in a serious road accident while on holiday there.

Warrington Wolves retained third spot in the table thanks to another great performance from halfback Lee Briers, who set up three of the Wolves' six tries at the Boulevard, also kicking four goals and field goal in a 33-22 win. A great second-half comeback from the Sharks, with youngster Paul Cooke having a great game at stand-off, saw them get to within four points of the Wolves but Scott Wilson and Mark Forster scored tries to keep Warrington safe.

In London, Castleford played their second draw of the week, as the Broncos ended their own run of five consecutive defeats. Illawarra prop Scott Cram arrived the day before to play a fine match and could have been the hero but he just lost control of the ball as he went over for what would have been the winning try.

"My message to all Broncos supporters is to stay strong in these difficult times for us," said coach Dan Stains.

Paul Sculthorpe halted by Adam Hughes as the Wildcats end Saints' 100% record

Friday night was Wakefield's big chance to impress in front of the TV cameras.

Their old Belle Vue ground wasn't considered suitable for the nation's eyes, so the home game against league-leaders St Helens was switched to Barnsley soccer club's Oakwell ground.

It was the shock of the season as winger Lynton Stott hammered over a 40-metre field goal with four minutes left on the clock to secure a 23-22 win. "We weren't going to let this one go," said Stott.

It was a stunning way for Saints to lose their 100% record as Wakefield shot into a 20-6 lead after 30 minutes and fought and harried for every scrap after that.

"Wakefield were a better football side than us tonight," concluded Saints coach Ellery Hanley.

The news that Andy Gregory and Salford Reds had parted company after

**JJB SUPER LEAGUE
ROUND TEN RESULTS**
Friday 14th May, 1999
Wakefield Trinity Wildcats 23 ....St Helens 22
Sunday 16th May, 1999
Castleford Tigers 10 ....Sheffield Eagles 6
Gateshead Thunder 12 ....Bradford Bulls 22
Halifax Blue Sox 30 ....Hull Sharks 12
Salford Reds 31..London Broncos 14
Warrington Wolves 10 ....Leeds Rhinos 28
Wigan Warriors 36 ....Huddersfield Giants 2
Wednesday 19th May, 1999
Castleford Tigers 14 ....St Helens 33
Gateshead Thunder 25 ....Hull Sharks 6

four years leaked out the previous Tuesday morning.

"I don't mind admitting that I am looking forward to getting up every morning, walking my dog, watching some TV, doing what I want to do and not having to go to Salford every day," Gregory said at a press conference later that day.

The news couldn't have come at a more crucial time for the Reds who were due to play the first of the many scheduled Wednesday night fixtures at home to the Rhinos, who needed to string some wins together if they were going to climb into the top-three.

The Reds - with John Foran and Steve O'Neill taking temporary charge of the team - were absolutely dead and buried on the hour mark when Francis Cummins went in for the Rhinos' seventh try and a 38-6 lead.

But an incredible four-try, 24-point comeback almost stunned the Rhinos, who were playing their fourth game in eleven days.

The Reds did end their losing run at last on the following Sunday when they bettered the struggling London Broncos 31-14 at the Willows, with the brilliant Steve Blakeley scoring a hat-trick of tries and kicking five goals and a field goal.

"That's lifted a big cloud over Salford," smiled Foran, who revealed that he had worked hard on defence in the days preceding the match.

Salford remained bottom but only on points difference as the Sharks came away with nothing from their visit to the New Shay.

Sox's talisman Gary Mercer was back from a neck injury incurred at the start of the season that had threatened to end his career and, once again, Gavin Clinch was at the heart of a win that saw Halifax edge into eighth place, only four points adrift of the top-five.

Sheffield Eagles boss John Kear was highly critical of referee Steve Nicholson after seeing his side go down 10-6 to Castleford Tigers at Wheldon Road, a game which marked a watershed for both clubs in 1999.

The Eagles had three tries disallowed, prompting Kear to suggest that Tigers' hooker Aaron Raper had "refereed the game....he was in the referee's face at all points".

Huddersfield Giants sign Paul Reilly on a new two-year deal ● Danny Peacock retires after suffering another knee injury ● Dean Lance is announced as Graham Murray's successor at Headingley ● London Broncos sign Illawarra prop Scott Cram ● Bobbie Goulding gets 240 hours community service for assault ● Auckland Warriors captain Matthew Ridge is suspended for eight weeks for gouging ● Wakefield Wildcats sign PNG international Alfred Songoro ● Sheffield Eagles sign French international Frederic Teixido ● London Broncos under fire for plans to stage home game with Bulls in Leicester ● Bulls sign Tongan World Cup player Phil Howlett ● Hull Sharks part company with coach Peter Walsh and put assistant Steve Crooks in charge ● Andy Farrell's record as the only ever-present in Super League comes to an end at 80 games ● RFL promise early decision on Super League entry for NFP Grand Final winners...

Jason Flowers was the standout for the Tigers, who kicked on to have a tremendous season, while Sheffield's form slumped from there on in.

The Tigers were quick to dispel rumours that 20 year old stand-off Danny Orr would be leaving the club at the end of the season because his father Paul - himself a former Castleford player - had resigned from the club's board - and set about tying up the young star to a four-year deal.

The Wolves meanwhile slipped below the Tigers into fifth spot as Iestyn Harris spearheaded Leeds Rhinos' 28-10 win against his old club at Wilderspool. Leeds led 16-0 at the break, endured a Wolves comeback which featured two tries from Toa Kohe-Love, and then stretched away, Francis Cummins completing a hat-trick.

Huddersfield Giants were no match for Wigan at Central Park, with eight Warriors scoring a try each in a 36-2 win.

And the Bulls got to within a league point of St Helens at the top of the table with a tough 22-12 win at the Thunderdome, 17 year old winger Leon Pryce scoring the clinching try nine minutes from time in front of a crowd of over six and a half thousand people.

Saturday Night Fever at Odsal Stadium as the Warriors attempted to halt the Bulls, whose stampede towards the play-offs was already starting to gather steam.

In an emotionally-charged night at Odsal Stadium, 13,000 Bradford fans stayed behind after their side's 19-2 win to say a fond farewell to Danny Peacock, who had played such a big part in the Bulls-phenomenon.

Greg Florimo, Gary Connolly and Andy Farrell all carried knocks into the crunch-game but the gamble back-fired as the Bulls pack got on top of the Wigan six right from the off. Behind that pack, young Paul Deacon, who had forced himself into the starting line up before having to retire in the 52nd minute with an ankle injury, put in a gamestar performance with his distribution and kicking game, and the Bulls were 11-2 up. When Robbie Paul scored a superb individual try on 49 minutes the game was up, although there was still time for an all-in brawl.

St Helens pulled three points clear of the Bulls at the top of the table next day though with their second win of the week against top-five contenders.

On the Wednesday they had bounced back from the Wakefield defeat with a magnificent 33-18 win at Wheldon Road, with Cas old boy Chris Smith scoring a hat-trick and Paul Newlove a pair of tries.

Smith, picking up a second gamestar rating, and Newlove were on

JJB SUPER LEAGUE ROUND ELEVEN RESULTS

Friday 21st May, 1999

Leeds Rhinos 70 ....Halifax Blue Sox 22

Saturday 22nd May, 1999

Bradford Bulls 19 ....Wigan Warriors 2
Sheffield Eagles 26 ....Salford Reds 26

Sunday 23rd May, 1999

Huddersfield Giants 22 ....Wakefield Trinity Wildcats 38
Hull Sharks 2 ....Castleford Tigers 30
London Broncos 18 ....Gateshead Thunder 18
St Helens 57 ....Warrington Wolves 20

the try-sheet again as Saints wupped the Wolves 57-20. "We were pathetic," blasted Wolves coach Darryl Van de Velde after the disappointment. "Every time we come here we fall apart. It must be something in the air."

Salford Reds, who announced their new boss was to be former Gold Coast coach John Harvey, clambered off the bottom of the table with a gutsy 26-all draw at the Don Valley Stadium.

It was the first time the Reds had avoided defeat away from home since an 18-18 draw at the Don Valley the previous August, and the feat was achieved after a week where a virus had struck down the bulk of the Salford squad.

And to cap it they had Darren Brown sent off for a high tackle on Sheffield winger Dale Cardoza on 17 minutes, just after the Aussie had returned from a spell in the sin bin after a bust up with Dave Watson!

In fact a late try from Paul Anderson salvaged a point for the Eagles after they had come back from 18-0 down to lead 20-18 at the break.

Hull Sharks sunk to the bottom with their eleventh defeat of the season - a

Paul Deacon collared by Mark Reber and Denis Betts as the Bulls charge on

30-2 hammering by Castleford Tigers. "I've got some soul-searching to do tonight," said coach Peter Walsh after the game.

Gateshead Thunder had Willie Peters' late try to thank for an 18-18 draw with London Broncos at the Stoop, although, with Ian Herron out with a groin strain, Ben Sammut missed a kickable conversion which would have won both points. The Thunder had also accounted for Hull Sharks in midweek, with Irishman Brian Carney on debut in a 25-6 success.

And Wakefield Wildcats were on a roll, beating the Giants at the McAlpine by 38-22, moving four points above Huddersfield in the table.

The on-field action was overshadowed by the news that the future of Halifax Rugby League club was in doubt after it faced a winding up order from the Inland Revenue, with Super League Europe reluctant to advance the club any more TV sponsorship money. They were running out of cash and the effect on team morale was boldly illustrated in Friday's televised clash with the Leeds Rhinos at Headingley.

"You can't show any mercy in this game," said Rhinos skipper Iestyn Harris after the 70-22 towelling.

"We have had a pretty disruptive and uncertain week off the field but to use that would be a lame excuse," said Sox coach John Pendlebury. Indeed, the Rhinos - who that week announced former Perth and Adelaide boss Dean Lance as Graham Murray's successor - were back to their Grand Final mood of '98, with Adrian Morley in outstanding form.

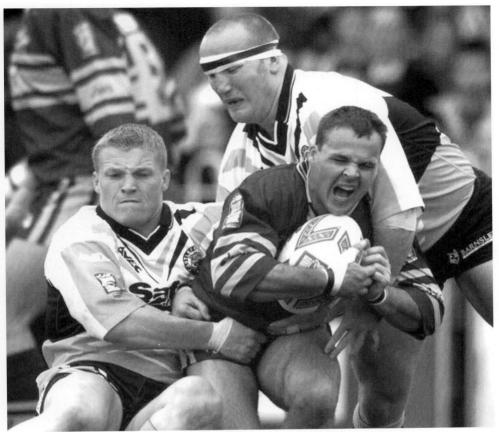

Brad Godden feels the force of Lee Harland and Nathan Sykes as the
Tigers and Rhinos fight out a 12-12 draw

Peter Walsh was fired the day after Hull's 12th defeat in 13 games, a week before the Sharks' crucial showdown with Salford Reds at the Willows.

Assistant Steve Crooks was put in charge and said: "It's going to take every waking hour of every waking day until Sunday to work on the things we have been doing wrong."

Crooks was aware that some names had already been put in the frame for Walsh's old job including local hero Lee Crooks, Dewsbury boss Neil Kelly and former overseas players Gary Kemble and Craig Coleman.

The pressure didn't pay, as Salford strode to a 38-18 win with Darren Brown - given a sending off sufficient verdict for his high tackle at Sheffield the week before - scoring a hat-trick of tries.

London Broncos suspended Shaun Edwards from the club after he allegedly attended the draw for the World Cup at the Savoy without permission, but it didn't seem to be affecting the Broncos as they raced into a 12-0 lead against Wigan on the Friday night. But a terrific second-half fightback capped by a try from Jon Clarke - playing his first Super League game since serving a custodial sentence for assault, saw the defending champions storm ahead. Greg Florimo was London's chief tormentor as Dominic Peters folded under the pressure of Wigan's kicking game, coming up with two crucial errors.

It was the first time Wigan had played a Super League match without their captain Andy Farrell, who had finally succumbed to the ankle injury he had carried into the Bradford game.

Leaders St Helens didn't have it all their own way at the Shay. The Blue Sox management had made a rallying-call to the fans at half-time in the light of their cash-crisis, but it was the club's players who responded immediately in an attempt to claw back from an 18-0 half-time deficit. An Apollo Perelini try on 65 minutes was enough to secure a 28-22 win for the Saints.

And Saints almost went five points clear, as the Bulls - who had announced they were signing Tongan Phil Howlett as replacement for Danny Peacock - almost stumbled against Huddersfield Giants, just edging their neighbours 22-20. After going in tied up at 12-all at the break, Stuart Spruce's try on the hour made it 22-14 before Andrew Tangata-Toa got the Giants within two points with two minutes to go.

JJB SUPER LEAGUE
ROUND TWELVE RESULTS
Friday 28th May, 1999
London Broncos 12 ....Wigan Warriors 30
Sunday 30th May, 1999
Bradford Bulls 22 ....Huddersfield Giants 20
Castleford Tigers 12...Leeds Rhinos 12
Gateshead Thunder 26 ....Sheffield Eagles 18
Halifax Blue Sox 22 ....St Helens 28
Salford Reds 38...Hull Sharks 18
Warrington Wolves 22 ....Wakefield Trinity Wildcats 36
Wednesday 2nd June, 1999
Wigan Warriors 28 ....Sheffield Eagles 0

Ten and a half thousand crammed into Wheldon Road for the best match of the round - a 12-12 draw between the Tigers and the Rhinos. It was Cas's third draw of the year. Loan signing Brad Hepi was in at hooker for the injured Aaron Raper and it was his high shot on Jamie Mathiou that allowed Iestyn Harris to kick a penalty that shared the points. Just after, Hepi was put on report for a high one on Harris. It was that sort of game, ferocious and exciting to the final whistle.

Shock of the round was at Warrington, where the Wolves' top-five ambitions took a real hammerblow as the Wildcats fought back from 22-6 to win their third game on a row, 36-22.

And Gateshead Thunder took full advantage with a hard-fought 26-18 win over the Eagles, Chook Herron's perfect five goals shooting Thunder into sixth spot.

JJB SUPER LEAGUE - *Monday 31st May, 1999*	P	W	D	L	F	A	D	PTS
St Helens	13	12	0	1	452	215	237	24
Bradford Bulls	12	10	1	1	253	171	82	21
Leeds Rhinos	13	8	1	4	356	274	82	17
Castleford Tigers	13	7	3	3	239	178	61	17
Wigan Warriors	12	8	0	4	318	159	159	16
Gateshead Thunder	13	7	1	5	285	219	66	15
Warrington Wolves	12	7	0	5	263	281	-18	14
Sheffield Eagles	12	5	1	6	236	270	-34	11
Wakefield Trinity Wildcats	12	5	0	7	257	271	-14	10
Halifax Blue Sox	12	5	0	7	214	269	-55	10
London Broncos	12	3	2	7	198	307	-109	8
Salford Reds	13	2	1	10	240	378	-138	5
Huddersfield Giants	12	2	0	10	189	320	-131	4
Hull Sharks	13	1	0	12	169	357	-188	2

JUNE
Bulls believe

As May turned into June St Helens's destiny as minor premiers looked almost assured, three points clear of Bradford at the top of Super League and combining steely defence aligned to their unquestioned attacking prowess.

But June was to be a true test of their credentials with trips to Gateshead and Bradford, plus a home tie with Wigan to come.

The Reds' run had to end sometime and there is no surer place for the pricking of bubbles than Knowsley Road.

Incredibly the Reds dominated the opening stages of their match at St Helens before succumbing to a nine-try blitz, Chris Smith scoring his second successive home hat-trick in a 48-0 win. Saints coach Ellery Hanley expressed his pleasure that his side had "zilled" Salford.

And when St Helens got their defence right in 1999 there was nothing most teams could do about their attack. Smith scored the first try on 18 minutes after a break by Sean Long, whose fifth goal of the afternoon took him to 500 points for the club, and it was 22-0, and all over, by the break.

The Bulls, after the scare by the Giants the week before, were looking ominous too.

On the Saturday afternoon they travelled to Chesterfield to play Sheffield Eagles at Saltergate. The Eagles were playing on the back of a 28-0 defeat at Central Park the previous Wednesday - the game in which Mark Aston, the linchpin of Sheffield's attack, finally had to submit to a groin injury which kept him out for almost the rest of the season.

But 52-2 on a "home" ground was almost too much for coach John Kear to bear.

"I'm humiliated and devastated," he blasted. "It's nothing to do with three games in a week. Other teams have to do it and they don't capitulate like we did."

Henry Paul - at stand-off, with brother Robbie on the bench - was inspirational and at the heart of nine Bulls tries in a power-packed attack. And significantly, the Bulls had kept Eagles tryless - in fact they had conceded only five tries in their latest five games.

JJB SUPER LEAGUE
ROUND THIRTEEN RESULTS
Friday 4th June, 1999

Leeds Rhinos 32	Gateshead Thunder 14
Warrington Wolves 31	Halifax Blue Sox 18

Saturday 5th June, 1999

Sheffield Eagles 2	Bradford Bulls 52

Sunday 6th June

Huddersfield Giants 20	London Broncos 21
Hull Sharks 12	Wigan Warriors 18
St Helens 48	Salford Reds 0
Wakefield Trinity Wildcats 11	Castleford Tigers 10

Wednesday 9th June, 1999

Bradford Bulls 74	London Broncos 12
Halifax Blue Sox 16	Wakefield Trinity Wildcats 36
Warrington Wolves 48	Huddersfield Giants 16

Darren Rogers and Adam Hughes meet head on during a fiery clash at Belle Vue

There was high drama at Belle Vue on the Sunday afternoon when Trinity met the Tigers. After 80 minutes of tough, at times spiteful football, the Wildcats were 11-10 to the good thanks to a 76th minute Tony Kemp field goal, and on course for an astonishing fourth successive victory. The final hooter sounded as the ball was played 25 metres out from the Wakefield line and the referee blew the whistle as Brad Davis sent a field goal attempt soaring towards the posts. In the mayhem, referee Bob Connolly stood firm, the kick came after full-time and Trinity had won the match.

Not for the first time Cas coach Stuart Raper found it hard to hide his feelings after the final whistle.

"I think Andy Kelly (Wakefield's coach) must have kissed a leprechaun with the luck he had today," he said. "They continually took out Danny Orr. I was very unhappy with some of the things that Tony Kemp was doing. I am absolutely furious about what went on today after Castleford had been chastised over Brad Hepi last week (the Tigers and the player had received a letter from the RFL after the Leeds match, warning Hepi to improve his tackling technique).

"Today there was a bloke out there trying to take everybody's head off. If Graham (Leeds coach Murray) can have a whinge about Hepi, then I am going to have a whinge about Kemp because it is disgusting what he did today. Adrian Vowles wanted to have him in the dressing room." Kemp was suspended for two matches after being spotted on video making a high tackle by the RFL Disciplinary Committee and Raper was called into to the RFL to "explain his comments".

On the Friday night the Wolves ended their three-match losing run with a 31-18 win against the Blue Sox at Wilderspool in which Jon Roper and Toa Kohe-Love got two tries each. But the game had much wider impact than just taking Warrington back into the top-five reckoning.

South African Jamie Bloem was put on report for allegedly biting Lee Briers two minutes from the end of the game and two days later was found guilty of the offence at the RFL Disciplinary Committee, and suspended for three months. Blue Sox football manger David Hobbs promised the club would appeal. "The evidence of Jamie's guilt wasn't conclusive because Lee Briers didn't present himself at the hearing. Given the severity of the sentence the Committee needs to be 100 per cent clear whether he did or did not commit the offence."

There were also doubts about the severity of the punishment even if Bloem were guilty - the most recent precedent being Paul Davidson's three-match ban when found guilty of biting while playing for Oldham Bears against North Queensland Cowboys.

Bloem's appeal eventually failed and he and his family headed off to France to play rugby union. It was just another problem among many for the Blue Sox, who were faced with having to sell some of their players - with Chris Chester and Gavin Clinch linked with moves to Wigan - to try and balance their books.

The same night Leeds Rhinos resisted a stiff challenge from the Thunder, who had former Sheffield player Danny McAllister on debut, at Headingley, 32-14. With Kerrod Walters still absent, fullback Ben Sammut filled in at hooker, but broke an arm after a challenge for the ball with Adrian Morley, who was later cleared of any foul play. Two more tries from Leroy Rivett and another top game from Ryan Sheridan were pivotal for the Rhinos, as Shaun McRae hailed his side's "worst defensive effort of the season".

Halifax Blue Sox ensure survival by agreeing Creditors Voluntary Agreement ● Wakefield Trinity agree new two-year deal with Paul and David March ● Hull Sharks cancel contracts of Martin Hall and Matt Calland ● Wigan linked with Shaun Edwards ● Bulls and Blue Sox merger floated ● Ellery Hanley openly criticises his football manager Eric Hughes ● Wakefield promised £550,000 from RFL for year 2000 ● Blue Sox's South African utility Jamie Bloem is banned for three months on biting charge ● London sack coach Dan Stains and promote assistant Les Kiss...

Clubs at the bottom were getting desperate, and Hull Sharks, with Steve Crooks in charge for his second game, gave the Wigan Warriors - on the back of their win against Sheffield in midweek - a big scare, the Warriors eventually coming through 18-12. Andy Farrell was still absent and Greg Florimo out but Gary Connolly filled in at stand-off and finally sealed the game with a try four minutes from time, putting two scores between the sides, which was a good job as Fili Seru scored again for Hull just before the final whistle.

"I asked them what they wanted to get out of the game...they insisted they wanted to bring some pride and respect back to the club," said Crooks, rightly proud of his side which included six local teenagers. "We know we can't expose them to Super League football every week, but that bodes extremely well for the future of this club."

There was similar commitment on the Sunday evening too at the McAlpine where the battlers Huddersfield Giants lost in heartbreaking fashion to the London Broncos. Glen Air's stunning field goal three minutes from time had coach Dan Stains exclaiming: "That is one big gorilla that has been ripped off my back!", despite losing another prop - Scott Cram with a suspected dislocated a shoulder - making it four for the season. Another refereeing decision, when Steve Presley disallowed a John Bentley try nine minutes from time for offside without consulting the video referee, caused plenty of debate in the week following

The pressure was building.

And no-one was feeling it more than Super League coaches.

London Broncos travelled to Odsal on the Wednesday night and in the wake of a 74-12 hammering, which featured a Mike Forshaw hat-trick, coach Dan

June

Stains was sacked.

Broncos chief executive Tony Rea went live on the internet to explain why the club had taken the action. "Dan is a fantastic human being but things have not worked out for a number of reasons," he said. Shaun Edwards, who had been banned from the club by Stains, immediately announced himself fit and ready to play against Sheffield on the Sunday and, with Les Kiss and Rea in joint charge, the Broncos looked a different outfit as they took the Eagles apart 44-12. Chris Ryan scored two tries in a gamestar performance.

Friday night's TV match turned out to be one of the most significant of the season.

The Rhinos 13-4 win at Central Park was a momentous effort, achieved after the injury withdrawal of Ryan Sheridan in the first half, with veteran Daryl Powell putting in a supreme effort. But it was the brilliant Iestyn Harris who won a game which could have gone either way when he popped out a pass from a two-man tackle to allow Paul Sterling to go over in the left corner, before running down the clock with a field goal.

"We've no complaints," said Wigan boss John Monie phlegmatically. "It was a good tough game with plenty of intensity and good defence and they just took their chances better than us."

The following Tuesday, Monie was asked to step down from the coaching job and move into a management role to make way for assistant Andy Goodway. Monie refused and left the club. It seemed harsh treatment for the man who had guided the club to its first Super League Championship the year before.

The heat was also increasing for John Pendlebury at Halifax Blue Sox, whose job was being made almost impossible by the financial situation at the club.

On the Wednesday night, the Wakefield Wildcats made it an incredible five wins in a row when they completed a 36-16 win at the New Shay, but on the Sunday, the Sox imposed a 51-18 thrashing on another coach not having the best of it - Malcolm Reilly.

"Appalled. I am absolutely appalled," Reilly said after watching Chris Chester, temporarily back in a Blue Sox shirt, score two-tries in a Halifax romp. The Giants had also lost in midweek - a 48-16 thumping at Warrington - and were looking an increasingly lost cause.

New Salford coach John Harvey arrived and switched second-rower Darren Brown to stand-off for the game against the Wildcats at the Willows. It worked a treat, as the Reds ran out 28-14 winners to end Trinity's winning run.

The Tigers put down a marker for the top-five when they ran over Warrington Wolves at Wheldon Road 39-6.

Dean Sampson once again led the Tigers pack superbly and Francis Maloney scored a hat-trick of tries after a four-match absence with a fractured cheekbone.

"It looked like eight blokes turned up to play and the rest just came over

JJB SUPER LEAGUE
ROUND FOURTEEN RESULTS
Friday 11th June, 1999

Wigan Warriors 4..Leeds Rhinos 13

Sunday 13th June, 1999

Bradford Bulls 42 ....Hull Sharks 14
Castleford Tigers 39 ....Warrington Wolves 6
Gateshead Thunder 32 ....St Helens 20
Halifax Blue Sox 51 ....Huddersfield Giants 18
London Broncos 44 ....Sheffield Eagles 12
Salford Reds 28 ....Wakefield Trinity Wildcats 14

70

Bobby Thompson brought down by Wakefield's Shane Kenward as the Salford Reds
earn new coach John Harvey his first win

for the drive," said Wolves boss Darryl Van de Velde.

It wasn't a great weekend for St Helens either who slipped off the top of the table for first time since the start of April when they found Gateshead too hot to handle at the Thunderdome. "We lost every single battle out there," said Saints boss Ellery Hanley after watching his side go down 32-20, late tries from Tommy Martyn and Fereti Tuilagi making the scoreline respectable.

Thunder had Mick Jenkins, a hooker from Newcastle, NSW that is, on debut after signing him from Workington two days before, and he played a big part in the win along with halfbacks Willie Peters and Will Robinson.

Saints' stumble allowed the Bulls to take up pole position - for the rest of the season as it turned out - as they registered their third win of the week, on Sunday night against the Sharks, 42-14. Nathan McAvoy scored four tries and Robbie Paul two as the Bulls warmed up for their tryst with the competition's other form team, Leeds Rhinos, the following Friday.

Round fifteen derby day...Leeds' Adrian Morley rounds Bradford's Henry Paul in front of a packed Headingley *(above)* and Wigan's Jason Robinson fends off Saints' Tommy Martyn at Knowsley Road *(below)*

A Super League record crowd awaited the clash of the Yorkshire giants on a beautiful summer's evening at Headingley on that Friday night.

What a night it was as the Rhinos' 45-16 win - the Bulls were on an eleven-match unbeaten run - convinced everybody that they were destined for the Grand Final in October. "That was as good a game as they've played," said Rhinos boss Graham Murray as his side ran in seven tries, three of the from second-rower Andy Hay.

Henry Paul gave the Bulls the lead when he timed his run onto Paul Deacon's kick to the in-goal perfectly, but Leeds had scored 33 points by the time the excellent Paul - brother Robbie was sidelined with a nagging lower leg injury - scored his second.

The Rhinos were unstoppable, with Daryl Powell again the key man in his 61 minutes of action - even producing Leeds' first 40/20 of the season. "You just feel so focused when things are going right for you," said Powell. Incredibly, the Rhinos produced such a dominant display without Richie Blackmore, Brad Godden, Ryan Sheridan, or Darren Fleary.

JJB SUPER LEAGUE
ROUND FIFTEEN RESULTS
Friday 18th June, 1999

Halifax Blue Sox 0	....	Castleford Tigers 24
Leeds Rhinos 45	....	Bradford Bulls 16

Sunday 20th June, 1999

Huddersfield Giants 37	....	Sheffield Eagles 18
Hull Sharks 6	....	London Broncos 47
St Helens 18	....	Wigan Warriors 24
Wakefield Trinity Wildcats 18	....	Gateshead Thunder 22
Warrington Wolves 28	....	Salford Reds 14

Wednesday 23rd June, 1999

Hull Sharks 18	....	Salford Reds 10
Leeds Rhinos 50	....	Castleford Tigers 22

There was also another tasty derby on the Sunday night, completing a magnificent TV double, when Saints faced up to Wigan Warriors, playing their first game with Andy Goodway as head coach, at Knowsley Road.

Both sides were coming off defeats, and St Helens knew that if they won they would leap over the Bulls back to the top of the table.

It proved to be a dream start for Goodway, who saw his Warriors pull off a magnificent 24-18 win, with Gary Connolly, moved up to stand-off for the second half, the stand-out. Connolly's try on the 75th minute finally settled a pulsating game. Paul Davidson's sin-binning on 58 minutes, for obstructing Tony Smith, was also crucial as, three minutes later, Simon Haughton crossed in style on the left to give Wigan a lead they never lost.

Wigan move John Monie aside and appoint his assistant Andy Goodway, and sign Gavin Clinch and Chris Chester from Halifax ● St Helens send home Phil Adamson ● Cash-crisis club Halifax Blue Sox chase Alfie Langer ● Steve Renouf tipped to join Leeds Rhinos ● Hull Sharks react angrily to rumours of a cash crisis ● Stuart Raper signs new two-year coaching deal at Wheldon Road ● Sheffield Eagles issue a hands-off Keith Senior warning to Leeds and Wigan and report £478,000 loss in 1998 to stock market ● Kerrod Walters returns to Gateshead ● John Pendlebury quits at Halifax....

It was a second consecutive defeat for the Saints where cracks were beginning to open up between coach Hanley and football manager Eric Hughes. With a daunting trip to the Bulls to come the following Friday, Hanley was banking on the return from injury of Paul Sculthorpe, Kevin Iro and Sonny Nickle.

On the night that Leeds put Bradford to the sword, the Tigers were also hitting their straps in a 24-0 whitewash of the Blue Sox at the Shay, making light of the absence of Adrian Vowles and Aaron Raper. "It was one of the best defensive efforts I have been associated with," said coach Stuart Raper after the game. "We know if we keep sides down to a minimum we will win a lot of tight games as we have the character to hold the line."

73

Not that the Blue Sox played badly without Wigan-bound Chris Chester and Gavin Clinch but, allied to an A1 defence, Danny Orr's attacking skills were enough to keep Cas in fifth spot.

Two days later coach Raper signed a new contract which would keep him at Wheldon Road for a further two years.

The Wolves were still hot on the Tigers' heels, after they beat the re-energised Salford Reds at Wilderspool 28-14, on the back of Lee Briers' excellent long kicking game. Toa Kohe-Love scored yet another pair of tries to go four clear at the top of the Super League try-scorers list with 16, as the Wolves stayed within one point of the top-five.

Things were going from very bad to worse for the Sheffield Eagles who went to the McAlpine on the back of two thrashings, to Bradford and London, and became the Giants' third victims of the season, 37-18.

Aussie centre Jim Lenihan scored a second-half hat-trick to seal Huddersfield's first win since their 15-14 success at the Willows on 18th April. Once again Bobbie Goulding's kicking game was crucial in a game in which the Giants introduced 19 year old debutant forward Jim Carlton just before half-time.

The win put the Giants four points clear of the relegation spot as Hull Sharks sank to a worrying 47-6 defeat at the hands of London Broncos at the Boulevard.

"To be 47 points to nil down with a minute left is inexcusable," blasted coach Steve Crooks. "I can only apologise to our supporters at what they had to witness out there this afternoon." Rob Roberts saved the whitewash with his late try but that was after eight from the re-vitalised Broncos, with Karle Hammond at the top of his form, grabbing two tries himself.

Gateshead kept their own top-five dream alive, while probably ending Wakefield's with a gutsy 22-14 win at Belle Vue.

The match had looked like ending all square at 18-all when, with only 15 seconds left on the clock, David Maiden's long pass allowed Brett Grogan to grab a late, late winner for the Tyneside club.

The Bulls gained sweet revenge for their mauling at Knowsley Road.

"We got slaughtered in the end, it was as simple as that," was Saints coach Ellery Hanley's assessment, after seeing his side fall to their third successive defeat by 46-22.

Henry Paul was involved in all three first-half Bulls tries, two to teenage sensation Leon Pryce and one to Stuart Spruce, as Bradford raced into a 16-8 lead at the break. Four more tries in 20 minutes after the turnaround had the Bulls 30-8 to the good before a three-try Saints rally was stemmed with three more Bulls tries - two to the irrepressible James Lowes.

JJB SUPER LEAGUE
ROUND SIXTEEN RESULTS
Friday 25th June, 1999

Bradford Bulls 46 ....St Helens 22
Gateshead Thunder 26 ....Warrington Wolves 20

Saturday 26th June, 1999

London Broncos 16 ....Leeds Rhinos 22
Sheffield Eagles 18 ....Hull Sharks 8

Sunday 27th June, 1999

Castleford Tigers 19 ....Huddersfield Giants 10
Salford Reds 20 ....Halifax Blue Sox 22
Wigan Warriors 40 ....Wakefield Trinity Wildcats 14

Tuesday 29th June, 1999

Sheffield Eagles 6 ....Gateshead Thunder 23

Wednesday 30th June, 1999

St Helens 46 ....Halifax Blue Sox 10

The reverse meant that Saints slipped a place into third spot but their

Paul Wellens tries to halt the progress of Stuart Spruce as the Saints cop a hiding at Odsal

coach was refusing to be ruffled. "Look, the season's not over yet," said Hanley.

Leeds Rhinos leapfrogged Saints with two crucial wins in the week. On the back of their romp against the Bulls the previous Friday, the Rhinos had given the Tigers the same treatment at Headingley on Wednesday night, in front of another bumper crowd of over 16,000. Unsung hero Marvin Golden collected a powerful hat-trick as 18 year old Kevin Sinfield took the gamestar rating.

Despite the setback, Cas coach Stuart Raper claimed: "We knew we were up against it from the word go but I still believe we can match Leeds."

The Rhinos looked tired when they made the trip to the capital at the weekend, but, as the Broncos discipline let them down, Iestyn Harris's four penalties proved crucial in a 22-16 win. Robbie Beazley's sin-binning for dissent ten minutes from time ended London's hopes as Leeds moved to within two points of the Bulls.

Halifax Blue Sox finally lost their coach John Pendlebury two days before their trip to Salford Reds. Pendlebury and football manager David Hobbs' contracts were cancelled before the club went into a Creditors Voluntary

Agreement which put a line under the bulk of the club's debts, while putting all their players over the age of 24 up for grabs.

Gary Mercer was given temporary charge of the team as player-coach and he led from the front in a 22-20 win - only Halifax's second win in seven games since the financial crisis blew up. Martin Moana had a standout game for the Blue Sox at stand-off, with Graham Holroyd moving up to scrum-half after Chris Chester joined Gavin Clinch at Central Park.

The defeat left John Harvey's Salford Reds looking slightly insecure following their 18-12 midweek loss at the Boulevard, Gary Lester getting two vital tries for the Sharks who moved within two points of Huddersfield Giants.

Sadly for Hull, they could not keep up the momentum when they travelled to South Yorkshire that Saturday. "The heat and the sheer effort after the Salford game did it for us," said hooker Andrew Purcell, a trademark darting try from Johnny Lawless turning the game in favour of the Eagles.

Chook Herron's five goals were crucial to the Thunder as they moved into sixth spot with a tough 26-20 win over Warrington Wolves at the Thunderdome.

Gateshead were 20-6 up at the break thanks to a try in the dying minutes from their skipper, Tony Grimaldi. Lee Briers orchestrated the Wolves comeback after the break with Lee Penny, Toa Kohe-Love and Alan Hunte getting tries. But a further try from Grimaldi just about wrapped it up.

With Brad Davis undergoing knee surgery, hooker Aaron Raper returned to the Tigers side as scrum-half and masterminded a scrappy rain-soaked 19-10 home victory over the Giants. "The main positive to take out of the game is that we didn't have any more injuries," said Huddersfield coach Mal Reilly as he looked ahead to the clash with the Sharks the following week.

The most bizarre match of the season took place at Central Park where Wigan, with skipper Andy Farrell back in action, beat Wakefield 40-14.

Referee Nick Oddy sin-binned five Wildcats players, reducing Trinity to nine men at one stage of the second half after they had clawed back to 18-14 just after half-time.

An RFL inquiry led by Geoff Berry, in the absence of Greg McCallum, away in Sydney on compassionate leave, decided to take no further action.

JJB SUPER LEAGUE - *Wednesday 30th June, 1999*

	P	W	D	L	F	A	D	PTS
Bradford Bulls	17	14	1	2	483	266	217	29
St Helens	18	14	0	4	606	327	279	28
Leeds Rhinos	18	13	1	4	518	346	172	27
Wigan Warriors	17	12	0	5	432	216	216	24
Castleford Tigers	18	10	3	5	353	255	98	23
Gateshead Thunder	18	11	1	6	402	315	87	23
Warrington Wolves	17	10	0	7	396	392	4	20
Wakefield Trinity Wildcats	17	7	0	10	348	387	-39	14
London Broncos	17	6	2	9	338	441	-103	14
Halifax Blue Sox	18	7	0	11	331	444	-113	14
Sheffield Eagles	18	6	1	11	292	462	-170	13
Salford Reds	18	3	1	14	314	508	-194	7
Huddersfield Giants	17	3	0	14	290	477	-187	6
Hull Sharks	18	2	0	16	227	494	-267	4

JULY
Ellery's back

St Helens duly climbed back into second place in Super League with an expected 46-10 defeat of Halifax Blue Sox in midweek at the start of what was to be the most remarkable period in the great club's history.

Coach Ellery Hanley and football manager Eric Hughes were rumoured to be not speaking to each other, with the dispute over Aussie prop Phil Adamson at the root of the problem. Hanley had never picked Adamson, who eventually went home to Sydney after wallowing in the Saints' Alliance season for most of the season.

Hull's win over Salford in June had raised hopes in the west side of the city that they could pull off the Great Escape and the first Sunday in July was a heaven sent opportunity to draw level on points with their opponents that day - Huddersfield Giants.

But the frustration of a disappointing season for Airlie Birds supporters was compounded as the Giants stunned the Sharks at the Boulevard with a 26-17 win that took them four points clear of their old rivals from division one days.

It had all looked to be turning out OK as the game entered the final quarter with the Sharks leading 13-6 but three Giants tries in seven minutes, from man of the match Dave Boughton, Darren Simpson and Craig Weston, turned the game around completely.

"I'm absolutely distraught," said Hull coach Steve Crooks, who had seen star fullback Steve Prescott led off with a dislocated elbow that threatened to keep him out for the rest of the season.

If Huddersfield were getting away, the Sharks still had Salford Reds in their sights, as John Harvey's side, missing injured halfback pairing Martin Crompton and Steve Blakeley, went down heavily at Castleford, 38-10.

Star turn Danny Orr missed the game through injury but the half-time announcement that he had signed a new four-year contract with the Tigers brought the biggest cheer of the afternoon.

But Adrian Vowles was back after a five-match lay-off and he led from the front in his inimitable style, as Jason Flowers pushed his claim for a Great Britain place with another top-notch performance.

JJB SUPER LEAGUE
ROUND SEVENTEEN RESULTS
Friday 2nd July, 1999

Leeds Rhinos 40.....................................Sheffield Eagles 16
Wakefield Trinity Wildcats 8 ....Bradford Bulls 36

Sunday 4th July, 1999

Castleford Tigers 38 ....Salford Reds 10
Halifax Blue Sox 35........................Gateshead Thunder 14
Hull Sharks 17 ....Huddersfield Giants 26
St Helens 22 ....London Broncos 24
Warrington Wolves 17 ....Wigan Warriors 17

Wednesday 7th July, 1999

Huddersfield Giants 0 ....Bradford Bulls 26
Wakefield Trinity Wildcats 8 ....Warrington Wolves 15
Wigan Warriors 22 ....London Broncos 4

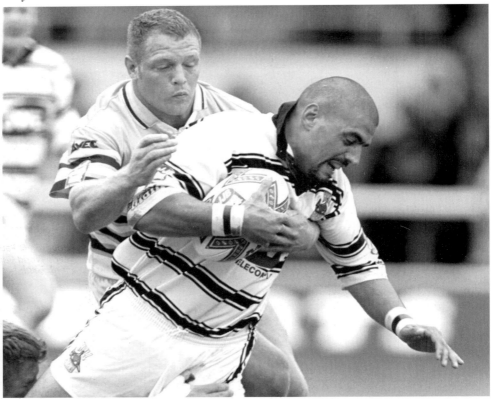

Steve Craven falls under the challenge of Huddersfield's Matt Sturm as the Sharks go
down at the Boulevard, and fall behind at the foot of Super League

The defeat left Salford just three points clear of the Sharks in bottom
position.

One other team still in danger of joining the relegation scramble was
Sheffield Eagles, whose midsummer form slump had been briefly halted with the
Hull win. But the following Tuesday night Gateshead Thunder put in a clinical 80
minutes against a side badly missing leader Mark Aston. Kerrod Walters was
back, coming on from the bench as Thunder's four tries confirmed their
superiority, before Rod Doyle scored a consolation for the Eagles four minutes
from the end to make it 23-6.

On the Friday night the Eagles, playing their third game in six days, were
given no chance at Headingley, against the form team of the competition.

Eagles started like a house on fire, shot into a 10-0 lead through two Bright
Sodje tries and if Paul Sterling hadn't raced back to just stop Keith Senior -
Senior, hotly tipped to join either Wigan or Leeds, had his best game of the
season that night - from going under the posts, it would have been 16-0. Then
Sterling went to the other end and got a try for the Rhinos who stretched out to
an eventual 40-16 win.

The Tuesday night game could have had a bigger effect on Gateshead, who
went to the New Shay expected to win, but were well beaten by the troubled
Blue Sox, 35-14.

Halifax themselves had had a hard game in midweek - on the Wednesday night at Knowsley Road. On the Sunday Blue Sox debuted teenager Danny Barnes at hooker, with Paul Rowley, himself on the transfer list, moved to scrum-half. Daryl Cardiss scored two second-half tries to bury the Thunder.

Also on the scoresheet was 17 year old centre David Hodgson, who the next day turned down a four-year deal to stay at the New Shay, instead signing for Wigan. Halifax claimed a clear breach of the Super League code of conduct agreed between the clubs, claiming that the player had been approached by Wigan before the July 1st cut off. They were never able to prove it, and Hodgson played out the rest of the season with the Blue Sox, before moving over the Pennines.

Kiwi Joe Vagana linked with move to Warrington Wolves, while Gary Chambers signs a new two-year deal at Wilderspool ● Jamie Bloem signs for French rugby union club ● Super League clubs admit a re-think on midweek fixtures is needed ● Danny Orr signs new four-year deal at the Tigers ● Paul Newlove stays away from Great Britain training camp ● Sheffield Eagles deny Keith Senior sale ● Leeds Rhinos sign up Barrie McDermott on three-year deal ● Ellery Hanley makes stinging attack on Saints directors in Total Rugby League magazine ● Halifax blast Wigan for signing their young star David Hodgson ● Paul Newlove opts to play for Ireland in next year's World Cup ● Ellery Hanley suspended by St Helens board, Leigh boss Ian Millward tipped to take over...

While Gateshead were dropping two points, the Wolves were gaining one as they fought out a rip-roaring draw with Wigan at Wilderspool. Lee Briers missed five kickable goal attempts but rescued a point in superb style with a field goal 57 seconds from the end of the game, six minutes after Phil Jones had kicked a simple penalty from in front of the sticks to give Wigan a 17-16 lead.

On a hot and sticky Friday night, the Bulls beat Wakefield Trinity Wildcats 36-8 at Belle Vue, storming away in the second half, with Scott Naylor in barnstorming form in the centre, and Tongan Phil Howlett, signed as a straight replacement for the retired Danny Peacock, getting his first try in Super League.

But the big shock of the day came at Knowsley Road where Karle Hammond played a dream game against his old club, leading the Broncos to a magnificent 24-22 win.

It was the first time that London had beaten Saints and enhanced their status as play-off dark horses. If the defeat was a shock to the Saints fans, it was nothing compared to what was to come in the following weeks.

St Helens had won only one game in their last five, and the simmering discontent behind the scenes at Knowsley Road boiled over on the Friday morning when coach Ellery Hanley blasted the Saints board of directors on the front page of Total Rugby League.

"We need fresh blood upstairs in the club's hierarchy," Hanley said. "If the directors had anything about them they would realise that we shouldn't be doing this to these young players," he continued, claiming that the board had refused his requests to strengthen his squad, meaning that Saints prodigious talent was exposed to too much Super League football too early.

There was more. "If the directors really do have the club's best interests at heart, and not just wearing the badge and walking around saying 'I'm a director of St Helens', they would do something about this and make money available."

Hanley also described the Saints directors as "ignorant and rude" after they failed to follow up Hanley's initial discussions with Halifax's Martin Moana.

He also revealed that negotiations with Kiwi Jarrod McCracken had broken down because of the board's intransigence.

It was all a mind-boggling backdrop for St Helens' visit to Sheffield Eagles on the Saturday afternoon. With fourth-placed Wigan beating the Broncos at Central Park in midweek, Saints' top-five aspirations were looking a little shaky.

Eagles were still missing Mark Aston, Dave Watson, Jeff Hardy, Daio Powell - out long term with a broken arm, injured against Gateshead - and Dale Laughton. Saints had their injury problems too of course, with Apollo Perelini missing his first game of the season, joining Kevin Iro and Anthony Stewart on the injury list.

But Tommy Martyn was back and he inspired Saints to a gritty 21-16 win, scoring the third and last try as early on 24 minutes.

"We weren't pretty in any aspect of our game," said Ellery Hanley in one of the more fascinating post-match press conferences of the season.

Hanley had been given a rapturous welcome from the travelling Saints support as he made his way off the field, which reflected the support for Hanley in his attacks on the board.

"I'm only here to win football games," said Hanley," to give the public what they want which is a very good football side. But at the same time I have to be honest with them, and tell them the truth about what is happening, because they pay the players' wages."

The Saints board's response was to call an emergency meeting the following Monday with Hanley tipped to get the sack. "Everybody's future is in doubt eventually," Saints chairman Howard Morris told League Express.

JJB SUPER LEAGUE
ROUND EIGHTEEN RESULTS
Friday 9th July, 1999
Hull Sharks 18 ....Leeds Rhinos 26
Saturday 10th July, 1999
Sheffield Eagles 16.................................St Helens 21
Sunday 11th July, 1999
Bradford Bulls 56 ....Warrington Wolves 6
Gateshead Thunder 24 ....Castleford Tigers 16
Huddersfield Giants 10 ....Salford Reds 24
London Broncos 36 ....Wakefield Trinity Wildcats 26
Wigan Warriors 30................................Halifax Blue Sox 4

It was an amazing weekend for St Helens that threatened to overshadow events on the field, and there were some big ones.

They were getting used to heartbreak at the Boulevard but the Friday night defeat to Leeds Rhinos hurt more than most.

The Sharks deserved at least a draw after matching Leeds' four tries, in what was Leeds' toughest battle in a twelve-match unbeaten run.

Iestyn Harris didn't have one of his best games but his five goals against Graeme Hallas's one were crucial and he scored a try two minutes from time to finally finish the Sharks off.

Rob Roberts - a product of junior football in Leeds - was at the centre of a rousing performance from the black and whites, who led 18-10 when Jamie Smith got his second try on 54 minutes.

But two controversial penalties aided the Rhinos' comeback, before Harris finished them off with his try.

Things got worse for the Sharks on Sunday as Salford Reds beat Huddersfield Giants 24-10, which made Hull's arrears in the table now four points.

Two Mark Johnson tries helped Salford into a 16-4 half-time lead, with star Aussie Darren Brown and Super League's oldest player, David Hulme, leading the way. To compound a frustrated Mal Reilly's problems - who had seen his side lose 26-0 at home to the Bulls the previous Wednesday - key Aussies Craig Weston and Jim Lenihan both suffered injuries.

The Bulls' march to the minor premiership continued to gather pace as Brian McDermott scored a prop's hat-trick in eleven minutes as the Wolves were annihilated at Odsal 56-6. "We put the white flag up," said Wolves boss Darryl Van de Velde after his side conceded nine tries, and Steve McNamara kicked ten goals.

With all the clubs having played 20 of their 30 games, the Bulls were now four points clear at the top of the table.

The Wolves had a hard midweek 15-8 win at Wakefield as part of their defence, and the Wildcats travelled to London at the weekend to meet the Broncos

Whipping up a storm - Ellery Hanley

who had their own tough Wednesday night experience at Central Park, where they had gone down 22-4 to Wigan.

But if there was any fatigue it didn't show at the Stoop as Wakefield registered their sixth successive defeat. Willie Poching gave Trinity the lead on the hour but Dean Callaway replied seven minutes later before a Karle Hammond 40/20 set up position for Greg Fleming's clinching try that, with Brett Warton's conversion - Warton was back for the first since breaking an arm - secured a 36-26 win for the Broncos. "People would say that the top-five is only mathematically possible," said Broncos coach Les Kiss, "but we are in control of our own destiny."

Gateshead brought the play-off race well and truly to life with a 26-16 win over fifth-placed Castleford. The win - achieved in front of another 6,000-plus crowd at the Thunderdome - brought them level on points with the Tigers. The Thunder controlled the ball better on the day with Ben Sammut, back at fullback, outshining an off-colour Jason Flowers for once.

Gavin Clinch made his debt for Wigan, ironically against the Blue Sox, and he had a hand in all six Wigan tries in a 30-4 win - three of them to fullback Kris Radlinski. Chris Chester also got his first start after making his debut from the bench against London the previous Wednesday. "I told the board Gavin and Chris Chester were the two we needed and they proved us right today," said coach Andy Goodway, still unbeaten since he took over from John Monie.

July

It was the weekend that Super League cubs started to panic with two totally one-sided matches firing the debate about reducing the size of Super League, despite Super League Europe announcing lass than a year before that 16 teams was the aim.

Friday night's match at Headingley started the debate when Huddersfield Giants, reeling from injuries to star Aussies Craig Weston and Jim Lenihan, and having suspended another overseas player, Andrew Tangata-Toa, after he was charged with attempting to pervert the course of justice after a road traffic accident, crumbled to an 86-6 mauling.

The Rhinos, who had coach Graham Murray back from Australia where he had spent two weeks after the death of his mother, scored 15 tries and Iestyn Harris smashed Greg Barwick's Super League points-in-a-match record set against Castleford in 1996 - with 42 individual points, with four tries and 13 goals, also a Super League record.

"I've never been so embarrassed in my life," said Giants' coach Mal Reilly. "There were one or two who had a go but the majority bottled it."

One Super League official who witnessed the mauling at first hand was Gary Hetherington. "This could turn out to be a very significant result, because over the next few weeks there are going to be quite a number of debates within Rugby League as to where the game is going at all levels. The outcome of the game will feature prominently in the minds of the people who will be making some fairly major decisions," he said.

"The Super League competition loses credibility with results like this."

At Knowsley Road the following Sunday, St Helens - with Nigel Ashley-Jones and John Myler in charge of the team - put Hull Sharks to the sword 74-16. Saints scored 13 tries and Tommy Martyn eleven goals before a group of around a thousand fans staged an hour long vigil at the ground in protest at the suspension of coach Ellery Hanley the previous Monday, chanting "Sack the Board" and "Bring back Ellery".

Chairman Howard Morris promised a swift decision by the board to end the impasse, with the clever money being on Hanley getting the sack the following Tuesday.

M'learned friends were hovering in the background too, with Saints football manger Eric Hughes considering legal action against Hanley for comments he had made in the press, while having accused Hanley of wanting to swap Keiron Cunningham for Richard Pachniuk of Hunslet and Tommy Martyn for Halifax's Graham Holroyd.

Meanwhile Wigan chairman Peter Norbury was keen to refute suggestions that Hanley was to return to Wigan, or that retiring Super League Europe managing director Maurice Lindsay was a target for the club.

With doubts fuelled about the quality of some Super League clubs, Salford Reds reacted to a proposal from Swinton Lions that the two clubs should merge into a Manchester club by re-launching themselves as the City Reds.

**JJB SUPER LEAGUE
ROUND NINETEEN RESULTS**
Friday 16th July, 1999

Castleford Tigers 33	Wigan Warriors 18
Leeds Rhinos 86	Huddersfield Giants 6

Sunday 18th July, 1999

Halifax Blue Sox 20	Bradford Bulls 34
Salford City Reds 18	Gateshead Thunder 31
St Helens 74	Hull Sharks 16
Wakefield Trinity Wildcats 6	Sheffield Eagles 24
Warrington Wolves 28	London Broncos 18

Wednesday 21st July, 1999

Sheffield Eagles 12	Wigan Warriors 36

The re-branding worked off the field as over five and half thousand people turned out at the Willows for their televised game on the Sunday evening against Gateshead. Thunder had the game sewn up at 21-0 at half-time, before withstanding a robust Salford comeback to emerge 31-18 winners.

Thunder had to win to keep the Tigers in sight after they had won a magnificent match against Wigan - who confirmed their signing of Steve Renouf from Brisbane that week - on Friday night.

"If those Wigan props are better than Dean Sampson then I don't know what I am doing here," said Tigers coach Stuart Raper after a 33-18 success, referring to Wigan coach Andy Goodway's decision to leave Sampson out of his Great Britain train-on squad.

Salford Reds change their name to Salford City Reds
● *Leeds coach Graham Murray heads for Australia on two weeks' passionate leave* ● *Super League salary cap comes down* ● *Wigan sign Steve Renouf* ● *Huddersfield Giants release loose forward Andrew Tangata-Toa after his arrest for a traffic accident* ● *Hull Sharks sign up local youngster Richard Horne on his 17th birthday on a four-year deal* ● *RFL chief executive Neil Tunnicliffe blasts Super League Europe in League Express* ● *Halifax Blue Sox target Kiwi Gene Ngamu and sign Balmain prop James Gannon* ● *Iestyn Harris shatters Super League pointscoring record with 42 in rout of Huddersfield Giants* ● *Ellery Hanley reinstated as coach of St Helens* ● *Gateshead Thunder sign Leeds prop Garreth Carvell on loan* ● *Halifax transfer list Paul Rowley at £95,000....*

Brad Davis was back from a four-match absence with a knee injury and he played a massive part in the win which included a brilliant chip and chase solo effort from him two minutes before half-time that gave Cas a 16-6 lead.

But it was the way that the Tigers won the game after Wigan had blitzed them to go into the lead in the 49th minute with tries to Brett Goldspink - as powerful a prop's try as you could wish to see - and Jason Robinson, that made this win so special. Tries from Richard Gay, Francis Maloney and Danny Orr and a Davis field goal had the home support on cloud nine.

Darren Rogers swamped by Jon Clarke and Denis Betts as the Tigers complete the double over Wigan

July

Warrington Wolves also stayed in touch with the play-off spots with a 28-14 victory over London Broncos at Wilderspool, which featured a hat-trick from the exemplary Simon Gillies.

Sheffield Eagles dispelled any lingering relegation fears with a 24-6 win after a spiteful 80 minutes against the Wildcats at Belle Vue. Six players spent time in the sin bin, three more were put on report and Glen Tomlinson was sent off after a bout of verbals aimed towards the referee. Tomlinson got a two-match ban for his outburst and Karl Lovell a three-match suspension for a late high tackle on Adam Hughes. It wasn't Sheffield's only casualty as Dale Laughton suffered a broken nose and Martin Pearson was alleged to have made gestures towards the crowd as he was leaving the field with a mouth wound.

Tevita Vaikona - back from an eleven-match absence - scored two vital tries as the Bulls ground out a 34-20 win against the battling Blue Sox at the Shay. Former Leeds hooker Mick Shaw was in the Blue Sox side after his signing from Rochdale to fill in for the still absent Paul Rowley, strongly tipped to join the Halifax exodus to Wigan.

The following Wednesday morning St Helens chairman Howard Morris faced the media to inform the world that the club had re-instated Ellery Hanley as coach.

Morris denied the board of directors had backed down to fan pressure or that they couldn't afford the financial pay-off to sack Hanley claiming simply that, "he is the best man for the job".

At the same time Hanley apologised for "any offence caused" maintaining that he had never had any problem with Morris. The future of football manager Eric Hughes now in doubt though, his absence from the press conference noted by all present.

On the Friday night, St Helens stunned the Rhinos at Headingley in one of the most important games of the season.

It was an absolutely explosive match right from the second minute when Adrian Morley was sensationally sent off by Russell Smith for a punch on Paul Davidson after playing the ball. Twenty-nine penalties followed as the two sides employed a physical approach to the game with five players sin-binned, including Leeds skipper Iestyn Harris for dissent.

JJB SUPER LEAGUE
ROUND TWENTY RESULTS
Friday 23rd July, 1999
Leeds Rhinos 12..St Helens 28
London Broncos 48 ....Halifax Blue Sox 12
Saturday 24th July, 1999
Sheffield Eagles 16 ....Warrington Wolves 48
Sunday 25th July, 1999
Bradford Bulls 24 ....Castleford Tigers 22
Huddersfield Giants 16 ....Gateshead Thunder 40
Hull Sharks 23 ....Wakefield Trinity Wildcats 18
Wigan Warriors 64...Salford City Reds 2
Wednesday 28th July, 1999
London Broncos 16 ....Bradford Bulls 19
at Welford Road, Leicester
Wakefield Trinity Wildcats 26................................Halifax Blue Sox 20

Three Chris Smith tries in the final 17 minutes finally settled a momentous match, that some commentators described as "disappointing" for failing to produce much open football, but the majority recognised as one of the best games of the season

"Ellery's back and that's superb," said gamestar Sean Long after he and the rest of the players had been taken over to the St Helens fans in the 16,000-plus crowd to take their applause.

In the post-match press conference Hanley blasted certain sections of the press for reporting he had climbed down in his dispute with the board.

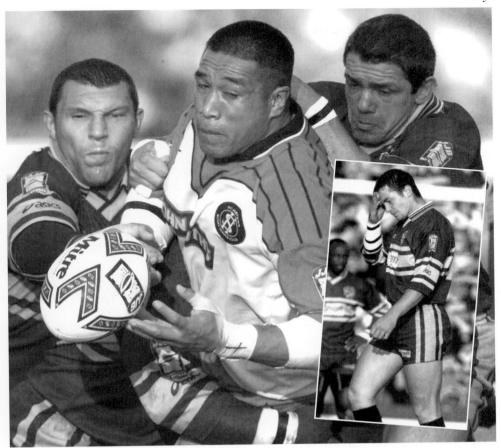

Apollo Perelini surrounded by the Leeds defence during an explosive clash at Headingley, which saw Adrian Morley sent off after only 90 seconds, *(inset)*, and Ellery Hanley's return to the Saints coaching role

"Before I touch on the football game, the first thing I want to talk about is this....Let me tell you something. Ellery Hanley did not climb down at all...Ellery Hanley doesn't eat humble pie, it's as simple as that."

Saints jumped into second spot as Leeds slipped to fourth after Wigan completed their second win of he week. On the Wednesday they had impressed at Sheffield Eagles with Denis Betts scoring a hat-trick of tries as Sheffield lost Martin Pearson with knee damage.

And on the Sunday, the Warriors showed little respect for Salford's big-city status as they wupped the City Reds 64-2, after leading only 16-2 at the break.

Wigan scored seven tries in 16 minutes after the turnaround, with Gavin Clinch kicking ten goals on the back of an 11-3 penalty count.

It was much closer at Odsal on the Sunday night, when James Lowes' 100th career try finally settled the game with the Tigers 24-22 in the Bulls favour.

The Tigers raced into a 12-0 lead after eleven minutes and led 18-12 at the break, but felt rightly aggrieved that they should have been further in front. Just before half-time, Danny Orr's mercurial run had been halted by a trip by Stuart Spruce, but incredibly, referee John Connolly ruled that it had been accidental.

At the Stoop on the Friday, Karle Hammond also registered a ton of career tries when he scored four in London's 48-12 win over the Blue Sox; and at the Don Valley, Sheffield Eagles, playing their third game in a week, were no match for the Wolves for the second time in the season, losing 48-16 as Lee Briers orchestrated the slaughter and Toa Kohe-Love registered a hat-trick to take him to 23 for the season.

At the bottom of the table, Huddersfield Giants were starting to get nervous as they lost heavily at home to Gateshead Thunder 40-16, while Hull Sharks were registering their third win of the season against Wakefield at the Boulevard.

The Giants slump had stories of merger with Halifax doing the rounds as Tony Grimaldi led Thunder superbly in front of a crowd of just over 2,000.

Jeff Hardy on the charge as the Eagles are savaged by the Wolves

Hulls' win left them just two league points adrift. The Sharks led 20-6 at the break with young hooker Paul King putting in a gamestar performance, before withstanding a Trinity comeback to hang on for the lifesaving points.

JJB SUPER LEAGUE - *Wednesday 28th July, 1999*

	P	W	D	L	F	A	D	PTS
Bradford Bulls	23	20	1	2	678	338	340	41
St Helens	22	17	0	5	751	395	356	34
Wigan Warriors	23	16	1	6	619	288	331	33
Leeds Rhinos	22	16	1	5	682	414	268	33
Gateshead Thunder	22	14	1	7	511	400	111	29
Castleford Tigers	22	12	3	7	462	331	131	27
Warrington Wolves	22	13	1	8	510	503	7	27
London Broncos	23	9	2	12	480	570	-90	20
Wakefield Trinity Wildcats	23	8	0	15	440	541	-101	16
Halifax Blue Sox	23	8	0	15	422	596	-174	16
Sheffield Eagles	23	7	1	15	376	613	-237	15
Salford City Reds	22	4	1	17	368	651	-283	9
Huddersfield Giants	22	4	0	18	348	670	-322	8
Hull Sharks	22	3	0	19	301	638	-337	6

AUGUST
Bulls on top

Super League's On the Road venture in 1999 wasn't quite as ambitious as the year before and involved just two matches, London Broncos' 'home' fixture against table-toppers Bradford Bulls and the following Sunday's Gateshead Thunder v Wigan game, which had to be played away from Gateshead any way as the Thunderdome was double booked.

Over 8,000 fans turned out at Welford Road, Leicester to see a tight tussle between the Broncos and the Bulls, which the leaders just edged 19-16. An estimated turnout of 3,000 locals had Super League Europe claiming a huge success.

"After tonight's success we'll be back for sure," said SLE managing director Maurice Lindsay, "but we are not pressing Leicester or anyone else into a franchise application."

It wasn't all smooth running as when many fans arrived at the ground, already delayed by a motorway accident, they found they had to queue for tickets, with no cash turnstiles open. "We'll take some blame for that," said Lindsay.

After the win, with Aussie Michael Withers producing one of several influential performances during August, Bradford moved seven points clear of the rest.

On the Sunday afternoon, Andy Goodway's dream run as head coach at Wigan came to an end as the super-charged Thunder beat them 20-16, after a whirlwind start which saw the Tynesiders race into an 18-0 lead with one try from Irish winger Brian Carney and two from Matt Daylight. Greg Florimo came off the bench to revive Wigan and after Denis Betts had pulled

JJB SUPER LEAGUE ROUND TWENTY ONE RESULTS

Friday 30th July, 1999

St Helens 64	Huddersfield Giants 16

Sunday 1st August, 1999

Castleford Tigers 52	London Broncos 16
Gateshead Thunder 20	Wigan Warriors 16
	at Tynecastle Stadium, Edinburgh
Halifax Blue Sox 24	Sheffield Eagles 43
Salford City Reds 20	Bradford Bulls 58
Wakefield Trinity Wildcats 10	Leeds Rhinos 34
Warrington Wolves 32	Hull Sharks 12

Wednesday 4th August, 1999

Hull Sharks 12	Gateshead Thunder 40

one try back, thought he had narrowed the margin to six points in first-half injury-time, but the video referee spotted the tiniest of knock-ons by Andy Farrell in the build-up.

The celebrations, in front of just under 5,000 people, a thousand of them from the North East, were a sight to see and Thunder coach Shaun McRae was naturally ebullient.

"Something special is evolving at Gateshead," he said. "We are on a learning curve but we have a team, a club and a set of supporters who are prepared to work and improve. It will take time but even in the short period that the club has been in existence we are making measurable progress. The win is a big boost for the organisation of Gateshead Thunder."

The Thunder set about signing three key players for 2000 in Great Britain prop Paul Broadbent, Hull KR's Stanley Gene and Wakefield's Wayne McDonald.

The Bulls' march continued on the Sunday at the Willows with their eighth win on a row, running in eleven tries in a 58-20 victory on a boiling hot afternoon. "I'm glad the week's over to be honest," said Bulls coach Matthew Elliott.

The City Reds had conceded 22 tries in two games. "I knew there was no quick fix

Jonathan Roper looks for space against Hull

when I got here. But we need to get a result," said their coach John Harvey.

Fortunately for the City Reds, the two clubs below them were also losing.

The Sharks went into their game at Wilderspool after owner David Lloyd threatened to withhold their wages unless they started winning. The 'motivation' didn't work as, after agreeing eventually to play the game, Hull lost 32-12.

But coach Steve Crooks was full of praise for his side. "I must give credit to all the players for the way they have rallied," he said. "The best part of Thursday's and Friday's preparation was ruined. We only got back to work yesterday and from an effort point of view they have done very well."

On the Friday night the Huddersfield Giants were looking increasingly ragged as St Helens did what they often do, score a bucketful of tries - eleven in all - in a 64-16 win.

To increase Huddersfield's worries, Bobbie Goulding, looking likely to be released by the club at the end of the season, was taken from the field with a suspected broken fibula.

Sean Long ran riot for the Saints, picking up a personal haul of 28 points on the back of a 9-1 penalty count.

In a mid-table match-up, Halifax Blue Sox, who lost in midweek 26-20 at Wakefield, were the victims of Newcastle youngster Chris Thorman, who was secured by the victorious Sheffield Eagles on a long term contract earlier that week.

Thorman's distribution and kicking were the keys to Eagles' 43-24 win at the Shay, with in-demand centre Keith Senior getting two tries.

Wigan's defeat in Edinburgh meant that the Leeds Rhinos went back into third place after their 34-10 win against the Wildcats at Belle Vue.

Richie Blackmore was back from injury for the Rhinos - "it was like signing a new international," said coach Graham Murray. Blackmore was awesome in attack and defence, scoring two tries in a comfortable win.

The Tigers ensured they stayed only two points behind Gateshead in sixth position with a 52-16 mauling of the tired-looking Broncos at Wheldon Road.

Francis Maloney scored his second hat-trick of the season in Cas's record home score as Stuart Raper's dad, Aussie legend Johnny Raper, enjoyed the special atmosphere that had evolved in 1999 at Tigertown.

Prospects didn't seem too bright for the Sharks going into the second weekend of August with only six games remaining to salvage their place in Super League and coming off the back of another defeat, this time in midweek at home to Gateshead Thunder. To compound the problems, prop Andy Ireland sustained ankle ligament damage in that defeat.

Another gutsy display from the Sharks wasn't enough to prevent a brilliant second-half display from Kerrod Walters take the Thunder home 40-12.

But on the Sunday, determination got its rewards as Hull relegated the Giants to bottom spot in the table with a 24-21 win over Halifax Blue Sox after the most amazing comeback of the season.

JJB SUPER LEAGUE
ROUND TWENTY TWO RESULTS
Friday 6th August, 1999

Leeds Rhinos 34 ....Warrington Wolves 30

Saturday 7th August, 1999

London Broncos 28 ....Salford City Reds 14
Sheffield Eagles 0 ....Castleford Tigers 22

Sunday 8th August, 1999

Bradford Bulls 30 ....Gateshead Thunder 14
Huddersfield Giants 10 ....Wigan Warriors 60
Hull Sharks 24 ....Halifax Blue Sox 21
St Helens 42 ....Wakefield Trinity Wildcats 34

Wednesday 11th August, 1999

Huddersfield Giants 12 ....Warrington Wolves 40

Going into the final quarter of the match the Sharks trailed by 20-0 but four late tries - from 17 year old Richard Horne, gamestar Steve Craven, Michael Smith and the winner in the dying seconds from Graeme Hallas - sent the Boulevard faithful into a state of delirium.

Iestyn Harris breaks Super League points-in-a-season record ● Gateshead Thunder sign Paul Broadbent from Halifax, Stanley Gene from Hull KR and Wayne McDonald from Wakefield for season 2000 ● St Helens' match against Castleford scheduled for January in Dubai is in doubt ● Salford deny they have been offered £1.25 million to drop out of Super League ● RFL boss Neil Tunnicliffe expects to receive confirmation of end-of-season Tri-Series ● Eric Hughes to stay as St Helens football manager ● Leeds Rhinos announce interest in signing rugby union player Jonah Lomu ● Super League Europe announce minimum criteria system for 2002, and offer £1.25million carrot for clubs to merge ● Maurice Lindsay says Widnes Vikings would be a welcome addition to Super League...

Hull had Ian Pickavance on debut from the bench after signing him that week from rivals Huddersfield Giants. It was sweet for the former Saints man who felt he hadn't been treated fairly by Giants coach Mal Reilly. "I can't see Huddersfield winning another game all season," he said. "I wouldn't mind playing my part in a couple more Hull wins to get them relegated."

The Giants were smashed on the same day by Wigan at the McAlpine Stadium 60-10, as Andy Farrell became one of the club's top-five all-time scorers. Mal Reilly had signed Dean Lawford from Leeds to fill in for the injured Bobbie Goulding and he made a fine debut, but it was another disappointing show from the Giants - the paltry crowd of just over 3,000 reflecting the gloom around the club.

Logan Campbell fends off Halifax's Nick Pinkney as the Sharks snatch a crucial victory

Neil Cowie had a terrific game for the Warriors in a ten-try rout, although the Giants were trailing only 18-10 midway through the second half.

The Rhinos kept their nose in front of Wigan with a 34-30 win against a battling Wolves outfit at Headingley on the Friday night. Veteran winger Paul Sterling scored a crucial hat-trick but the game was decided in controversial fashion in the 75th minute when Alan Hunte released the ball as he was tackled over his own line to gift Andy Hay a try, though the Wolves claimed the tackle was complete when he let the ball go.

Saints also had a close game at home to the Wakefield Wildcats.

They looked to be cruising 32-6 up until Tony Kemp inspired a fantastic Trinity comeback to grab a 34-32 lead midway through the second half, before late tries to Paul Newlove and Gareth Price sealed a 42-34 win for the second-placed side.

Salford City Reds were beginning to get nervous, only one point clear of bottom spot after their 28-14 defeat at the Stoop on the Saturday night, in a dour game that didn't thrill either coach.

The Bulls proved too strong for Gateshead, ending the Tynesiders' winning run at five with a 30-14 win at Odsal. Leon Pryce and David Boyle each scored two tries for the Bulls with Robbie Paul returning after a nine-match injury absence to partner brother Henry at halfback.

The defeat left Gateshead only two points clear of the Tigers who had a game in hand and a superior points difference. Cas had whitewashed the Eagles at the Don Valley Stadium the previous evening 22-0. "I'm happy with the way we are going," said Tigers coach Stuart Raper, "and I'd be disappointed if we keep playing this well and don't make the top-five." It was the first time Sheffield had been prevented from scoring at home in four seasons of Super League, as Darren Rogers scored the 100th try of his career.

At least Eagles coach John Kear was keeping his sense of humour. When asked to respond to Stuart Raper's complaints of niggling tactics by Sheffield, Kear laughed: "Well he always does that, he's an Aussie."

At a crunch meeting, Super League clubs rejected a proposal to implement a franchise system for 2002, deciding instead that all clubs must apply for their Super League place from that year onwards, with applications to be in by 31 March 2000. Any clubs that failed to satisfy criteria would be relegated to the Northern Ford Premiership.

The meeting also approved a cash inducement to Super League clubs who merged of £1.25million, if clubs could agree merger by September 30th 1999. It would go down to a million pounds if they did it after that.

One club who were already intimating that they could be on course for such a move was Sheffield Eagles, who were speaking to soccer clubs about groundshare. "We would not go into an alliance as tenants," said chief executive Ralph Rimmer. "Any alliance would depend purely on what is the best deal for Sheffield Eagles."

With the Eagles making cutbacks in the front office, on the field they were struggling and on the Sunday went down to Salford City Reds at the Willows. Salford were more than relieved to put daylight between themselves and the bottom two as Mark Johnson and Bobby Thompson scored late tries to halt an Eagles comeback inspired by Mark Aston, returning off the bench after a lengthy injury.

JJB SUPER LEAGUE
ROUND TWENTY THREE RESULTS
Friday 13th August, 1999
Halifax Blue Sox 21 ....Leeds Rhinos 20
Wigan Warriors 14 ....Bradford Bulls 0
Sunday 15th August, 1999
Castleford Tigers 44 ....Hull Sharks 16
Gateshead Thunder 22 ....London Broncos 28
Salford City Reds 26..Sheffield Eagles 12
Wakefield Trinity Wildcats 40 ....Huddersfield Giants 12
Warrington Wolves 12 ....St Helens 35
Wednesday 18th August, 1999
Leeds Rhinos 50 ....Salford City Reds 16

But the return of Salford halfback Martin Crompton after a nine-game lay-off was just as crucial and the Reds could breathe more easily.

The Giants had Kiwi Test stand-off Gene Ngamu and signing from Wigan, Andy Johnson, on debut at Belle Vue but they couldn't stop Wakefield getting the two points that ensured it was mathematically impossible for them to be relegated.

Dean Lawford again looked impressive but Wakefield's four quick tries around the hour mark took them out to a 40-12 win. "I think it's in their heads - it's desire," said coach Mal Reilly, whose side had lost their midweek game against the Wolves at the McAlpine by exactly the same score.

The Sharks were no match for Castleford Tigers, losing 44-16. Hull couldn't repeat their heroics of the previous Sunday, after they trailed 28-4 at half-time.

Gateshead kicked off at 2.00pm that Sunday afternoon and the biggest roar of the day at Wheldon Road came when the PA man announced the result from the Thunderdome - where London Broncos stunned the Thunder with a 28-22 win. "We didn't deserve to win," admitted Thunder coach Shaun McRae, after

Paul Rowley gets the ball away as the Sox shock the Rhinos at the New Shay

Chris Ryan's try a minute from time sealed it.

Cas, now level on points with Gateshead but with a much better points difference, were looking a good bet for the play-offs.

At the top of the table, Wigan ended the Bulls' winning run at nine matches in an absolutely intense match at Central Park.

A rain-drenched night didn't spoil the entertainment and a 14-0 Wigan win was finally capped seven minutes from time when Gary Connolly stole the ball one-on-one from Nathan McAvoy to slide over for the only try of the match. "We were outstanding from one to 17," said coach Andy Goodway, who had struck a blow for the upcoming play-offs.

The Bulls also saw forward David Boyle put on report for punching Lee Gilmour, and he was later suspended for one match.

There was a big shock at the Shay on Friday night as the Blue Sox, with Paul Rowley restored to the starting line-up, stunned Leeds Rhinos 21-20. It was Rowley's field goal - though it came in the fourth minute of the game - that eventually separated the two sides as the Blue Sox limited Leeds to a solitary penalty goal in the second half. The game ended with Adrian Morley being sent off for the second time in four matches for a head-butt on Rowley. Morley got a two-match ban the following Tuesday.

St Helens stayed three points ahead of third-placed Wigan with a resounding 35-12 win at Wilderspool, severely damaging the Wolves' own play-off hopes. It was another convincing display by Ellery Hanley's side, led superbly by Chris Joynt, but utility forward Vila Matautia picked up another suspension - three matches - for a high tackle on Danny Nutley.

Leeds Rhinos recaptured third place from Wigan on the Wednesday night with an eventual overwhelming of Salford City Reds by 50-16.

Incredibly the Rhinos had trailed the determined Reds 16-10 at the break in front of another 10,000-plus crowd at Headingley. But Lee Jackson, not for the first time this season, came off the bench to inspire Leeds as tries by Andy Hay and Francis Cummins started a second-half rout. Cummins, though unable to agree a new contract with the Rhinos, scored two tries to maintain his position as top-scorer at Leeds with 20 tries, and there was also a brace for 16 year old Chev Walker, who had played three minutes from the bench against Halifax, but was given a full debut that Wednesday. The youngster's massive frame and speed marked him down as one to watch in the future as he finished off his chances in style.

Leeds had to stage a comeback again on Sunday night at Gateshead, who were desperate to revive their top-five chances. 18-8 down at half-time, marshalled superbly again by Daryl Powell, they scored 22 points without reply after the break with tries to

Warrington Wolves linked with Martin Offiah ● Super League welcomes its one millionth fan at Tynecastle in Edinburgh ● Bradford Bulls linked with former Kangaroo Brad Mackay ● Warrington Wolves sign Alfie Langer and Andrew Gee from Brisbane ● Huddersfield Giants sign Gene Ngamu from Auckland, Mark Sibson from Bramley and Troy Slattery from South Sydney ● Sheffield Eagles investigate groundshare option with Chesterfield ● St Helens and Wigan announce Boxing Day game will be revived in 1999 ● Karl Harrison announces he will retire from Super League at end of season ● Halifax Blue Sox hooker Paul Rowley returns to the club, Gary Mercer appointed coach on permanent basis...

Anthony Farrell, Leroy Rivett and Ryan Sheridan, to stretch out to a 30-18 win.

After the game, Leeds coach Graham Murray accused the Thunder of deliberately diving at the feet of the tackler to get a quick play the ball, claiming it was an unfair tactic outside the spirit of the game.

Thunder coach Shaun McRae countered: "I'm not sure what Graham is getting at. But if you are being intimidated with high shots, what are you supposed to do - run around with your head in the air and get it taken off."

In the week, Anthony Farrell received a one-match suspension for a high tackle on Matt Daylight and Terry Newton copped two matches for punching Luke Felsch, while in Friday's Total Rugby League, refs' boss Greg McCallum said he had no concerns about runners diving into the tackle.

St Helens continued their amazing winning run, but were not that convincing against the City Reds at the Willows, tries from Steve Hall and Sean Long in the closing quarter and a Tommy Martyn field goal wrapping up a 23-10 win. The City Reds were inspired by a brilliant performance

JJB SUPER LEAGUE
ROUND TWENTY FOUR RESULTS
Friday 20th August, 1999
Castleford Tigers 30 ....Wakefield Trinity Wildcats 18
Halifax Blue Sox 23 ....Warrington Wolves 22
Wigan Warriors 58 ....Hull Sharks 0
Sunday 22nd August, 1999
Bradford Bulls 52 ....Sheffield Eagles 4
Gateshead Thunder 18 ....Leeds Rhinos 30
London Broncos 40 ....Huddersfield Giants 4
Salford City Reds 10...St Helens 23
Wednesday 25th August, 1999
St Helens 42 ....Castleford Tigers 14

from Steve Blakeley and Saints had skipper Chris Joynt placed on report after a late challenge on the Salford stand-off. Joynt received a written warning from the RFL after Blakeley attended the disciplinary to aid his defence.

The Bulls were back on song with Steve McNamara returning to lead them to a 52-4 thrashing of Sheffield Eagles at Odsal.

"It was a good result even though we didn't play as well as we could," said Bulls boss Matthew Elliott. "Over there on the horizon we can see the prize."

August

There was a third terrific derby of 1999 between the Tigers and the Wildcats at Wheldon Road on the Friday night, which Cas eventually won 30-18. A 54th minute penalty try for Danny Orr, who was clearly obstructed by Glen Tomlinson as he chased a kick through, certain to score, and another hotly disputed try by Brad Hepi five minutes from time, proved crucial.

Cas's hold on fifth spot now looked sure, but Warrington Wolves said goodbye to their hopes as they were pipped by Halifax at the New Shay, who were winning by one point for the second week in a row, this time 23-22. It took a Graham Holroyd field goal, with 70 seconds left on the clock, to decide this tie.

Gateshead's Craig Wilson tries to shrug off Leeds' Daryl Powell

The Broncos and Huddersfield Giants had been well matched in their two previous meetings that season but the re-match at the Stoop was a one-sided affair. The Giants had signed Andy Hill from Castleford to bolster their squad but they folded to a 40-4 defeat. Sporadic flashes of brilliance from Karle Hammond were enough to sink the low-on-confidence Giants.

The Sharks were lacking in that department too when they returned to Central Park - having suffered a 58-4 humiliation there in Round One back in March.

That night Peter Walsh was the subject of abuse from Hull fans, some of whom he described as having half a brain, and this time it was the turn of his successor as coach, Steve Cooks, who was advised for his own safety to leave for the tunnel ten minutes before the end.

Wigan deny offering Sheffield cash plus Gavin Clinch for Keith Senior ● Chester Wolves win Rugby League Conference Grand Final ● Great Britain great Garry Schofield announces his retirement ● Thunder prop Danny Lee announces his retirement ● Sheffield Eagles give free transfers to Michael Jackson and Paul Anderson ● Leeds Rhinos sign Melbourne Storm centre Paul Bell and Roosters prop David Barnhill ● Tri-Series in doubt as Aussies threaten to pull plug ● Huddersfield Giants rubbish claims they are about to merge with Sheffield Eagles...

Denis Betts scored a four-timer as the Warriors prepared for the battle for third spot that was scheduled for Headingley the following Friday.

The Headingley showdown let no-one down. It was sport at its best as Wigan seemed to be taking a grip, only to see the game turned on one incident.

Wigan had raced into a 12-4 lead on the half hour and after some searing pressure seemed certain to score again when Andy Farrell, playing at stand-off, fired a long pass to the left.

The quick-thinking Leroy Rivett plucked the ball from the air before racing

Neil Cowie battles through the Leeds ranks as the Rhinos down the Warriors

80-metres up the South Stand side for a thrilling try. A typical side-stepping try from Iestyn Harris had the Rhinos 16-12 up at the break. When Wigan clawed their way back to 22-16 with five minutes to go, it was Harris again who interjected, this time sending Ryan Sheridan in for the try.

Mal Reilly had judged that the Giants had to win two of their last three games to escape relegation and they won the first in dramatic style against local rivals Halifax Blue Sox at the McAlpine.

The Blue Sox had won their last two games with field goals and the irony was noted when they lost 19-18, courtesy of a Dean Lawford one-pointer struck seven minutes from time.

Blue Sox player-coach Gary Mercer missed the game with injury and gave Aussie Andrew Dunemann his debut at scrum-half

Reilly admitted afterwards that he rated this game as crucial as Tests and Cas's win at Wembley in 1986, and was delighted with the form of new signing from South Sydney, Troy Slattery, who had a hand in all three Giants tries in a first half which they won 18-6. Other debutant, Mark Sibson, signed from Bramley via Student Rugby League, was on hand for the first of them.

The Giants were now two points clear of Hull Sharks, with only an eleven-point's worse points difference.

The Sharks had pushed the Bulls at the Boulevard in round two but there was no shock this time as the leaders strode to a 44-12 win, with Michael Withers, deputising for the injured Stuart Spruce at fullback, scoring four tries. The Sharks were running out of time.

Just over 2,000 folk turned out at the Don Valley Stadium on the Saturday night to see Sheffield Eagles regain some pride with a 20-16 win over the London Broncos. Fijian Waisale Sovatabua broke a 13-month try-drought with a score in each half, the second settling the outcome after the lead changed hands four times in the second half.

Wakefield Wildcats scored 26 second-half points without reply against the City Reds at Belle Vue to stretch out 36-10 winners - their tenth win of Super League IV, ten more than most people predicted they would win at the start of the campaign. Once again Willie Poching was the key to Trinity's success.

The Wolves were virtually out of the Championship for 1999 but they were out to prove a point in the Sunday night game against the Tigers.

Cas had crashed to a 42-14 defeat at St Helens midweek and were desperate for the two points to keep their noses in front of sixth-placed Gateshead. The Tigers produced a clinical display, and even when Scott Wilson's try on 62 minutes brought the Wolves back to 8-6, they never looked like losing their defensive composure, with Dale Fritz at the centre of a mighty effort.

JJB SUPER LEAGUE
ROUND TWENTY FIVE RESULTS
Friday 27th August, 1999
Leeds Rhinos 28......................................Wigan Warriors 22
Saturday 28th August, 1999
Sheffield Eagles 20 ....London Broncos 16
Sunday 29th August, 1999
Huddersfield Giants 19 ....Halifax Blue Sox 18
Hull Sharks 12 ....Bradford Bulls 44
Wakefield Trinity Wildcats 36 ....Salford City Reds 10
Warrington Wolves 6 ....Castleford Tigers 8
Monday 30th August, 1999
St Helens 32 ....Gateshead Thunder 36

On the Bank Holiday Monday, St Helens were confidently predicted to see off Gateshead Thunder, but Saints' winning sequence of nine games came to an end in a 36-32 Thunder success.

It was all the more remarkable as Tommy Martyn scored six points with only seven minutes to go to give Saints what looked like a 32-30 winning lead. But Deon Bird crashed over at the other end and Ian Herron kicked his sixth conversion from six attempts to steal it. Bradford Bulls were minor premiers.

Had the Ellery Hanley bubble burst?

JJB SUPER LEAGUE - *Monday 30th August, 1999*								
	P	W	D	L	F	A	D	PTS
Bradford Bulls	28	24	1	3	862	402	460	49
St Helens	28	22	0	6	989	517	472	44
Leeds Rhinos	28	21	1	6	878	531	347	43
Wigan Warriors	28	19	1	8	789	346	443	39
Castleford Tigers	28	17	3	8	632	429	203	37
Gateshead Thunder	28	17	1	10	661	548	113	35
Warrington Wolves	28	15	1	12	652	627	25	31
London Broncos	28	12	2	14	608	682	-74	26
Wakefield Trinity Wildcats	28	10	0	18	578	669	-91	20
Halifax Blue Sox	28	10	0	18	529	724	-195	20
Sheffield Eagles	28	9	1	18	455	753	-298	19
Salford City Reds	28	5	1	22	464	858	-394	11
Huddersfield Giants	28	5	0	23	421	932	-511	10
Hull Sharks	28	4	0	24	377	877	-500	8

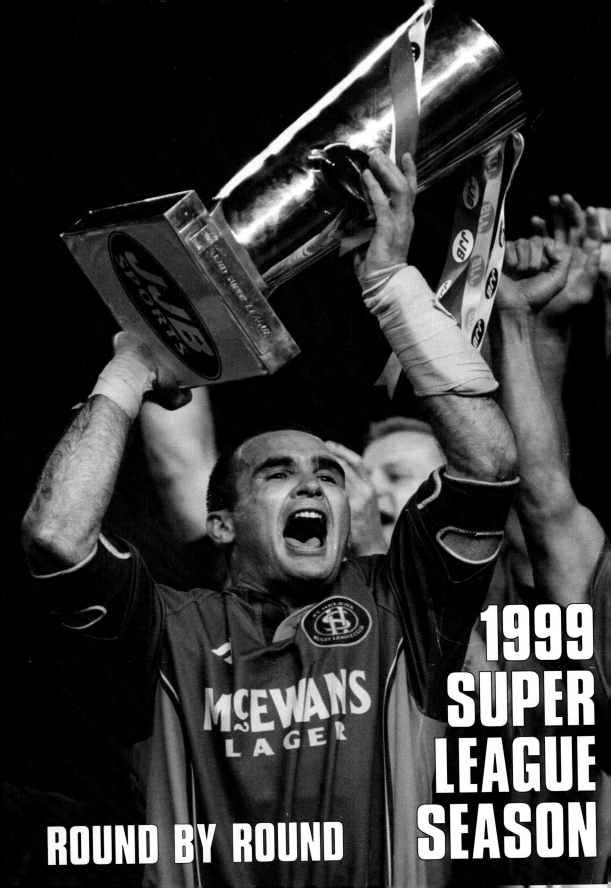

ROUND BY ROUND

1999 SUPER LEAGUE SEASON

RIGHT: Leeds Rhinos Richie Blackmore blasts through Stuart Spruce.

BOTTOM LEFT: Leeds players celebrate their passage through to the Silk Cut Challenge Cup Final.

RIGHT (INSET): Leeds coach Graham Murray and captain Iestyn Harris salute the fans.

BOTTOM RIGHT (INSET): Ryan Sheridan scores for Leeds.

CHALLENGE CUP SEMI FINALS

EFT: London's Steele Retchless scores the atch winning try to beat Castleford Tigers.

OTTOM (INSET): Martin Offiah and Shaun dwards celebrate another trip to Wembley, is time with the London Broncos.

TOP: Iestyn Harris lifts the Silk Cut Challenge Cup as Leeds smash the records at Wembley.
TOP (INSET): Leeds' Barrie McDermott celebrates his try with Lee Jackson.
LEFT: Richard Branson leads out the London Broncos.
BOTTOM: Four-try hero Leroy Rivett scores his first.

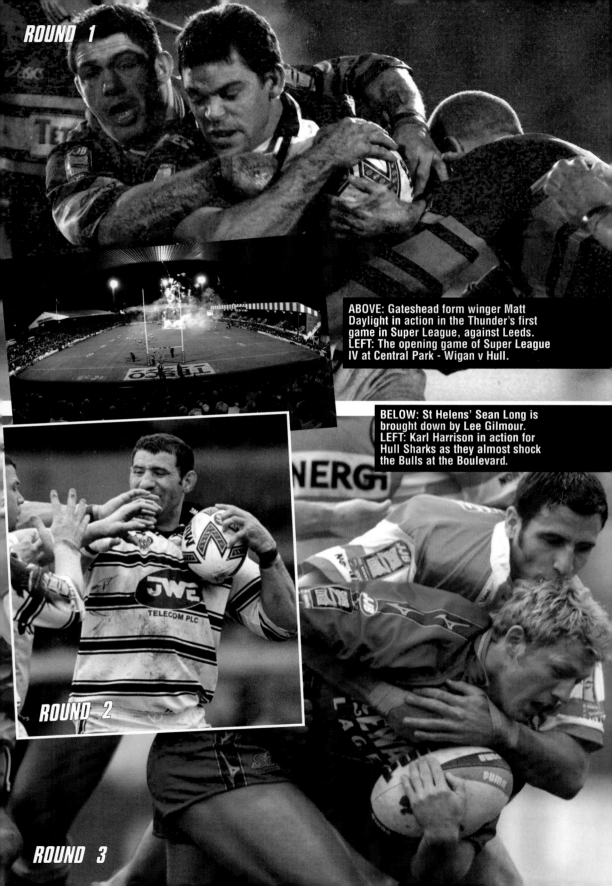

ROUND 1

ROUND 2

ROUND 3

ABOVE: Gateshead form winger Matt Daylight in action in the Thunder's first game in Super League, against Leeds.
LEFT: The opening game of Super League IV at Central Park - Wigan v Hull.

BELOW: St Helens' Sean Long is brought down by Lee Gilmour.
LEFT: Karl Harrison in action for Hull Sharks as they almost shock the Bulls at the Boulevard.

ABOVE: St Helens' Fereti Tuilagi brought crashing down by Danny Peacock.
BELOW RIGHT: Iestyn Harris has nowhere to go as Leeds are beaten by Sheffield Eagles.

ROUND 5

ROUND 6

LEFT: Jamie Bloem leaves Denis Betts flailing as Halifax record their first win in Super League.

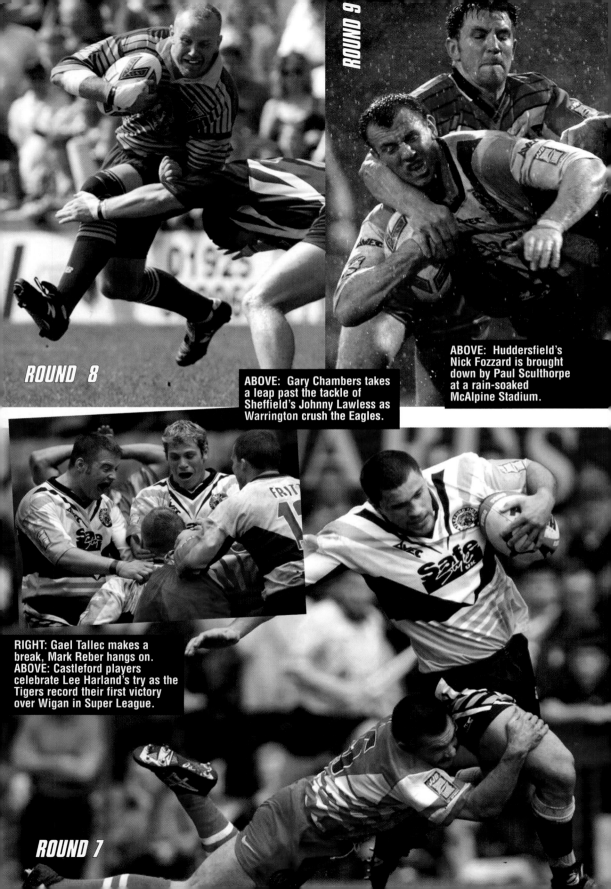

ROUND 8

ROUND 9

ABOVE: Gary Chambers takes a leap past the tackle of Sheffield's Johnny Lawless as Warrington crush the Eagles.

ABOVE: Huddersfield's Nick Fozzard is brought down by Paul Sculthorpe at a rain-soaked McAlpine Stadium.

RIGHT: Gael Tallec makes a break, Mark Reber hangs on.
ABOVE: Castleford players celebrate Lee Harland's try as the Tigers record their first victory over Wigan in Super League.

ROUND 7

ROUND 10

ABOVE: Wakefield's Gary Price shrugs off the challenge of Sean Long as St Helens' winning run is brought to an end at Barnsley's Oakwell Stadium.

ROUND 12

ROUND 11

ABOVE LEFT: Gateshead's Steve Collins bursts past Mat Toshack as London Broncos draw with the Thunder.
ABOVE RIGHT: Warren Jowitt on the charge as Bradford just shade Huddersfield Giants.

LEFT: Halifax's Damian Gibson is dumped by Mike Wainwright.

RIGHT: Willie Peters scores for Gateshead as they beat St Helens.
BELOW: Andy Hay scores a hat-trick for Leeds as they hammer the Bulls.

ROUND 15

ROUND 14

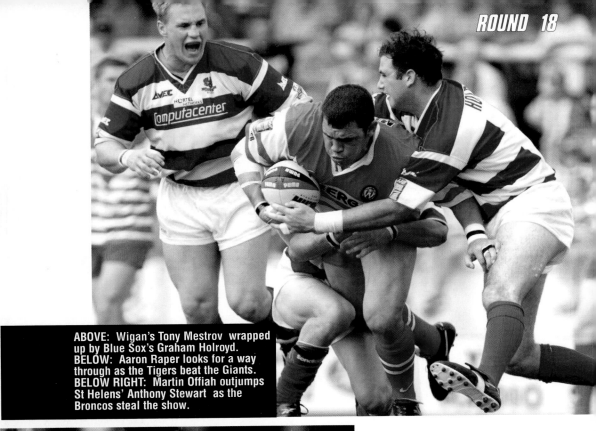

ABOVE: Wigan's Tony Mestrov wrapped up by Blue Sox's Graham Holroyd.
BELOW: Aaron Raper looks for a way through as the Tigers beat the Giants.
BELOW RIGHT: Martin Offiah outjumps St Helens' Anthony Stewart as the Broncos steal the show.

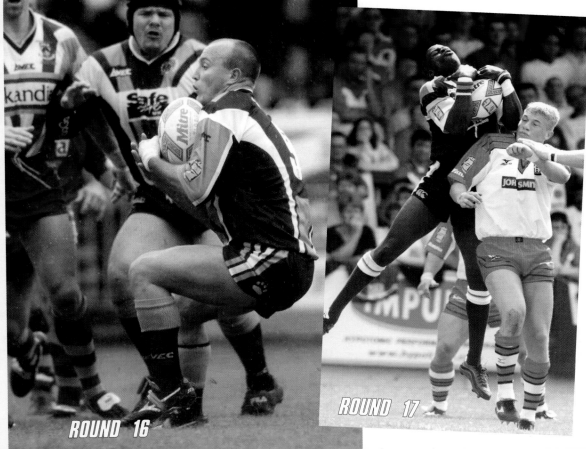

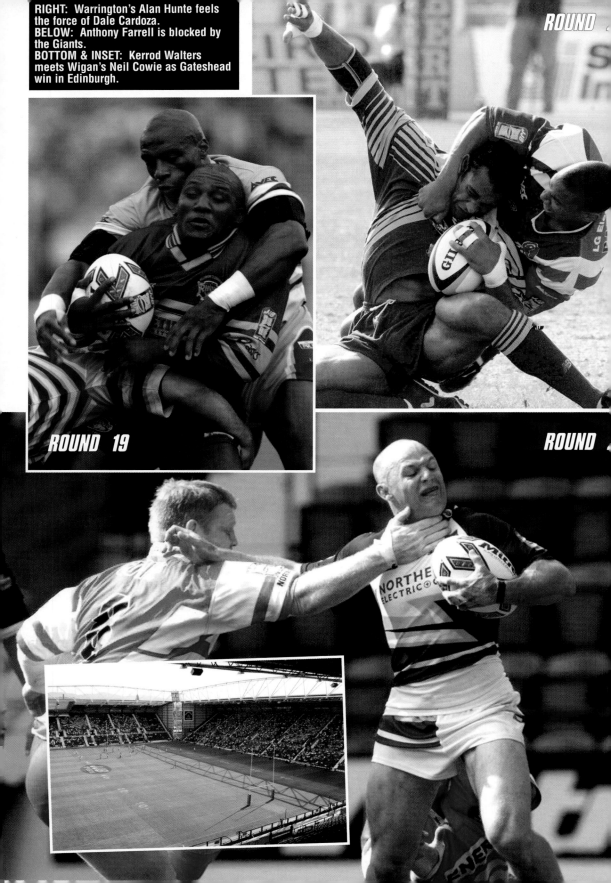

RIGHT: Warrington's Alan Hunte feels the force of Dale Cardoza.
BELOW: Anthony Farrell is blocked by the Giants.
BOTTOM & INSET: Kerrod Walters meets Wigan's Neil Cowie as Gateshead win in Edinburgh.

ROUND 19

ROUND

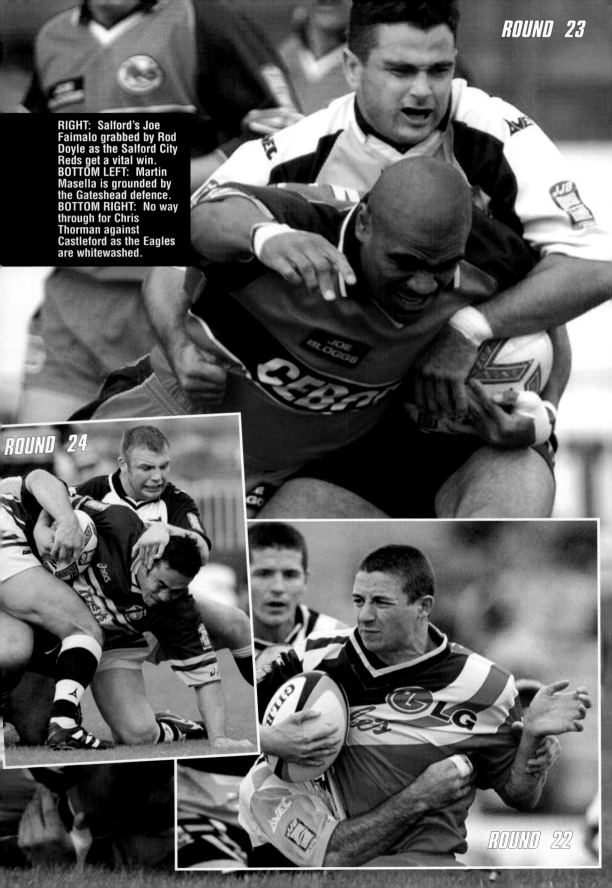

RIGHT: Salford's Joe Faimalo grabbed by Rod Doyle as the Salford City Reds get a vital win.
BOTTOM LEFT: Martin Masella is grounded by the Gateshead defence.
BOTTOM RIGHT: No way through for Chris Thorman against Castleford as the Eagles are whitewashed.

ROUND 24

ROUND 22

RIGHT: Denis Betts scores the first try of the last game at Central Park.
BOTTOM RIGHT: A young fan sits alone on the empty terraces.
BOTTOM LEFT: Sheffield's Matt Crowther proves a handful for the Broncos.

ROUND 25

ROUND 27

LEFT: Huddersfield players in despair as they lose their final game to Castleford and remain bottom of the table.

RIGHT: Butch Fatnowna on the charge for Hunslet.
BOTTOM RIGHT: Hunslet captain Shaun Irwin lifts the Northern Ford Premiership trophy.
BOTTOM LEFT: Hunslet celebrate their victory over Dewsbury.

BOTTOM LEFT: Anthony Murray on the burst as West of Pennines have the edge over Easts.
BOTTOM RIGHT: Latham Tawhai gets the ball away for Hunslet.

EAST v WEST

ELIMINATION PLAY-OFF

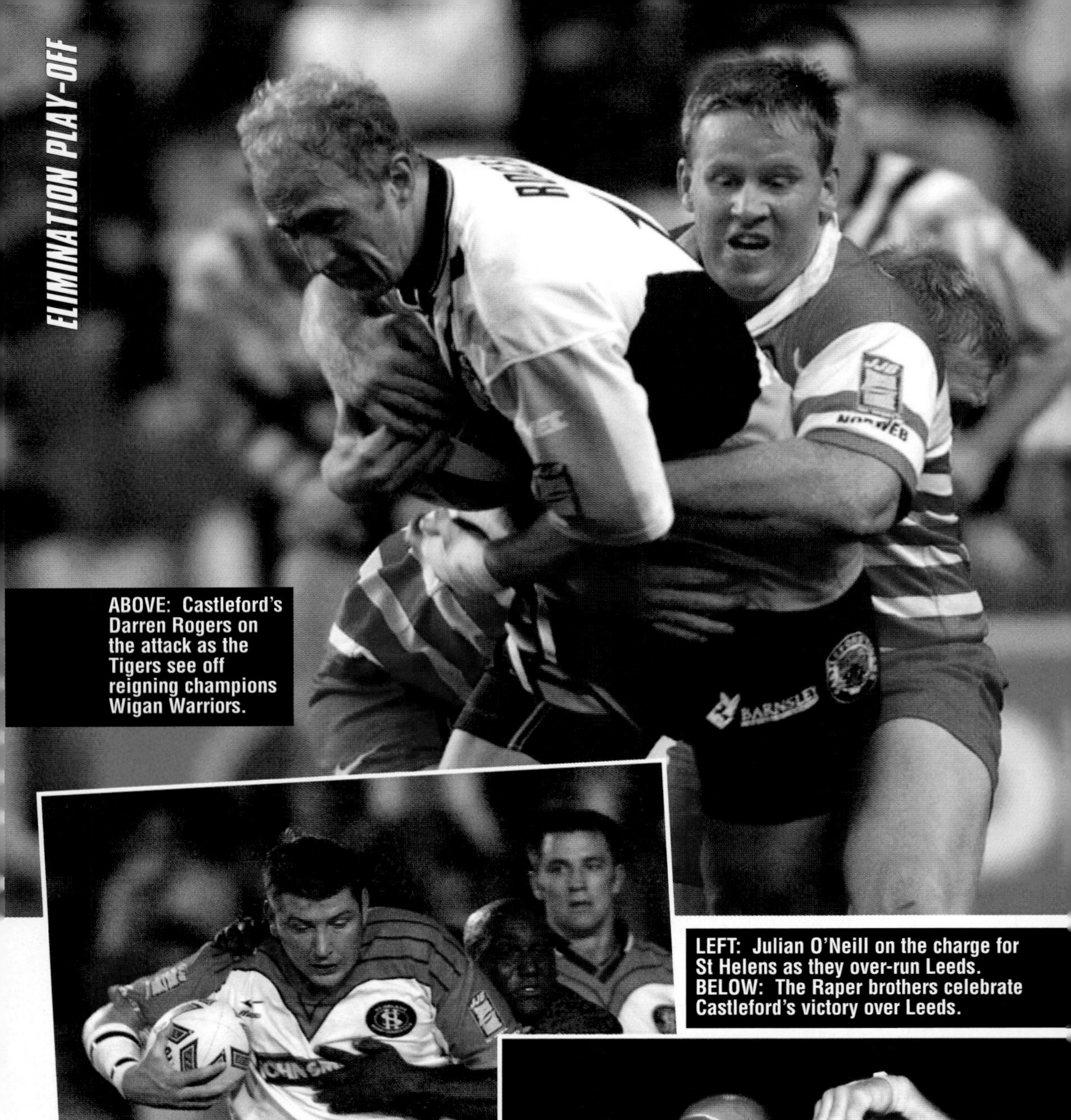

ABOVE: Castleford's Darren Rogers on the attack as the Tigers see off reigning champions Wigan Warriors.

QUALIFYING PLAY-OFF

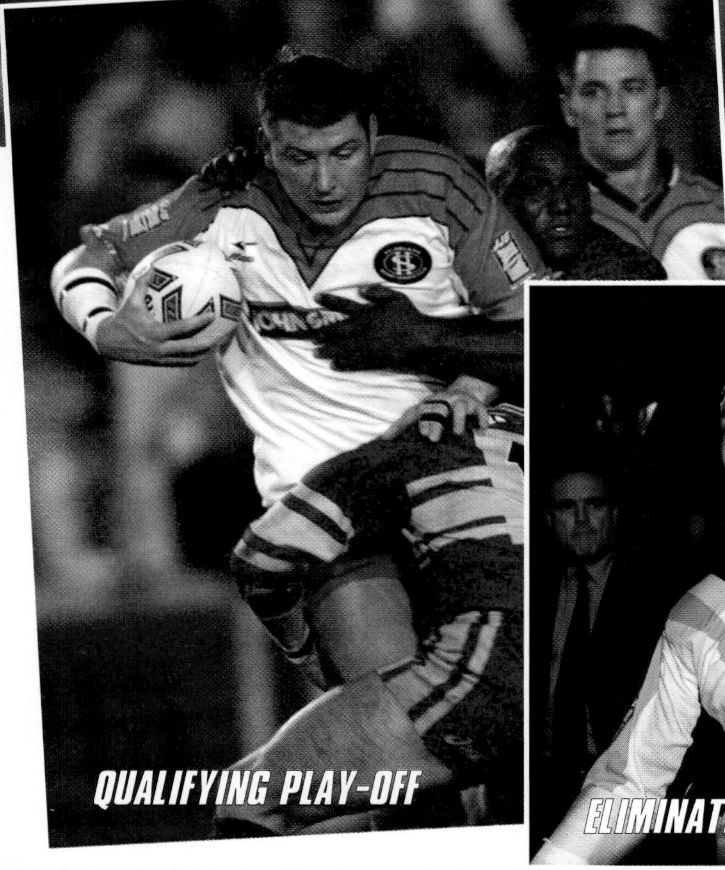

LEFT: Julian O'Neill on the charge for St Helens as they over-run Leeds.
BELOW: The Raper brothers celebrate Castleford's victory over Leeds.

ELIMINATION SEMI FINAL

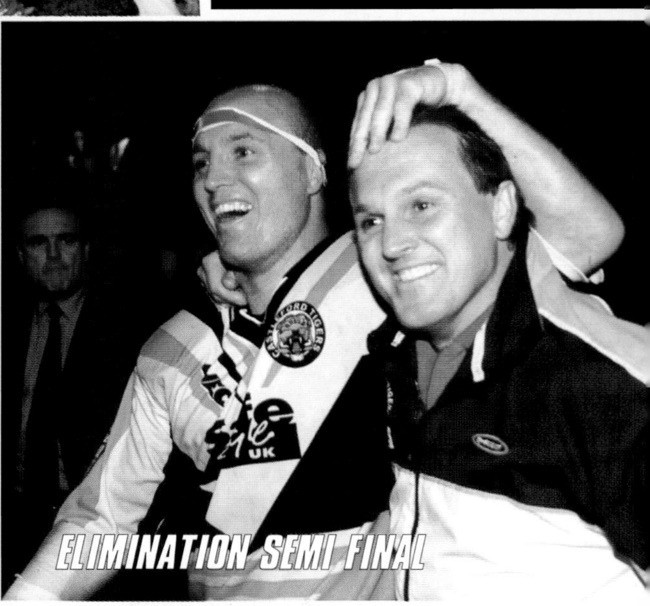

TOP LEFT: St Helens coach Ellery Hanley congratulates his captain Chris Joynt as they make it to the JJB Super League Grand Final.
RIGHT: Paul Newlove powers his way through the Castleford defence as the Tigers dream is shattered.
BOTTOM: Paul Anderson caught by Sean Long and Kevin Iro.
BOTTOM (INSET): Bradford's Stuart Fielden celebrates with Scott Naylor at the final whistle as the Bulls take their place at Old Trafford.

QUALIFYING SEMI FINAL

JJB SUPER LEAGUE GRAND FINAL

BRADFORD BULLS 6   ST HELENS 8

CLOCKWISE FROM TOP: St Helens Sean Long powers through the Bulls defence; Ellery Hanley holds the trophy; Chris Smith and Fereti Tuilagi celebrate at the final whistle; Chris Joynt holds up the trophy as the Saints team celebrate; James Lowes on his knees after the final whistle.

SEPTEMBER
Tiger feat

On the Sunday night of the penultimate round of Super League, the last ever game was played at Wigan's Central Park.

The match - it had to be against St Helens - was sold out weeks before as people clamoured to be part of a great occasion.

18,179 got in as Wigan Rugby League Club said goodbye to its home of 97 years, beating the old rival 28-20 in another stunning game.

"With all due respect to St Helens," said Maurice Lindsay, then still managing director of Super League Europe, "this was one that Wigan had to win."

There was a parade of old Wigan favourites before the kick-off and one of the modern greats, Jason Robinson, played a major role in Wigan's win that confirmed they would finish at least fourth in the table.

Saints drew level on the hour mark, only for tries from Robinson and Paul Johnson to pull Wigan away before Tommy Martyn became the last player to score a try at the great old ground.

"It's just been an emotional day," said Denis Betts, before leaving Central Park for the last time before it was knocked down to make way for a supermarket.

There was plenty of drama elsewhere, particularly at the bottom end of the table, where a life or death situation was developing.

Steve Prescott recovered early from his dislocated elbow in a desperate attempt to get the Hull Sharks off the bottom with a win at London Broncos..

JJB SUPER LEAGUE
ROUND TWENTY SIX RESULTS
Friday 3rd September, 1999
Bradford Bulls 19...Leeds Rhinos 18
Saturday 4th September, 1999
Sheffield Eagles 47...Huddersfield Giants 32
Sunday 5th September, 1999
Castleford Tigers 48...Halifax Blue Sox 12
Gateshead Thunder 66 ....Wakefield Trinity Wildcats 6
London Broncos 28...Hull Sharks 12
Salford City Reds 42 ....Warrington Wolves 26
Wigan Warriors 28 ....St Helens 20

Prescott starred, but the Sharks never recovered from a nightmare start that saw them 16-0 down on 23 minutes. The frustration showed during three minutes of mayhem when London's Dominic Peters was red-carded for running in and punching Steve Craven during a flare-up, with three others being sin-binned. Craven's cheekbone was fractured and Peters got himself banned until April 2000.

It was disappointment for the Sharks who now had one last chance for Super League survival.

"We thought we had done enough to win this match," said skipper Karl Harrison. "If we show that kind of spirit next week we have good chance of beating Sheffield Eagles."

A Super League record crowd of 24,020 witnesses a titanic Odsal struggle between Bradford and Leeds

The Giants' hopes of securing a lifeline evaporated in 16 minutes either side of half-time at the Don Valley Stadium where Sheffield Eagles ran in 31 unanswered points to lead 41-8, Mark Aston showing what the Eagles had been missing during his twelve-match absence. Eagles shrugged off the dismissal of Dale Laughton for a retaliatory head-butt on Gene Ngamu just before the break and the Giants couldn't get back, despite three tries in the last ten minutes, finishing 47-32 losers.

The players and over 2,000 newly converted League fans stayed behind to celebrate Gateshead Thunder's last match in a real party atmosphere at the Thunderdome.

The Thunder gave Wakefield their first thrashing of the season, 66-6 as they ran in eleven tries, matched by Ian Herron's eleven goals.

Barring a miracle it wasn't enough to deny the Tigers their place in the play-offs, as they beat the Blue Sox 48-12 at Wheldon Road, with Danny Orr scoring 20 points with two tries and six goals in front of a crowd of over 7,000.

Salford completed their home season with a surprise 42-26 over the Wolves at the Willows, with Steve Blakeley once again great form.

But the big event in terms of Super League took place on the Friday night at Odsal Stadium, where the Bulls took on the Rhinos and the Super League attendance record was beaten for the second time in the season with 24,020 seeing Michael Withers' field goal three minutes from time snatch a dramatic win for the Bulls.

The Rhinos had appeared to be on course for a third victory of the season

Farewell...Wigan and St Helens play out the last ever game at Central Park, watched by an emotional crowd

against the Bulls after a magnificent defensive effort in the first half. A side-stepping individual effort from Anthony Farrell, back from suspension, and three Iestyn Harris goals had Leeds 10-0 up before Steve McNamara pulled a penalty back before half-time.

Harris banged over a penalty just after the turnaround before, on the hour, Leon Pryce just got to Robbie Paul's grubber into the left corner and three minutes later Nathan McAvoy scored one of the most remarkable tries in Rugby League history.

It was Steve McNamara who turned the game on its head. First he took the Bulls downfield with a superb 40/20 and then on the last play he put a high kick across field from the right centre. It looked too flat, but the rangy McAvoy ran through at speed and plucked the ball out of the air to race in and give McNamara the chance to level at 12-12.

The Rhinos hit back almost instantly when, minutes later, 16 year old Chev Walker supported a Andy Hay break for another six-pointer. With only ten minutes to go, some of the Bradford fans began to drift away, not realising what was to come.

With James Lowes having left the field injured before the break the Bulls attacking edge could have been blunted but his replacement, Paul Deacon, got them back into the match when his dart and inside pass sent Tevita Vaikona tearing through for the equalising score. There was just time for Withers' field goal to bring the house down. "If I had another ten shots at goal I don't think I'd kick one," admitted Withers after a remarkable game.

September

Sky TV's decision to televise Huddersfield Giants' last game of the season on the Sunday night had Hull Sharks officials pressing for a delay to their kick-off too so as not to give the Giants any advantage by knowing their result against Sheffield Eagles.

As it unfolded, they need not have worried as the Sharks put in a passionate 80 minutes against the Eagles, whose players faced the threat of drifting into limbo with rumours increasing about the imminent merger of their club.

Hull had to win to get off the bottom of the table and rely on the Giants losing their game against the in-form Tigers.

From the moment that Eagles prop Steve Molloy knocked on from the kick-off there was never really any doubt that the Sharks would grab a lifeline. Sharks coach Steve Crooks described it as "Boys Own" stuff as he took the plaudits from the five and a half thousand black and whiters who shouted their side home.

The Sharks raced into a 30-4 half-time lead against a Sheffield side lacking Keith Senior, who had finally moved to Leeds that week. "I would now like to see some of that money we received from Leeds," said a disappointed Eagles coach John Kear, in charge of the Eagles team for the very last time as it turned out.

Chris Thorman sparked a mini-revival when he came off the bench but it was Hull's night.

The Giants couldn't match the Sharks' heroics as they went down 32-10 to Castleford Tigers, who were just too good on the night, leading 20-4 by half-time. Dean Sampson was once again in magnificent form up front as the Tigers geared up for a sudden death play-off against Wigan at the new JJB Stadium.

A season's worth of frustration had Giants coach Mal Reilly promising he would not stay on if Huddersfield didn't retain a place in Super League.

Bradford Bulls confirm they have signed Western Suburbs utility back Justin Brooker for 2000 season ● New Zealand Rugby League save Tri-Series by staging final ● Jarrod McCracken turns down move to St Helens ● London Broncos rumoured to be moving back to the Valley in time for 2000 ● Wigan deny they are to sign St Helens' Sean Long ● Super League scraps midweek fixtures for 2000 ● Dale Laughton suspended for two matches for head-butt on Gene Ngamu ● Keith Senior leaves Sheffield for Leeds Rhinos ● Bulls back another plan to redevelop Odsal Stadium ● Total Rugby League columnist Graeme Bradley is banned from involvement in Rugby League for 12 months ● Halifax Blue Sox tie Damian Gibson to a new two-year deal ● St Helens chase Kiwi Bryan Henare ● Warrington Wolves release Jason Roach and Dean Hanger...

"I feel angry," he said. "The club hasn't had any foundation and we have had nothing to build on. I'm not making any excuses but the irony is that the plans and the prospects for this club are very good if we can stay in Super League."

Gateshead confirmed they deserved to finish above Warrington in sixth when they beat the Wolves 48-22 at Wilderspool. Danny Farrar scored two tries from scrum-half, but it wasn't enough to stop the Wolves finishing the 1999 season with five straight losses.

An interesting personal battle that day was the race to finish top try-scorer in Super League with Gateshead winger Matt Daylight and Wolves centre Toa Kohe-Love level at the top with 24 tries going into the match. They both got one try each to finish joint top with 25.

The agony and the ecstacy...Huddersfield's Matt Sturm in despair as the Giants stare relegation in the face *(below)* and *(above)* Hull's Gary Lester and Logan Campbell celebrate the Sharks' last day escape

September

In the only other Sunday game Wigan were on the rack at Wakefield where the Wildcats led 18-10 after 24 minutes and were 24-22 ahead at half-time.

The final score was 60-24 which is a measure of Wigan's dominance after the break, with Kris Radlinski and Danny Moore both getting second-half hat-tricks. It was Trinity's second 60-point beating in two weeks and a rough way to finish what had been an excellent first season in Super League under trying circumstances.

On the Friday night another club which had had a traumatic season was signing off with a win, Halifax Blue Sox beating the Salford City Reds 32-20 at the New Shay to become the inaugural holders of the newly instituted Colin Dixon Memorial Trophy.

Gateshead Thunder extend deal with hooker Mick Jenkins and name playing squad for 2000 ● St Helens sign Sean Hoppe from Auckland Warriors ● Salford City Reds tie up coach John Harvey for another season ● Huddersfield Giants forward Dave Boughton heads home to Australia ● Tony Smith signs two-year contract with Wigan ● Captain Thunder selected as Mascot of the Year ● Rob Roberts signs a two-year extension to his contract at the Boulevard ● London Broncos hand Martin Offiah a free transfer ● Salford City Reds sign Nick Pinkney from Halifax ● Blue Sox sign former Leeds centre Phil Hassan ● Daryl Powell announces retirement from international football ● Wakefield Trinity release Papuan Alfred Songoro and Andy Hodgson....

Over at Headingley, the Rhinos - who gave a debut to big signing Keith Senior - just held on to third spot after a heck of a fright from the London Broncos. There was a party atmosphere at Headingley before the game but the Broncos almost pooped it as they had Leeds under pressure, only 10-8 down going into the last ten minutes. But Leeds had come to rely on Iestyn Harris and they could do so again, as he stole over from dummy-half to clinch the win.

With an eye on the play-offs, the Bulls and second-placed St Helens clashed at Knowsley Road in a tremendous match which the Saints won 25-16. Saints had Kiwi international Sean Hoppe on debut as Sonny Nickle put in a storming performance against his old club.

Bulls shot into a 10-2 lead through Steve McNamara and Robbie Paul touchdowns before tries to Apollo Perelini and Kevin Iro plus three Tommy Martyn goals gave Saints a 16-10 half-time lead.

Martyn - playing scrum-half with Sean Long still out with a sprung shoulder incurred against Gateshead at the end of August - was the architect of St Helens' second-half dominance and scored the winning try on 63 minutes.

JJB SUPER LEAGUE - FINAL TABLE 1999

	P	W	D	L	F	A	D	PTS
Bradford Bulls	30	25	1	4	897	445	452	51
St Helens	30	23	0	7	1034	561	473	46
Leeds Rhinos	30	22	1	7	910	558	352	45
Wigan Warriors	30	21	1	8	877	390	487	43
Castleford Tigers	30	19	3	8	712	451	261	41
Gateshead Thunder	30	19	1	10	775	576	199	39
Warrington Wolves	30	15	1	14	700	717	-17	31
London Broncos	30	13	2	15	644	708	-64	28
Halifax Blue Sox	30	11	0	19	573	792	-219	22
Sheffield Eagles	30	10	1	19	518	818	-300	21
Wakefield Trinity Wildcats	30	10	0	20	608	795	-187	20
Salford City Reds	30	6	1	23	526	916	-390	13
Hull Sharks	30	5	0	25	422	921	-499	10
Huddersfield Giants	30	5	0	25	463	1011	-548	10

The Play-offs

The Bulls' reward for finishing minor premiers was a weekend off as the four challengers battled it out.

On the Monday before the action started, refs' controller Greg McCallum called a meeting of his senior referees and the coaches of all five clubs to agree on how referees would interpret rules, mostly around the play-the-ball and the kick-off, where plenty of controversy in earlier games had arisen. The contested kick-off had been a regular feature in 1999 and the meeting agreed a clamp down on chasers getting in front of the kicker.

Offences around the play-the-ball had multiplied and the refs, and the coaches, wanted them cleaning up, as well as warnings to players who overstepped protocol questioning referees' decisions.

On the Friday night the qualifier between St Helens and Leeds was expected to provide fireworks, after the controversial last meeting between the two sides at Headingley.

Saints delivered a hammer blow to Leeds Championship chances with a 38-14 rout, running in eight high-speed tries - four of them in the last ten minutes, and two in the first ten.

In between, it was two apiece and an even battle.

And that was the part of the game that didn't quite satisfy Saints coach Ellery Hanley.

JJB SUPER LEAGUE
PLAY-OFF RESULTS (WEEKEND ONE)
Friday 17th September, 1999
Qualifying Play-off
St Helens 38..Leeds Rhinos 14
Sunday 19th September, 1999
Elimination Play-off
Wigan Warriors 10 ....Castleford Tigers 14

"The players all gathered round well together. but to be quite honest I thought we played under par in particular parts of the game," Hanley said, straight after the match.

"In the overall picture we came away with what we wanted, which was the victory, but there's areas we have got to improve on.

"There's a long way to go in this competition yet, so we are not going to get carried away."

It was a fine team effort by St Helens, but at the forefront was skipper Chris Joynt, who threatened to bust every time he had the ball. Joynt created both the opening tries and scored the crucial try on 70 minutes that settled the game.

It came less than two minutes after the Rhinos looked to have drawn level, with a conversion to come, when Daryl Powell burrowed for the line on the sixth, only to be denied a try by a five-man tackle

Joynt's try was a Saints classic.

From just inside his own half, Tommy Martyn spun the ball to the left; Paul Sculthorpe, playing another magnificent game at stand-off, missed out two men and hit Paul Newlove in the left centre and, before the flailing Keith Senior could do anything about it, Newlove was streaking away, drawing Iestyn Harris and sending Joynt in on his inside.

Three minutes later, Anthony Sullivan, on half-way, picked up the ball at dummy-half, jinked his way past the markers and the first line and hared for the tryline with two coverers to beat. A change of pace, a swerve, a sidestep, who knows how he did it, but the two covering tacklers - Iestyn Harris and Marcus St

Sean Hoppe tussles with Ryan Sheridan as the Saints get the drop over the Rhinos

Hilaire - ran into each other as Sullivan sprinted in untouched.

Three minutes passed again and Martyn popped a ball out of the tackle to Freddie Tuilagi, who raced in on the right and, disorientated, veered to the right along the dead-ball line to get nearer to the posts. When he looked up and saw the perimeter wall and the crowd coming towards him he realised his mistake and hurriedly got the ball down.

And then right on time, as the Rhinos threw caution to the wind, Chris Smith plucked a long Harris pass out of the air to race into the right corner.

Twenty points in the last ten minutes - Paul Wellens converted two of the tries - gave the score a one-sided look.

Saints faced the pleasure of a trip to Odsal the following Sunday night as Murray remained phlegmatic about the defeat.

'We've been well and truly smacked," he said, "but it's on again next week."

On the Sunday night Castleford Tigers christened the superb JJB Stadium by completing a third victory of the season, 14-10, knocking out reigning champions Wigan Warriors.

QUALIFYING PLAY-OFF

ST HELENS 38 ....**LEEDS RHINOS 14**
Knowsley Road - Friday 17th September, 1999

SAINTS: Paul Atcheson; Chris Smith; Kevin Iro; Paul Newlove; Anthony Sullivan; Paul Sculthorpe; Tommy Martyn; Apollo Perelini; Keiron Cunningham; Julian O'Neill; Des Clark; Sonny Nickle; Chris Joynt. *Subs:* Fereti Tuilagi for O'Neill (19); Sean Hoppe for Clark (28); Vila Matautia for Perelini (22); Paul Wellens for Atcheson (61).
Perelini for Matautia (50); O'Neill for Perelini (63bb); Clark for Nickle (74).
Tries: Newlove (2,55), Sullivan (9,73), Smith (28,79), Joynt (70), Tuilagi (76); **Goals:** Martyn, Wellens 2

RHINOS: Iestyn Harris; Leroy Rivett; Brad Godden; Keith Senior; Francis Cummins; Daryl Powell; Ryan Sheridan; Martin Masella; Lee Jackson; Barrie McDermott; Adrian Morley; Anthony Farrell; Marc Glanville. *Subs:* Andy Hay for McDermott (24); Jamie Mathiou for Masella (30); Marcus St Hilaire for Godden (ht); Kevin Sinfield for Glanville (53).
McDermott for Farrell (47bb, rev 71); Masella for Mathiou (65).
Tries: Harris (39), Jackson (61); **Goals:** Harris 3

League Express Men of the Match -
Saints: Chris Joynt; **Rhinos:** Iestyn Harris
Penalties: 10-9; **HT:** 12-8; **Ref:** S Presley (Castleford); **Att:** 9,585

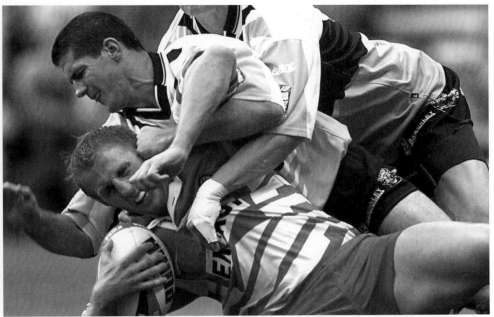

Denis Betts falls to the challenge of Michael Eagar as Castleford stun Wigan at the JJB Stadium

Danny Orr was instrumental in the sensational win that stunned a near-capacity crowd, creating both first-half tries with his astute tactical kicking, adding three goals from four attempts, and defending like...a Tiger!

The Tigers pack, with skipper Adrian Vowles, hooker Aaron Raper, Ian Tonks and Dale Fritz all outstanding, put in a magnificent defensive effort too, particularly under spells of intense pressure in the first half.

ELIMINATION PLAY-OFF

WIGAN WARRIORS 10 ....CASTLEFORD TIGERS 14
JJB Stadium - Sunday 19th September, 1999

WARRIORS: Kris Radlinski; Jason Robinson; Lee Gilmour; Paul Johnson; Danny Moore; Gavin Clinch; Tony Smith; Neil Cowie; Mark Smith; Terry O'Connor; Mick Cassidy; Denis Betts; Andy Farrell. *Subs:* Tony Mestrov for Cowie (49bb); Brett Goldspink for O'Connor (34); Simon Haughton for M Smith (32); Chris Chester for T Smith (15).
O'Connor for Goldspink (62); Cowie for O'Connor (73); Goldspink for Mestrov (73).
Try: Betts (8); **Goals:** Farrell 3

TIGERS: Jason Flowers; Richard Gay; Francis Maloney; Michael Eagar; Darren Rogers; Danny Orr; Brad Davis; Dean Sampson; Aaron Raper; Nathan Sykes; Dale Fritz; Lee Harland; Adrian Vowles. *Subs:* Ian Tonks for Sykes (34); Brad Hepi for Harland (56); James Pickering for Sampson (51); Jon Wells for Vowles (75). Sampson for Pickering (66); Sykes for Tonks (71).
Tries: Eagar (16), Vowles (25); **Goals:** Orr 3

League Express Men of the Match -
Warriors: Kris Radlinski; **Tigers:** Danny Orr
Penalties: 8-8; **HT:** 6-12; **Ref:** S Cummings (Widnes); **Att:** 13,374

The early withdrawal of Tony Smith who carried a groin injury into the game - Gary Connolly was out with a back injury - meant Wigan were unable to turn large spells of pressure into points after Denis Betts had opened the scoring in the eighth minute.

Tigers coach Stuart Raper admitted that his thoughts drifted back to their Challenge Cup semi-final defeat at the hands of London Broncos during the agonising last few minutes.

"It was the longest last five minutes I've ever had," said Raper. "At times in the second half we almost pushed the self-destruct button but we called on our defence to win the game for us."

Warriors coach Andy Goodway said: "Obviously losing Tony Smith didn't help us but fair play to Castleford, their defence was outstanding."

ELIMINATION SEMI-FINAL

LEEDS RHINOS 16......................................**CASTLEFORD TIGERS 23**
Headingley - Friday 24th September, 1999

RHINOS: Iestyn Harris; Paul Sterling; Keith Senior; Brad Godden; Francis Cummins; Daryl Powell; Ryan Sheridan; Martin Masella; Andy Speak; Darren Fleary; Adrian Morley; Anthony Farrell; Marc Glanville. *Subs:* Lee Jackson for Speak (19); Barrie McDermott for Masella (25); Andy Hay for Fleary (40); Marcus St Hilaire for Sterling (4bb, rev 11).
St Hilaire for Glanville (46); Masella for Powell (74).
Tries: Cummins (62, 66); **Goals**: Harris 4

TIGERS: Jason Flowers; Richard Gay; Francis Maloney; Michael Eagar; Darren Rogers; Danny Orr; Brad Davis; Dean Sampson; Aaron Raper; Nathan Sykes; Lee Harland; Dale Fritz; Adrian Vowles. *Subs:* Ian Tonks for Sykes (26); Brad Hepi for Fritz (59); James Pickering for Raper (79); Jon Wells for Rogers (30bb, rev 36). Sykes for Sampson (64); Sampson for Harland (76); Fritz for Tonks (69).
Tries: Eagar (7), Vowles (11), Fritz (76); **Goals**: Orr 5; **Field goal:** Raper

League Express Men of the Match -
Rhinos: Francis Cummins; **Tigers:** Aaron Raper
Penalties: 9-10; **HT**: 2-14; **Ref:** S Cummings (Widnes); **Att:** 16,912

Five days after killing off Wigan, Castleford Tigers put arch-rivals Leeds Rhinos to the sword in the Elimination Semi-final at Headingley by 23-16.

Rhinos fans were saying goodbye to favourites Brad Godden and Marc Glanville, and to coach Graham Murray, but the Tigers didn't mind ruining the occasion for them.

A compelling match was decided when Castleford second-rower Dale Fritz darted over for his first ever try for the club with only minutes remaining, to finally deny a brave Leeds fightback, and leave Murray angrily pointing the finger at referee Stuart Cummings.

"I have a lot of admiration for my team, and I thought they were very, very harshly treated," he glowered. "With a 50-50 crack at things we would have won, but there were too many barriers put in front of us. It was gut-wrenching.

"We got a directive that the ten metres was going to be policed. I didn't think we'd have to wait until the 73rd minute. At 16-16 I thought the tide was turning."

Man of the match, particularly in those early stages when Castleford roared into a twelve-point lead in as many minutes, was Aaron Raper. An influential figure in the Tigers pack all season, the hooker tormented an uncharacteristically hesitant Rhinos front six with his forceful running and clever kicking.

Cas led 14-2 at the break, thanks to tries from Michael Eagar and Adrian Vowles, and three goals from Danny Orr

A Iestyn Harris penalty opened the scoring for the Rhinos in the second half in controversial circumstances.

Barrie McDermott appeared to release the ball in the tackle on the Castleford 30-metre line, Orr picked the loose ball up and sped away for what would surely have been a length of the field try. Referee Cummins, however, had detected a phantom

JJB SUPER LEAGUE
PLAY-OFF RESULTS (WEEKEND TWO)
Friday 24th September, 1999
Elimination Semi-final
Leeds Rhinos 16..............................Castleford Tigers 23
Sunday 26th September, 1999
Qualifying Semi-final
Bradford Bulls 40 ....St Helens 4

knock on, and Orr's protests went on just too long, giving Harris the chance to bag two much needed points.

Orr then grabbed another two-pointer of his own, but, as the Leeds fans went berserk, Francis Cummins got two tries back in the space of five minutes and Harris converted both to level the scores.

Brad Davis can't hide his delight as the Tigers shock the Rhinos at Headingley

Orr put a 70th minute penalty wide, after Andy Hay had drifted offside right under the referee's nose, but Raper landed a potentially crucial field goal with only seven minutes remaining.

Leeds simply couldn't get out of their own half, and after Sterling had miraculously chased back to deny Eagar, the pressure finally told. Senior dropped a pass, Rogers picked it up, and Fritz pounced like a cat through a tattered Rhinos defence from the play-the-ball.

On the Sunday night the Bulls marched gloriously into the Grand Final at Old Trafford to stay on course for their second Super League title in three years.

Saints were overwhelmed by 40-4, after a decisive opening quarter when the Bulls ruthlessly exploited Saints' defensive weaknesses and opened up a 26-0 lead on 21 minutes.

Saints winger Chris Smith, outstanding all season, endured a miserable evening, three times fumbling kicks in the build up to Bulls tries, while the Bulls incisive backs, with Scott Naylor and Michael Withers prominent, cut the visitors' defence to shreds.

Steve McNamara, at his most influential, piled on the agony with seven goals from as many attempts before sitting out most of the second half.

"Semi-finals football is all about winning. Whether you win by a thousand points or two points it doesn't matter as long as you get to Old Trafford," said

123

Michael Withers tries to escape the clutches of Keiron Cunningham as the Bulls reach Old Trafford

Bulls coach Matthew Elliott.

The Bulls, defending a 21-match unbeaten home record stretching back to the previous August, made a sensational start, scoring two converted tries - by Stuart Fielden and Scott Naylor - inside the first six minutes.

When Henry Paul scored another converted try after ten minutes the game as a contest was over.

Ellery Hanley put a brave face on what seemed to be a fatal blow for his side's Championship chances. Even if they bettered the Tigers the following Sunday, they'd have to face the rampant Bulls again in the Grand Final. "When you dissect the game it is easy to see that we made too many fundamental errors," Hanley said. "If you do that against a good side you will pay the penalty.

"But none of my players threw in the towel. Collectively as a group we came up with a bad game together but we will come back next week fired up."

Hanley insisted that Sean Long won't be playing despite rumours around the ground that the star halfback would return.

QUALIFYING SEMI-FINAL

BRADFORD BULLS 40 ....**ST HELENS 4**
Odsal Stadium - Sunday 26th September, 1999

BULLS: Stuart Spruce; Tevita Vaikona; Scott Naylor; Michael Withers; Leon Pryce; Henry Paul; Robbie Paul; Stuart Fielden; James Lowes; Paul Anderson; David Boyle; Bernard Dwyer; Steve McNamara. *Subs:* Paul Deacon for McNamara (54); Nathan McAvoy for Spruce (49); Jamie Peacock for R Paul (54); Brian McDermott for Anderson (25). Anderson for Dwyer (60).
Tries: Fielden (3), Naylor (6), H Paul (10, 18), Withers (45), Vaikona (58);
Goals: McNamara 7, Deacon

SAINTS: Paul Atcheson; Chris Smith; Kevin Iro; Paul Newlove; Anthony Sullivan; Paul Sculthorpe; Tommy Martyn; Apollo Perelini; Keiron Cunningham; Julian O'Neill; Des Clark; Sonny Nickle; Chris Joynt. *Subs:* Fereti Tuilagi for Clark (20); Sean Hoppe for C Smith (48); Vila Matautia for O'Neill (24); Paul Wellens for Cunningham (69). Clark for Nickle (50); Nickle for Tuilagi (52).
Try: Newlove (37)

League Express Men of the Match -
Bulls: Steve McNamara; **Saints:** Sonny Nickle
Penalties: 6-10; **HT:** 26-4; **Ref:** S Presley (Castleford); **Att:** 16,126

OCTOBER
Saints in heaven

Sean Long did make it back to fitness for Sunday night's Final Eliminator, after two weeks of speculation that Wigan had persuaded their former player to return up the A58.

But the rumours were dispelled when it was announced before the game that he had signed a four-year extension to his Saints contract.

Long was only on the pitch for 44 minutes, but his contribution to Saints' march to Old Trafford was immense, as the Tigers' fairytale came to an end, for 1999 at least.

Returning after four matches out with shoulder trouble, Long, who had been voted the player of 1999 by his fellow professionals, scored two tries, kicked five goals and made a try for Tommy Martyn during his vital contribution to Saints' victory.

Saints were trailing 4-6 when Long entered the fray on 23 minutes.

When he left the field with 13 minutes remaining Saints were leading 30-6 and their fans making plans for their trip to Old Trafford.

JJB SUPER LEAGUE
PLAY-OFF RESULT (WEEKEND THREE)
Sunday 3rd October, 1999
Final Eliminator
St Helens 36 ....Castleford Tigers 6

Long admitted afterwards that the decision on whether or not he was fit was left to him. "I knew I'd be fit for the grand final if we got there," he said. "But today was a bonus.

"I've done everything in training apart from taking bangs and tackling. But it needed someone to come on and give the side direction."

It was disappointment for the Tigers but the way their big travelling support stayed right to the very end of the match to cheer their heroes, reflected the mood of optimism at the club.

"They are terrific supporters, a great bunch of people," coach Stuart Raper said straight after the game.

"This season we've played poorly in only three or four games, but unfortunately three of them have been against St Helens.

"We've had a good season and I'm pretty happy. Now we must re-group and there's always next season and hopefully we will beat Saints next year."

Ellery Hanley hadn't panicked after the mauling at Odsal seven days before and made one only starting change and brought in Fereti Tuilagi for Des Clark - signed from Halifax Blue Sox mid-season - while Long was on the bench.

The Tigers were unchanged again, but went into the game knowing that their last win at Knowsley Road was way back in December 1992.

Saints, attacking towards the Castleford fans massed opposite the clubhouse, hit the front when Darren Rogers fumbled a Paul Sculthorpe grubber kick to set up a scrum ten metres out.

Martyn and Paul Sculthorpe combined and Kevin Iro, taking on Flowers, flung out a long overhead pass to the left which Anthony Sullivan collected to go over by the corner flag, despite Danny Orr's despairing cover tackle. The try was confirmed by the video referee, but Martyn was unable to convert from the touchline.

After Tuilagi was held over the line on his back by a combined effort from Jason Flowers, Adrian Vowles and Aaron Raper, Castleford took the lead in virtually their first attack. A charge by mighty prop Dean Sampson had the Saints defence back-pedalling; Raper sent Danny Orr to attack a small hole in the home defence for the supporting Flowers to take the inside pass and go over in Sonny Nickle's tackle by the side of the posts. Orr converted for a 6-4 lead.

Richard Gay looked to have scored his 100th career try in the 29th minute, but the video referee ruled that a miraculous tackle from Paul Atcheson had prevented the winger from grounding the ball.

Five minutes later Long dabbed a brilliant kick through the close range Castleford defence and Tommy Martyn beat Flowers to get the vital touch and score a try that put Saints into a half-time lead. Long, resuming the kicking duties from Martyn, managed the conversion.

Just 45 seconds after the restart Long made another indelible mark on the game with a superb 50-metre try. Chris Smith made the opportunity with a darting run from dummy-half and Long took the pass to dart inside two defenders and speed past the covering Vowles and Flowers before adding the conversion.

With Long at the heart of everything, and he scored his second try to open up daylight, added the conversion for a 22-6 lead; then tagged on a 30-metre penalty when Tigers' sub Brad Hepi, just seconds after taking the field, was placed on report for a high tackle on Apollo Perelini.

Two more converted tries from skipper Chris Joynt and Martyn gave Saints a 30-point winning margin.

Now for the Bulls, with Hanley determined to reverse last weekend's defeat at Odsal.

"Bradford deserve to be favourites and we are the underdogs," Hanley said. "But I knew that you do not become a poor side after six or seven days and we showed that tonight."

FINAL ELIMINATOR

ST HELENS 36 ....**CASTLEFORD TIGERS 6**

Knowsley Road - Sunday 3rd October, 1999

SAINTS: Paul Atcheson; Chris Smith; Kevin Iro; Paul Newlove; Anthony Sullivan; Paul Sculthorpe; Tommy Martyn; Apollo Perelini; Keiron Cunningham; Julian O'Neill; Fereti Tuilagi; Sonny Nickle; Chris Joynt. *Subs:* Sean Long for O'Neill (23); Sean Hoppe for Perelini (62); Vila Matautia for Nickle (32); Paul Wellens for Long (67). O'Neill for Matautia (55); Matautia for Tuilagi (70).
Tries: Sullivan (5), Martyn (34), Long (41, 57), Joynt (65), Martyn (73);
Goals: Long 5, Wellens

TIGERS: Jason Flowers; Richard Gay; Francis Maloney; Michael Eagar; Darren Rogers; Danny Orr; Brad Davis; Dean Sampson; Aaron Raper; Nathan Sykes; Lee Harland; Dale Fritz; Adrian Vowles. *Subs:* Ian Tonks for Sykes (32); Brad Hepi for Harland (39); James Pickering for Tonks (67); Jon Wells for Gay (41). Sykes for Sampson (44).
Try: Flowers (14); **Goal:** Orr

League Express Men of the Match -
Saints: Sean Long; **Tigers:** Adrian Vowles

Penalties: 4-5; **HT:** 10-6; **Ref:** S Cummings (Widnes); **Att:** 11,212

JJB SUPER LEAGUE GRAND FINAL
Bradford Bulls 6 ....St Helens 8

A new chapter was added to the Ellery Hanley legend on Saturday October 9th, 1999.

50,717 people crammed into Old Trafford to witness a remarkable Grand Final victory by Hanley's St Helens, that was testament to the team spirit and defensive mettle instilled into the side by their enigmatic coach of only one season.

The 8-6 scoreline full reflected a tense and at times unbearably exciting Grand Final.

By the time Kevin Iro scored their try in the right corner in the 65th minute, Saints should have already been dead and buried, but Hanley's side was prepared to hang on and grind out an incredible win.

Hot favourites, the Bulls contributed to their own downfall, as they failed to convert plenty of pressure into points on the board.

And when Sean Long, coming off the bench for the second time in a week, hammered over an incredibly cool touchline conversion to Iro's try to edge his side ahead, many of the huge Bulls support knew deep down that Saints were about to kill their Championship hopes.

Coming on the back of the 1996 and 1997 Silk Cut Challenge Cup defeats at Wembley, this was supposed to be third time lucky for the Bulls. And for a while it looked like it might be as they created most of the attacking opportunities.

They thought they had done enough in the 42nd minute when Leon Pryce roared in at the side of the posts off a Michael Withers pass for a dream 18th birthday present.

127

But, referee Stuart Cummings wasn't sure. He suspected a Withers knock-on in the build-up and passed the decision over to video ref David Campbell. All eyes turned to the big screen where Paul Atcheson was attempting to move the ball out wide to Iro on half-way as Withers attempted the interception. He either touched or missed the ball by a fingernail, collected it on the bounce, and tore off en-route to what looked a crucial Bulls score.

The call of "No Try - Scrum Defence" was the turning point.

Harry Sunderland Trophy winner Henry Paul - a magnificent man of the match - had struck the first blow for Bradford on 18 minutes when he stepped Sonny Nickle and Atcheson straight from a scrum before scorching away for a 60-metre solo special, minus one boot. Nickle gave pursuit, but Paul's momentum and the wet surface saw him slide over under the posts.

Both packs put in a monumental effort in the rain, with Bulls' Bernard Dwyer losing for the third time in a major final to his old club. The delirious Saints fans still found time amid their after-match celebrations to applaud their old favourite as he trudged his weary way down the tunnel.

It was on right from the word go.

In the very first tackle of the game Saints prop Apollo Perelini found himself hammered by four Bradford defenders, and the pressure didn't let up throughout a tense, frenetic first half of passion, pace and intensity.

The Bulls' first chance came via the out-of-sorts Steve McNamara, who had spent a sleepless night ill with a stomach complaint. The loose forward put up a cross-field kick, centre Scott Naylor pounced on the loose ball, but his desperate flick back in-field as he was heading for touch went forward.

The Bulls pack was aggressive in these early stages, but the Saints front-six matched them pound for pound with Perelini, Fereti Tuilagi and Julian O'Neill in the thick of it. In the three-quarters, Iro and winger Chris Smith - keen to erase his Odsal play-off nightmare - were also a handful.

But the Bulls looked the most likely to score. Paul Sculthorpe, starting the

Sean Long fires over the winning conversion from the touchline

match at halfback ahead of Long, put up a bomb. Withers took it on the full, fed his fullback Stuart Spruce, and Spruce pinned back his ears for 60 metres with Tevita Vaikona in support.

The giant Tongan took the inside pass and looked all over a scorer, but the Saints cover scrambled back in numbers and the winger was panicked into off-loading straight into the arms of the back-tracking Tommy Martyn.

Then James Lowes charged down another Sculthorpe kick, but Paul Atcheson got back to hack the ball safe.

The slippery conditions played their part, too, as young Bulls prop Stuart Fielden was bundled into touch by Smith and Iro, then Anthony Sullivan went the same route with the help of Scott Naylor.

With Iro having his best attacking performance in ages, Martyn found himself in position for a field goal attempt, but his low shot hardly left the ground

JJB SUPER LEAGUE GRAND FINAL

BRADFORD BULLS 6 ....**ST HELENS 8**
Old Trafford, Manchester - Saturday 9th October, 1999

BULLS: Stuart Spruce; Tevita Vaikona; Scott Naylor; Michael Withers; Leon Pryce; Henry Paul; Robbie Paul; Paul Anderson; James Lowes; Stuart Fielden; David Boyle; Bernard Dwyer; Steve McNamara. *Subs:* Paul Deacon for R Paul (53); Nathan McAvoy (not used); Mike Forshaw for McNamara (18); Brian McDermott for Anderson (18).
Anderson for Fielden (61); Fielden for Dwyer (65); R Paul for Deacon (72).
Try: H Paul (18); **Goal:** H Paul

SAINTS: Paul Atcheson; Chris Smith; Kevin Iro; Paul Newlove; Anthony Sullivan; Paul Sculthorpe; Tommy Martyn; Apollo Perelini; Keiron Cunningham; Julian O'Neill; Fereti Tuilagi; Sonny Nickle; Chris Joynt. *Subs:* Paul Wellens for Martyn (52); Sean Hoppe for Newlove (43); Vila Matautia for O'Neill (20); Sean Long for Perelini (24). Perelini for Matautia (46); O'Neill for Perelini (69)
Try: Iro (65); **Goals:** Long 2

League Express Men of the Match -
Bulls: Henry Paul; **Saints:** Kevin Iro
Penalties: 4-7; **HT:** 6-2; **Ref:** Stuart Cummings (Widnes); **Att:** 50,717

After Henry Paul's try Saints brought on Long, and the nippy little scrum-half made an immediate impact for the second week running, after Fielden had spilled the ball with an overlap out wide.

Long's twisting and turning prised a hole in the Bradford defence, but his run to the line was halted prematurely when referee Cummings failed to play advantage after the Bulls had strayed offside. Long slotted the penalty anyway and, after another Spruce break had fizzled to nothing, after the fullback chose to go it alone with Vaikona clear out wide, another Bradford chance was lost.

Super League paraded its "Man of Steel" - Castleford's Adrian Vowles - at half-time, and if the first half had been full of incident, it was nothing on the second.

Video ref Campbell disallowed a second Bradford effort when Lowes was brilliantly held up under the posts by Nickle, Tuilagi and Atcheson and this time there was no disputing his decision.

In between those two video-calls, chances for the Bulls continued to rain down. Spruce and Henry Paul combined to send Naylor on a run to the corner after sub Sean Hoppe had failed to deal with a Lowes bomb, but the centre was slid into touch by Martyn, who didn't produce his usual magic in attack but defended like a man possessed.

Atcheson was again on hand to clear another Lowes kick; Spruce was bundled over the sidelines; and second-rower David Boyle spilled a Robbie Paul pass with the line at his mercy.

It appeared the gods had deemed the Bulls would not score again. Or at least the St Helens will to win had.

Naylor spurned yet another good scoring opportunity near the line and St Helens sprayed it wide. Iro knocked on with only the wide open spaces of Old Trafford before him, but the warning signs of a Saints breakaway were clear.

A penalty for laying on enabled Saints to sweep upfield. Atcheson almost went in at the corner but England's young vice-captain Paul Deacon produced a superb cover tackle to stop him in his tracks.

Bradford were again penalised, Paul Anderson not standing square at the play the ball, and Saints went for the kill. The ball whizzed through the hands of Cunningham, Long and Atcheson, before Iro roared in, despite the attentions of Pryce and sub Mike Forshaw. The video referee decision was a formality and when Long converted from the touchline with only 15 minutes left the Saints fans began to sense victory.

Bradford were desperate. A Spruce pass to Forshaw bounced forward, Vaikona was held short, and a trademark Lowes stab through close to the line was picked up by Cunningham.

The Saints hooker sped away, but was stopped by up Naylor. From the play-the-ball Long almost sealed matters but for a desperate Pryce tackle and, with Super League's Young Player of the Year now out of position, Iro thought he had gone in for his second but the video ref, after an age, spotted a Tuilagi knock on in the build up.

An unhappy night for Bradford was summed up when the otherwise impressive Spruce spilled Long's clearing kick under little or no pressure.

What scenes followed for the cock-a-hoop Saints as they celebrated their second Super League Championship in four years.

Saints skipper Chris Joynt summed up the feeling of the players, just before heading straight home to pack his bags for the Lions' trip down under.

"I feel like I have been run over by a bus. It was brutal out there and the defence of both sides was awesome," he said.

Huddersfield Giants and Sheffield Eagles merge to become Huddersfield-Sheffield Giants ● Warrington Wolves sign Tawera Nikau from Melbourne ● St Helens Sean Long and Keiron Cunningham sign three-year extensions to their contracts at Knowsley Road ● Bradford Bulls deny link with Andy Farrell ● Chief executive Steve Ferres leaves Wakefield Trinity ● Castleford Tigers sign Sheffield Eagles skipper Darren Shaw ● Steve McNamara in contract talks at the Bulls ● Hunslet Hawks threaten legal action after being refused Super League entry ● Adrian Vowles chosen as Man of Steel for 1999 ● Blue Sox sign former Leeds centre Phil Hassan ● New Zealand win the Independent Student World Cup ● Terry Newton agrees to leave Leeds for Wigan ● World Club Challenge between St Helens and Melbourne Storm scheduled for JJB Stadium in January ● Paul Anderson signs new two-year contract and fellow prop Stuart Fielden a four-year deal at Bradford ● Huddersfield Giants fans march to protest against merger ● Former Hull chairman Roy Waudby dies as club faces extinction ● Phil Veivers appointed assistant to coach John Kear at Huddersfield-Sheffield ● Les Kiss leaves coaching job at London Broncos, John Monie is appointed ● Wigan ordered to pay Halifax up to £85,000 for David Hodgson by RFL Tribunal ● Steve Blakeley threatens Huddersfield-Sheffield with legal action for going back on contract ● Salford Reds sign Mike Wainwright ● Wakefield Trinity Wildcats sign Francis Maloney, Tony Tatupu, Warren Jowitt, Martin Masella and Ryan Hudson....

Joy and pain...Henry Paul touches down for the Bulls' only try, and
Brian McDermott reflects on just how Bradford managed to come out second best *(inset)*

"Ellery has instilled in us all season that defence wins games, and we worked for one another, made our one-on-one tackles and that is what has brought us victory.

"Our win is testimony to our team spirit and the way that the lads have stuck together.

"We were called a soft set of forwards and people said we would not be able to match the Bradford set, but we matched them and then finished on top."

A soft set of forwards, what did he mean?

In fact Joynt was referring to the extra bit of motivation the players had received from an unlikely source.

In the post-match press conference, coach Hanley told Rugby League Express editor Martyn Sadler: "You played a big part in the game.

"In your column you actually said that our forwards were very soft. My forwards were very disappointed in your comment, and you riled all our players up. ("I don't see St Helens being tough enough in the forwards to hold Bradford's charge down the middle", Sadler had written).

"My forwards are not soft at all. If you go on the football field, you are not soft, whether you play in the forwards or the backs. You have to show respect to the players because they put their bodies on the line and I think that is a very important issue.

"My players were very upset that they were called soft and accused of being overcome by the occasion."

Hanley was keen to credit his players for the fantastic win, while showing no sympathy for the Bulls.

"I take no personal satisfaction from the win," he said. "You have to be able to handle a win or a loss in the same breath. The people who should get all the credit and all the plaudits are the players. This game is very, very brutal and I stand back and give the players all the plaudits.

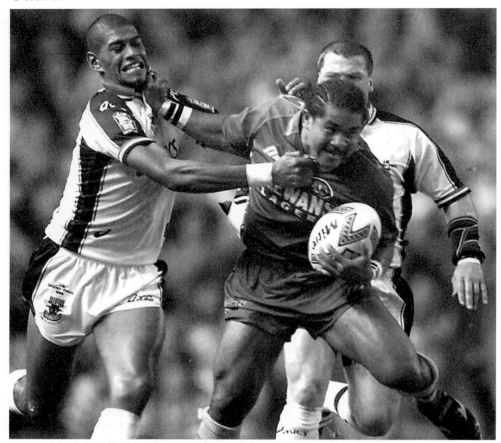

Fereti Tuilagi charges through Leon Pryce and James Lowes

"I have no sympathy for Matthew Elliott. There is no sympathy in this game, it is all about winning trophies or getting two points. If you look back and start feeling sorry for people it may have an adverse affect on your game. You have stay focused and concentrate on your own game.

"I felt very, very comfortable throughout the game. Not comfortable in the sense of being cocky, or over-confident, but I knew that we had enough resolve to win. We had been through a lot of trying times together, good and bad, but we stick together very tightly and I always thought that would see us through."

AND IN NOVEMBER......Andy Goodway sacked as coach of Wigan on his return from the Tri-Series ● MPs condemn mergers in Commons debate ● Bernard Dwyer signs one-year deal at Bradford ● Halifax Blue Sox sign Brett Goldspink and Marvin Golden ● Gateshead and Hull merge and move to Boulevard, the Thunder is dead ● Tigers sign Logan Campbell from Hull ● Wakefield sign Steve McNamara....

An emotional Bulls coach Matthew Elliott was clearly shaken by the heartbreaking defeat.

"I can analyse it until next week if I like, but that won't change the result," he said. "Grand Finals are about winners, not about people who came second - and we came second."

NORTHERN FORD PREMIERSHIP
Rams on top of the pile

Dewsbury Rams' coach Neil Kelly followed in the footsteps of elder brother, Wakefield Trinity coach Andy, by guiding his club to the summit of the Premiership table, as the Rams lost just five of their 28 league games.

Of those five defeats, two came in the opening three rounds and the other three in a disastrous run in June when they won just once in five, but otherwise they were incredibly consistent, and put together two winning runs of ten matches.

The entire Rams' squad played their full part in the success, and although the halfback pairing of Barry Eaton and Richard Agar gained many deserved plaudits for their performances in the middle of the park, Dewsbury's free-scoring three-quarter line and hard-working pack should also be remembered.

David Plange's Hunslet Hawks continued their own progression over the last three seasons, and their highly talented squad secured a second-placed finish, which would have been first had it not been for a 10-6 defeat at Dewsbury late in the campaign.

They had in their ranks the NFP Player of the Year in brilliant hooker Richard Pachniuk, who finished the season as the top try-scorer outside Super League - breaking the Rugby League record for tries on a season by a hooker - after an outstanding campaign in which he terrorised defences throughout the NFP.

But the Hawks were anything but a one-man team, and Kiwi halfback Latham Tawhai and former London fullback Butch Fatnowna both had big seasons, while the tireless pair of Steve Pryce and Richie Hayes were kingpins in a robust, mobile pack.

Fourteen wins from their final 15 league games transformed the Widnes Vikings from play-off outsiders into a top-three side, as Colin Whitfield and his men looked to live up to the club's bold ambitions.

Whitfield recruited a vastly experienced pack that included the likes of George Mann, Lee Hansen, Paul Hulme, Phil Cantillon and Gareth Adams, and they were complimented in the backs by skilful Kiwi Paul Mansson and prolific fullback Damian Munro, among others.

A poor first half of the season denied them any chance of topping the Premiership, but on their day they looked as good as anyone, and they were buoyed by their increasing crowds at the superb Auto Quest Stadium.

Defeat in the penultimate league game of the season at Keighley denied Leigh Centurions top spot in the table, but no-one can deny that Ian Millward and his players were the success story of the season.

Wooden-spoonists in the old Division One in 1998, they were transformed into genuine title-contenders by a combination of the enthusiasm of their primarily young squad, and the work of Australian Millward, the NFP Coach of the Year.

The whole squad played their full part in the Centurions' success, but NFP

Northern Ford Premiership

Young Player of the Year Stuart Donlan, inspirational prop Timmy Street and Aussies Heath Cruckshank and Jamie Kennedy were all outstanding.

Another incredible late-season recovery saw Featherstone Rovers snatch a top-five spot on the last day of the season for the second consecutive year.

Their dramatic last day win against Hull KR confirmed their play-off spot, and sealed a superb revival that was led by experienced coach Peter Roe, who took over at the newly-named Lionheart Stadium mid-way through the campaign following the resignation of Kevin Hobbs

And with the help of the likes of overseas stars Hitro Okesene, Brendon Tuuta and Wayne Simonds, and local boys Danny Evans and rookie scrum-half Jamie Rooney, Roe managed to turn around the club's fortunes, and was rewarded with a shot at the play-offs.

Hull Kingston Rovers appeared to be on course to make up for last season's play-off disappointments as they prepared for their 23rd game of the campaign at Bramley, three points clear at the top of the Premiership with just four defeats.

But a stunning collapse saw Dave Harrison's side lose five of their last six matches, culminating in that final-day defeat at Featherstone which ultimately sent them crashing out of the top-five.

Up until that point, Rovers had looked to be one of the strongest sides in the competition, thanks to the consistency of Kiwi centre Whetu Taewa, the evergreen Paul Fletcher and livewire hooker Mike Dixon, but they undoubtedly missed the multi-talented Stanley Gene, who was injured for most of the run-in.

JANUARY...Ford are unveiled as sponsors of first division for 1999 ● Garry Schofield joins Doncaster Dragons ● Lancashire Lynx return to Chorley ● Barrow sign Dave Clark from Gold Coast Chargers ● Hunslet sign David Mycoe ● Bramley sign Maea David from Hull ● Widnes re-sign Jason Critchley....

FEBRUARY...Bramley sign Papuan Tom O'Reilly from Gold Coast ● David Plange signs new two-year contract at Hunslet ● Workington Town sign Mick Jenkins from Newcastle Knights....

MARCH...Bob Scott quits as manager of Northern Ford Premiership ● Widnes Vikings re-sign Richie Eyres ● Swinton Lions sign Richard Henare ● Lancashire Lynx sign Andy Bennett from Warrington ● Garry Schofield joins Bramley ● Rochdale Hornets sign Brad Hepi ● Oldham lose giant centre Josh Bostock through injury....

APRIL...York Wasps sign former Hull winger Leroy McKenzie ● Doncaster sack coach Colin Maskill ● Mike Gregory joins Swinton as assistant coach ● Hull KR coach Dave Harrison signs new two-year deal ● Widnes Vikings apply for place in Super League ● Keighley Cougars fire coach Lee Crooks....

MAY...Mike Gregory appointed coach at Swinton Lions after Les Holliday resigns ● York's future in doubt under financial crisis ● Keighley Cougars appoint Frank Punchard as coach ● Widnes Vikings sign winger Simon Verbickas ● Evan Cochrane fractures skull in freak accident at Cougar Park....

York Wasps were another of the Premiership's big success stories - on the field at least - as they improved on finishing second in the old Division Two by attaining seventh place.

And they could easily have been challenging for the play-offs had it not been for the suspension of head coach Dean Robinson mid-way through the campaign, a period in which the Wasps lost crucial matches and fell off the top-five pace.

But generally the Wasps enjoyed a highly profitable year, with the displays of young halfback pairing Mark Cain and Darren Callaghan a major boost, along with the form of Jamie Benn and Fata Sini.

A disappointing start to the season for the Whitehaven Warriors meant that they were never really in contention to make the five, but, guided by respected coach Kevin Tamati, they finished the season in fine style to climb into eighth spot.

The turning point in their campaign arrived after a shocking performance away at York in May, when they lost 46-0 and found themselves fourth bottom.

But they improved dramatically after that, and - with Kiwis Aaron Lester and David Fatialofa in their ranks - they ended the year more like Grand Final contenders.

Keighley Cougars failed to live up to their pre-season billing for the second consecutive year, and a start that saw them win just two of their opening six games virtually ruled them out of a serious challenge, and cost coach Lee Crooks his job.

He was replaced by his assistant Frank Punchard mid-season, but he had too much ground to make up, and despite some excellent wins - notably against Leigh at Cougar Park - the club were disappointed with a ninth-placed finish.

On the positive side winger Jason Lee enjoyed a productive season on the flanks, finishing as the NFP's second top try-scorer with 22.

Bramley enjoyed a season of considerable improvement under new player-coach Mike Ford, and they surprised several teams on their way to an impressive tenth-placed finish.

And had it not been for the loss of influential overseas pair Tom O'Reilly (to injury) and Danny McAllister (to Gateshead Thunder), they could have finished even higher up the NFP table.

Ford recovered from defeat to amateurs Leigh Miners in the Challenge Cup to get his side playing as a unit, with rookie Mark Sibson, a highly impressive and prolific fullback from the Student Rugby League, and Anthony Gibbons, Maea David and Dan Potter all standing out.

Paul Charlton explained before the start of the season that 1999 would effectively be a new start for Barrow Border Raiders, but his talented young side probably exceeded even his own expectations in finishing mid-table.

And in goal-kicking scrum-half Darren Holt - picked as the outstanding number seven in the NFP's All Star team - they had one of the shining lights outside Super League.

A poor finish marred what was a creditable season for David Ward's Batley Bulldogs, who started the year strongly and provided a stern challenge for every side in the competition.

Three draws and a series of close defeats against the NFP's top clubs were the main reasons for the Bulldogs not finishing higher up the league ladder, although they will no doubt have been disappointed with their home form as well, as they lost eight of their 14 games at Mount Pleasant. Their star performers came in the shape of prop Chris McWilliam and loose forward Paul Harrison.

Eight defeats from their opening eleven games got Swinton Lions off on the wrong foot, and resulted in coach Les Holliday making way for former Great Britain International Mike Gregory.

But Gregory was left with little time to emulate 1998's fifth-placed finish, and a combination of persistent injury problems and inability to perform for the full 80 minutes meant the Lions never made it past mid-table.

However they were undoubtedly starting to show signs of responding to their new coach's demands by the end of the campaign, and Gregory had two of the NFP's outstanding performers in the shape of scrum-half Ian Watson and fullback Mark Welsby.

Workington Town started the year brightly under new player-coach Andy Platt, and looked set for at least a mid-table finish after losing just six of their first 15 games.

But things started to fall apart after that, and Town finished the year struggling to get a team on the park after a period of terrible luck, in which they lost influential overseas stars Evan Cochrane (to a freak accident) and Mick Jenkins (signed by Gateshead Thunder) within weeks of each other, while highly-rated forward Barry Williams played hardly any football all year and Aussie scrum-half Josh White never even arrived!

All this resulted in Platt departing to Australia, and Town struggled badly in the latter stages of the campaign, although there were promising signs under new coach, Ellenborough's former Carlisle halfback Gary Murdock.

Rochdale Hornets were once again extremely inconsistent, and that cost the popular Deryck Fox his coaching job mid-way through the campaign.

A series of close defeats early in the year got Fox's side into a losing habit that they were never quite able to shake off, and despite excellent wins at Batley and Dewsbury and a gritty home victory against York, they put in several disappointing performances and were always destined for the lower reaches of the competition.

The main plus point for Hornets was the form of the front row, with Matt Knowles, David Stephenson and Jon Aston superb throughout, while they appear to have three highly promising youngsters on their hands in the shape of Danny Sculthorpe, Chris Newall and Darren Robinson.

Steve Hampson's Lancashire Lynx side was plagued by injuries throughout the season, and the loss

JUNE...Whitehaven's Leroy Joe gets six-match ban ● Peter Roe is appointed coach of Featherstone Rovers ● York coach Dean Robinson suspended by club ● Cougars deny suggestions of a cash crisis ● Martin Offiah turns down move to Leigh ● Swinton boss Malcolm White proposes merger with Salford ● Doncaster sack Colin Maskill and then Carl Sanderson as coach ● Paul Cook joins Hunslet Hawks....Rochdale sack Deryck Fox....

JULY...NFP clubs plan to return to winter season ● East v West rep' match panned for NFP Grand Final day ● Andy Platt quits Workington Town ● Hull KR ground sale flounders and five directors get the sack....

AUGUST...Featherstone Rovers rumoured to be under threat because of financial trouble ● merger talks are back on between Whitehaven and Workington ● Takeover of York Wasps falls through ● Keighley Cougars pair Christian Tyrer and David Larder are suspended by club for fighting with each other during game against Barrow ● NFP clubs vote for RFL proposal to start season in December ● Dewsbury chairman Bob McDermott threatens legal action if Rams win NFP Grand Final and are not promoted...

of last year's Second Division Player of the Year Phil Jones to Wigan prevented them from having any real chance of building on the success of 1998.

But although they finished third bottom of the whole Rugby League, they certainly ended the season in much better shape than they started it, with their performances improving considerably once Hampson had a full strength squad to work with.

Prolific stand-off Neil Alexander had a big year after moving from Salford, finishing with a tally of 16 tries that included two four-try hauls.

1999 has to go down as one of the most difficult years in the recent history of professional Rugby League in Oldham, with the team struggling, playing outside of the town at Spotland, and crowds plummeting.

Coach Mick Coates battled admirably through a turbulent campaign that ended with one win from their last twelve NFP games, including four 60-plus defeats and a particularly embarrassing 0-84 humiliation at Widnes.

It could have been even worse was it not for the efforts of inspirational veteran Leo Casey and barnstorming prop Jason Clegg in the front row, while former Warrington hooker John Hough gave his all throughout what was a season to forget for the Roughyeds.

A year that started with so much promise for the Doncaster Dragons finished with failure and the NFP wooden spoon, but to have remained in business is a big achievement itself, with the club receiving no TV sponsorship money.

To have finished bottom of the whole Rugby League for the second consecutive season has to be a big disappointment for their loyal fans, as they watched three different coaches in the hot seat for the Dragons.

But the club has big plans now, and in St John Ellis have a coach with the enthusiasm and will to succeed. He will no doubt have been pleased with the efforts of full back Lee Maher - who made the NFP All Star team at fullback - Guy Adams John Okul and Tony Miller during a campaign in which the Dragons only won on four occasions.

The Play-offs

Featherstone Rovers destroyed Leigh Centurions' hopes of a fairy-tale finish to their outstanding campaign, as a superb performance saw them record a 17-4 win at Hilton Park in front of over 3,000 fans on the opening day of the NFP play-offs.

The Centurions went into the game with several of their star players carrying injuries, and the gamble back-fired as Rovers built up an 11-0 half-time lead thanks to tries from centre Richard Newlove and Kiwi Brendon Tuuta.

The Centurions did manage to get themselves back in the game when Paul Wingfield crossed 17 minutes from time, but substitute Richard Chapman's try sealed the win in the 72nd minute.

"The players are very disappointed," said Leigh coach Ian Millward after the game. "A couple of things didn't come off for us, we took gambles on some busted players too but we've learned a lot this year. We were one win off finishing top of the league, one win from a Grand Final, but this is the end of the road for us."

Meanwhile, Widnes Vikings' scrum-half Mark Hewitt almost single-handedly transformed the qualifying semi-final at Hunslet, masterminding a thrilling 24-21 win.

Two tries in five minutes from Hewitt - who also kicked six goals from as many attempts - helped the Vikings to victory, despite the fact that the Hawks scored four tries to three.

Two Shaun Irwin tries had given the Hawks a 10-4 half-time lead, and when Butch Fatnowna cancelled out Damian Munro's 43rd minute try eight minutes into the second half, the home side looked set to win. But Hewitt's interventions were crucial, and despite a late Chris Ross try, David Plange's side had to face defeat, and the prospect of elimination football all the way to the Grand Final.

The first of those matches came a week later, as the Hawks took on play-off specialists Featherstone at the South Leeds Stadium.

And Plange's Hawks eventually emerged victorious, as this time it was their turn to overcome a half-time deficit, coming back from 0-9 down to record a 17-9 win.

A Martin Law try and five points from the boot of Jamie Rooney had given Rovers their useful half-time lead but thanks to two tries from Richard Pachniuk and one from Richard Baker and a field goal from creative halfback Latham Tawhai, the Hawks powered through to the final eliminator.

Their opponents there would be Widnes Vikings, as Colin Whitfield's side had been sent crashing to earth by the Dewsbury Rams, who booked their place in the

Grand Final with a brilliant 28-6 win in the qualifying semi-final at Ram Stadium.

At the heart of their win was a brilliant display of tactical kicking, underpinned by a record seven 40/20 kicks, including five from man of the match Richard Agar. Agar also booted three field goals, as the Rams - who scored tries through Nathan Graham, Brendon O'Meara, Damian Ball (2) and Andy Spink - never looked in danger of losing.

The showdown between the Hawks and the Vikings to decide who would meet the Rams at Headingley could hardly have been any closer - particularly as it came at the end of two weeks of wrangling over who should have home advantage - and in the end a controversial 78th minute penalty from the boot of Hunslet's Chris Ross decided a titanic battle, 10-8, played at South Leeds Stadium.

Referee Russell Smith awarded the penalty after the intervention of a touch judge, after initially ruling that George Mann's tackle on Lee St Hilaire had first hit the shoulder.

SEPTEMBER...Oldham sack coach Mick Coates ● Rochdale Hornets appoint Newcastle Knights assistant coach Steve Linnane as coach ● Peter Roe agrees a one-year deal as coach of Featherstone Rovers ● West of Pennines beat East 38-22 ● Swinton sign Chris Highton from Warrington....

OCTOBER...Karl Harrison appointed new coach at Keighley Cougars, Abi Ekoku becomes managing director ● Hull KR sign Whitehaven's Kiwi halfback Leroy Joe ● Doncaster's Lee Maher, Salford's Scott Martin and Aussies Dane Dorahy and Shayne McMannemy sign for Rochdale Hornets ● Dewsbury Rams coach Neil Kelly signs new three-year contract ● Batley Bulldogs sign Craig Barker and Davy Kimmel ● Mark Aston announces plan to relaunch Sheffield Eagles ● Doncaster back as full members of RFL and sign Peter Edwards, Fata Sini, Latham Tawhai, Joe Berry and Carl Gillespie, Craig Weston, Lynton Stott, Basil Richards and old boy Carl Hall ● Matt Sturm joins Workington Town ● Oldham appoint Mike Ford as coach and sign British Students prop Chris Naylor ● Mick Higgins resigns from Leigh....

Winger Ross coolly stepped up to convert the penalty from 25 metres out, and Plange and his team were in the Grand Final.

They had started the game perfectly with a first-minute try from Richard Baker, and when Ross added a penalty to his early conversion, they held an 8-0 lead. But the Vikings levelled the score with tries from James Briers and scrum-half Hewitt, who later hit the post with a field goal attempt in those dramatic dying minutes.

NORTHERN FORD PREMIERSHIP - FINAL TABLE 1999

	P	W	D	L	F	A	D	PTS
Dewsbury Rams	28	21	2	5	710	449	261	44
Hunslet Hawks	28	21	0	7	845	401	444	42
Widnes Vikings	28	21	0	7	792	415	377	42
Leigh Centurions	28	21	0	7	802	524	278	42
Featherstone Rovers	28	19	1	8	714	466	248	39
Hull Kingston Rovers	28	19	1	8	573	425	148	39
York Wasps	28	17	1	10	697	425	272	35
Whitehaven Warriors	28	16	0	12	651	620	31	32
Keighley Cougars	28	14	1	13	584	612	-28	29
Barrow Border Raiders	28	12	0	16	660	718	-58	24
Bramley	28	11	1	16	489	596	-107	23
Batley Bulldogs	28	9	3	16	546	553	-7	21
Swinton Lions	28	10	0	18	645	641	4	20
Workington Town	28	9	1	18	468	813	-345	19
Rochdale Hornets	28	9	0	19	539	724	-185	18
Lancashire Lynx	28	7	0	21	544	889	-345	14
Oldham	28	5	2	21	449	999	-550	12
Doncaster Dragons	28	4	1	23	473	911	-438	9

GRAND FINAL
Hawks swoop to conquer

Dewsbury Rams 11 ....**Hunslet Hawks 12**

THE showcase event of the Northern Ford Premiership season provided almost 6,000 supporters and a big television audience with a Grand Final to remember, as the Hunslet Hawks secured victory by the narrowest of margins in a classic match.

In the end, Jamie Leighton's 62nd minute field goal proved to be the difference between two very well matched sides, who had supplied the Headingley crowd with 80 minutes of pulsating Rugby League.

The Final could easily have gone either way, and Neil Kelly's Dewsbury Rams certainly created enough chances to win. They can look back on Butch Fatnowna's superb cover tackle on Adrian Flynn close to the line in the second half, and Barry Eaton's break down the left side late in the game, as well as the fact that they managed to build up a 7-0 lead late in the first period.

Flynn's well-worked try on 26 minutes, added to a Richard Agar field goal and an Eaton penalty, had put the Rams in firm control, only for the Hawks to draw level by half-time through Paul Cook's determined try, Chris Ross's conversion and a Latham Tawhai one-pointer.

NORTHERN FORD PREMIERSHIP GRAND FINAL

Headingley, Leeds - Saturday 25th September, 1999

RAMS: Nathan Graham; Alex Godfrey; Paul Evans; Brendan O'Meara; Adrian Flynn; Richard Agar; Barry Eaton; Alan Boothroyd (C); Paul Delaney; Matthew Long; Andrew Spink; Mark Haigh; Damian Ball. *Subs:* Brendan Williams for Eaton (5bb, reversed 15); Sean Richardson for Haigh (50); Simon Hicks for Long (25); Paul Medley for Spink (50). Williams for Evans (61); Long for Boothroyd (71); Spink for Long (78). **Tries:** Flynn (27), Ball (54); **Goals:** Eaton; **Field goal:** Agar

HAWKS: Butch Fatnowna; Chris Ross; Shaun Irwin (C); Paul Cook; Iain Higgins; Marcus Vassilakopoulos; Latham Tawhai; Richie Hayes; Richard Pachniuk; Steve Pryce; Rob Wilson; Jamie Leighton; Lee St Hilaire. *Subs:* Mick Coyle for Wilson (57); Phil Kennedy for Pryce (35); Jamie Thackray for St Hilaire (25); Richard Baker for Higgins (55). Higgins for Fatnowna (62); Pryce for Kennedy (65). **Tries:** Cook (31), Higgins (46); **Goal:** Ross; **Field goals:** Tawhai, Leighton

League Express Men of the Match -
Rams: Barry Eaton; **Hawks:** Latham Tawhai
Penalties: 8-5; **HT:** 7-7; **Ref:** S Ganson (St Helens); **Att:** 5,783

The Hawks then took the lead for the first time in the match four minutes after the break when Iain Higgins crossed out wide, before Damian Ball tied the scores up again at 11-all with a try in the corner after a towering Agar bomb.

Leighton's match-winning intervention came with just 18 minutes remaining, and signalled the start of an incident-packed final quarter, as the Hawks just hung on despite almost relentless Rams' pressure.

"There was a lot of emotion out there tonight," said Hawks coach David Plange, who ranked the success alongside his Challenge Cup win with Castleford in the 1986 final.

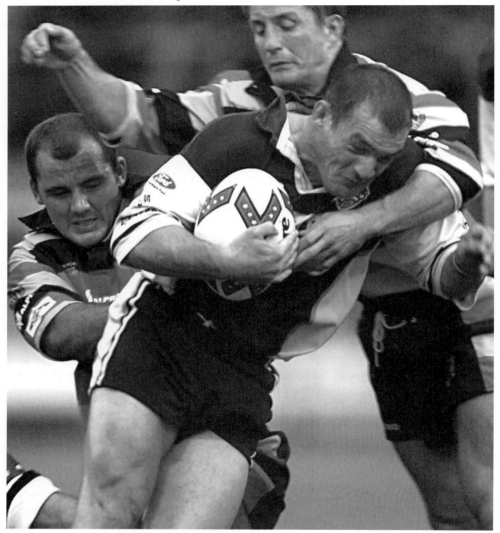

No way through the Dewsbury defence for Hunslet skipper Shaun Irwin

"We've been in tight situations before, and if there's one thing I know about my side, then it's that they do not lack character, and I was confident it would come to the fore if we needed it to."

Rams' coach Neil Kelly, meanwhile, was left to reflect on the bitter disappointment of defeat after a year's hard work.

"I was as much disappointed with the fact that we didn't perform to our full abilities, as with the defeat itself," he said.

"But at the end of the day, there was just one point separating these two sides, and they have won the Grand Final with a drop goal from a player that you would not usually expect to be there. I think they deserved the win over the 80 minutes, but the scoreline reflected the closeness of the game and we could have won it in the end."

RL CONFERENCE
Spreading the word

From the high profile announcement of the inclusion of six new teams at the Hilton Hotel, Leeds in January; through the prestigious season's launch at the Rugby Club of St James in late April and 14 weeks of intense competition; to the dramatic, cliffhanging climax in the last 90 seconds of the Grand Final in August, it was another momentous year for the burgeoning Rugby League Conference.

The second full summer of competition spread across the length and breadth of England fulfilled and, in many cases, exceeded expectations. A move to four divisions to accommodate the increase from 14 to 20 sides - as Nottingham Outlaws, Derby City, Crewe Wolves, Wolverhampton Wizards, Manchester Knights and Hemel Stags were admitted - produced some superb tussles which saw over half the teams still in contention for the play-offs going into the final week of regular season.

Although some struggled with the intensity of the competition, there was early encouragement for all when Wolverhampton centre Parminder Tutt was snapped up by Warrington Academy after starring in the Wizards' season of defeat.

Significantly, all clubs, irrespective of league standing, reported increased enthusiasm, interest and numbers as the league gained higher profile for the game outside its traditional heartlands. That was partly achieved by the relaying of fixtures, results and occasional news items on teletext, ceefax and consequently in the majority of the national press, gaining the Conference visibility and more importantly greater credibility and commercial clout.

In their own localities local media interest in the clubs as the season progressed intensified with such as defending Champions Crawley commandeering the back pages of the West Sussex papers to record their exploits, especially as the Jets played their opening three home fixtures at the impressive new all-seater Broadfield Stadium at the invitation of the local council.

Local radio, and, in Oxford's case, television, stations took live broadcasts and updates of matches as the summer season intensified.

The Northern, Western and Eastern divisions rapidly turned into three-team dogfights for the two play-off spots available with Manchester and Nottingham in the north making massive impressions in their debut years and Cheltenham earning the tag of most improved team as they went on a long unbeaten run on the back of some enterprising, free-flowing rugby.

In the south, five evenly-matched teams made it impossible to separate the combatants throughout an enthralling three months, with each capable of beating any other. In the end only points difference separated the top three with West London again the unluckiest side in the tournament as they just missed out on the run-in despite beating the sides above them.

Alongside the progress at open age level, two junior festival weekends in June and July staged by seven of the Conference clubs were resounding successes. In all, over 750 children were encouraged to try their hand at the game, with local sponsorships ensuring that they received mementoes of their efforts. Some outstanding talents were unearthed as were several under-16 and under-18 players who look destined for big futures after attracting the notice of representative scouts and professional clubs.

The rest of the Rugby League world were shown the progress the RLC was making when Leicester Phoenix played aspiring applicants Coventry Bears in the curtain-raiser to the London Broncos v Bradford Bulls Super League fixture held in Leicester - a night that was a resounding success for the 'on the road' experiment.

The regionalised play-offs were eagerly anticipated as the season boiled up to its frantic finale.

Ipswich Rhinos qualified for the first time but were just unable to quell the greater all-round experience of the Oxford Cavaliers in the South/East and although Hemel downed Crawley in an encounter dubbed as one of the finest southern amateur Rugby League had seen, the Stags' inadvertent fielding of two ineligible players meant that they had to forfeit the tie. In the Preliminary Final, staged superbly at the Stoop, Crawley hit top form to blast their way back to the Grand Final.

RUGBY LEAGUE CONFERENCE 1999

FINAL LEAGUE TABLES

Northern Division

	P	W	L	D	F	A	D	PTS
Chester	12	10	2	0	603	155	448	20
Manchester	12	10	2	0	526	172	354	20
Nottingham	12	8	4	0	400	230	170	16
Derby	12	2	10	0	128	431	-303	4
Crewe	12	0	12	0	132	690	-558	0

Western Division

	P	W	L	D	F	A	D	PTS
Cheltenham	12	10	2	0	540	133	407	20
Leicester	12	9	3	0	494	204	290	18
Birmingham	12	7	5	0	358	184	174	14
W'stershire	12	4	7	0	240	351	-111	8
W'hampton	12	0	12	0	46	907	-861	0

Eastern Division

	P	W	L	D	F	A	D	PTS
Ipswich	12	7	5	0	449	385	64	14
Hemel ●	12	8	4	0	535	248	287	12
Sth Norfolk	12	6	0	6	438	418	20	12
Cambridge	12	1	11	0	170	698	-528	2
Bedford	12	1	11	0	145	680	-535	2

● Hemel deducted four points for breach of rules

Southern Division

	P	W	L	D	F	A	D	PTS
Crawley	12	9	3	0	606	226	380	18
Oxford	12	9	3	0	458	224	234	18
West London	12	9	3	0	410	231	179	18
Nth London	12	6	6	0	344	395	-51	12
St Albans	12	4	8	0	314	375	-61	8

PLAY-OFFS

Weekend of 1st August, 1999

SOUTH/EAST SEMI-FINALS:
Crawley Jets 16 Hemel Stags 18 *(Hemel were later expelled for fielding two eligble players)*; Ipswich Rhinos 16 Oxford Cavliers 31.

Weekend of 8th August, 1999

SOUTH/EAST PRELIMINARY GRAND FINAL: Crawley Jets 54 Oxford Cavaliers 16.

NORTH/WEST SEMI-FINALS:
Cheltenham Warriors 41 Manchester Knights 6; Chester Wolves 30 Leicester Phoenix 10.

Weekend of 15th August, 1999

NORTH/WEST PRELIMINARY GRAND FINAL: Chester Wolves 27 Cheltenham Warriors 16.

Saturday 21st August, 1999

GRAND FINAL: Crawley Jets 24 Chester Wolves 26

In the North/West, both the sides with home advantage in the semi-finals won through, Chester accounting for Leicester with a decisive late rally and Cheltenham imperiously brushing aside Manchester.

In the Preliminary Final played at Woolston, Chester's big match players in key positions saw them just hold on to a decisive lead against opponents who showed commendable resolve throughout.

The Grand Final on the 21 August at the New River Stadium, North London was a truly superb encounter. Crawley and Chester had never met previously but the champions of the North and South served up a memorable classic. The gripping contest was enthralling, exciting, dramatic and unpredictable, the Wolves coming from 4-18 down to snatch a 26-24 victory with a try in the corner with virtually the final play.

The sportsmanship, spirit and standard on display were a credit to the fledgling competition in 1999. Already, with the season just over, major plans were in hand for the Millennium season, with a revamped administration and support from all strata of the game being formed to cope with the deluge of interest and applications nation-wide.

3
INTERNATIONAL SCENE

TRI-NATIONS
Still playing catch up

The 1999 Great Britain & Ireland Tri-Nations squad

Any British hopes that the game in the Northern Hemisphere was catching up with that in Australasia were shattered by the performance of the Lions in the inaugural Tri-Nations Tournament at the end of the 1999 season.

For every stride forward in England it seems there have been two south of the Equator.

And the Lions who flew south full of confidence returned home shattered by the record defeat in history at the hands of the Kiwis and the second most humiliating loss to the traditional foe - Australia.

Indeed, the 42-6 defeat by Australia at Brisbane's Suncorp Stadium (Lang Park) was more embarrassing than the one that sits in the history books as the worst on record.

For when the Great Britain side was beaten 50-12 at Swinton in 1963, it was a case of playing two men short for much of the match in the days when injured players could not be replaced.

At Suncorp in 1999, the Lions had their full compliment of 13 on the field at all times. And, with unlimited interchange, weary legs could be regularly rested.

Their struggle to emerge victorious against a makeshift Maoris' side and an injury-depleted Burleigh Bears' club team on the Gold Coast (one that was little more than a reserve-grade combination), posed serious questions again about the administration of British Rugby League.

144

Lions coach Andy Goodway originally announced a squad of 35 from which he planned to choose the touring party. But, with the Tri-Nations Tournament many months away, he stressed that others who showed outstanding form could be added. And they were.

The original squad was:

● Paul Anderson, Paul Deacon, Stuart Fielden, Mike Forshaw, James Lowes (Bradford).

● Danny Orr (Castleford).

● Francis Cummins, Darren Fleary, Iestyn Harris, Lee Jackson, Barrie McDermott, Adrian Morley, Terry Newton, Leroy Rivett, Ryan Sheridan (Leeds).

● Keiron Cunningham, Chris Joynt, Sean Long, Paul Newlove, Anthony Sullivan, Paul Sculthorpe (St Helens).

● Dale Laughton, Keith Senior, Darren Turner (Sheffield).

● Jon Roper (Warrington).

● Denis Betts, Gary Connolly, Andy Farrell, Lee Gilmour, Simon Haughton, Paul Johnson, Terry O'Connor, Kris Radlinski, Jason Robinson, Tony Smith (Wigan).

Lions skipper - Andy Farrell

In June, Goodway added Andy Hay (Leeds) and a month later Mick Cassidy (Wigan).

The squad was pruned to 29 in September with the omission of Deacon, Jackson, Newton, Rivett, Sullivan, Roper, Gilmour and Turner.

Sullivan was a surprise axing as he had been scoring a swag of tries for St Helens.

Goodway was to perform a back somersault after the Old Trafford grand final.

When the final squad of 24 was announced, Sullivan suddenly found himself back in favour.

Paul Newlove was unavailable through injury and gone were Cassidy, Fleary, Haughton, O'Connor and Orr.

THE 1999 LIONS

(With number of caps, before Tri-Nations Tournament)

	GB	Eng	Wales	Ire	Scot
Paul Anderson (Bradford Bulls)	0	0	0	0	0
Denis Betts (Wigan Warriors)	30	4	0	0	0
Gary Connolly (Wigan Warriors)	20	4	0	0	0
Francis Cummins (Leeds Rhinos)	2	2	0	0	0
Keiron Cunningham (St Helens)	7	0	5	0	0
Andy Farrell (Wigan Warriors), (c)	16	5	0	0	0
Stuart Fielden (Bradford Bulls)	0	0	0	0	0
Mike Forshaw (Bradford Bulls)	3	0	0	0	0
Iestyn Harris (Leeds Rhinos)	7	0	9	0	0
Andy Hay (Leeds Rhinos)	0	0	0	0	0
Paul Johnson (Wigan Warriors)	0	0	0	0	0
Chris Joynt (St Helens)	18	6	0	0	0
Dale Laughton (Sheffield Eagles)	3	0	0	0	1
Sean Long (St Helens)	2	0	0	0	0
James Lowes (Bradford Bulls)	3	0	0	2	0
Barrie McDermott (Leeds Rhinos)	3	1	0	3	0
Adrian Morley (Leeds Rhinos)	5	1	0	0	0
Kris Radlinski (Wigan Warriors)	11	5	0	0	0
Jason Robinson (Wigan Warriors)	10	7	0	0	0
Paul Sculthorpe (St Helens)	11	2	0	0	0
Keith Senior (Leeds Rhinos)	5	0	0	0	0
Ryan Sheridan (Leeds Rhinos)	0	0	0	0	0
Tony Smith (Wigan Warriors)	5	5	0	0	0
Anthony Sullivan (St Helens)	6	0	13	0	0

Goodway was circumspect about the British hopes.

"We were never going to be favourites," he said before leaving for Australasia, stating the obvious. "We've got to make sure we get it right straight away."

Sadly, Great Britain and Ireland didn't. And, in the words of the well-worn cliché, the rest is history.

New Zealand 24 ....Australia 22

There has been an attitude among some Australian Test players in recent years that there is not a team in the world capable of beating them.

To say they often underestimate the opposition is like saying Julia Roberts is a pretty woman.

As a result, they've regularly found out that there is more than just turning up for the kick-off if they are to win Tests.

Witness Wembley in 1990 and 1994 and that 33-10 drubbing at the hands of the 1992 Lions in Melbourne.

Did this complacency affect the Aussies at Ericsson Stadium in the opening clash of the first Tri-Nations Tournament? Or was it, in the letdown after a hard domestic season, their minds weren't firmly focused on the job ahead of them.

At the very least, the Kiwis caught them on the hop and claimed a most unexpected victory

Admittedly it was by just two points. But, for a while, the pundits were reaching for their history books when a record defeat for the Australians loomed.

The Kiwis had taken a 20-point lead and the previous best effort had been a 49-25 success at the Gabba (the Brisbane Cricket Ground) back in 1952.

But the Australians fought back and for a while looked as if they might even, Phoenix-like, rise from the ashes and fly to victory.

The ferocity of the Kiwis' early efforts stunned the visitors.

NEW ZEALAND 24 ....**AUSTRALIA 22**
Ericsson Stadium, Auckland - Friday 15th October, 1999

NEW ZEALAND: Richie Barnett (Sydney City) (C); Nigel Vagana (Auckland); Ruben Wiki (Canberra); Willie Talau (Canterbury); Lesley Vainikolo (Canberra); Robbie Paul (Bradford); Stacey Jones (Auckland); Joe Vagana (Auckland); Henry Paul (Bradford); Craig Smith (St Geo-Illawarra); Stephen Kearney (Melbourne); Matt Rua (Melbourne); Logan Swann (Auckland). *Subs:* David Kidwell (Parramatta); Jason Lowrie (Balmain); Nathan Cayless (Parramatta); Richard Swain (Melbourne).
Tries: Talau (4), Lowrie (10), Kearney (18), N Vagana (39); **Goals:** H Paul 4

AUSTRALIA: Robbie Ross (Melbourne); Mat Rogers (Sharks); Matthew Gidley (Newcastle); Russell Richardson (Sharks); Wendell Sailor (Brisbane); Brad Fittler (Sydney City) (C); Brett Kimmorley (Melbourne); Darren Britt (Canterbury); Craig Gower (Penrith); Rodney Howe (Melbourne); Bryan Fletcher (Sydney City); Nik Kosef (Manly); Jason Smith (Parramatta). *Subs:* Darren Lockyer (Brisbane); Darren Smith (Canterbury); Jason Stevens (Sharks); Michael Vella (Parramatta).
Tries: Gidley (36), Rogers (57), Fittler (60), Richardson (78); **Goals:** Rogers 3

HT: 24-4; **Ref:** R Smith (England); **Att:** 25,392
League Express Men of the Match -
New Zealand: Stacey Jones; **Australia:** Wendell Sailor

After 18 minutes New Zealand led 18-0 through a display that mixed tough forward play with clever attack.

And 'the little general' Stacey Jones led the charge.

The match had been underway for just four minutes when he darted from dummy-half some 30 metres out from the tryline.

The Australian defence was completely bamboozled as Jones then slipped a neat pass to Willie Talau.

In his 12-metre run for the line, the Canterbury centre shrugged off a would-be tackle by the normally reliable Jason Smith before touching down and leaping into the air with delight.

Exactly six minutes later Jones produced some more magic, with a 20-metre burst from just inside the Australian half. Stephen Kearney backed up before unloading to big replacement prop Jason Lowrie who was over under the posts for the first try of his senior career (129 first-grade matches for the Roosters and Balmain and 13 Tests for New Zealand and the Rest of the World).

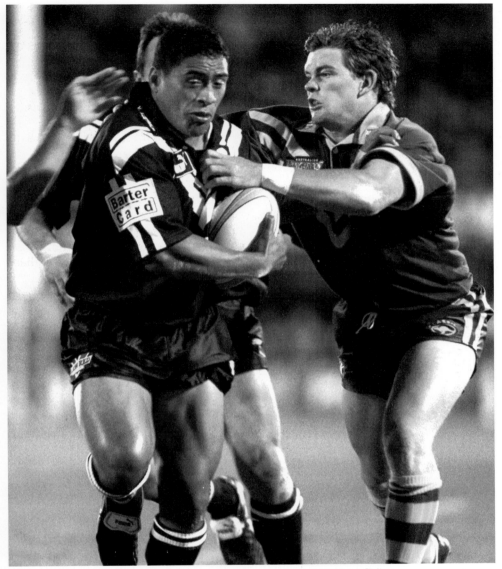

Willie Talau tries to escape the attentions of Matthew Gidley

There was no end to Jones' five-star effort.

In the 19th minute of the game he positioned Kearney perfectly and the rangy second-rower ripped through first Brett Kimmorley and then Robbie Ross on his way to the tryline.

The Australians had no answer to the 'up-in-your-face' play by the Kiwis.

The two exceptions were hooker Craig Gower, who was trying everything from dummy-half, and Wendell Sailor, who carved up the Kiwi defence every time he touched the ball.

Sailor had been denied a possible try midway through the first half after a copybook tackle by new Kiwi captain Richie Barnett.

147

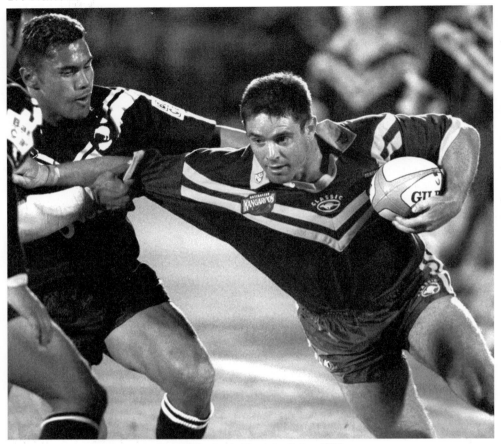

Brad Fittler hauled back by Ruben Wiki

And the big Brisbane Broncos' winger was not just excelling in attack.

He prevented what looked like a certain try with a memorable tackle of his own just eight minutes before the break.

The Kiwi loose forward Logan Swann would have scored had he continued to the try-line himself. But he unselfishly passed to centre David Kidwell.

Kidwell stormed towards the line with visions of a try that would most certainly have put the result beyond doubt. But ten metres out his progress was brought to an abrupt halt by the jolting Sailor tackle.

With four minutes remaining in the half Australia looked as if they were getting back into the match after yet another fine run by Sailor.

From the ensuing play-the-ball Test debutant Matthew Gidley scored off a cut-out pass from Jason Smith.

However, from the kick-off, Gidley undid all his good work with a fumble that led to another New Zealand try.

Jones...for it was that genius again...ran from 20 metres out, threw a perfect dummy, and sent the ball on to Kidwell. The Parramatta 'Find of the Year' calmly flicked it out to Nigel Vagana to score adjacent to the sideline.

Henry Paul, immaculate with the boot, kicked his fourth conversion from as many attempts and the Kiwis went to the break 20 points clear.

One could only wonder at the smile that creased the face of Aussie captain Brad Fittler as he returned for the second half, apparently unperturbed by the enormity of the lead.

It had a certain ring of confidence about it.

That confidence was not misplaced - despite the Kiwis almost scoring soon after the resumption of play.

But video referee, Chris Ward, ruled that winger Lesley Vainikolo had scraped the sideline just before he touched down in the corner.

In the 56th minute, with a remarkable leap Sailor defused a bomb behind his own line.

It was a vital take. Within a minute Australia had scored at the other end of the field, Brad Fittler running at the defence before sending on to Gidley. The Newcastle youngster caught and passed in one movement to send Mat Rogers over the line.

Three minutes later and Australia had scored again - this time it was Fittler who dummied his way through the defence to touch down.

These were ominous times for the Kiwis. The Australians were on a roll.

Two minutes later Gower finished a fine movement by inexplicably passing to the Kiwi Kidwell 10 metres from the New Zealand line.

Then came what proved to be a vital moment.

With the Australians trailing by eight and with 12 minutes remaining, fullback Ross looked likely to score.

But Kiwi centre Ruben Wiki stopped him dead in his tracks with a bonecruncher that shook not only the Australian fullback but the confidence of his teammates.

With seven minutes remaining, the video referee refused a Russell Richardson touchdown, ruling the Aussie centre's arm had touched the sideline before he could ground the ball over the try-line.

Richardson was eventually to score two and a half minutes later and the Australians trailed by just two points.

But it was all too late.

When play belatedly restarted there were only 15 seconds remaining. Not enough for any fairytale comeback victory.

In the final wash-up, the difference turned out to be Mat Rogers' conversion attempt of Gidley's try from wide out.

The ball hit the right upright and bounced the wrong way for the Australians.

Had it gone over the match would have ultimately ended in a draw.

"I think we tried too hard in the first half," was the way Australian coach Chris Anderson analysed the defeat. "We made too many mistakes and there were too many missed tackles. Later we settled down and played some decent football."

Reporters kept asking Kiwi coach Frank Endacott about the narrowness of the victory and the way, early in the game, that a record winning-margin had beckoned.

The reply was gruff and to the point: "I'm not into records...just wins."

Australia 42 ....Great Britain & Ireland 6

For three-quarters of a century Australian fans would look forward eagerly to clashes between their green and gold heroes and the cream of British manhood.

They were battles fought with pride - the honour of both nations on the line.

All that changed in 1999.

The British may have travelled south buoyed by the belief that the game in England was catching up with that in the Southern Hemisphere. But, the fans, it seems believed otherwise.

And only 12,511 bothered to turn up for the only Tri-Nations' clash in Australia.

It was the smallest crowd for an Anglo-Australian international in Australia, even less than the 12,944 at the Sydney Football Stadium for the 'dead' Third Test of the 1988 series.

And this on the same ground in which many of the 45,057 spilled over to within inches of the sideline for the 1966 clash that has become known as the Battle of Brisbane Mark II.

AUSTRALIA 42 ....**GREAT BRITAIN & IRELAND 6**
Suncorp Stadium, Brisbane - Friday 22nd October, 1999

AUSTRALIA: Darren Lockyer (Brisbane); Mat Rogers (Sharks); Shaun Timmins (St Geo-Illawarra); Matthew Gidley (Newcastle); Wendell Sailor (Brisbane); Matthew Johns (Newcastle); Brett Kimmorley (Melbourne); Darren Britt (Canterbury); Craig Gower (Penrith); Rodney Howe (Melbourne); Bryan Fletcher (Sydney City); Nik Kosef (Manly); Brad Fittler (Sydney City) (C). *Subs:* Ryan Girdler (Penrith); Darren Smith (Canterbury); Jason Smith (Parramatta); Michael Vella (Parramatta).
Tries: Fittler (13), J Smith (17), Kimmorley (44), Sailor (63), Gidley (66), Lockyer (74, 77); **Goals:** Rogers 6, Girdler

GREAT BRITAIN & IRELAND: Kris Radlinski (Wigan); Jason Robinson (Wigan); Gary Connolly (Wigan); Keith Senior (Leeds); Anthony Sullivan (St Helens); Iestyn Harris (Leeds); Ryan Sheridan (Leeds); Dale Laughton (Sheffield); Keiron Cunningham (St Helens); Barrie McDermott (Leeds); Denis Betts (Wigan); Adrian Morley (Leeds); Andy Farrell (Wigan) (C). *Subs:* Sean Long (St Helens); Paul Anderson (Bradford); Paul Sculthorpe (St Helens); Andy Hay (Leeds).
Try: Harris (38); **Goal:** Harris

HT: 10-6; **Ref:** D Pakieto (NZ); **Att:** 12,511
League Express Men of the Match -
Australia: Darren Lockyer; **GB & Ireland:** Adrian Morley

The fans obviously suspected the final outcome - a scoreline of 42-6 in favour of the home team.

It topped the previous most humiliating defeat on Australian soil - when Doug Laughton's Lions went down 35-0 in the First Test of the 1979 Ashes Series.

That, too, was at Lang Park, since renamed in deference to the vast sponsorship of a Queensland insurance company.

The Tri-Nations' scoreline was also just two points short of the record 38-point victory when the Kangaroos beat Great Britain 50-12 at Swinton in the Second Test of the 1963 series.

However, that loss was in the days when there were no substitutes and Britain finished with only 11 men after losing captain Eric Ashton in the sixth minute and stand-off Frank Myler in the 25th, both with broken ribs.

To be fair, the final score was not a true indication of the relative merits of the two sides. The Lions were still in the game at the break, trailing by just four points after having the better of the first half.

And this against all the odds.

At one stage they'd been caned 6-1 in the penalties. And they had second-rower Denis Betts despatched to the sin bin in what was nothing less than a piece of nit-picking by New Zealand referee David Pakieto.

But give Australia the mere whiff of victory and those green and gold

Iestyn Harris upends Darren Lockyer, who spills the ball

Andy Farrell congratulates Iestyn Harris on his try

champions make you pay dearly.

And as the shattered Lions' captain Andy Farrell was quick to point out: "It's just that we didn't play well for the full 80 minutes. Everybody was confident at half-time.

"We competed strongly for 40 minutes and were making inroads into the Australian defence. But we dropped too much ball in the second half and you can't defend all day against Australia."

The British most certainly did hold their own in a scrappy first half.

Leeds' backrower Adrian Morley showed they meant business with a crunching tackle on Aussie hard-man Rodney Howe in the opening minutes of the game.

Morley was a stand-out for the British although, like his teammates, he did seem to tire and was subdued late in the game when the Australians ran riot.

It was a tribute to the British that they held out the Australians when, several times early in the game, they looked likely to score.

On one occasion, fullback Darren Lockyer, promoted from the bench into the starting lineup to provide some flair in the Australian attack, sped 40 metres before his pass to supports was knocked down by Anthony Sullivan.

It was a try-saving effort by the St Helens' winger.

Some 12 minutes into the game there was that crucial refereeing decision.

Betts was sent to the sin bin for holding down young centre Matthew Gidley in a tackle.

The ruling by New Zealand referee David Pakieto, in his Test debut, seemed unduly harsh. And it cost the Lions dearly.

While Betts was off the field, the Australians ran in two tries.

The first came before Betts had even made it out of the arena. Scrum-half Brett Kimmorley send a long pass to new stand-off Matthew Johns, who in turn popped a clever ball to captain Brad Fittler who was through a gap and over the try-line before the British defence could reach him.

Four minutes later Lockyer made another slashing 30-metre break before flicking a reverse pass to substitute Jason Smith to score.

When St Helens' Super League grand final hero Sean Long was brought off the bench the British attack was instantly uplifted.

Andy Hay touched down for what he thought was Britain's first try, but was called back for a forward pass.

Just before half-time international debutant Paul Anderson livened up the proceedings when he fended off Howe with his forearm. The jolt brought an audible gasp from the crowd. And trainers were needed to help Howe from the field, his rubbery legs having trouble walking a straight line.

While he was departing, some Iestyn Harris magic put the Lions back into the match. The Welshman stepped around both Bryan Fletcher and Jason Smith, making both look quite pedestrian, to score what subsequently proved to be the visitors' only try.

As in their first match, the Aussies returned to the field after half-time brimming with confidence. And with good reason.

Just four minutes into the second half, the brilliant Lockyer cut the defence to ribbons and sent Kimmorley over to score. The scrum-half hit the turf in the field of play after a tackle by Gary Connolly but he then bounced over the line.

This was confirmed by the video replay. It showed Connolly had lost his grip on Kimmorley after bringing him to ground. There was no double-movement.

Britain may have got back into the match had a rehearsed move come to fruition.

Farrell made a great break before sending Long on his way to the line.

But Lockyer...yes it was that man again...swooped with a try-saving tackle. Whether it be in attack or defence, Lockyer seems to make every aspect of Rugby League look so easy.

Ten minutes later the rot well and truly set in.

It all started when Lockyer leaped high to defuse a bomb behind his own line.

The ball was thrown for a quick 20-metre tap restart and Wendell Sailor shrugged off an insipid attempted tackle by Long before racing almost the length of the field to score.

"When you get Sailor going 80 metres, it does break you," Farrell said later, with a shake of the head.

Three minutes later a tackle by Keith Senior failed to prevent a try to the exciting young centre Gidley.

Then, to cap off the evening Britain would rather forget, Lockyer scored two tries himself, including one in which he raced 62 metres.

There was not an Australian who disappointed, with Lockyer and Sailor giving stand-out performances.

For the visitors Morley could hold his head high despite his team's thrashing.

Hooker Keiron Cunningham also worked tirelessly all evening.

When Pakieto mercifully blew the whistle for full-time, the dispirited Lions trooped off the field knowing they would have to produce a minor miracle against New Zealand if they were to make the final.

They would need a 20-point victory over the Kiwis.

Not impossible but as Fittler was wont to suggest: "That would be some performance, wouldn't it!"

New Zealand 26 ....Great Britain & Ireland 4

Just when the Lions thought things couldn't get any worse...they did. They flew across the Tasman Sea to New Zealand with the knowledge that nothing less than a 20-point success over the Kiwis would satisfy the fans back home.

They were optimistic, especially after the news that star Kiwi scrum-half Stacey Jones, the man who had destroyed them in the home series 12 months before and had orchestrated the shock victory over Australia, had broken an arm the previous week in a 'Test' against Tonga.

The optimism was misplaced. It was the Kiwis who were to emerge with a decisive victory. The Lions were left demoralised and wondering how they were going to regroup for the World Cup in 2000.

In Auckland they managed to turn in their worst effort in history against New Zealand. And to rub salt into the wound, the defeat meant there was the ignominy of playing a curtain-raiser to the Tri-Nations Series final, against a spare-parts Maori side of semi-professionals.

The Lions' defeat was the sixth from their last seven matches against the Kiwis.

The performance of the 1999 crop of Lions' players against New Zealand was so inept that the final score could well have matched the previous week's 42-6 defeat by the Australians.

"Bumbling" was the word used in the local newspaper headlines on Saturday morning.

For that's exactly what it was.

The need for a big win seemed to affect the Lions' play.

NEW ZEALAND 26 ....**GREAT BRITAIN & IRELAND 4**
Ericsson Stadium, Auckland - Friday 29th October, 1999

NEW ZEALAND: Richie Barnett (Sydney City) (C); Nigel Vagana (Auckland); Ruben Wiki (Canberra); Willie Talau (Canterbury); Lesley Vainikolo (Canberra); Henry Paul (Bradford); Robbie Paul (Bradford); Joe Vagana (Auckland); Richard Swain (Melbourne); Craig Smith (St Geo-Illawarra); Matt Rua (Melbourne); Stephen Kearney (Melbourne); Logan Swann (Auckland). *Subs:* Gene Ngamu (Huddersfield); Jason Lowrie (Balmain); Nathan Cayless (Parramatta); David Kidwell (Parramatta).
Tries: Rua (9), N Vagana (20, 51), J Vagana (67); **Goals:** H Paul 5

GREAT BRITAIN & IRELAND: Kris Radlinski (Wigan); Jason Robinson (Wigan); Gary Connolly (Wigan); Keith Senior (Leeds); Francis Cummins (Leeds); Iestyn Harris (Leeds); Ryan Sheridan (Leeds); Dale Laughton (Sheffield); Keiron Cunningham (St Helens); Barrie McDermott (Leeds); Adrian Morley (Leeds); Chris Joynt (St Helens); Andy Farrell (Wigan) (C). *Subs:* Sean Long (St Helens); Denis Betts (Wigan); Mike Forshaw (Bradford); Andy Hay (Leeds)
Try: Long (46)

HT: 14-0; **Ref:** T Mander (Australia); **Att:** 11,961
League Express Men of the Match -
New Zealand: Stephen Kearney; **GB & Ireland:** Keiron Cunningham

From the kick-off they were on the back foot with big Joe Vagana making a 30-metre burst at his first touch of the ball, dragging three Lions with him.

The Paul brothers, together as halves following Jones' injury, routinely settled into the role they play in club rugby with Bradford. They taunted the British players with their clever play.

Henry Paul put first points on the board with a penalty in the seventh minute after the Lions, frustrated after keeping the Kiwis at bay for 20 tackles, were penalised for holding down.

Less than two minutes later Paul ran the ball from ten metres out before sending Matt Rua charging over for a try. Paul's conversion made it 8-0 and the prospects were ominous.

When Sean Long was included off the bench, he managed to put some spark into the British attack. Why Goodway didn't have the St Helens' half on the field from kick-off is anyone's guess for Long was to later show out as the Lions'

Stephen Kearney gets the ball away despite the attentions of the Great Britain defence

lone attacking weapon.

It was in the early stages of the match that the Kiwi pack laid the foundations for victory. Rua was devastating with his hit-ups. Stephen Kearney showed why he is one of the finest ball-players in the world. And Vagana, Craig Smith and substitute Jason Lowrie rampaged through the rucks.

When the Lions had the ball they were savaged by the Kiwi forwards, who drove them onto the back foot with crunching tackles.

Former Warrington three-quarter Nigel Vagana shattered any hope of a Lions' revival when, in the 21st minute, he intercepted a lobbed pass from Harris, who had hoped to find Keith Senior.

Vagana sped 30 metres to score and Paul's conversion had the home side ahead 14-nil. The Lions' fate was as good as sealed.

New Zealand went close to scoring on a couple of other occasions in the first half.

Richie Barnett raced around Senior in a 35-metre run only to see his pass to supports go astray.

Then with just three seconds left on the clock, Logan Swann was grassed centimetres from the line. He passed to Nigel Vagana who touched down. But the video referee ruled Swann had been legitimately held and his pass off the ground was illegal.

Long gave the Lions some hope with a try just after the break.

It was a spectacular effort. Winger Francis Cummins was racing for the corner when he realised the cover was about to knock him into touch. He flicked the ball infield to the waiting Long, who dived under a Henry Paul tackle to touch down.

Barrie McDermott trudges from the Ericsson Stadium pitch

It was a brief, but forlorn, moment of hope for the British.

Five minutes later Henry Paul took a kick from Cunningham two metres out from the New Zealand line.

He ran to the 10-metres, before sending Nigel Vagana on a 90-metre gallop to score at the other end of the field.

It was very similar to the gut-wrenching effort by Aussie Wendell Sailor that demoralised the Lions a week earlier.

The Kiwis mocked the visitors for the rest of the match.

But the Lions hardly helped their own cause.

With just over 13 minutes left for play, Wigan fullback Kris Radlinski made an unforced knock-on.

His head went down with embarrassment. And with real justification. A few seconds later Joe Vagana joined his cousin on the scoreboard.

TRI-NATIONS FINAL TABLE

	P	W	D	L	F	A	D	Pts
New Zealand	2	2	0	0	50	26	24	4
Australia	2	1	0	1	64	30	34	2
Great Britain & Ireland	2	0	0	2	10	68	-58	0

Even with the match firmly in their grasp, the Kiwis kept hammering at the British defences. Indeed, Henry Paul looked like scoring from a great run with just a few minutes remaining, but he was bundled into touch 15 metres out.

It didn't matter, the Kiwis had posted their record win.

A defiant Great Britain and Ireland coach, Andy Goodway, put on a brave face after the game as he palmed off questions about his future.

"I only do what I think is right for Great Britain and the players and that's how it will stay unless I'm told otherwise," he said.

But as far as the understatement of the tournament was concerned it was left to the dejected captain Andy Farrell: "We've got to make ourselves better players for next year."

Andy Hay meets Ruben Wiki head on

TRI-NATIONS FINAL

New Zealand 20 ....Australia 22

What a thriller to end the inaugural Tri-Nations. For the second time in three weeks there was just two points between the two Southern Hemisphere rivals - Australia and New Zealand.

And, sadly for the Kiwis, they found out the truth of the adage about counting chickens before they are hatched.

They were ecstatic when, with just over ten minutes left in the final, big Joe Vagana dragged three defenders with him as he bullocked his way towards Australia's try-line and with a magnificent offload sent cousin Nigel Vagana over to score.

The New Zealanders jumped in the air and embraced each other as if the match had been won there and then. They were convinced the 46-year drought since their most recent series victory over the Australians was approaching an end.

But the Australians had learned a salutary lesson when beaten by the Kiwis in the opening match of the tournament.

There was no way they were going to give up their crown as the best in the world without a fight.

Just over three minutes later there was a bit of magic from Australia's scrum-half, Brett Kimmorley, who had asked for a pain-killing injection to get himself back onto the field after a thigh injury that looked likely to prematurely end his evening.

He sliced through the Kiwi defence in a run that took him from just inside their half right up to the 20-metre line.

The ball went on to captain Brad Fittler and thence to stand-off Matthew Johns who positioned Wendell Sailor to dance the last ten metres to score wide out.

TRI-NATIONS FINAL

NEW ZEALAND 20 ....**AUSTRALIA 22**
Ericsson Stadium, Auckland - Friday 5th November, 1999

NEW ZEALAND: Richie Barnett (Sydney City) (C); Nigel Vagana (Auckland); Ruben Wiki (Canberra); Willie Talau (Canterbury); Lesley Vainikolo (Canterbury); Henry Paul (Bradford); Robbie Paul (Bradford); Joe Vagana (Auckland); Richard Swain (Melbourne); Craig Smith (St Geo-Illawarra); Matt Rua (Melbourne); Stephen Kearney (Melbourne); Logan Swann (Auckland). *Subs:* Gene Ngamu (Huddersfield); Jason Lowrie (Balmain); Nathan Cayless (Parramatta); David Kidwell (Parramatta).
Tries: R Paul (10), N Vagana (70); **Goals:** H Paul 6

AUSTRALIA: Darren Lockyer (Brisbane); Mat Rogers (Sharks); Darren Smith (Canterbury); Matthew Gidley (Newcastle); Wendell Sailor (Brisbane); Matthew Johns (Newcastle); Brett Kimmorley (Melbourne); Darren Britt (Canterbury); Craig Gower (Penrith); Jason Stevens (Sharks); Bryan Fletcher (Sydney City); Nik Kosef (Manly); Brad Fittler (Sydney City) (C). *Subs:* Ryan Girdler (Penrith); Shaun Timmins (St Geo-Illawarra); Jason Smith (Parramatta); Michael Vella (Parramatta).
Tries: Rogers (3, 54), Johns (17), Sailor (74); **Goals:** Rogers 3

HT: 10-14; **Ref:** R Smith (England); **Att:** 22,500
League Express Men of the Match -
New Zealand: Robbie Paul; **Australia:** Mat Rogers

The try wasn't the most spectacular the Brisbane Broncos' winger has scored in his marvellous career. However there would be few that were more significant.

It helped Australia pull off a remarkable victory. Ericsson Stadium went silent as the realisation set in on a stunned Auckland crowd.

New Zealand's national sporting pride had never been so low.

In previous weeks their netball side had been beaten by a lone Australian goal in the closing seconds of the World Championship' final, their cricketers humbled by India and...shock of shocks...the All Blacks bundled out of rugby

Mat Rogers and Brad Fittler celebrate Australia's Tri-Nations success

union's World Cup by outsiders France.

Now the Kiwi Rugby League team had seen victory snuffed out in the dying moments.

"Pride...that's what got us home," said Fittler.

It was a pride that seemed sadly lacking in the third nation in the tournament, Great Britain and Ireland.

The Tri-Nations Tournament showed just how close Australia and New Zealand had become (with the Lions trailing a distant third). Australia had won the Anzac Test in April by six points, New Zealand the opening game of the Tri-Nations by two and Australia the final by two.

It would be some time before the Australians ever again took the Kiwis lightly.

The final was certainly different to the earlier encounters when Australia had been caught on the hop by the Kiwis.

This time it was the Kiwis who were caught unawares.

Three minutes into the game, Bradford stand-off Henry Paul made his one mistake of the match, flinging a stray pass behind his supports.

Winger Mat Rogers pounced for an intercept and raced 58 metres unopposed to touch down for the simplest of tries. His conversion gave Australia a handy 6-nil lead.

If the visitors thought this was to be the start of a romp they were sadly mistaken.

An embarrassed Paul soon made amends for his uncharacteristic lapse, capitalising on a brilliant burst from near his own line by captain Richie Barnett.

The champion stand-off suddenly split the Australians in a 15-metre run from just inside his own half. Brother Robbie loomed up inside and cut the Australian defence to pieces in an unimpeded race to touch down.

Henry Paul's conversion squared up the score after ten minutes of play.

The Bulls Brothers were all smiles.

Three minutes later it seemed as if Robbie may have scored again after he had sliced through the defence with remarkable ease. A desperation tackle by fullback Darren Lockyer brought him to ground just short of the line. But it seemed to many that his momentum might just have carried him across the line with the ball under his chest.

The video referee ruled Paul had, in fact, lost the ball.

Rogers was not content with his intercept try. He eagerly sought out the ball and with 16 minutes on the clock made a sensational run that provided field position for Australia's second touchdown.

The ball was flung out to the centres, where Darren Smith had an overlap. As the regrouped defence came at him, he turned the attack back inside to Lockyer who positioned Johns for a try.

The video referee was unable to reach a decision when the ball went loose as Henry Paul got over the tryline in the 26th minute. It was back to English referee Russell Smith for the final decision.

In a controversial ruling, Smith denied Paul a try but despatched one of the tacklers, Lockyer, to the sin bin for a professional foul (raking the ball out of Paul's hands).

Lockyer was not the only Aussie to cool his heels for ten minutes during the final.

On the second occasion, 15 minutes from full-time, prop Darren Britt was

TRI-NATIONS TOP POINTSCORERS

	T	G	FG	Pts
Mat Rogers (Australia)	3	12	0	36
Henry Paul (New Zealand)	0	15	0	30
Nigel Vagana (New Zealand)	4	0	0	16
Brad Fittler (Australia)	2	0	0	8
Matthew Gidley (Australia)	2	0	0	8
Darren Lockyer (Australia)	2	0	0	8
Wendell Sailor (Australia)	2	0	0	8
Iestyn Harris (GB & Ireland)	1	1	0	6

sin-binned for holding down in a tackle. While he was in the sheds, that try to Nigel Vagana put the Kiwis in front.

Needless to say, Aussie coach Chris Anderson was upset by both sin-binnings as well as the final 14-7 penalty count in favour of the Kiwis. Henry Paul took full advantage of the string of penalties regularly raising the flags to keep the home side within striking distance.

The penalty goal after Britt's dismissal brought the Kiwis back to 18-16. And then came the exciting finish that stunned the Kiwi supporters and players alike.

Such was the commitment by both sides that neither deserved to lose.

The two packs matched each other with fire for the entire 80 minutes.

The Paul brothers again shone out. And not just in attack - although they were quite exhilarating when it came to scoring tries or providing the opportunities to do so.

That they were able to find cracks in the wonderful Australian defence was testimony to their talents.

As for their defence...

One lost count of the number of promising Australian sorties that were brought to a swift halt by their efforts.

Lesley Vainikolo made amends for a horror display in the previous match against the Australians with several terrifying bursts. Comparison with Jonah Lomu was obvious. On his display in the Tri-Nations' final Vainikolo lost nothing by such comparison.

Richie Barnett was an inspiring captain and showed himself to be up there with the great fullbacks of the past. For so long New Zealand has relied on Matthew Ridge. Barnett's display was the equal of any by the former Test custodian.

For Australia none was better than Rogers, who has come so far in such a short time. Could it only have been April when he played so badly in the Anzac Test?

He has always been talked about as Steve Rogers' son. How long before the fans will instead be describing Steve as Mat Rogers' father?

Kimmorley came of age in the closing weeks of the 1999 season, emerging from Andrew Johns' shadow. His gallant effort in the closing minutes of the final most certainly kept Australia's record intact and will be talked about in years to come.

The rookies Matthew Gidley and Bryan Fletcher showed the promise that should keep them on the international scene for many a year to come.

It would be a brave man who would tip against anything but an all-Australasian final in the 2000 World Cup.

As for the British... it is very much a case of back to the drawing board.

LIONS TOUR MATCHES

Burleigh Bears 6 ....Great Britain & Ireland 10

A friendly against the Queensland Cup champions, the Burleigh Bears, was a sombre preview of what was to later unfold in the Tri-Nations Tournament.

The Lions turned in a lack-lustre performance and were only saved from the humiliation of defeat by the injury-ridden 'park' side by some late magic by Jason Robinson and Andy Farrell.

Granted, the tourists were caned 16-6 in the penalties by local referee David Allsop.

But they had a lineup that should have run up a cricket score against the Bears who were missing five of their best players, including goal-kicking utility star Ben Lythe, who was later signed by the Auckland Warriors as a back-up to their Test half Stacey Jones.

The Bears had led 6-4 at three-quarter time and the mood was ominous as a mistake-ridden Lions' attack kept faltering.

Then Robinson made a long run to put the visitors in a good attacking position.

Seconds later Farrell burst through a gap wide out to score. And he converted his own try to give his side a four-point victory.

Coach Andy Goodway made excuses: "This was only a warm-up match. We achieved what we wanted to achieve."

Unfortunately, while the tourists may have got warm - they never got hot, as their subsequent displays against Australia and New Zealand proved.

Sean Long charges through the Burleigh Bears defence

Barrie McDermott brought to earth by the Maori defence

Aotearoa Maoris 12.............................Great Britain & Ireland 22

The final embarrassment for the Lions on their jaunt Down Under came when they were forced to play in the curtain-raiser to the Tri-Nations' final, against a makeshift Maoris' combination.

Backrower Denis Betts summed up the attitude of his teammates: "There's just no dignity. Maybe it's a punishment....it's no way to treat a side."

It could have been worse. The Lions could have been beaten by the Maoris.

And for much of the match such an upset looked quite on the cards. This was especially the case when, in the 65th minute, Paul Anderson was sent to the sin-bin for his second play-the-ball offence in less than a minute.

At the time the Lions were clinging to a 16-12 lead and the loss of Anderson could very well have given the Maoris the chance to snatch a winning lead.

But in the end it was left to scrum-half Sean Long, one of the few Britons to emerge from the tour with reputation untarnished, to race onto a James Lowes' pass and sprint away for his second try of the match.

The Maori side welcome the Lions with the haka

At 22-12 the Lions had been saved from complete humiliation.

Betts was probably right when he said the game should never have been played.

But this British attitude only served as an inspiration to the Maoris, flung together at just six days notice and with most of their best players unavailable through injury.

Coach Cameron Bell, who once had charge of Carlisle, gave warning about the World Cup in which he will have a much stronger Maori combination to work with.

"(Kiwi coach) Frank Endacott will have first choice when it comes to players," Bell noted. "But the determination of Maoris to play will be written in blood. And we wouldn't care if we only got third or fourth choice of players. We'd still be playing for the pride of our people."

BURLEIGH BEARS 6 .... **GREAT BRITAIN & IRELAND 10**
Pizzey Park, Burleigh - Saturday 16th October, 1999

BEARS: Jamie Mahon; Graham Lyons; Frank Napoli; Reggie Cressbrook; Aaron Douglas; Craig Freer; Grant Adamson (C); Ali Brown; Jamie O'Connor; Shane O'Flanagan; Bill Dunn; Justin Bryant; Dean Allan. *Subs:* Todd Lester; Adam McKenzie; Frank Johnson; Ali Davys; Stan Kennedy.
Try: Davys; **Goal:** Kennedy

GREAT BRITAIN & IRELAND: Kris Radlinski (Wigan); Jason Robinson (Wigan); Gary Connolly (Wigan); Keith Senior (Leeds); Francis Cummins (Leeds); Iestyn Harris (Leeds); Ryan Sheridan (Leeds); Stuart Fielden (Bradford); James Lowes (Bradford); Barrie McDermott (Leeds); Denis Betts (Wigan); Adrian Morley (Leeds); Andy Farrell (Wigan) (C). *Subs:* Paul Anderson (Bradford); Keiron Cunningham (St Helens); Andy Hay (Leeds); Paul Johnson (Wigan); Chris Joynt (St Helens); Dale Laughton (Sheffield); Sean Long (St Helens); Paul Sculthorpe (St Helens); Tony Smith (Wigan); Anthony Sullivan (St Helens); Mike Forshaw (Bradford).
Tries: Lowes, Farrell; **Goal:** Farrell

HT: 6-4; **Ref:** D Allsop; **Att:** 4,760

AOTEAROA MAORIS 12 .... **GREAT BRITAIN & IRELAND 22**
Ericcson Stadium, Auckland - Friday 5th November, 1999
(Tri-Nations Final curtain raiser)

MAORIS: Alex Chan (Wentworthville); Steve Matthews (Glenora); Peter Lewis (Auckland); Steve Berryman (Waikato); Jared Mills (Western Subs); Luke Goodwin (Western Subs); Willie Rangi (Kellyville); Paul Rauhihi (Newcastle); Tukere Barlow (Kellyville) (C); John Edmonds (Northcote); Robert Henare (St George); Darren Rameka (Western Subs); Andrew Wynyard (London). *Subs:* Gavin Bailey (Glenora); Martin Moana (Halifax); Frank Watene (Wakefield); Wairangi Koopu (Auckland).
Tries: Rameka (32), Chan (52); **Goals:** Rangi, Goodwin

GREAT BRITAIN & IRELAND: Kris Radlinski (Wigan); Jason Robinson (Wigan); Keith Senior (Leeds); Anthony Sullivan (St Helens); Francis Cummins (Leeds); Andy Farrell (Wigan) (C); Sean Long (St Helens); Paul Anderson (Bradford); James Lowes (Bradford); Dale Laughton (Sheffield); Adrian Morley (Leeds); Paul Sculthorpe (St Helens); Chris Joynt (St Helens). *Subs:* Stuart Fielden (Bradford); Barrie McDermott (Leeds); Mike Forshaw (Bradford); Andy Hay (Leeds).
Tries: Sullivan (5), Long (11, 64), Lowes (46); **Goals:** Farrell 3

HT: 6-12; **Ref:** D Pakieto

ANZAC Day Test

A Rush trip halfway across the world by the Paul brothers almost paid dividends for their native New Zealand - as the Kiwis went within a whisker of pulling off an upset in the annual Anzac Test.

The international encounter, instigated in 1997 during the Super League conflict, is held on the weekend nearest to Anzac Day (April 25) when the two nations remember those who died fighting for their country in hostilities from the Boer War to the Vietnam conflict.

The Australian Super League side won in 1997 and the Kiwis turned the tables a year later. And there was to be nothing between the 1999 sides.

The headlines in the lead-up to the match had little to do with what was going to happen on the field. Australian hooker Craig Gower was sent packing by team officials after a drunken incident in a Sydney nightclub.

At first the management and coach Chris Anderson tried to hush up the whole incident saying Gower had been dropped from the team after being injured in training. But the attempted whitewash didn't work.

With eleven internationals missing, the Kiwis were 7-1 outsiders in the betting. But once play got underway you would never have believed it.

The game had been in progress for less than two minutes when Robbie Paul, playing stand-off outside Stacey Jones, scored from a scrum 15 metres out. The scrum had come after Mat Rogers dropped a bomb. The young Sharks' winger had a wretched night - but it was to the selectors' credit that they persevered with him later in the season, when his form could not be faulted.

Henry Paul, playing hooker, was the best player on the field. His clever runs from dummy-half had the Australian forwards continually on the back foot. The performances of both Henry and Robbie Paul drew unabashed praise from Aussie skipper Brad Fittler: "They are two very talented blokes, aren't they!" Australia had to wait until the second half before taking the lead when Darren Smith snapped up a bouncing ball from a bomb that the Kiwis had failed to defuse. Then newcomer Bryan Fletcher made a 60-metre burst that opened a hole for Fittler to score.

The Aussies were also well served by two of the Brisbane Broncos, Wendell Sailor and Gorden Tallis. And when you have experienced talent like that in a side, it's very difficult to post a victory over the Australians. Robbie Paul set up a late try to blockbusting winger Lesley Vainikolo but there was to be no Kiwi revival.

The crowd of 30,245 looked a trifle sparse in the huge new Olympic stadium. But it was the best attendance at a Trans-Tasman clash since 32,000 packed Lang Park to watch the Third (and deciding) Test of the 1993 series.

As such it brought a hopeful smile to the faces of ARL officials who had little good news since the Super League conflict broke out in 1995.

AUSTRALIA 20 ....**NEW ZEALAND 14**

Stadium Australia - Friday 23rd April, 1999

AUSTRALIA: Darren Lockyer (Brisbane); Mat Rogers (Sharks); Laurie Daley (Canberra); Darren Smith (Canterbury); Wendell Sailor (Brisbane); Brad Fittler (Sydney City) (C); Allan Langer (Brisbane); Shane Webcke (Brisbane); Andrew Johns (Newcastle); Glenn Lazarus (Melbourne); Robbie Kearns (Melbourne); Gorden Tallis (Brisbane); Jason Smith (Parramatta). *Subs:* Matt Sing (Sydney City); Steve Price (Canterbury); Nik Kosef (Manly); Bryan Fletcher (Sydney City). **Tries:** Sailor (28), D Smith (42), Fittler (58); **Goals:** Rogers 4

NEW ZEALAND: Richie Barnett (Sydney City); Sean Hoppe (Auckland); Willie Talau (Canterbury); Ruben Wiki (Canberra); Lesley Vainikolo (Canberra); Robbie Paul (Bradford); Stacey Jones (Auckland); Joe Vagana (Auckland); Henry Paul (Bradford); Jason Lowrie (Balmain);

Jarrod McCracken (Parramatta) (C); Nathan Cayless (Parramatta); Logan Swann (Auckland). *Subs:* David Kidwell (Parramatta); Matt Rua (Melbourne); Terry Hermansson (Auckland); Richard Swain (Melbourne). **Tries:** R Paul (2), Swann (49), Vainikolo (63); **Goal:** H Paul

HT: 6-6; **Ref:** S Cummings (England); **Att:** 30,245
League Express Men of the Match -
Aust: Gorden Tallis; **NZ:** Henry Paul

Craig Gower (Penrith) was chosen as hooker for Australia but was sacked after a nightclub incident. Johns came off the bench and was in turn replaced by Sing. Quentin Pongia (Sydney City) was chosen as the Kiwi captain but withdrew through injury and was replaced by Lowrie. Other New Zealanders to fail fitness tests after being chosen in the original squad of 18 were Craig Smith (St George-Illawarra) and Tony Puletua (Penrith). Hermansson was added to the squad.

ANGLO-FRENCH CHALLENGE
England on the up

The success of French sides, both at club and national team levels, against their cross channel counterparts in 1998, paved the way for a welcome renewal of full internationals between England and France in '99. That new spirit of optimism did not, however, stretch far enough for the Treize Tournoi to be repeated, despite what appeared to have been a big success as far the French could see.

Villeneuve were even denied the opportunity to defend their 'European Cup' against the British Premiership winners, and instead had to settle for a special challenge match against a hastily-assembled Northern Ford Premiership XIII played at Widnes. The French Champions won plenty of friends for their attractive attacking football as they came back from a half-time deficit to beat the Premiership XIII by 24-14.

That growing respect for the improvements made in French Rugby League gathered even more momentum when England travelled to Carcassonne for the opening encounter in the two-match Lincoln Financial Group International Challenge. A new look English team, despite lacking several first choice stars who were on Tri-Series duty down-under with Great Britain, were confidently expected to win comfortably - but they came away relieved to have a 28-20 victory in the bag.

England coach John Kear was the first to pay tribute to the improvement of the French team he himself had coached back in 1997. "They played very well and were highly committed, and there were some marvellous performances from their players, especially in the pack," said Kear. "Thirteen of their 17 were players who I had worked with - their team hasn't changed much for three years so they know each other inside out and are very well organised."

Kear's praise for the work of French coaches Patrick Pedrazzani and Gilles Dumas, was matched by English admiration for the play of emerging young forwards Abderazzak Elkhalouki and Jerome Guisset which set the visitors on

EMAP EUROPEAN CHALLENGE

NFP SELECT XIII 14 ....VILLENEUVE LEOPARDS 24
Auto Quest Stadium, Widnes - Sunday 3rd October, 1999

NFP XIII: Mark Sibson (Bramley); Matt Bramald (Featherstone Rovers); Phil Atkinson (Barrow Border Raiders); Stuart Magorian (Barrow Border Raiders); Paul Wingfield (Leigh Centurions); Paul Mansson (C) (Widnes Vikings); Latham Tawhai (Hunslet Hawks); Lee Hansen (Widnes Vikings); Anthony Murray (Leigh Centurions); Steve Pryce (Hunslet Hawks); Steve Gee (Lancashire Lynx); Gareth Adams (Widnes Vikings); Jamie Leighton (Hunslet Hawks). *Subs (all played):* Darren Callaghan (York Wasps); Darren Holt (Barrow Border Raiders); Richard Pachniuk (Hunslet Hawks); Asa Amone (Featherstone Rovers).
Tries: Gee (11), Callaghan (63); **Goals:** Wingfield 3

LEOPARDS: Freddy Banquet (C); Ludovic Perolari; David Despin; Gilles Cornut; Richard Doste; Laurent Frayssinous; Julien Rinaldi; David Collado; Vincent Wulf; Vea Bloomfield; Grant Doorey; Artie Shead; Laurent Carrasco. *Subs (all played):* Pierre Sabatie; Regis Brioux; Christophe Canal; Romain Gagliazzo.
Tries: Doste (17), Banquet (53), Cornut (73), Despin (78); **Goals:** Banquet 4

League Express Men of the Match - **NFP:** Mark Sibson; **Leopards:** Freddy Banquet
Penalties: 10-9; **HT:** 8-6; **Ref:** G Shaw (Wigan); **Att:** 1,017

166

the back foot in a first half France deserved to lead.

The famous medieval city of Carcassonne, used to basking in rich autumn sunshine, had saved its worst weather for the visit of the English, and torrential rain made handling mistakes inevitable. Whether it was difficulty adapting to the wet conditions, or nervousness among a side that had a complete backline of full international debutants, England needed a vast improvement after half-time to save the game - and they got it with the experienced Lee Jackson and Steve McNamara providing the momentum.

After a soft try from dummy-half by prop Dean Sampson in the opening minutes of the game made French fans fear the worst, the young 'Tricolours' stormed ahead with fine passing and support play leading to tries from Sylvain Houles and Gael Tallec, to go alongside Freddy Banquet's goals, and put France firmly in command as half-time approached. Danny Orr's solo dash from a scrum made England more comfortable, just four points down, at the interval.

But when young centre Jean-Emmanuel Cassin, on as a substitute for injured captain Jean-Marc Garcia, brushed off Nathan McAvoy and sprinted 60 metres to score, France were 20-10 up and a shock was on the cards. That's when the English pack took control and, with a tiring French side pegged in their own quarter,

LINCOLN FINANCIAL GROUP INTERNATIONAL CHALLENGE

FRANCE 20 ....ENGLAND 28
Std Albert Domec, Carcassonne
Wednesday 13th October, 1999

FRANCE: Freddy Banquet (Villeneuve); Patrice Benausse (Carcassonne); Jean-Marc Garcia (C) (St-Esteve); Arnaud Dulac (St-Gaudens); Sylvain Houles (XIII Catalan); Laurent Frayssinous (Villeneuve); Fabien Devecchi (Villeneuve); Jason Sands (Villefranche); Vincent Wulf (Villeneuve); Abderazzak Elkhalouki (Toulouse); Jerome Guisset (Canberra Raiders); Gael Tallec (Castleford Tigers); Laurent Carrasco (Villeneuve). *Subs (all played):* Frederick Teixido (Limoux); David Collado (Villeneuve); Jean-Emmanuel Cassin (Toulouse); Jean-Christophe Borlin (St-Gaudens).
Tries: Houles (21), Tallec (25), Cassin (44); **Goals:** Banquet 4

ENGLAND: Marcus St Hilaire (Leeds Rhinos); Paul Sterling (Leeds Rhinos); Francis Maloney (Castleford Tigers); Jon Roper (Warrington Wolves); Darren Rogers (Castleford Tigers); Danny Orr (Castleford Tigers); Paul Deacon (Bradford Bulls); Steve Molloy (C) (Sheffield-Huddersfield); Terry Newton (Leeds Rhinos); Dean Sampson (Castleford Tigers); Anthony Farrell (Leeds Rhinos); Simon Haughton (Wigan Warriors); Steve McNamara (Bradford Bulls). *Subs (all played):* Lee Jackson (Leeds Rhinos); Lee Harland (Castleford Tigers); Nathan McAvoy (Bradford Bulls); Mark Hilton (Warrington Wolves).
Tries: Sampson (6), Orr (36, 47), Sterling (50), St Hilaire (80); **Goals:** McNamara 4

League Express Men of the Match - **France:** Laurent Frayssinous; **England:** Danny Orr
Penalties: 5-3; **HT:** 14-10; **Ref:** R Connolly (Wigan); **Att:** 3,000

ENGLAND 50 ....FRANCE 20
The Boulevard, Hull
Saturday 23rd October, 1999

ENGLAND: Marcus St Hilaire (Leeds Rhinos); Leon Pryce (Bradford Bulls); Francis Maloney (Wakefield Wildcats); Nathan McAvoy (Bradford Bulls); Darren Rogers (Castleford Tigers); Danny Orr (Castleford Tigers); Paul Deacon (Bradford Bulls); Steve Molloy (C) (Sheffield-Huddersfield); Terry Newton (Leeds Rhinos); Dean Sampson (Castleford Tigers); Anthony Farrell (Leeds Rhinos); Simon Haughton (Wigan Warriors); Steve McNamara (Bradford Bulls). *Subs (all played):* Lee Jackson (Leeds Rhinos); Lee Harland (Castleford Tigers); Nathan Sykes (Castleford Tigers); Steve Blakeley (Salford City Reds).
Tries: Pryce (4) Deacon (10), Sampson (24), Maloney (39, 66), St Hilaire (49, 52, 80), Jackson (72); **Goals:** McNamara 7

FRANCE: Stephane Millet (St-Gaudens); Patrice Benausse (Carcassonne); Jean-Marc Garcia (C) (St-Esteve); Arnaud Dulac (St-Gaudens); Sylvain Houles (XIII Catalan); Laurent Frayssinous (Villeneuve); Fabien Devecchi (Villeneuve); Jason Sands (Villefranche); Vincent Wulf (Villeneuve); Abderazzak Elkhalouki (Toulouse); Jerome Guisset (Canberra Raiders); Gael Tallec (Castleford Tigers); Laurent Carrasco (Villeneuve). *Subs (all played):* Frederick Teixido (Limoux); Jean-Emmanuel Cassin (Toulouse); Romain Sort (Carpentras); Jean-Christophe Borlin (St-Gaudens).
Tries: Dulac (16), Sands (32), Frayssinous (42), Garcia (77); **Goals:** Millet 2

League Express Men of the Match - **England:** Paul Deacon; **France:** Abderazzak Elkhalouki
Penalties: 5-9; **HT:** 24-10; **Ref:** T Alibert (Tarn); **Att:** 3,068

a lucky bounce gave Orr his second try, rapidly followed by some fine passing that put Paul Sterling over in the corner for McNamara's superb conversion to put England 22-20 ahead. Marcus St Hilaire added an injury-time try as he snapped up a fluffed last desperate kick by France, and the English were home ... but certainly not dry.

The return match at Hull's Boulevard ground ten days later had coach Kear and his English team on their guard, having seen the improved organisation of the French team at first hand in Carcassonne. In the event, it was a much more relaxed 80 minutes for England, as they stormed to a 50-20 win and threatened to overwhelm France in the final quarter.

Joining the debutants from the first encounter was Bradford's 18 year old winger Leon Pryce, and within four minutes he had posted his first full international try. With his fellow Bulls, Paul Deacon and Steve McNamara, at the hub of everything, England always looked in control.

A happy coach Kear had no doubts about the reason for his team's big improvement.

"The extra week's preparation was the key," he said. "That, coupled with a gameplan that exploited the French weaknesses and nullified their strengths, gave us the win."

Lee Harland takes on Fabien Devecchi

The drier conditions allowed full reign to the English players' talents and the mix of youth and experience was perfectly illustrated by the fact that the two outstanding performers were teenage scrum-half Deacon and, inevitably, the country's most experienced Test player Lee Jackson.

Skipper Steve Molloy recognised that positive mix. "There are some great young players just starting to emerge. I just wish I was five years younger so I could be playing with these lads when they hit their full potential."

Nine tries to four summed up England's superiority, with Marcus St Hilaire posting a hat-trick from fullback.

The French were very disappointed with their effort. "I was sure we would do much better," said their joint-coach Gilles Dumas. "But we made too many errors due to lack of concentration, particularly in defence around the rucks."

Dumas summed it up perfectly. Going forward France showed they could still score tries, but their defence allowed Jackson and Deacon all the room they needed to turn the game. The French also badly missed the big kicking game of their injured fullback Banquet.

Nevertheless, the two-match series put European international Rugby League back on the agenda, and left both countries counting the positives from two entertaining encounters both played in a wonderful spirit.

WORLD CUP QUALIFIERS
Eastern promise

Lebanon claimed the 16th place in World Cup 2000 with a convincing 62-8 win against the USA in the qualifying play-off final at Disney World in Florida.

The team, made up of Lebanese players from Sydney, produced an 11-try romp against their relatively inexperienced opponents, and earned the Middle Eastern side a spot in Group Two of World Cup 2000 alongside Wales, New Zealand and the Cook Islands

Lebanon captain Darren Maroon was even talking about beating the Welsh to get into the last eight. "We've looked at the draw and obviously the Kiwis are going to be the favourites," said 33 year old Maroon, who spent ten years in Australian first-grade League.

"But we have a lot of great players from Sydney and we have guys to come into the side. If we can make second in the group, we could have a chance of playing against Australia in the quarter-finals."

The Americans found Canterbury's free-scoring back Hazem El Masri - he grabbed another 22 points in the play-off final - Sydney City scrum-half Paul Khoury - who scored two tries - and North Queensland loose forward Michael Coorey - who grabbed a second-half hat-trick - too hot to handle.

The Lebanese shrugged off the disappointment of seeing their enigmatic team manager John Elias refused entry into the States because of his criminal past and are now hoping their success will kick-start Rugby League in the Lebanon, with matches against France and Italy being lined up for Beirut in the build-up to the 2000 Lincoln World Cup.

America were devastated by the set-back, although they will play in the Emerging Nations tournament to run side by side with the World Cup proper.

"This is a real kick in the guts for a lot of people," admitted coach Shane Millard, the London Broncos star who was recruited by nephew David Niu, the US League's leading light.

"It was imperative that we won and we realise what a great opportunity it was for us."

But the United States, despite coming to the final unbeaten, found themselves completely out of their depth against the streetwise Lebanese.

Two early penalty goals from Niu kept them in touch at 6-4 but the pace and class of Lebanon was always likely to tell, even when they were down to eleven men for a time after Sami Chamoun and Maroon were sin-binned in separate incidents for dissent. But America also paid the price for foul play.

St Helens' Vila Matautia was sent to the sin bin just ten minutes into the game for a high tackle and Salford forward Joe Faimalo was shown the red card six minutes into the second half when he repeated the offence on second-rower Chris Salem.

Faimalo escaped a ban when a three-man disciplinary panel ruled that his dismissal was sufficient punishment.

Despite the disappointing loss, US captain Jeff Preston insists that efforts will continue to take the game into new areas like Arizona and Texas and he predicted that America will win the Emerging Nations Championship.

The USA had won the Pacific play-offs in fine style with two whitewashes of both Canada and Japan.

All the games were played at the Disney Wide World of Sports complex in Orlando, Florida, with the backing of the Philadelphia-based Lincoln Financial Group.

In the group opener, America beat Japan 54-0, but the game was in no way as one-sided as the scoreline suggests, even though the US were boosted by the inclusion of British-based players Matautia, Julian O'Neill and Faimalo, who qualified under the grandparents rule.

Japan regained their honour in the same week when they beat Canada 14-0 amid delirious scenes and on the last day of the Pacific group, USA overpowered the Canadians 68-0 to raise their hopes.

Lebanon had won the right to travel to Florida when they won the double-edged competition that ran in the south of France, parallel to the Pacific group.

After having secured their place in the World Cup qualifying final, they were also crowned inaugural Mediterranean Cup champions in Avignon, as favourites France went down to a shock 10-14 defeat to Italy, after needing only a draw to claim the silverware.

The competition had started well for the hosts in Perpignan, where they cruised past a beleaguered and outclassed Morocco 80-8 in their opening game.

The Lebanon squad celebrate reaching the 2000 World Cup

Lebanon's Sami Chamoun surrounded by the USA defence during the Qualifying Tournament final

Morocco manager Hussein M'Barki later slammed the French Federation for their organisation of the event, and claimed his side were being "treated like a second class country."

His main cause for concern was the fact that many of the players he was expecting to use, homegrown Moroccans currently playing First Division rugby a treize, had failed to be given letters by their clubs informing them of their international call-up.

Star of the show for France was young fullback Yacine Dekkiche, who picked up five tries and ten goals in his debut international appearance, and marked himself down as a real star of the future.

Morocco's next opponents Italy, meanwhile, had just been in a bruising encounter with Lebanon. Many had expected that the winners of this match, the competition's opener, would go on to take that qualifying final place and they were to be proved right.

Inspired by the presence of the cancer-stricken John Elias, Lebanon won a bruising match 16-36, although the importance of the game was put into perspective later. Returning from a night out over the nearby Spanish border, the Italian squad were alarmed to find their Lezignan hotel flooded with water.

The South of France had just suffered its worst floods in over 60 years, with over 20 people dead or missing amid scenes of utter devastation and carnage.

At 1.30am, a wall of water had crashed into and destroyed the ground floor completely, but fortunately all the Italy players had yet to return to their beds. "I'm just glad I made the trip compulsory," said coach Craig Salvatori, "or we would have lost at least one of them for sure."

Unsurprisingly, a jaded Italian side only managed to beat Morocco 34-0 in their hastily rearranged second round match the following day in Toulouse. The Moroccans deserved praise however, their commitment and refusal to buckle under pressure helped them produce the performance of their tournament.

In the day's second game, also originally intended for Lezignan, France played superbly to beat the ultra-physical Lebanese 38-24, and put themselves in pole position for finishing top of the table.

Three days later, however, that hope had turned to tears of disappointment as a mixture of big night nerves and ferocious Italian defending turned up the shock of the tournament. Lebanon - who notched up an incredible 104-0 win over a brave but physically shattered Morocco in the evening's first game - had pipped the French to the first ever Mediterranean Cup championship.

LINCOLN FINANCIAL GROUP WORLD CUP 2000 QUALIFYING TOURNAMENT

MEDITERRANEAN GROUP

Thursday 11th November, 1999

FRANCE 80 ....**MOROCCO 8**
France: Tries: Yacine Dekkiche (14, 26, 41, 54, 72), Roman Gag,gliazo (18), Arnaud Dulac (21), Gilles Cornut (23), Abderazzak Elkahlouki (33), Stephane Millet (36, 58), Pascal Jampy (39), Romain Sort (51), Claude Sirvent (68, 75); Goals: Yacine Dekkiche 10
Morocco: Try: Hicham Laaribi (29); Goals: Hussein El Bouchti 2
at Stade Jean Laffon, Perpignan

ITALY 16 ....**LEBANON 36**
Italy: Tries: David Riolo (42), Carmine Barbaro (65), Mick Salafia (68); Goals: Mick Salafia 2
Lebanon: Tries: Michael Coorey (10), David Lambert (14), Chris Salem (28, 72), Mohamed Chalal (61), Ray Daher (79); Goals: Hazem El Masri 6
at Stade Jean Laffon, Perpignan

Sunday 14th November, 1999

FRANCE 38 ....**LEBANON 24**
France: Tries: Yacine Dekkiche (6, 22), Fabien Devecchi (16), Jean-Marc Garcia (31), Patrice Benausse (44), Abderazzak Elkahlouki (56); Goals: Yacine Dekkiche 7
Lebanon: Tries: Hazem El Masri (26), Michael Coorey (34, 75), Chris Salem (39); Goals: Hazem El Masri 4
at Stade de Minimes, Toulouse

ITALY 34 ....**MOROCCO 0**
Italy: Tries: David Riolo (13, 38, 44), Simon Margheritini (30), Frank Napoli (63), Brendon Di Paolo (79); Goals: Simon Margheritini 5
at Stade de Minimes, Toulouse

Wednesday 17th November, 1999

FRANCE 10 ....**ITALY 14**
France: Tries: Patrice Benausse (36), Arnaud Dulac (64); Goal: Yacine Dekkiche
Italy: Tries: Daniel Paolini (28), Damien Sonego (51), Simon Margheritini (60); Goal: Mick Salafia
at Parc Des Sports, Avignon

LEBANON 104 ....**MOROCCO 0**
Lebanon: Tries: Chris Salem (4, 10, 46, 52, 77), Hazem El Masri (7, 43, 57, 72), David Lambert (12), Mohammed Chalal (16, 25, 62), Paul Khoury (37), Travis Touma (65), Nadol Saleh (68), Michael Coorey (74), Rabbie Chehade (79); Goals: Hazem El Masri 16
at Parc Des Sports, Avignon

Final Group Standings

	P	W	D	L	F	A	D	PTS
Lebanon	2	2	0	0	140	16	124	4
Italy	2	1	0	1	50	36	14	2
Morocco	2	0	0	2	0	138	-138	0

Coupe de la Mediterranée

	P	W	D	L	F	A	D	PTS
Lebanon	3	2	0	1	164	54	110	4
France	3	2	0	1	128	46	82	4
Italy	3	2	0	1	64	46	18	4
Morocco	3	0	0	3	8	218	-210	0

PACIFIC GROUP

Tuesday 9th November, 1999

UNITED STATES 54 ....**JAPAN 0**
United States: Tries: Chris Craig (2), Bob Balachandran (11), Loren Broussard (13, 68, 76), Shayne Mains (24), Vila Matautia (27), David Niu (38), Cory Sheridan (47), Tony Fabri (54), Joe Faimalo (65); Goals: David Niu 4, David Bowe
at Disney's Wide World of Sports, Orlando

Thursday 11th November, 1999

JAPAN 14 ....**CANADA 0**
Japan: Tries: Jeff Bannister (9), Kyohei Ueda (20), Yusuke Kanemura (69); Goal: Ike Tateyama
at Disney's Wide World of Sports, Orlando

Monday 15th November, 1999

UNITED STATES 68 ....**CANADA 0**
United States: Tries: Tony Fabri (5), Cory Sheridan (17, 36, 41), Loren Broussard (25, 50, 75), Ryan Warren (27, 79), Shayne Mains (38), Vila Matautia (48, 58), Joe Faimalo (63); Goals: David Niu 7, David Bowe
at Disney's Wide World of Sports, Orlando

Final Group Standings

	P	W	D	L	F	A	D	PTS
USA	2	2	0	0	122	0	122	4
Japan	2	1	0	1	14	54	-40	2
Canada	2	0	0	2	0	82	-82	0

FINAL

Sunday 21st November, 1999

UNITED STATES 8 ....**LEBANON 62**
United States: Tries: Shayne Mains; Goals: David Niu 2
Lebanon: Tries: Michael Coorey 3, Paul Khoury 2, Rabbie Chehade, Mohamed Chalal, David Lambert, Travis Touma, Hazem El Masri, Chris Salem; Goals: Hazem El Masri 9
at Disney's Wide World of Sports, Orlando

172

TRIANGULAR TOURNAMENT
The pluck of the Irish

Rugby League's long cherished hope of an annual Five Nations Championship took a step towards reality in October 1999, as Scotland, Ireland and Wales took part in the Lincoln Triangular Series, with the Irish emerging triumphant.

With Great Britain & Ireland on tour down under, and England and France engaged in a two-match international series of their own, the stage was set for any players harbouring hopes of an appearance in the World Cup 2000 proper to stake their claim.

Many seized their chance with both hands, in three games held over three weekends which helped further push back the boundaries of top flight, international Rugby League.

The series began on Friday 15th October at the Vetch Field, Swansea, where a Welsh side which had second rower Richie Eyres sent off in the 10th minute battled well but eventually went down 17-24 to the eventual Champions.

An entertaining, if somewhat scrappy game saw encouraging performances from two of Wigan's ignored potential Lions, Neil Cowie for Wales, and Mick Cassidy for the Irish.

Biggest talking point of the field, though, was the pitifully low crowd of 812. Out came the excuses; we were bang in the middle of the rugby union World Cup, the local union side were playing away that night in a televised match at Neath, to name but two.

A distinct lack of promotion for the competition might well have had more to do with the "frenzy of apathy" in South Wales, as League Express reporter Tony Hannan described it, although those involved were at pains to point out that massive attendances weren't the real aim of the tournament.

WALES 17 ....**IRELAND 24**
Vetch Field, Swansea - Friday 15th October, 1999

WALES: Wes Davies (Wigan Warriors) Jason Lee (Keighley Cougars); Damian Gibson (Halifax Blue Sox); Steve Thomas (Bradford Bulls); Lenny Woodard (Pontypridd RU); Martin Pearson (Sheffield Eagles); Lee Briers (Warrington Wolves); Craig Makin (Salford City Reds); Gareth Price (St Helens); Neil Cowie (Wigan Warriors) (C); Chris Morley (Salford City Reds); Richie Eyres (Swinton Lions); Karle Hammond (London Broncos). *Subs:* Barry Eaton (Dewsbury Rams) for Briers (40); Ian Watson (Swinton Lions) for Price (20); Paul Highton (Salford City Reds) for Morley (20); David Luckwell (Hull Kingston Rovers) for Makin (44).
Price for Cowie (62); Cowie for Luckwell (69); Morley for Highton (46); Highton for Hammond (66); Hammond for Lee (78); Makin for Morley (58); Morley for Makin (71).
Tries: Thomas (19), Gibson (71), Pearson (79); **Goals:** Pearson 2; **Field goal:** Briers

Dismissal: Eyres (10) - high tackle

IRELAND: Steve Prescott (Hull Sharks); Ian Herron (Gateshead Thunder); Richard Smith (Hull Kingston Rovers); Rob Smyth (London Broncos); Mark Forster (Warrington Wolves); Tommy Martyn (St Helens); Martin Crompton (Salford City Reds) (C); Terry O'Connor (Wigan Warriors); Johnny Lawless (Sheffield Eagles); Jamie Mathiou (Leeds Rhinos); Paul Southern (Salford City Reds); Mick Cassidy (Wigan Warriors); Bernard Dwyer (Bradford Bulls). *Subs:* Brian Carney (Gateshead Thunder) for Smith (59); Neil Harmon (Bradford Bulls) for Mathiou (19); Liam Bretherton (Wigan Warriors) for Smyth (71); David Bradbury (Salford City Reds) for Southern (27). Mathiou for O'Connor (52); O'Connor for Harmon (61); Southern for Bradbury (50)
Tries: Cassidy (3), Crompton (27), Martyn (46); **Goals:** Herron 6

League Express Men of the Match -
Wales: Neil Cowie; **Ireland:** Mick Cassidy
Penalties: 10-12; **HT:** 7-14; **Ref:** N Oddy (England); **Att:** 812

173

David Bradbury races away from the Welsh defence

The match, they said, was more about the players, and solid, long term development rather than a one-off exhibition.

"We've got to keep going," said Ireland coach Steve O'Neill. "We can't keep missing a year whatever's going on elsewhere. If our ultimate aim is a Rugby League Five Nations we've got to keep plugging away at it."

Welsh coach Clive Griffiths agreed. "There were a lot more plusses than minuses," he insisted. "There was a lot of pride and passion out there, and lads like Steve Thomas, Gareth Price and Lenny Woodard will have only gained from it."

That faith in the venture was again to be tested the following Friday evening, where 667 people turned up to Glasgow's Firhill to see Scotland compound the Welsh misery by beating them 36-16 and set up a Lincoln Financial Group Triangular Tournament decider in Dublin.

By scoring 20 unopposed points in the last 28 minutes of the game, Shaun McRae's side ensured that they won the first-ever international between the two countries in convincing style. And Dewsbury Rams fullback Nathan Graham, the only player from outside a Super League club in the Scots starting line-up, capped an outstanding display with the man of the match award.

SCOTLAND 36 ....**WALES 16**
Firhill Stadium, Glasgow - Friday 22nd October, 1999

SCOTLAND: Nathan Graham (Dewsbury Rams); Jason Roach (Warrington Wolves); David Maiden (Gateshead Thunder); Andy Craig (Halifax Blue Sox); Danny Arnold (Huddersfield-Sheffield Giants); Matt Crowther (Huddersfield-Sheffield Giants); Scott Rhodes (Leeds Rhinos); Scott Cram (London Broncos); Danny Russell (Huddersfield-Sheffield Giants) (C); Wayne McDonald (Gateshead Thunder); Darren Shaw (Castleford Tigers); Paul Anderson (Huddersfield-Sheffield Giants); Mike Wainwright (Warrington Wolves). *Subs (all used):* Andrew Lambert (Workington Town); John Duffy (Warrington Wolves); Joe Berry (Huddersfield-Sheffield Giants); Neil Lowe (Featherstone Rovers).
Tries: Arnold (9, 78), Russell (29), Lambert (36, 72), Wainwright (52), Crowther (60); **Goals:** Crowther 4

WALES: Wes Davies (Wigan Warriors); Chris Smith (St Helens); Damian Gibson (Halifax Blue Sox); Steve Thomas (Bradford Bulls); Jason Lee (Keighley Cougars); Martin Pearson (Huddersfield-Sheffield Giants); Lee Briers (Warrington Wolves); Craig Makin (Salford City Reds); Ian Watson (Swinton Lions); Neil Cowie (Wigan Warriors) (C); Chris Morley (Salford City Reds); Paul Highton (Salford City Reds); Karle Hammond (London Broncos). *Subs (all used):* Barry Eaton (Dewsbury Rams); Gareth Price (St Helens); Richie Eyres (Swinton Lions); David Luckwell (Hull KR).
Tries: Pearson (21), Cowie (32), Briers (47); **Goals:** Briers 2

League Express Men of the Match -
Scotland: Nathan Graham; **Wales:** Neil Cowie
Penalties: 6-3; **HT:** 16-10; **Ref:** J Connolly (England); **Att:** 667

"We came into the game as underdogs because we hadn't played as a combination before," pointed out McRae. "But I was pleasantly surprised. Our attack was superb at times and I was pleased with our scrambling defence. There wasn't a bad player out there."

"You've got to applaud the Rugby League for trying to encourage the game up here," Scotland manager Shane Richardson continued. "I know from my own experience (at Gateshead) that you have to start from somewhere."

Even fewer fans - a paltry 385 - were at Dublin's Tolka Park nine days later, as the home side saw off a spirited Scotland challenge to win the deciding match 31-10, and lift the Lincoln Financial Triangular Tournament trophy.

On a wild, blustery Halloween afternoon on the Emerald Isle, the two countries - who will next meet in the same World Cup 2000 group - were locked at 10-10 in a fierce competitive encounter. Ireland halfbacks Martin Crompton and Tommy Martyn then seized control, as the home side ran in 21 points without reply in the last 25 minutes.

"We have had two really good weeks and the lads' attitude has been spot on," O'Neill said after the game. "We realise that when we play Scotland in the World Cup it will be a totally different game but it was an important victory for us ahead of that competition."

"Before the tournament many people saw us as the favourites but I couldn't see that," admitted inspirational Ireland skipper Martin Crompton. "All the three sides had a lot of good individuals in their ranks and we knew we were in for two really tough games.

"But we have come a long way in the last five years and now we want to keep up the good work. We have reached the stage in our progress where we are now recognised as a good team and the World Cup in 2000 is now our target."

Scotland coach McRae, meanwhile, called for an increase in international competition after watching his Scotland side finish second.

Joe Berry looks for support as Scotland condemn Wales to the wooden spoon

No way through for Ireland's Steve Prescott against Scotland

"It is absolutely essential that we develop this triangular tournament into a five-nations competition," McRae said. "We won't improve the national side until there is a go-between between Super League and International football. But the question is where you fit the five nations into the schedule.

"I would prefer a time out in the league programme during the season with split rounds, so that we could play international football at that stage and continue our improvement at this level."

IRELAND 31 ....**SCOTLAND 10**

Tolka Park, Dublin - Sunday 31st October, 1999

IRELAND: Steve Prescott (Hull Sharks); Ian Herron (Gateshead Thunder); Richard Smith (Hull Kingston Rovers); Rob Smyth (London Broncos); Mark Forster (Warrington Wolves); Tommy Martyn (St Helens); Martin Crompton (Salford City Reds) (C); Neil Harmon (Bradford Bulls); Johnny Lawless (Sheffield Eagles); Terry O'Connor (Wigan Warriors); Paul Southern (Salford City Reds); Tim Jonkers (St Helens); Mick Cassidy (Wigan Warriors). *Subs (all used):* Brian Carney (Gateshead Thunder); Paul Salmon (Barrow Border Raiders); Liam Bretherton (Wigan Warriors); Garett Molloy (Dublin Blues). **Tries:** Lawless (4), Herron (23), Prescott (55), Carney (65), Forster (70), Smyth (71); **Goals:** Herron, Martyn 2; **Field goal:** Martyn

SCOTLAND: Nathan Graham (Dewsbury Rams); Jason Roach (Warrington Wolves); David Maiden (Gateshead Thunder); Andy Craig (Halifax Blue Sox); Danny Arnold (Huddersfield-Sheffield Giants); Matt Crowther (Huddersfield-Sheffield Giants); Scott Rhodes (Leeds Rhinos); Scott Cram (London Broncos); Danny Russell (Huddersfield-Sheffield Giants) (C); Jon Neill (Huddersfield-Sheffield Giants); Darren Shaw (Castleford Tigers); Wayne McDonald (Gateshead Thunder); Mike Wainwright (Salford City Reds). *Subs (all used):* Andrew Lambert (Workington Town); Paul Anderson (Huddersfield-Sheffield Giants); Joe Berry (Doncaster Dragons); Neil Lowe (Featherstone Rovers). **Tries:** Russell (14), Arnold (47); **Goal:** Crowther

League Express Men of the Match -
Ireland: Martin Crompton; **Scotland:** Danny Russell
Penalties: 4-5; **HT:** 10-6; **Ref:** K Kirkpatrick (England); **Att:** 385

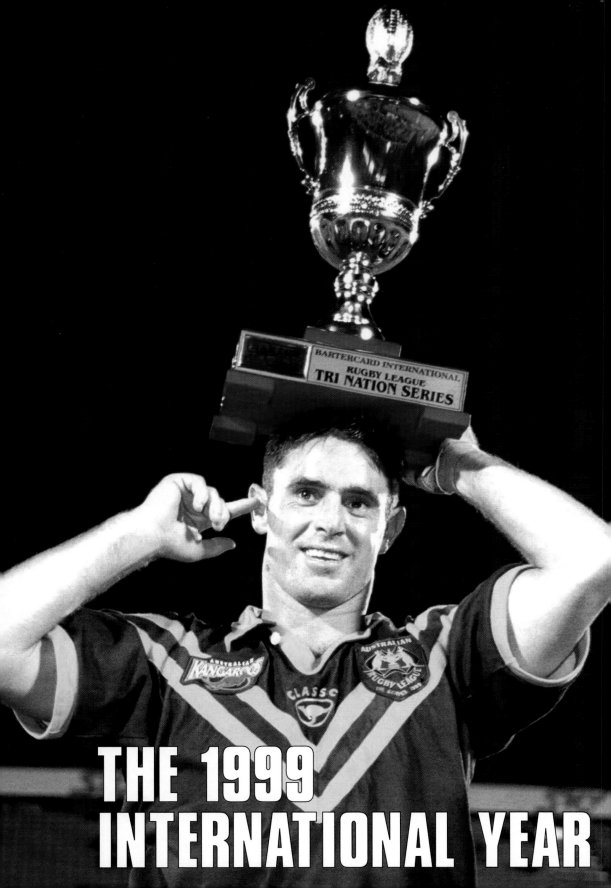

THE 1999
INTERNATIONAL YEAR

NEW ZEALAND 24 AUSTRALIA 22

TOP: Stacey Jones holds off Brett Kimmorley at the Ericsson Stadium in the first game against Australia.
TOP (INSET): Nigel Vagana dives over to give the Kiwis a 20-point lead.
LEFT: Nigel Vagana gets a hold of Darren Smith.

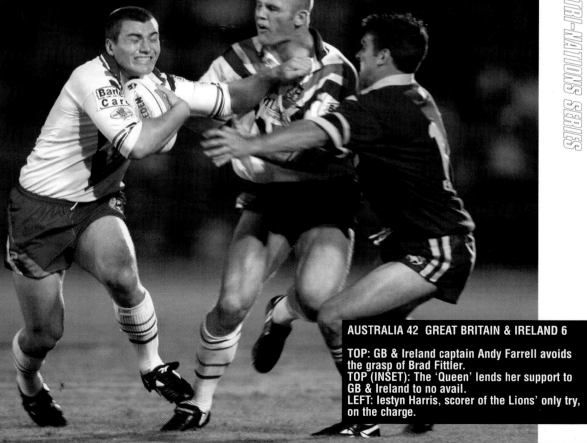

AUSTRALIA 42 GREAT BRITAIN & IRELAND 6

TOP: GB & Ireland captain Andy Farrell avoids the grasp of Brad Fittler.
TOP (INSET): The 'Queen' lends her support to GB & Ireland to no avail.
LEFT: Iestyn Harris, scorer of the Lions' only try, on the charge.

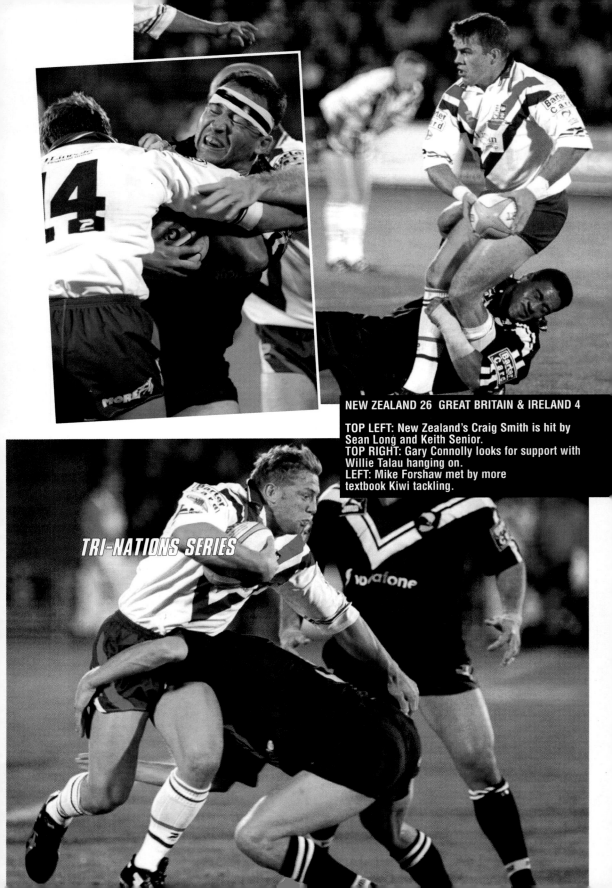

NEW ZEALAND 26 GREAT BRITAIN & IRELAND 4

TOP LEFT: New Zealand's Craig Smith is hit by Sean Long and Keith Senior.
TOP RIGHT: Gary Connolly looks for support with Willie Talau hanging on.
LEFT: Mike Forshaw met by more textbook Kiwi tackling.

TRI-NATIONS SERIES

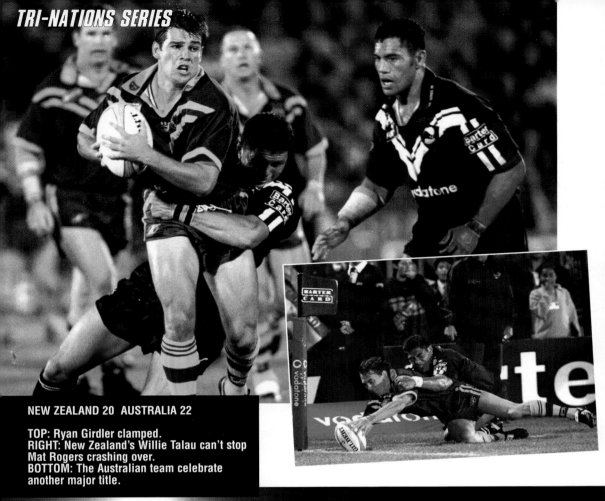

NEW ZEALAND 20 AUSTRALIA 22

TOP: Ryan Girdler clamped.
RIGHT: New Zealand's Willie Talau can't stop Mat Rogers crashing over.
BOTTOM: The Australian team celebrate another major title.

TOP: Gary Connolly in action for Great Britain & Ireland in their warm up match against Queensland Cup champions the Burleigh Bears.
BOTTOM: Barrie McDermott (left) and captain Andy Farrell (right) take it up for Great Britain & Ireland as they take on the New Zealand Maoris.

LEFT: France's Jason Sands gets his collar felt by Terry Newton at the Stade Albert Domec, Carcassonne.
BOTTOM: Danny Orr breaks past Jean-Marc Garcia and Freddie Banquet as England come away with a win.
TOP: England's Leon Pryce looks for support at the Boulevard in the return match against France.

LINCOLN FINANCIAL GROUP INTERNATIONAL CHALLENGE

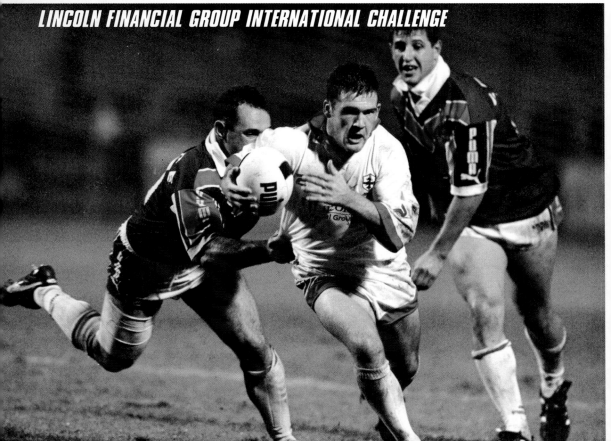

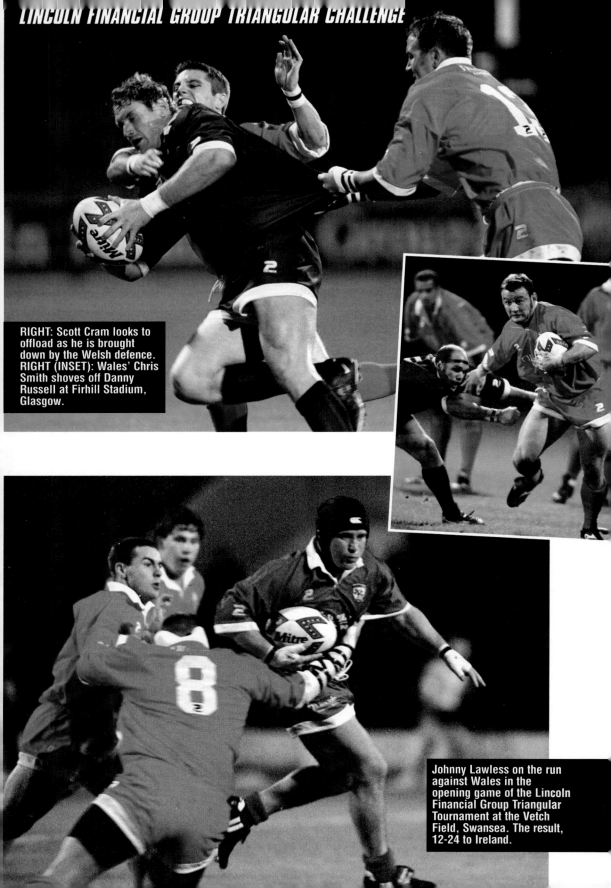

RIGHT: Scott Cram looks to offload as he is brought down by the Welsh defence.
RIGHT (INSET): Wales' Chris Smith shoves off Danny Russell at Firhill Stadium, Glasgow.

Johnny Lawless on the run against Wales in the opening game of the Lincoln Financial Group Triangular Tournament at the Vetch Field, Swansea. The result, 12-24 to Ireland.

ABOVE: Ireland's Johnny Lawless celebrates his try as Ireland overcome Scotland.
BELOW: Terry O'Connor meets the Scots at Tolka Park, Dublin.

LEFT: No way through for Mick Cassidy.

LINCOLN FINANCIAL GROUP TRIANGULAR CHALLENGE

TOP: Lee Hansen is held by the Villeneuve defence.
TOP RIGHT: Villeneuve's David Collado forces his way through.

EMAP EUROPEAN CHALLENGE

LEFT: Gareth Adams in action for the NFP Select XIII against French Champions Villeneuve Leopards at the Auto Quest Stadium, Widnes. Villeneuve overcame the NFP 24-14.

CLOCKWISE FROM TOP LEFT: Japan's Nakashima takes the ball up. Daryl Howland in action for the USA. Canada's Mike Brown is halted. Matthew Tunstall looks for support from his Scottish teammates as they defeat Canada in the Student World Cup Plate Final. New Zealand's Gavin Welsh celebrates winning the World Cup after defeating England.

MEDITERRANEAN CUP

PACIFIC CUP

CLOCKWISE FROM TOP: Action from the Mediterranean Cup in Toulouse as Morocco's Houcine El Bouchti takes on the Italian defence. Lebanon's Anthony Mansour swamped by the French defence. From the Pacific Cup, USA in action against Japan. St Helens' teammates Julian O'Neill and Vila Matautia celebrate USA's victory over Japan.

RIGHT: Henry Paul in magnificent form for New Zealand who lost to Australia 20-14 at Stadium Australia.

RIGHT: Laurie Daley leaves Henry Paul in his wake.
TOP (INSET): New Zealand's Jarrod McCracken and Brad Fittler collide.

CLOCKWISE FROM TOP: Queensland celebrate their series win. Adrian Lam lifts the trophy. Queensland's Shane Webcke is 'tackled'. Tonie Carroll is brought crashing down by the NSW defence. Terry Hill has a minor disagreement with Gorden Tallis!

CLOCKWISE FROM TOP RIGHT:
Cronulla Sharks' Martin Lang is hit by the Sydney City defence. Brisbane Broncos' Tonie Carroll gets airborne, just missing a try. Andrew Frew is halted by a diving challenge during the Manly v Wests game. Canberra's Brett Mullins takes a bomb in the defeat by St George-Illawarra. Parramatta Eels' Jim Dymock wrapped up by the Cronulla Sharks.

CLOCKWISE FROM TOP RIGHT:
Melbourne's Craig Smith is collared by Jamie Ainscough and awarded the match winning penalty try. St George Illawarra's Anthony Mundine is closed down. Melbourne celebrate their 20-18 Grand Final win. Glen Lazarus lifts the trophy and is chaired off by his team mates.

SEASON DOWN UNDER
Storm-ing finish

D-Day, October 15, 1999. The day when the axe was to fall on three of the NRL clubs.

Three of the 17 wouldn't be around to contest the 2000 Premiership.

It had all been part of the peace deal negotiated at the end of the Super League war in December 1997.

The traditionalists believed the NRL would back down. After all, they argued, how could the game's leaders face the inevitable public backlash that would follow the axing of pioneer clubs that had set up the game way back in 1908?

But 1999 was not 1908. And best business practice was all that counted when it came to the cull. Tradition counted for nothing.

So what if South Sydney, the club they dubbed 'The Pride of the League', had won more Premierships (20) than any other side.

Who cared if Wests had provided a record three captains of Kangaroo sides that toured Britain?

And why worry about the Balmain Tigers, once dubbed the Watersiders after the tough dockers who used to live in the suburb, whose coach Wayne Pearce was currently in charge of the NSW State of Origin side?

Some clubs saw the writing on the wall and acted accordingly.

Balmain had contemplated legal action to stop being axed. But lawyers told them they had no hope of winning.

And, after a brief flirtation with Parramatta, the Tigers' chiefs decided on a merger with the Western Suburbs Magpies.

Enter a new side with an assured immediate future - the Wests Tigers.

The rest decided to go it alone.

At least, they did until the North Sydney board found the Bears were so far in debt that they called in a financial administrator. He, in turn, arranged a hasty merger with the Manly Sea Eagles, who were also in dire financial straits. Welcome to another new side, the Northern Eagles.

Souths, meanwhile, stood defiant and on D-Day received the inevitable news - they were the final team to go.

The Rabbitohs did not take it lying down with a crowd of around 20,000 marching in protest through the streets of Sydney.

And, despite the fact that all but five of their senior players had left for a secure future with other clubs, Souths began court action against the NRL and its two owners, News Limited and the ARL.

As the 1990s drew to a close the only winners were the lawyers.

The game's first merger had been an outstanding success.

At the end of 1998, the St George Dragons and the Illawarra Steelers had decided upon a marriage of convenience.

Many believed Illawarra had chosen the short straw.

The jokers reckoned it was only Illawarra's socks that were running around in 1999.

But, after the initial dismay at losing their club, the Illawarra fans were happy enough with their new side - especially when it clawed its way into the Grand Final with victories over the Melbourne Storm, Sydney City Roosters and the Sharks in the finals' series.

Wayne Bartrim, showing a new lease of life, was among the top NRL pointscorers. Livewire Aboriginal winger Nathan Blacklock finished as the top try-scorer with 24 touchdowns.

Prop Craig Smith, one of the quiet achievers of the game, made the Kiwi Test side and established himself as one of the finest front-rowers in the game.

And centre Shaun Timmins, another much underrated player, shocked everyone, including himself, by making the Australian squad for the Tri-Nations Tournament.

The other side in the grand final was the Melbourne Storm.

What a success story that was!

Twelve months earlier in the Storm's debut season they had reached the play-offs - no mean feat in itself.

NRL - FINAL TABLE 1999

	P	W	D	L	B	F	A	PTS
Sharks	24	18	0	6	2	586	332	40
Parramatta Eels	24	17	0	7	2	500	294	38
Melbourne Storm	24	16	0	8	2	639	392	36
Sydney City Roosters	24	16	0	8	2	592	377	36
Canterbury Bulldogs	24	15	1	8	2	520	462	35
St George-Illawarra Dragons	24	15	0	8	2	588	416	34
Newcastle Knights	24	14	1	9	2	575	484	33
Brisbane Broncos	24	13	2	9	2	510	368	32
Canberra Raiders	24	13	1	10	2	618	439	31
Penrith Panthers	24	11	1	12	2	492	428	27
Auckland Warriors	24	10	0	14	2	538	498	24
South Sydney Rabbitohs	24	10	0	14	2	349	556	24
Manly Sea Eagles	24	9	1	14	2	454	623	23
North Sydney Bears	24	8	0	16	2	490	642	20
Balmain Tigers	24	8	0	16	2	345	636	20
North Queensland Cowboys	24	4	1	19	2	398	588	13
Western Suburbs Magpies	24	3	0	21	2	285	944	10

TOP POINTSCORERS 1999

	T	G	FG	PTS
Matt Geyer *(Storm)*	20	81	0	242
Ryan Girdler *(Panthers)*	18	75	3	229
Daryl Halligan *(Bulldogs)*	7	91	0	210
Andrew Johns *(Knights)*	7	76	4	184
Luke Williamson *(Raiders)*	5	74	2	174
Clinton Schifcofske *(Eels)*	9	64	0	164
Wayne Bartrim *(Dragons)*	5	71	0	162
Jason Taylor *(Bears)*	3	72	2	158

TOP TRYSCORERS 1999

Nathan Blacklock *(Dragons)* 24
Matt Geyer *(Storm)* 20
Robbie Ross *(Storm)* 20
Ryan Girdler *(Panthers)* 18
Brett Howland *(Sharks)*..............18
David Peachey *(Sharks)* 18
Rod Silva *(Bulldogs)* 18

DALLY M AWARDS

Player of the Year:
Andrew Johns *(Knights)*
Runner-up:
David Peachey *(Sharks)*
Captain of the Year:
Brad Fittler *(Roosters)*
Coach of the Year:
John Lang *(Sharks)*
Rookie of the Year:
Michael Vella *(Eels)*
Representative Player of the Year:
Mat Rogers *(Sharks)*
Provan-Summons Medal
(People's Choice):
Andrew Johns *(Knights)*

QUEENSLAND CUP GRAND FINAL

BURLEIGH 12 ....REDCLIFFE 10
Burleigh: T - D Anderson, J Mahon;
G - B Lythe 2
Redcliffe: T - T Leis, R Hewinson;
G - T Leis
Ref: T Maksoud At Suncorp Std *(Sept 11)*

This time they excelled themselves after finishing third on the table at the conclusion of the regular competition rounds.

They were thoroughly outplayed by the Dragons in their first finals' appearance but then regrouped and stormed past Canterbury and Parramatta to reach the season's finale.

A new world record crowd for a game of either code of rugby, 107,961, turned up at Stadium Australia to see a team win their first Premiership.

Okay, so the St George half of the Dragons had won 15 Premierships. But this was the newly merged combination.

The Dragons seemed to have the game all wrapped up when they led 14-0 at the break.

And ten minutes into the second half they should have extended that lead to 20-2.

But stand-off Anthony Mundine decided to go for a try himself when he had two teammates unmarked outside him. He lost the ball as he tried to touch down and in doing so lost the Dragons their chance of victory.

For then came what the League Express headline dubbed 'the greatest comeback since Lazarus'.

The pun was well founded even though it was Kiwi loose forward Tawera Nikau and not captain Glenn Lazarus who inspired the fightback by the Storm.

When the Dragons' skipper Paul McGregor scored in the 56th minute, his side looked to be cruising at 18-6.

But within moments, halves Brett Kimmorley and Matt Geyer had found a gap for substitute Ben Roarty to score for Melbourne. Melbourne's Craig Smith added the extras and suddenly there was just a converted try between the two sides.

A penalty goal to Smith narrowed the difference to just four.

Then came the most dramatic end to a grand final in the history of the game.

With six minutes remaining Kimmorley put up a bomb. Smith leaped high and took it cleanly.

As he was coming down, wide out behind the try-line, he was hit high by his opposite number Jamie Ainscough. Smith was knocked unconscious and the ball came loose.

Referee Bill Harrigan asked his colleague in the grandstand, Chris Ward, to check the video and adjudicate on whether there had been foul play that had prevented a try.

The replays left Ward in no doubt.

A penalty try - the first in a grand final since St George's John Bailey was awarded one in the 1977 replay against Parramatta. But that one made no difference to the result.

The penalty try to Smith meant the conversion attempt would be taken from in front of the posts - and it was a mere formality for Geyer to pot the winning goal (Smith was in no condition to attempt a conversion).

The match was a personal triumph for Lazarus, in the last match of his illustrious 16-year career.

He went into the history books as the only player to have won Premierships with three different clubs.

And not only that...with each he had been part of the respective club's first titles.

Canberra in 1989 and 1990, Brisbane in 1992 and 1993 and finally Melbourne in 1999.

Kimmorley won the official Man of the Match award and the Clive Churchill Medal that went with it.

Nikau must have pushed him close for that honour. And the Kiwi had achieved his aim of winning Premierships in his native New Zealand and now Australia and was soon to sign with Warrington in the hope to taste similar success in Britain.

What of the other clubs?

The Sharks, who decided to dispense with the Cronulla part of their name mid-season, had been near the top for the entire season but faltered at the penultimate hurdle.

After leading 8-0 at half-time in their preliminary final they were beaten 24-8 by the Dragons.

They were sunk by the enigmatic stand-off Anthony Mundine who scored a second-half hat-trick of tries for St George-Illawarra.

Parramatta had also wasted a handy first-half lead in their preliminary final clash with the Storm.

The Eels had led 16-6 but ultimately went down 18-16.

The Roosters disappointed in the finals' series once again, with successive losses to the Bulldogs and the Dragons.

As the season ended they were to lose goal-kicking ace Ivan Cleary to the Auckland Warriors and talented fullback Andrew Walker to rugby union and coach Phil Gould decided to call it a day.

The Canterbury Bulldogs couldn't match the wonderful finish that took them to the grand final in 1998. But they were without clever Test hooker Jason Hetherington for the important end-of-season games.

And Newcastle and Brisbane went out in the first week of the play-offs.

For defending Premiers Brisbane it was a near miracle that they even reached the finals.

After ten rounds they were running last - behind even Western Suburbs - with a lone victory against Souths and a draw with North Queensland.

But they then strung together an unbeaten sequence of twelve matches and, although losing to Parramatta in the second last round, scraped into the play-offs.

Once there it became obvious that the long run of sudden-death matches had taken its toll and they were thrashed by the Sharks.

One of the real disappointments was North Sydney.

QUALIFYING QUARTER-FINALS

CANTERBURY BULLDOGS 12
SYDNEY CITY ROOSTERS 8
Bulldogs: T - Bradley Clyde, Willie Talau; G - Daryl Halligan 2
Roosters: T - Ivan Cleary; G - Ivan Cleary 2
HT: 6-8; **Ref:** S Hampstead
Att: 23,417 at SFS *(Sept 3)*

ST G-ILLAWARRA DRAGONS......34
MELBOURNE STORM 10
Dragons: T - Nathan Blacklock 3, Paul McGregor, Rod Wishart, Jamie Ainscough; G - Wayne Bartrim 4, Brad Macka
Storm: T - Aaron Moule, Stephen Kearney; G - Matt Geyer
HT: 10-4; **Ref:** B Harrigan
Att: 15,653 at Olympic Park *(Sept 4)*

PARRAMATTA EELS 30
NEWCASTLE KNIGHTS 16
Eels: T - Clinton Schifcofske, Jason Smith, Nathan Cayless, Eric Grothe; G - Clinton Schifcofske 7
Knights: T - Tony Butterfield, Matthew Gidley, Darren Albert; G - Andrew Johns 2
HT: 14-10; **Ref:** S Clark
Att: 22,053 at P'matta Std *(Sept 4)*

SHARKS 42
BRISBANE BRONCOS.................20
Sharks: T - Mat Rogers 2, Adam Dykes 2, Andrew Ettingshausen, David Peachey, Brett Howland; G - Mat Rogers 7
Broncos: T - Kevin Walters, Darren Lockyer; G - Ben Walker 6
HT: 16-2; **Ref:** T Mander
Att: 17,713 at Shark Park *(Sept 5)*

SEMI-FINALS

ST G-ILLAWARRA DRAGONS......28
SYDNEY CITY ROOSTERS 18
Dragons: T - Anthony Mundine, Brad Mackay, Wayne Bartrim, Rod Wishart, Nathan Brown; G - Wayne Bartrim 3, Craig Fitzgibbon
Roosters: T - Brad Fittler 2, Ivan Cleary; G - Ivan Cleary 3
HT: 12-12; **Ref:** B Harrigan
Att: 31,506 at SFS *(Sept 11)*

MELBOURNE STORM 24
CANTERBURY BULLDOGS 22
Storm: T - Matt Geyer 2, Marcus Bai, Robbie Ross; G - Craig Smith 4
Bulldogs: T - Rod Silva, Hazem El Masri, Steven Hughes, Brent Sherwin; G - Daryl Halligan 3
HT: 18-12; **Ref:** S Clark
Att: 20,075 at SFS *(Sept 12)*

PRELIMINARY FINALS

MELBOURNE STORM 18
PARRAMATTA EELS 16
Storm: T - Brett Kimmorley, Aaron Moule, Richard Swain; G - Craig Smith 3
Eels: Daniel Wagon, Stuart Kelly; G - Clinton Schifcofske 4
HT: 16-6; **Ref:** B Harrigan
Att: 27,555 at SFS *(Sept 18)*

ST G-ILLAWARRA DRAGONS......24
SHARKS 8
Dragons: T - Anthony Mundine 3, Luke Patten; G - Wayne Bartrim 4
Sharks: T - David Peachey; G - Mitch Healey, Mat Rogers
HT: 0-8; **Ref:** S Clark
Att: 51,637 at Std Australia *(Sept 19)*

Melbourne's Kiwi contingent celebrate the Storm's success with the haka

You would never have realised they were fighting for their very existence, slumping from the top five in 1998 to 14th of the 17 clubs.

Their 1999 efforts included a losing sequence of eight straight games and another of six on the trot as the players plotted the downfall of coach Peter Louis instead of concentrating on their on-field task.

Twice they had more than a half-century of points scored against them.

They were disadvantaged by the fact that their new home ground, Grahame Park on the Central Coast, was not finished.

But there was little pride from players in a club that was one of the pioneers.

Wests' players should have also hung their heads in shame.

The once proud club had a Premiership record of 944 points scored against it - an average of 39 per game.

The Magpies finished their last year as a single entity with an inglorious run of twelve straight losses including a 60-16 hammering in their final appearance.

It was a sad finish to the coaching career of one of the greats of the game - Tom Raudonikis.

NRL GRAND FINAL

MELBOURNE STORM 20.......ST GEORGE-ILLAWARRA DRAGONS 18
Stadium Australia - Sunday 26th September, 1999

STORM: Robbie Ross; Craig Smith; Aaron Moule; Tony Martin; Marcus Bai; Matt Geyer; Brett Kimmorley; Tawera Nikau; Paul Marquet; Stephen Kearney; Glenn Lazarus; Richard Swain; Rodney Howe. *Interchange:* Matt Rua; Danny Williams; Russell Bawden; Ben Roarty.
Tries: Martin, Roarty, Smith (penalty try); **Goals:** Smith 3, Geyer

DRAGONS: Luke Patten; Nathan Blacklock; Paul McGregor; Shaun Timmins; Jamie Ainscough; Anthony Mundine; Trent Barrett; Wayne Bartrim; Darren Treacy; Lance Thompson; Chris Leikvoll; Nathan Brown; Craig Smith. *Interchange:* Craig Fitzgibbon, Colin Ward, Brad Mackay, Rod Wishart.
Tries: Fitzgibbon, Blacklock, McGregor; **Goals:** Bartrim 2, Fitzgibbon

Ref: B Harrigan; **Video ref:** C Ward
HT: 0-14; **Att:** 107,961 *(World record)*
Clive Churchill Medal (Man of the Match): Brett Kimmorley *(Storm)*

Season Down Under

The State of Origin series was one of the closest in the 20-year history of the interstate clashes.

And for the first time the series was shared. Queensland won the first clash by just one point, NSW the second by four and what should have been the decider was a 10-all draw.

After the split series, there were calls for a sudden-death finish to the third encounters if the result of the series hinged on the result, but the officials decided to continue with the status quo.

Mat Rogers set something of a record by scoring all of Queensland's points in the first two matches. But a cruciate injury that plagued him in Origin I and saw him leave the field at half-time and not return in Origin II prevented him from trying for a similar feat in the third game.

He kicked four goals and a field goal as the Maroons scraped home 9-8 in the first match, at Suncorp Stadium.

Rogers booted the match-winner with six minutes to go and attempts by NSW captain Brad Fittler and scrum-half Andrew Johns to match his effort failed to find the posts.

The pre-match headlines largely centred on a botched bonding session aimed at lifting the team morale of the Blues. Coach Wayne Pearce had taken them horse riding in the Blue Mountains, west of Sydney.

When some of the horses took fright, two players, Bradley Clyde and Robbie Kearns were thrown. Kearns was to miss most of the rest of the season with a broken collarbone.

STATE OF ORIGIN SERIES

ORIGIN I

QUEENSLAND 9
NSW 6
Qld: G - Mat Rogers 4;
FG - Mat Rogers
NSW: T - Anthony Mundine;
G - Ryan Girdler

Queensland: Robbie O'Davis (Newcastle), Mat Rogers (Sharks), Matt Sing (Sydney City), Darren Smith (Canterbury), Wendell Sailor (Brisbane), Kevin Walters (Brisbane), Adrian Lam (Sydney City) (c), Shane Webcke (Brisbane), Jason Hetherington (Canterbury), Craig Greenhill (Penrith), Gorden Tallis (Brisbane), Chris McKenna (Sharks), Jason Smith (Parramatta). *Interchange:* Ben Ikin (North Sydney), Steve Price (Canterbury), Tonie Carroll (Brisbane), Martin Lang (Sharks). **Coach:** Mark Murray

NSW: Robbie Ross (Melbourne), Darren Albert (Newcastle), Terry Hill (Manly), Laurie Daley (Canberra), Matt Geyer (Melbourne), Brad Fittler (Sydney City) (c), Andrew Johns (Newcastle), Jason Stevens (Sharks), Craig Gower (Penrith), Rodney Howe (Melbourne), Bryan Fletcher (Sydney City), David Barnhill (Sydney City), Nik Kosef (Manly). *Interchange:* Ryan Girdler (Penrith), Luke Ricketson (Sydney City), Glenn Lazarus (Melbourne), Anthony Mundine (SG-Illawarra). **Coach:** Wayne Pearce

Ref: B Harrigan; **HT:** 4-6
Man of the Match:
Jason Hetherington (Qld)
Att: 38,093 at Suncorp Std *(May 26)*

Robbie Kearns (Melbourne) and Bradley Clyde (Canterbury) were both chosen for NSW but were injured in a team 'bonding' session. They were replaced by Lazarus and Ricketson.

ORIGIN II

NEW SOUTH WALES 12
QUEENSLAND 8
NSW: T - Robbie Ross, Laurie Daley;
G - Ryan Girdler 2
Qld: T - Mat Rogers; G - Mat Rogers 2

NSW: Robbie Ross (Melbourne), Matt Geyer (Melbourne), Ryan Girdler (Penrith), Terry Hill (Manly), Adam MacDougall (Newcastle), Laurie Daley (Canberra), Andrew Johns (Newcastle), Mark Carroll (Souths), Geoff Toovey (Manly), Rodney Howe (Melbourne), Nik Kosef (Manly), Bryan Fletcher (Sydney City), Brad Fittler (Sydney City) (c). *Interchange:* Luke Ricketson (Sydney City), Michael Vella (Parramatta), Ben Kennedy (Canberra), Anthony Mundine (SG- Illawarra)

Queensland: Robbie O'Davis (Newcastle), Mat Rogers (Sharks), Matt Sing (Sydney City), Darren Smith (Canterbury), Wendell Sailor (Brisbane), Kevin Walters (Brisbane)

(c), Paul Green (North Qld), Shane Webcke (Brisbane), Jason Hetherington (Canterbury), Craig Greenhill (Penrith), Gorden Tallis (Brisbane), Chris McKenna (Sharks), Jason Smith (Parramatta). *Interchange:* Ben Ikin (North Sydney), Steve Price (Canterbury), Tonie Carroll (Brisbane), Martin Lang (Sharks).

Ref: S Clark; **HT:** 12-8
Man of the Match: Laurie Daley (NSW)
Att: 88,336 *(Origin record)*
at Stadium Australia *(June 9)*

David Barnhill (Sydney City) was chosen but failed a fitness test. His replacement, Bradley Clyde (Canterbury), also failed his fitness test and was replaced by Kennedy.

ORIGIN III

QUEENSLAND 10
NSW 10
Qld: T - Paul Green, Darren Lockyer;
G -Darren Lockyer
NSW: T - Matt Geyer 2;
G - Ryan Girdler

Queensland: Darren Lockyer (Brisbane), Robbie O'Davis (Newcastle), Tonie Carroll (Brisbane), Darren Smith (Canterbury), Wendell Sailor (Brisbane), Ben Ikin (North Sydney), Adrian Lam (Sydney City) (c), Shane Webcke (Brisbane), Jason Hetherington (Canterbury), Craig Greenhill (Penrith), Gorden Tallis (Brisbane), Chris McKenna (Penrith), Jason Smith (Parramatta). *Interchange:* Steve Price (Canterbury), Brad Thorn (Brisbane), Martin Lang (Sharks), Paul Green (North Qld).

NSW: Robbie Ross (Melbourne), Adam MacDougall (Newcastle), Ryan Girdler (Penrith), Terry Hill (Manly), Matt Geyer (Melbourne), Laurie Daley (Canberra) (c), Andrew Johns (Newcastle), Mark Carroll (South Sydney), Geoff Toovey (Manly), Rodney Howe (Melbourne), Bryan Fletcher (Sydney City), David Furner (Canberra), Nik Kosef (Manly). *Interchange:* Luke Ricketson (Sydney City), Michael Vella (Parramatta), Ben Kennedy (Canberra), Anthony Mundine (SG-Illawarra).

Ref: S Clark; **HT:** 6-6
Man of the Match:
Wendell Sailor (Qld)
Att: 37,500 at Suncorp Std *(June 23)*

Brad Fittler and Matt Sing (both Sydney City), who played in the first two Origin encounters, were not considered for their respective teams because of injury. David Barnhill (Sydney City) was chosen for NSW but suspended by the judiciary and replaced by Furner. Kevin Walters (Brisbane) was chosen for Queensland but withdrew through injury. Ikin came off the bench as his replacement and Green was added to the squad.

ORIGIN SERIES DRAWN

Clyde, who had gained a new lease of life after switching from Canberra to Canterbury, missed the whole Origin series with a shoulder injury, the result of him being dragged 20 metres along the ground.

Origin II was the first played at the new Olympic stadium in Sydney and predictably drew a record inter-state attendance.

Some 88,336 packed into the arena as Laurie Daley, in his last Origin match before a home crowd, turned back the clock with a display that inspired his fellow New South Welshmen to a narrow 12-8 victory.

Had the weather not been so shocking - torrential rain all day and during the match - the world record crowd set at the NRL opening round double-header might have been beaten.

But the weather didn't stop Daley.

Said coach Pearce: "Before the match if you had to choose the bloke who was going to be the outstanding player it was Laurie. There was no way he wasn't going to come off the field as one of the best."

There was another almost certain record.

Almost from the kick-off Daley speared a wonderful pass to centre Ryan Girdler, who raced 40 metres to set up fullback Robbie Ross for a NSW try.

As Ross touched down, the Stadium clock clicked on to 40 seconds.

There are no official records, but historians are pretty certain that it is the fastest Origin touchdown in history.

As well as setting up the Ross try, Daley scored one himself just before half-time and made a remarkable 30 tackles. Man of the Match? You betcha!

And a typical Daley response after the match when he thought only of his teammates: "I'm so happy we've had a win. It's bloody beautiful."

"You can't beat class - and this man has it," was the way former Queensland captain Paul Vautin summed up Daley's display.

It was atrocious conditions yet again for Origin III with rain bucketing down on Suncorp Stadium.

But the excitement was still very evident as the two sides fought out the first draw in Origin history.

There was a pre-match furore when Sydney City claimed their star scrum-half Adrian Lam was injured and unable to play but the Queensland doctor ruled him fit.

Angry Roosters' officials took the legal step of advising Lam in writing that if his injured shoulder was damaged further he would lose a percentage of his contract money - between $15,000 and $20,000 - for every missed match.

The big NSW forwards targeted Lam's shoulder, but to no avail.

Despite the match finishing in a draw, the Maroons were the better side.

Wendell Sailor was the official Man of the Match, but fellow Queenslanders Gorden Tallis and Jason Smith must have pushed him close for that honour.

The shared series set everyone wondering.

The Queenslanders claimed that because they held the Origin trophy they had remained champions.

Daley, in his final series, would beg to differ.

But as Total Rugby League noted in its match report: "In the words of the cliché - Rugby League was the winner."

It was a pity the same could not be said for the off-field machinations in 1999!

INTERNATIONAL ROUND-UP

It was a busy year, eventually, for international Rugby League as the build-up to the 2000 World Cup got under way.

It wasn't until June that the first signs of representative football sprung into life in the Papua New Guinean town of Lae, as the locals went down 22-18 to the New Zealand Maoris in the first of three matches, before a crowd almost 6,000.

The Maoris sneaked home in the second encounter 28-24 in Wabag, witnessed by more than 8,000 spectators. But PNG regained some pride with a crushing 38-10 win in Port Moresby, though the series was dealt a cruel blow when one of the PNG players, Willie Gabriel was killed in a plane crash while returning home early because of a broken hand.

American champions Glen Mills toured Australia for a three-match tour in July, beating the NSW Police 30-28 before going down 28-22 to Bondi United and 40-32 to an Aboriginal Selection.

Fiji beat Samoa 3-0 in the series held in Fiji. The home side edged out the Samoans 10-6 and 22-16 in the opening two encounters before the visitors relaxed for the final match which Fiji won easily 30-4 at the National Stadium in Suva before 3,200 onlookers.

Bowed out - Cliff Lyons

Tonga also emerged victorious in their series against the Cook Islands in Rarotonga. More than 1,500 turned up for the opening clash in which Tonga unleashed powerful attacking raids to crush the home nation 42-4. The visitors won the next two 28-12 and 34-4, with all three clashes held at the Tereora National Stadium.

Lebanon got ready for the World Cup play-offs with a 26-4 win over a French Invitational XIII that featured Paul Sironen as captain and rugby union international Jason Madz at five-eighth in his first ever game of Rugby League. The game was played as a curtain-raiser to the Canterbury-Balmain NRL match at Stadium Australia in front of a crowd of 21,031.

The Italians prepared by travelling to the New South Wales country town of Griffith to take on a Riverina Selection. Italy won 32-0 in a match played in atrocious conditions. The town was hit by torrential rain on the day of the game restricting a predicted crowd of 5,000 to only 500. Former Australian international and current coach of the Italians, Craig Salvatori, pulled on his boots to play the final ten minutes of the game.

During the Tri-Nations series, New Zealand also hosted Tonga and gave the neighbours a lesson and a half when they thrashed them 74-0 at Carlaw Park in a victory that was overshadowed by the injury to magical Kiwi halfback and playmaker Stacey Jones.

The Australian Aborigines hosted Papua New Guinea to a two-match international series in October with the Aborigines thrashing the visitors 58-12 at Campbelltown Stadium, with Manly's Albert Torrens scoring a hat-trick of tries. The second encounter was staged at Cairns' Barlow Park in North Queensland before a decent turnout of more than 3,000. PNG performed a touch better but still went down 32-10 in a game that was Cliff Lyons final match - yet again - before retiring for good.

INTERNATIONAL RESULTS

FRANCE

CHAMPIONNAT DE FRANCE
(for the Max Roussie Trophee)
FINAL

VILLENEUVE LEOPARDS 33
SAINT-GAUDENS 20
Villeneuve: T - Sebastien Gauffre, Laurent Frayssinous, Freddy Banquet, David Collado, Michael Van Snick, Julien Rinaldi; G - Freddy Banquet; FG - Julien Rinaldi
Saint-Gaudens: T - Jean-Christophe Borlin 2, Stephane Millet; G - Stephane Millet 4
HT: 16-6; **Ref:** C Alba
Att: 7,592 at Stade Charlety, Paris *(May 22)*

COUPE DE FRANCE
(for the Lord Derby Trophee)
FINAL

VILLENEUVE LEOPARDS 20
LEZIGNAN 5
Villeneuve: T - Gilles Cornut 2, Stephen Plath, Vincent Wulf; G - Freddy Banquet, Laurent Frayssinous
Lezignan: T - Jerome Sarda; FG - Didier Foulquier
HT: 6-1; **Ref:** M Alibert; **Att:** 10,000 at Stade L'Egassirial, Narbonne *(May 30)*

PLAYER OF THE YEAR
Pascal Jampy (XIII Catalan)
Runners-up: Gilles Cornut (Villeneuve) & Stephane Millet (Saint-Gaudens)

NEW ZEALAND

NATIONAL PROVINCIAL CUP FINAL

AUCKLAND SOUTH..................................24
AUCKLAND NORTH.................................22
South: T - Adrian Smith 2, Eddie Toby, Te Rangi; G - Daniel Mildenhall 4
North: T - Peter Lewis, Alan Lid, Richard White, Harry Kapi; G - Peter Lewis 3
HT: 12-10 ....At Carlaw Park *(October 10)*

AUCKLAND PREMIERSHIP *(Fox Memorial)*
GRAND FINAL

GLENORA BEARS 24
OTAHUHU LEOPARDS 4
Glenora: T - Shannon Lee, Aaron Tucker, Ben Valeni, Greg Ashby; G - Steve Buckingham 4
Otahuhu: T - Bryan Henare
At Carlaw Park (September 19)

CANTERBURY PREMIERSHIP
(Pat Smith Trophy)
GRAND FINAL

HALSWELL 30
HORNBY 12
Halswell: T - Lusi Sione2, Malcolm Aldridge, Benton Parata, Bryan Reeves, Mike Dorreen; G - Kauiri Pirika 2, Aaron Whittaker
Hornby: T - Jermaine MacDonald, Clayton Harris; G - Scott Codyre 2
At Hornby Rugby League Park

PAPUA NEW GUINEA

SP INTERCITY CUP GRAND FINAL

GOROKA LAHINIS....................................26
ISLAND GURIAS 0
Goroka: T - Lawrence Goive, Fatty Buka, Kenneth Livayong, Martin Wilson, Nima Kapo; G - Winnis Moihae 3
HT: 10-0; **Ref:** Sari Fareho; **Att:** 8,500 at Lloyd Robson Oval, Port Moresby *(August 8)*

CAMBRIDGE CUP *(Knockout comp involving Premiers of PNG's 21 Leagues)*
FINAL

MT HAGEN RAIDERS 16
PORT MORESBY SOUTHS 12
Raiders: T - Kuli Jacob 2, Steven Pungium, Robert Benny
Souths: T - Luke Minjuku, Robert Tende; G - Roy Amburi 2
HT: 12-6; **Ref:** Luxie Meta; **Att:** 5,000 at Sir Danny Leahy Oval, Goroka *(October 24)*

FIJI

FIJIAN PREMIERSHIP GRAND FINAL

NAUSORI BULLDOGS...............................16
NADERA PANTHERS 4
Nausori: T - Apilmelieki Katonibau, Ilikana Bicinavlu; G - Marika Waqa 4
Nadera: T - Lepani Soro
At Churchill Park, Lautoka (September 4)

SAMOA

SAMOAN PREMIERSHIP FINAL

MATAFALA TUNAULA BOYS 18
SAAGA 4

APIA PREMIERSHIP FINAL TABLE
MARIST 10, Falefa 7, Apia 4, Vaimoso 3
(No finals series)

(Apia clubs did not compete in Samoan Premiership because they were considered too strong for those in other Leagues)

TONGA

TONGAN PREMIERSHIP GRAND FINAL

HOUMA TIGERS d HA'ATEIHO CRUSADERS
(on forfeit - Crusaders refused to play after their second division side was disqualified for fielding a first division player in finals' series)

COOK ISLANDS

RED LION CUP GRAND FINAL

AVIATIU EELS 26
ARORANGI BEARS 25

4
STATISTICAL REVIEW

Paul Deacon

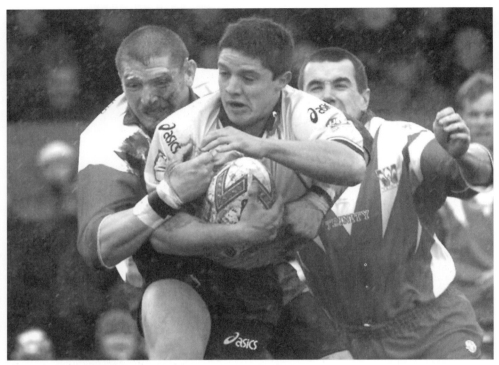

SEASON'S HIGH POINT:
Going through the season unbeaten at home was one of our targets back in March, so we have to be pleased with that.

SEASON'S LOW POINT:
I don't think there can be any doubt when that was. It has to be losing the Grand Final when we could have won it. I still can't bring myself to watch the video of the game.

MOST IMPRESSIVE TEAMMATE:
I'd have to say there are probably two. Firstly Mick Withers. When he came here he was a virtual unknown and he has been a revelation. And Scott Naylor has been a model of consistency all year.

MOST IMPRESSIVE OPPONENT:
A tough one but I would have to say Adrian Vowles. He was chosen the Man of Steel and I don't think anybody would argue with that. His 100% efforts seemed to lift Castleford all season.

HOPES FOR 2000:
We have to aim high and aim to win both prizes after having gone so close last season - the Challenge Cup and the Championship.

204

BRADFORD BULLS

DATE	FIXTURE	RESULT	SCORERS	LGE	ATT
14/2/99	Workington (h) (CCR4)	W92-0	t:Withers(4),McAvoy(4),Zisti(2),Lowes(2),McDermott,R Paul,Deacon, Fielden,Vaikona g:Deacon(12)	N/A	7,593
28/2/99	Wakefield (a) (CCR5)	W8-26	t:H Paul,Fielden,McNamara,Lowes g:Deacon(3),McNamara(2)	N/A	7,385
7/3/99	Sheffield (h)	W18-6	t:Lowes,McAvoy,Withers g:H Paul(3)	N/A	12,044
14/3/99	Warrington (h) (CCQF)	W52-16	t:Vaikona(4),Boyle,Forshaw,Naylor,R Paul,Withers,Spruce g:H Paul(6)	N/A	10,430
21/3/99	Hull (a)	W3-8	t:McAvoy g:McNamara(2)	3rd	6,577
28/3/99	Leeds (CCSF)	L10-23	t:Boyle,Lowes g:H Paul	N/A	23,438
1/4/99	Leeds (h)	W18-14	t:Forshaw,H Paul,R Paul g:H Paul(2),McNamara	2nd	16,049
5/4/99	St Helens (a)	L58-14	t:Dwyer,Harmon g:Deacon(3)	5th	15,042
11/4/99	Wakefield (h)	W26-16	t:Naylor,D Peacock,Boyle,Lowes g:McNamara(5)	5th	11,802
18/4/99	Warrington (a)	W14-22	t:Spruce,Withers,Naylor,Boyle g:H Paul(3)	2nd	7,591
23/4/99	Halifax (h)	W20-2	t:Vaikona,Withers,Fielden,McAvoy g:McNamara(2)	2nd	11,103
3/5/99	Castleford (a)	D18-18	t:McNamara,R Paul g:McNamara(5)	2nd	10,122
9/5/99	Salford (h)	W46-6	t:Spruce(2),McAvoy,McNamara,R Paul,Pryce,Jowitt,McDermott g:McNamara(4),Deacon(3)	2nd	11,863
16/5/99	Gateshead (a)	W12-22	t:H Paul,Jowitt,Pryce g:Deacon(2),H Paul(2),McNamara	2nd	6,631
22/5/99	Wigan (a)	W19-2	t:Withers,R Paul g:Deacon(4),McNamara fg:Deacon	2nd	13,476
30/5/99	Huddersfield (h)	W22-20	t:Fielden,Lowes,Pryce,Spruce g:Deacon(3)	2nd	11,032
5/6/99	Sheffield (a)	W2-52	t:Spruce(2),Boyle,J Peacock,McAvoy,Pryce,R Paul,Lowes,McDermott g:Deacon(3),H Paul(3),McNamara(2)	2nd	4,801
9/6/99	London (h)	W74-12	t:Forshaw(3),Spruce(2),J Peacock(2),R Paul,Fielden,McAvoy,Deacon, Withers,Naylor g:Deacon(6),H Paul(5)	2nd	9,575
13/6/99	Hull (h)	W42-14	t:McAvoy(4),R Paul(2),Fielden g:McNamara(5),Deacon(2)	1st	11,757
18/6/99	Leeds (a)	L45-16	t:H Paul(2),Boyle g:McNamara,H Paul	1st	21,666
25/6/99	St Helens (h)	W46-22	t:Pryce(2),Lowes(2),Spruce,Forshaw,H Paul,Naylor,McAvoy g:Deacon(3),McNamara(2)	1st	15,107
2/7/99	Wakefield (a)	W8-36	t:Lowes(2),J Peacock,Donougher,Boyle,Howlett g:McNamara(5),Deacon	1st	5,321
7/7/99	Huddersfield (a)	W0-26	t:Lowes,McNamara,Withers,Naylor g:McNamara(5)	1st	6,581
11/7/99	Warrington (h)	W56-6	t:McDermott(3),Pryce(2),Jowitt,Anderson,Spruce,Lowes g:McNamara(10)	1st	13,063
18/7/99	Halifax (a)	W20-34	t:Vaikona(2),Lowes(2),Spruce,Fielden g:McNamara(5)	1st	9,342
25/7/99	Castleford (h)	W24-22	t:McAvoy,Spruce,H Paul,Lowes g:McNamara(4)	1st	13,824
28/7/99	London (a)	W16-19	t:Boyle,Withers,McAvoy g:McNamara(3) fg:McNamara	1st	8,233
1/8/99	Salford (a)	W20-58	t:Withers(2),Spruce(2),J Peacock(2),Boyle,H Paul,Howlett,McNamara, McAvoy g:McNamara(6),Deacon	1st	6,680
8/8/99	Gateshead (h)	W30-14	t:Boyle(2),Pryce(2),Withers,Lowes g:H Paul(2),McNamara	1st	12,492
13/8/99	Wigan (a)	L14-0	No Scorers	1st	10,734
22/8/99	Sheffield (h)	W52-4	t:Vaikona(2),Naylor,McDermott,Forshaw,H Paul,Donougher,Anderson, Withers g:McNamara(8)	1st	11,029
29/8/99	Hull (a)	W12-44	t:Withers(4),Pryce(2),Vaikona,Boyle g:McNamara(5),Deacon	1st	5,031
3/9/99	Leeds (h)	W19-18	t:Pryce,McAvoy,Vaikona g:McNamara(3) fg:Withers	1st	24,020
10/9/99	St Helens (a)	L25-16	t:McNamara,R Paul,Fielden g:McNamara(2)	1st	8,490
26/9/99	St Helens (h) (QSF)	W40-4	t:H Paul(2),Fielden,Naylor,Withers,Vaikona g:McNamara(7),Deacon	N/A	16,126
9/10/99	St Helens (GFN)	L6-8	t:H Paul g:H Paul	N/A	50,717

	APP		TRIES		GOALS		FG		PTS	
	ALL	SL	ALL	SL	ALL	SL	ALL	SL	ALL	SL
Paul Anderson	24(5)	24(3)	2	2	0	0	0	0	8	8
David Boyle	27(3)	24(3)	12	10	0	0	0	0	48	40
Paul Deacon	16(14)	14(14)	2	1	48	33	1	1	105	71
Jeremy Donougher	3(15)	3(11)	2	2	0	0	0	0	8	8
Bernard Dwyer	20(3)	17(3)	1	1	0	0	0	0	4	4
Stuart Fielden	18(14)	14(14)	9	7	0	0	0	0	36	28
Mike Forshaw	24(3)	22(2)	7	6	0	0	0	0	28	24
Neil Harmon	5(14)	5(12)	1	1	0	0	0	0	4	4
Phil Howlett	5(1)	5(1)	2	2	0	0	0	0	8	8
Warren Jowitt	11(18)	10(16)	3	3	0	0	0	0	12	12
James Lowes	34	30	18	14	0	0	0	0	72	56
Nathan McAvoy	25(3)	23(2)	19	15	0	0	0	0	76	60
Brian McDermott	26(9)	22(9)	7	6	0	0	0	0	28	24
Steve McNamara	27(3)	25(3)	6	5	97	95	1	1	219	211
Scott Naylor	30(1)	26(1)	8	7	0	0	0	0	32	28
Henry Paul	31(2)	27(2)	12	11	29	22	0	0	106	88
Robbie Paul	23(1)	20(1)	11	9	0	0	0	0	44	36
Danny Peacock	10(1)	7(1)	1	1	0	0	0	0	4	4
Jamie Peacock	2(16)	2(16)	6	6	0	0	0	0	24	24
Leon Pryce	23(4)	23(4)	13	13	0	0	0	0	52	52
Lee Radford	1(4)	1(3)	0	0	0	0	0	0	0	0
Stuart Spruce	25(2)	23(1)	15	14	0	0	0	0	60	56
Paul Sykes	3(1)	3(1)	0	0	0	0	0	0	0	0
Tevita Vaikona	22	18	13	8	0	0	0	0	52	32
Michael Withers	26(3)	22(3)	21	16	0	0	1	1	85	65
Nick Zisti	7(3)	6(1)	2	0	0	0	0	0	8	0

LEAGUE RECORD
P30-W25-D1-L4
(1st, SL/Grand Final Runners Up)
F897, A445, Diff+452
51 points.

CHALLENGE CUP
Semi Finalists

ATTENDANCES
Best - v Leeds (SL - 24,020)
Worst - v Workington (CC - 7,593)
Total (SL, inc play-offs) - 214,362
Average (SL, inc play-offs) - 13,398
(Up by 372 on 1998)

MOST TACKLES
James Lowes 803

MOST CLEAN BREAKS
Michael Withers 29

MOST METRES GAINED
Brian McDermott 3306

Dean Sampson

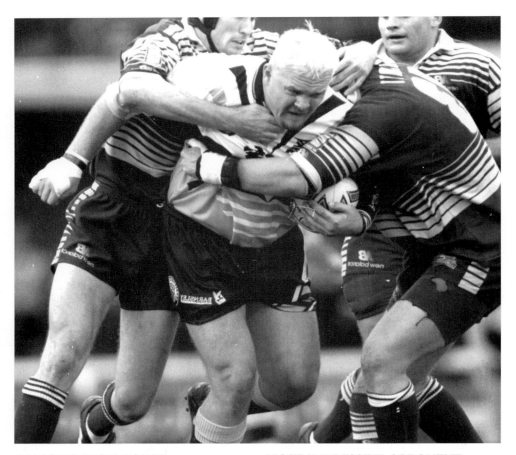

SEASON'S HIGH POINT:
Winning at Wigan in the first play-off game. It was the third time we had beaten Wigan in the season and made us all realise just how far we can really go.

SEASON'S LOW POINT:
The Challenge Cup semi-final defeat by London. We were ten minutes away from Wembley.

MOST IMPRESSIVE TEAMMATE:
For sheer doggedness and leadership it has to be Adrian Vowles.

MOST IMPRESSIVE OPPONENT:
I wasn't convinced at the start of the season but by the time I played with him for England at the end of the year I certainly was - Leon Pryce, he could be anything.

HOPES FOR 2000:
Ten minutes from Wembley, 40 minutes from the Grand Final. We have just got to better that.

CASTLEFORD TIGERS

DATE	FIXTURE	RESULT	SCORERS	LGE	ATT
14/2/99	Hull (h) (CCR4)	W36-22	t:Davis(2),Flowers(2),Orr,Rogers,Gay g:Tonks(4)	N/A	6,107
26/2/99	York (h) (CCR5)	W28-2	t:Davis,Eagar,Maloney,Harland g:Orr(6)	N/A	5,411
7/3/99	Wakefield (h)	W12-10	t:Maloney g:Orr(4)	N/A	7,233
13/3/99	Salford (h) (CCQF)	W30-10	t:Rogers(2),Maloney,Raper,Davis g:Orr(5)	N/A	5,236
21/3/99	Warrington (a)	L19-14	t:Gay,Eagar,Davis g:Orr	8th	4,738
27/3/99	London (CCSF)	L27-33	t:Gay(2),Eagar(2),Rogers g:Orr(3) fg:Orr	N/A	7,561
2/4/99	Halifax (h)	W14-10	t:Eagar(3) g:Orr	6th	7,210
7/4/99	Huddersfield (a)	W14-36	t:Rogers(2),Eagar(2),Maloney(2),Vowles g:Orr(4)	4th	3,882
11/4/99	Salford (a)	W17-29	t:Eagar,Gay,Maloney,Flowers g:Orr(4),Tonks(2) fg:Orr	3rd	3,663
18/4/99	Gateshead (h)	L14-17	t:Rogers(2),Davis g:Orr	4th	6,489
25/4/99	Wigan (a)	W8-24	t:Davis,Wells,Vowles,Harland g:Orr(3),Tonks	3rd	8,856
3/5/99	Bradford (h)	D18-18	t:Sampson,Rogers,Tallec g:Orr(2),Maloney	4th	10,122
9/5/99	London (a)	D12-12	t:Raper,Rogers g:Maloney(2)	5th	2,347
16/5/99	Sheffield (h)	W10-6	t:Maloney,Vowles g:Orr	4th	5,748
19/5/99	St Helens (h)	L14-33	t:Rogers,Davis,Gay g:Tonks	5th	6,633
23/5/99	Hull (a)	W2-30	t:Rogers(2),Davis,Hepi,Sampson,Gay g:Tonks(2),Orr	4th	4,564
30/5/99	Leeds (h)	D12-12	t:Wells,Eagar g:Orr(2)	4th	10,462
6/6/99	Wakefield (a)	L11-10	t:Harland,Sampson g:Orr	5th	6,596
13/6/99	Warrington (h)	W39-6	t:Maloney(3),Gay(2),Orr,Ellison g:Orr(5) fg:Davis	5th	5,551
18/6/99	Halifax (a)	W0-24	t:Flowers,Orr,Ellison,Wells g:Orr(4)	5th	3,582
23/6/99	Leeds (a)	L50-22	t:Orr,Rogers,Wells,Eagar g:Orr(3)	5th	16,371
27/6/99	Huddersfield (h)	W19-10	t:Ellison(2),Orr g:Raper(2),Orr fg:Flowers	5th	5,379
4/7/99	Salford (h)	W38-10	t:Gay(2),Wells,Hepi,Eagar,Flowers g:Maloney(7)	5th	5,786
11/7/99	Gateshead (a)	L24-16	t:Flowers,Tonks,Sampson g:Orr(2)	5th	6,108
16/7/99	Wigan (h)	W33-18	t:Orr(2),Harland,Davis,Gay,Maloney g:Orr(4) fg:Davis	5th	7,089
25/7/99	Bradford (a)	L24-22	t:Gay(2),Orr,Maloney g:Orr(3)	6th	13,824
1/8/99	London (h)	W52-16	t:Maloney(3),Davis(2),Eagar(2),Gay,Vowles,Harland g:Orr(6)	6th	5,693
7/8/99	Sheffield (a)	W0-22	t:Rogers(2),Eagar,Raper,Sampson g:Orr	6th	3,750
15/8/99	Hull (h)	W44-16	t:Gay(2),Flowers,Maloney,Davis,Rogers,Smith,Orr g:Orr(6)	5th	6,078
20/8/99	Wakefield (h)	W30-18	t:Vowles(2),Gay,Orr,Hepi,Rogers g:Orr(3)	5th	6,322
25/8/99	St Helens (a)	L42-14	t:Davis,Wells,Rogers g:Orr	5th	7,976
29/8/99	Warrington (a)	W6-8	t:Wells g:Orr(2)	5th	4,864
5/9/99	Halifax (h)	W48-12	t:Orr(2),Harland(2),Gay,Rogers,Wells,Vowles,Tallec g:Orr(6)	5th	7,367
12/9/99	Huddersfield (a)	W10-32	t:Rogers(3),Eagar,Vowles,Wells,Raper g:Orr(2)	5th	4,405
19/9/99	Wigan (a) (EPO)	W10-14	t:Eagar,Vowles g:Orr(3)	N/A	13,374
24/9/99	Leeds (a) (ESF)	W16-23	t:Eagar,Vowles,Fritz g:Orr(5) fg:Raper	N/A	16,912
3/10/99	St Helens (a) (FE)	L36-6	t:Flowers g:Orr	N/A	11,212

	APP		TRIES		GOALS		FG		PTS	
	ALL	SL	ALL	SL	ALL	SL	ALL	SL	ALL	SL
Brad Davis	33	29	14	10	0	0	2	2	58	42
Gareth Dobson	(6)	(5)	0	0	0	0	0	0	0	0
Michael Eagar	36	32	19	16	0	0	0	0	76	64
Danny Ellison	2(13)	2(12)	4	4	0	0	0	0	16	16
Jason Flowers	37	33	8	6	0	0	1	1	33	25
Dale Fritz	34(1)	31(1)	1	1	0	0	0	0	4	4
Richard Gay	30(1)	26(1)	19	16	0	0	0	0	76	64
Spencer Hargrave	(2)	(2)	0	0	0	0	0	0	0	0
Lee Harland	26(1)	24(1)	7	6	0	0	0	0	28	24
Brad Hepi	8(17)	8(17)	3	3	0	0	0	0	12	12
Andy Hill	4(5)	4(4)	0	0	0	0	0	0	0	0
Andy Lynch	(11)	(9)	0	0	0	0	0	0	0	0
Francis Maloney	28	24	16	14	10	10	0	0	84	76
Danny Orr	35	31	12	11	97	83	2	1	244	211
James Pickering	2(21)	1(19)	0	0	0	0	0	0	0	0
Aaron Raper	30(1)	27(1)	4	3	2	2	1	1	21	17
Darren Rogers	37	33	23	19	0	0	0	0	92	76
Dean Sampson	36	32	5	5	0	0	0	0	20	20
Paul Smith	1(10)	1(10)	1	1	0	0	0	0	4	4
Nathan Sykes	33(1)	30	0	0	0	0	0	0	0	0
Gael Tallec	14(17)	13(14)	2	2	0	0	0	0	8	8
Ian Tonks	8(19)	5(18)	1	1	10	6	0	0	24	16
Adrian Vowles	32	28	10	10	0	0	0	0	40	40
Jon Wells	15(15)	15(12)	9	9	0	0	0	0	36	36

LEAGUE RECORD
P30-W19-D3-L8
(5th, SL/Final Eliminator)
F712, A451, Diff+261
41 points.

CHALLENGE CUP
Semi Finalists

ATTENDANCES
Best - v Leeds (SL - 10,462)
Worst - v Salford (CC - 5,236)
Total (SL only) - 103,162
Average (SL only) - 6,877
(Up by 482 on 1998)

MOST TACKLES
Dean Sampson 732

MOST CLEAN BREAKS
Darren Rogers 33

MOST METRES GAINED
Jason Flowers 4589

Deon Bird

SEASON'S HIGH POINT:
The trip to Edinburgh. We took the game on the road, blitzed Wigan early on and then showed grit to hang on. And to see all those Thunder fans - it was the best atmosphere I have ever played in.

SEASON'S LOW POINT:
Not getting one over on London. They seem to be our bogey team. We drew down there and lost at home which was the end of our play-off chances.

MOST IMPRESSIVE TEAMMATE:
Luke Felsch was chosen as the players' player of the year and he deserved it. He was almost ever present and because of the position he plays in he really pushed his body to the limits.

MOST IMPRESSIVE OPPONENT:
Iestyn Harris. Completely unpredictable on the ball and then he has got this great long pass which can create tries. He virtually beat us on his own up here.

HOPES FOR 2000:
With the merger with Hull, nothing really changes. We finished sixth last year and we have got to go out and improve on that. And we are in the Challenge Cup for the first time so we'll aim to do well in that too.

GATESHEAD THUNDER

DATE	FIXTURE	RESULT	SCORERS	LGE	ATT
7/3/99	Leeds (h)	L14-24	t:Simon(2),Daylight g:Herron	N/A	5,960
21/3/99	St Helens (a)	L34-22	t:Bird(2),Robinson g:Herron(5)	12th	5,910
2/4/99	Wakefield (h)	W24-6	t:Sammut(2),Daylight,Peters g:Herron(4)	8th	3,460
5/4/99	Warrington (a)	L23-18	t:Daylight,Felsch,Maiden g:Herron(3)	10th	4,919
10/4/99	Halifax (h)	W22-14	t:Walters,Simon,Sammut,Peters g:Herron(3)	10th	2,340
18/4/99	Castleford (a)	W14-17	t:Sammut,Grimaldi g:Herron(4) fg:Peters	8th	6,489
25/4/99	Salford (h)	W38-14	t:Collins(2),Sammut,Maher,Walters,Robinson,Daylight g:Herron(5)	7th	1,780
3/5/99	Huddersfield (h)	W36-10	t:Hick(2),Daylight(2),Collins,Grogan g:Herron(6)	6th	2,616
9/5/99	Wigan (a)	L16-13	t:Daylight g:Herron(4) fg:Peters	6th	7,717
16/5/99	Bradford (h)	L12-22	t:Collins,Maiden g:Herron(2)	7th	6,631
19/5/99	Hull (h)	W25-6	t:Carney,Collins,Daylight,S Allwood g:Sammut(3),Peters fg:Peters	7th	1,580
23/5/99	London (a)	D18-18	t:Peters(2),Daylight,Sammut g:Sammut	7th	1,788
30/5/99	Sheffield (h)	W26-18	t:Robinson,Felsch,Wilson,Maher g:Herron(5)	6th	1,880
4/6/99	Leeds (a)	L32-14	t:McAllister,Daylight,Robinson g:Herron	7th	10,821
13/6/99	St Helens (h)	W32-20	t:Daylight,Peters,Grimaldi,Herron,Collins g:Herron(6)	7th	6,220
20/6/99	Wakefield (a)	W18-22	t:Bird,Daylight,Grimaldi,Grogan g:Herron(3)	7th	3,400
25/6/99	Warrington (h)	W26-20	t:Grimaldi(2),Collins,Jenkins g:Herron(5)	6th	3,457
29/6/99	Sheffield (a)	W6-23	t:Grogan,Bird,Wilson,Collins g:Herron(3) fg:Peters	6th	2,319
4/7/99	Halifax (a)	L35-14	t:Peters(2) g:Herron(3)	6th	3,305
11/7/99	Castleford (h)	W24-16	t:Maher,Bird,Collins g:Herron(5),Sammut	6th	6,108
18/7/99	Salford (a)	W18-31	t:Daylight(2),Simon,Peters,Robinson g:Herron(4),Sammut fg:Peters	5th	5,611
25/7/99	Huddersfield (a)	W16-40	t:Bird(3),Grimaldi,Collins,Peters,Carvell,Maiden g:Sammut(4)	5th	2,219
1/8/99	Wigan (h)	W20-16	t:Daylight(2),Carney,Wilson g:Sammut fg:Wilson,Peters	5th	4,978
4/8/99	Hull (a)	W12-40	t:Daylight(2),Wilson,Grimaldi,Peters,Simon,Maiden g:Sammut(6)	5th	3,321
8/8/99	Bradford (a)	L30-14	t:Daylight,Herron g:Herron(3)	5th	12,492
15/8/99	London (h)	L22-28	t:Robinson,Bird,Herron,Grimaldi g:Herron(3)	6th	2,631
22/8/99	Leeds (h)	L18-30	t:Daylight(2),Collins g:Herron(3)	6th	5,498
30/8/99	St Helens (a)	W32-36	t:Jenkins(2),Daylight,Peters,Maiden,Bird g:Herron(6)	6th	5,993
5/9/99	Wakefield (h)	W66-6	t:Robinson(2),Daylight(2),Wilson,Herron,Bird,Simon,Maiden, Grimaldi,Collins g:Herron(11)	6th	3,286
12/9/99	Warrington (a)	W22-48	t:Bird(2),Maiden(2),Daylight,Robinson,Collins,Grimaldi g:Herron(7),Walters	6th	4,834

	APP		TRIES		GOALS		FG		PTS	
	ALL	SL	ALL	SL	ALL	SL	ALL	SL	ALL	SL
Richard Allwood	(4)	(4)	0	0	0	0	0	0	0	0
Sean Allwood	3(17)	3(17)	1	1	0	0	0	0	4	4
Deon Bird	19(3)	19(3)	13	13	0	0	0	0	52	52
Brian Carney	3(2)	3(2)	2	2	0	0	0	0	8	8
Garreth Carvell	4(4)	4(4)	1	1	0	0	0	0	4	4
Steve Collins	20(4)	20(4)	13	13	0	0	0	0	52	52
Matt Daylight	30	30	25	25	0	0	0	0	100	100
Luke Felsch	28(1)	28(1)	2	2	0	0	0	0	8	8
Brett Green	10(2)	10(2)	0	0	0	0	0	0	0	0
Tony Grimaldi	27(2)	27(2)	10	10	0	0	0	0	40	40
Brett Grogan	14(7)	14(7)	3	3	0	0	0	0	12	12
Ian Herron	25	25	4	4	105	105	0	0	226	226
Andrew Hick	12(5)	12(5)	2	2	0	0	0	0	8	8
Mick Jenkins	16	16	3	3	0	0	0	0	12	12
Danny Lee	16(2)	16(2)	0	0	0	0	0	0	0	0
Adam Maher	21(5)	21(5)	3	3	0	0	0	0	12	12
David Maiden	5(16)	5(16)	8	8	0	0	0	0	32	32
Danny McAllister	3(3)	3(3)	1	1	0	0	0	0	4	4
Steve O'Neill	1(1)	1(1)	0	0	0	0	0	0	0	0
Willie Peters	27	27	11	11	1	1	6	6	52	52
Will Robinson	28	28	9	9	0	0	0	0	36	36
Ben Sammut	26(2)	26(2)	6	6	17	17	0	0	58	58
Craig Simon	25(4)	25(4)	6	6	0	0	0	0	24	24
Kerrod Walters	10(12)	10(12)	2	2	1	1	0	0	10	10
Craig Wilson	17(11)	17(11)	5	5	0	0	1	1	21	21

LEAGUE RECORD
P30-W19-D1-L10
(6th, SL)
F775, A576, Diff+199
39 points.

CHALLENGE CUP
N/A (Did not enter)

ATTENDANCES
Best - v Bradford (6,631)
Worst - v Hull (1,580)
Total - 58,425
Average - 3,895

MOST TACKLES
Luke Felsch 942

MOST CLEAN BREAKS
Matt Daylight 29

MOST METRES GAINED
Luke Felsch 3407

Martin Moana

SEASON'S HIGH POINT:
Probably the two one-point wins we produced against Leeds and Warrington at the end of the season. It had been a shocker of a season because of the off-field stuff and it was great how we as a team were able to stand up and be counted.

SEASON'S LOW POINT:
All the uncertainty in the middle of the season when we lost our coach and some key players. We just didn't know what the future was going to bring.

MOST IMPRESSIVE TEAMMATE:
Daryl Cardiss. He's not a big bloke but he went well all year for us.

MOST IMPRESSIVE OPPONENT:
There's plenty of great players out there, but if I had to pick one it would have to be Toa Kohe-Love. He cut us up a few times in 1999.

HOPES FOR 2000:
With the financial stuff hopefully out of the way we are building up a good squad, so a top-five place shouldn't be beyond us.

HALIFAX BLUE SOX

DATE	FIXTURE	RESULT	SCORERS	LGE	ATT
13/2/99	F'stone Lions (a) (CCR4)	W6-74	t:Mercer(3),Bloem(2),Holroyd(2),Clark,Skerrett,Gibson,Pinkney, Clinch,Moana g:Holroyd(11)	N/A	1,533
28/2/99	Warrington (a) (CCR5)	L34-4	g:Holroyd(2)	N/A	5,102
7/3/99	Warrington (h)	L14-16	t:Moana,Pinkney g:Holroyd(3)	N/A	4,687
21/3/99	Huddersfield (a)	W14-17	t:Holroyd,Gibson g:Holroyd(4) fg:Holroyd	7th	4,667
2/4/99	Castleford (a)	L14-10	t:Pinkney,Craig g:Clinch	7th	7,210
6/4/99	Salford (h)	W30-14	t:Pinkney(2),Bloem,Gibson,Rowley g:Holroyd(5)	6th	3,724
10/4/99	Gateshead (a)	L22-14	t:Clinch,Cardiss,Hodgson g:Holroyd	9th	2,340
16/4/99	Wigan (h)	W19-8	t:Chester,Gillespie g:Holroyd(4) fg:Holroyd(2),Clinch	7th	5,107
23/4/99	Bradford (a)	L20-2	g:Holroyd	9th	11,103
5/5/99	London (h)	W26-24	t:Moana(2),Bouveng,Rowley,Broadbent g:Holroyd(2),Clinch	7th	3,650
8/5/99	Sheffield (a)	L27-8	t:Clinch g:Clinch(2)	9th	3,901
16/5/99	Hull (h)	W30-12	t:Chester,Broadbent,Mercer,Moana g:Bloem(3),Clinch(2),Holroyd fg:Moana,Clinch	8th	3,779
21/5/99	Leeds (a)	L70-22	t:Clinch,Bloem,Hobson,Gibson g:Clinch(3)	9th	12,649
30/5/99	St Helens (h)	L22-28	t:Bouveng,Clinch,Gibson,Moana g:Bloem(2),Clinch	10th	4,857
4/6/99	Warrington (a)	L31-18	t:Bouveng,Cardiss,Hobson g:Bloem(3)	10th	3,298
9/6/99	Wakefield (h)	L16-36	t:Gibson,Cardiss,Seal g:Holroyd(2)	10th	3,466
13/6/99	Huddersfield (h)	W51-18	t:Chester(2),Pinkney(2),Clinch(2),Gibson,Seal g:Holroyd(9) fg:Clinch	9th	3,291
18/6/99	Castleford (h)	L0-24	No Scorers	10th	3,582
27/6/99	Salford (a)	W20-22	t:Rowley,Mercer,Gillespie,Cardiss g:Holroyd(3)	9th	3,536
30/6/99	St Helens (a)	L46-10	t:Cardiss g:Holroyd(3)	10th	5,788
4/7/99	Gateshead (h)	W35-14	t:Cardiss(2),Gibson,Rowley,Pinkney,Hodgson g:Holroyd(5) fg:Rowley	8th	3,305
11/7/99	Wigan (a)	L30-4	g:Holroyd(2)	9th	6,836
18/7/99	Bradford (h)	L20-34	t:Shaw,Moana,Randall g:Holroyd(4)	9th	9,342
23/7/99	London (a)	L48-12	t:Pinkney,Randall g:Holroyd,Craig	9th	2,044
28/7/99	Wakefield (h)	L26-20	t:Pinkney(2),Hodgson,Marns g:Holroyd(2)	10th	3,082
1/8/99	Sheffield (a)	L24-43	t:Gannon(2),Clark,Moana g:Holroyd(4)	11th	3,441
8/8/99	Hull (a)	L24-21	t:Hodgson,Pinkney,Holroyd g:Holroyd(4) fg:Holroyd	11th	3,461
13/8/99	Leeds (a)	W21-20	t:Holroyd,Pinkney,Holroyd g:Holroyd(4) fg:Rowley	10th	5,144
20/8/99	Warrington (h)	W23-22	t:Gibson(2),Randall,Cardiss g:Holroyd(3) fg:Holroyd	9th	4,106
29/8/99	Huddersfield (a)	L19-18	t:Dunemann,Hobson,Pinkney g:Holroyd(3)	10th	3,836
5/9/99	Castleford (a)	L48-12	t:Moana,Mercer g:Craig(2)	11th	7,367
10/9/99	Salford (h)	W32-20	t:Cardiss(2),Hobson,Mercer,Hodgson,Randall g:Holroyd(4)	9th	5,764

	APP		TRIES		GOALS		FG		PTS		
	ALL	SL	ALL	SL	ALL	SL	ALL	SL	ALL	SL	
Danny Barnes	2	2	0	0	0	0	0	0	0	0	
Jamie Bloem	15	13	4	2	8	8	0	0	32	24	
David Bouveng	26(1)	24(1)	3	3	0	0	0	0	12	12	
Paul Broadbent	27(1)	26(1)	2	2	0	0	0	0	8	8	
Daryl Cardiss	27(2)	27	10	10	0	0	0	0	40	40	
Chris Chester	10(2)	8(2)	4	4	0	0	0	0	16	16	
Des Clark	20(5)	19(4)	2	1	0	0	0	0	8	4	
Gavin Clinch	17	15	7	6	10	10	3	3	51	47	
Andy Craig	14(7)	13(7)	1	1	3	3	0	0	10	10	
Andrew Dunemann	3	3	1	1	0	0	0	0	4	4	
Danny Fearon	5(5)	5(5)	0	0	0	0	0	0	0	0	
Jim Gannon	6(2)	6(2)	2	2	0	0	0	0	8	8	
Damian Gibson	32	30	11	10	0	0	0	0	44	40	
Carl Gillespie	16(11)	15(10)	2	2	0	0	0	0	8	8	
Andy Hobson	2(24)	2(24)	4	4	0	0	0	0	16	16	
David Hodgson	10(3)	10(3)	5	5	0	0	0	0	20	20	
Graham Holroyd	26(2)	24(2)	5	3	87	74	5	5	199	165	
Simon Knox	(6)	(6)	0	0	0	0	0	0	0	0	
Oliver Marns	12(6)	12(6)	1	1	0	0	0	0	4	4	
Richard Marshall	19(13)	17(13)	0	0	0	0	0	0	0	0	
Wes McGibbon	1	1	0	0	0	0	0	0	0	0	
Gary Mercer	22	20	7	4	0	0	0	0	28	16	
Lee Milner	(1)	(1)	0	0	0	0	0	0	0	0	
Martin Moana	23(4)	22(3)	9	8	0	0	1	1	37	33	
Nick Pinkney	27(2)	26(2)	14	13	0	0	0	0	56	52	
Craig Randall	8(11)	8(11)	4	4	0	0	0	0	16	16	
Paul Rowley	24	22	4	4	0	0	2	2	18	18	
Danny Seal	4(11)	4(11)	2	2	0	0	0	0	8	8	
Mick Shaw	5	5	1	1	0	0	0	0	4	4	
Kelvin Skerrett	12	10	1	0	0	0	0	0	4	0	

LEAGUE RECORD
P30-W11-D0-L19
(9th, SL)
F573, A792, Diff-219
22 points.

CHALLENGE CUP
Round Five

ATTENDANCES
Best - v Bradford (SL - 9,342)
Worst - v Huddersfield (SL - 3,291)
Total (SL only) - 67,245
Average (SL only) - 4,483
(Down by 1,168 on 1998)

MOST TACKLES
Paul Broadbent 629

MOST CLEAN BREAKS
Daryl Cardiss 34

MOST METRES GAINED
Paul Broadbent 3248

Nick Fozzard

SEASON'S HIGH POINT:
Difficult one that. The win away at Hull was pretty good, it's always hard to go and play at the Boulevard, and also the win over Sheffield at home. But that was about it.

SEASON'S LOW POINT:
The thrashing at Leeds. Malcolm was absolutely devastated by it. I don't think he will ever recover from that game. Leeds were red-hot that night and we were poor.

MOST IMPRESSIVE TEAMMATE:
Dave Boughton. I've got a lot of respect for him as a forward, and Bobbie Goulding showed us the way too. We missed him a lot when he was out with a broken leg at the end of the season.

MOST IMPRESSIVE OPPONENT:
Either Iestyn Harris or Adrian Morley. They are just top class players.

HOPES FOR 2000:
To have an opposite type of season to this one and get up in the top five. I'm certainly optimistic we can have a shout this year.

HUDDERSFIELD GIANTS

DATE	FIXTURE	RESULT	SCORERS	LGE	ATT
14/2/99	Swinton (h) (CCR4)	W78-4	t:Weston(3),Cook(2),Arnold(2),Loughlin,Goulding,Boughton,Sturm, Cheetham,Lenihan,Wright g:Goulding(10),Cook	N/A	2,277
28/2/99	Salford (h) (CCR5)	L14-22	t:Arnold,Lenihan g:Goulding(3)	N/A	4,992
7/3/99	London (a)	L24-18	t:Cheetham(2),Weston g:Goulding(3)	N/A	2,278
21/3/99	Halifax (h)	L14-17	t:Cheetham(2),Bentley g:Goulding	10th	4,667
2/4/99	Sheffield (a)	L32-28	t:Loughlin(2),Cheetham,Weston,Reilly g:Goulding(4)	12th	3,621
7/4/99	Castleford (h)	L14-36	t:Lenihan,Wright g:Weston(2),Goulding	12th	3,882
11/4/99	Hull (h)	W26-12	t:Goulding,Richards,Cheetham,Russell g:Goulding(5)	11th	3,187
18/4/99	Salford (a)	W14-15	t:Russell,Bentley g:Goulding(3) fg:Goulding	12th	4,125
25/4/99	Leeds (h)	L20-42	t:Lenihan(3),Sturm g:Goulding(2)	12th	5,346
3/5/99	Gateshead (a)	L36-10	t:Fozzard,Arnold g:Goulding	12th	2,616
7/5/99	St Helens (h)	L0-11	No Scorers	12th	4,060
16/5/99	Wigan (a)	L36-2	g:Goulding	12th	6,634
23/5/99	Wakefield (h)	L22-38	t:Weston(2),Cheetham,Bentley g:Goulding(3)	12th	4,149
30/5/99	Bradford (a)	L22-20	t:Lenihan,Tangata-Toa g:Goulding(5),Weston	13th	11,032
6/6/99	London (h)	L20-21	t:Berry,Boughton,Arnold g:Goulding(4)	13th	2,685
9/6/99	Warrington (a)	L48-16	t:Boughton,Lenihan,Gleeson g:Goulding(2)	13th	3,941
13/6/99	Halifax (a)	L51-18	t:Tangata-Toa,Loughlin,Cheetham g:Goulding(3)	13th	3,291
20/6/99	Sheffield (h)	W37-18	t:Lenihan(3),Goulding(2),Simpson,Reilly g:Goulding(4) fg:Goulding	13th	2,363
27/6/99	Castleford (a)	L19-10	t:Simpson,Lenihan g:Goulding	13th	5,379
4/7/99	Hull (a)	W17-26	t:Weston(2),Boughton,Simpson g:Goulding(5)	12th	4,066
7/7/99	Bradford (h)	L0-26	No Scorers	12th	6,581
11/7/99	Salford (h)	L10-24	t:Weston,Carlton g:Goulding	13th	3,191
16/7/99	Leeds (h)	L86-6	t:Cheetham g:Goulding	13th	11,625
25/7/99	Gateshead (h)	L16-40	t:Gleeson,Fozzard,Arnold g:Goulding(2)	13th	2,219
30/7/99	St Helens (a)	L64-16	t:Sturm,Weston,Gleeson g:Goulding(2)	13th	5,213
8/8/99	Wigan (h)	L10-60	t:Boughton g:Weston(3)	14th	3,137
11/8/99	Warrington (h)	L12-40	t:Carlton,Arnold g:Weston,Lawford	14th	2,183
15/8/99	Wakefield (a)	L40-12	t:Ngamu,Gleeson g:Lawford(2)	14th	3,200
22/8/99	London (a)	L40-4	t:Weston	14th	2,011
29/8/99	Halifax (h)	W19-18	t:Sibson,Berry,Slattery g:Lawford(3) fg:Lawford	13th	3,836
4/9/99	Sheffield (a)	L47-32	t:Weston,Cheetham,Sibson,Johnson,Gleeson g:Ngamu(6)	13th	3,500
12/9/99	Castleford (h)	L10-32	t:Ngamu,Gleeson g:Ngamu	14th	4,405

	APP		TRIES		GOALS		FG		PTS		
	ALL	SL	ALL	SL	ALL	SL	ALL	SL	ALL	SL	
Danny Arnold	19(5)	17(5)	7	4	0	0	0	0	28	16	
John Bentley	13(4)	13(4)	3	3	0	0	0	0	12	12	
Joe Berry	20(3)	19(2)	2	2	0	0	0	0	8	8	
Steve Booth	7(2)	7(2)	0	0	0	0	0	0	0	0	
David Boughton	28(1)	26(1)	5	4	0	0	0	0	20	16	
James Bunyan	1(4)	1(4)	0	0	0	0	0	0	0	0	
Shane Byrne	1(2)	1(2)	0	0	0	0	0	0	0	0	
Jim Carlton	3(11)	3(11)	2	2	0	0	0	0	8	8	
Andy Cheetham	21	19	11	10	0	0	0	0	44	40	
Paul Cook	3	1	2	0	1	0	0	0	10	0	
Nick Fozzard	23(6)	21(6)	2	2	0	0	0	0	8	8	
Martin Gleeson	8(6)	8(6)	6	6	0	0	0	0	24	24	
Bobbie Goulding	24	22	4	3	67	54	2	2	152	122	
Andy Hill	(4)	(4)	0	0	0	0	0	0	0	0	
Ryan Hudson	12(7)	12(6)	0	0	0	0	0	0	4	4	
Andy Johnson	5	5	1	1	0	0	0	0	4	0	
Dave King	(11)	(11)	0	0	0	0	0	0	0	0	
Dean Lawford	6(1)	6(1)	0	0	6	6	1	1	13	13	
Jim Lenihan	21(1)	19(1)	12	10	0	0	0	0	48	40	
Paul Loughlin	24(1)	22(1)	4	3	0	0	0	0	16	12	
Adrian Moore	1	1	0	0	0	0	0	0	0	0	
Mark Moxon	5(1)	5	0	0	0	0	0	0	0	0	
Jonathan Neill	12(10)	12(10)	0	0	0	0	0	0	0	0	
Gene Ngamu	5	5	2	2	7	7	0	0	22	22	
Ian Pickavance	3(16)	3(14)	0	0	0	0	0	0	0	0	
Paul Reilly	24(2)	24(2)	2	2	0	0	0	0	8	8	
Basil Richards	14(12)	12(12)	1	1	0	0	0	0	4	4	
Danny Russell	21	19	2	2	0	0	0	0	8	8	
Gary Shillabeer	(2)	(2)	0	0	0	0	0	0	0	0	
Mark Sibson	2	2	2	2	0	0	0	0	8	8	
Darren Simpson	12(1)	12(1)	3	3	0	0	0	0	12	12	
Troy Slattery	3	3	1	1	0	0	0	0	4	4	
Matt Sturm	25	23	3	2	0	0	0	0	12	8	
Andrew Tangata-Toa	16	15	2	2	0	0	0	0	8	8	
Craig Weston	30	28	13	10	7	7	0	0	66	54	
Nigel Wright	4(8)	4(6)	2	1	0	0	0	0	8	4	

LEAGUE RECORD
P30-W5-D0-L25
(14th, SL)
F463, A1011, Diff-548
10 points.

CHALLENGE CUP
Round Five

ATTENDANCES
Best - v Bradford (SL - 6,581)
Worst - v Warrington (SL - 2,183)
Total (SL only) - 55,891
Average (SL only) - 3,727
(Down by 1,415 on 1998)

MOST TACKLES
Danny Russell 615

MOST CLEAN BREAKS
Craig Weston 17

MOST METRES GAINED
David Boughton 2250

Karl Harrison

SEASON'S HIGH POINT:
Had to be the last day of the season when we blitzed Sheffield to come off the bottom of the table.

SEASON'S LOW POINT:
All the injuries that we incurred at the start of the year made it a very long season for us.

MOST IMPRESSIVE TEAMMATE:
I can't separate three - Rob Roberts, Paul King and Richard Horne. There are a lot of great youngsters at the Boulevard.

MOST IMPRESSIVE OPPONENT:
The man I had the biggest tussles against this year was Bradford Bulls' Paul Anderson, a mate of mine. He's the hardest player I came up against in 1999.

HOPES FOR 2000:
I sincerely hope that Hull can get all the support they deserve to rekindle the glory days of the '80s. There's no better place to play when there is a full house than the Boulevard.

HULL SHARKS

DATE	FIXTURE	RESULT	SCORERS	LGE	ATT
14/2/99	Castleford (a) (CCR4)	L36-22	t:Prescott(2),Hall,Baildon g:Prescott(3)	N/A	6,107
5/3/99	Wigan (a)	L58-6	t:Prescott g:Prescott	N/A	9,186
21/3/99	Bradford (h)	L3-8	g:Prescott fg:Prescott	14th	6,577
2/4/99	London (a)	L12-10	t:Leatham,Roberts g:Hallas	14th	3,472
5/4/99	Sheffield (h)	L21-23	t:Campbell,Lester,Hallas g:Prescott(4) fg:Roberts	14th	3,995
11/4/99	Huddersfield (a)	L26-12	t:Lester,Roberts g:Prescott,Hallas	14th	3,187
16/4/99	Leeds (a)	L22-18	t:Nolan,Windley,Purcell g:Roberts(3)	14th	10,009
25/4/99	St Helens (h)	L10-30	t:Nolan(2) g:Prescott	14th	5,879
3/5/99	Wakefield (a)	W22-29	t:Nolan(2),Lester,King,Prescott g:Prescott(4) fg:Prescott	13th	4,546
9/5/99	Warrington (h)	L22-33	t:Lester(2),Campbell(2) g:Prescott(3)	13th	4,679
16/5/99	Halifax (a)	L30-12	t:Hallas,Prescott g:Prescott(2)	13th	3,779
19/5/99	Gateshead (a)	L25-6	t:Murdock g:Prescott	13th	1,580
23/5/99	Castleford (h)	L2-30	g:Prescott	14th	4,564
30/5/99	Salford (a)	L38-18	t:Poucher,Cooke,Seru g:Prescott(3)	14th	3,699
6/6/99	Wigan (h)	L12-18	t:Cooke,Seru g:Prescott(2)	14th	4,117
13/6/99	Bradford (a)	L42-14	t:Horne,Barrow g:Prescott(3)	14th	11,757
20/6/99	London (h)	L6-47	t:Roberts g:Prescott	14th	3,833
23/6/99	Salford (h)	W18-12	t:Lester(2),M Smith g:Prescott(3)	14th	3,100
26/6/99	Sheffield (a)	L18-8	t:Hallas g:Cooke,Hallas	14th	3,449
4/7/99	Huddersfield (h)	L17-26	t:Prescott,Murdock,J Smith g:Prescott,Hallas fg:Roberts	14th	4,066
9/7/99	Leeds (a)	L18-26	t:J Smith(2),Lester,Harrison g:Hallas	14th	3,522
18/7/99	St Helens (a)	L74-16	t:Purcell(2),Booth g:Hallas(2)	14th	5,972
25/7/99	Wakefield (h)	W23-18	t:Leatham,Lester,Parker g:Roberts(4),Hallas fg:Roberts	14th	3,602
1/8/99	Warrington (a)	L32-12	t:Baildon,Campbell g:Cooke(2)	14th	4,028
4/8/99	Gateshead (h)	L12-40	t:Poucher,Purcell g:Cooke(2)	14th	3,321
8/8/99	Halifax (h)	W24-21	t:Horne,Craven,M Smith,Hallas g:Roberts(4)	13th	3,461
15/8/99	Castleford (a)	L44-16	t:Roberts,Pickavance,Leatham g:Roberts(2)	13th	6,078
20/8/99	Wigan (a)	L58-0	No Scorers	13th	6,866
29/8/99	Bradford (h)	L12-44	t:M Smith,Parker g:Hallas(2)	14th	5,031
5/9/99	London (a)	L28-12	t:Parker,Prescott g:Prescott(2)	14th	2,538
12/9/99	Sheffield (h)	W33-16	t:Lester,Pickavance,Harrison,Parker,Campbell g:Prescott(6) fg:Roberts	13th	5,447

	APP		TRIES		GOALS		FG		PTS	
	ALL	SL	ALL	SL	ALL	SL	ALL	SL	ALL	SL
David Baildon	13(1)	12(1)	2	1	0	0	0	0	8	4
Steve Barrow	3(16)	3(16)	1	1	0	0	0	0	4	4
Simon Booth	3(6)	3(6)	1	1	0	0	0	0	4	4
Lee Brown	(1)	(1)	0	0	0	0	0	0	0	0
Matt Calland	2	1	0	0	0	0	0	0	0	0
Logan Campbell	31	30	5	5	0	0	0	0	20	20
Paul Cooke	10(6)	10(6)	2	2	5	5	0	0	18	18
Steve Craven	22(4)	21(4)	1	1	0	0	0	0	4	4
Richard Fletcher	(12)	(12)	0	0	0	0	0	0	0	0
Martin Hall	8	7	1	0	0	0	0	0	4	0
Graeme Hallas	17(4)	17(3)	4	2	10	10	0	0	36	36
Karl Harrison	27	26	2	2	0	0	0	0	8	8
Stephen Holgate	2	1	0	0	0	0	0	0	0	0
Richard Horne	9(9)	9(9)	2	2	0	0	0	0	8	8
Andy Ireland	13(7)	12(7)	0	0	0	0	0	0	0	0
Chico Jackson	(4)	(4)	0	0	0	0	0	0	0	0
Paul King	17(5)	17(5)	1	1	0	0	0	0	4	4
Andy Last	(1)	(1)	0	0	0	0	0	0	0	0
Jim Leatham	17(6)	17(5)	3	3	0	0	0	0	12	12
Robert Lee	4(3)	4(3)	0	0	0	0	0	0	0	0
Gary Lester	25	24	10	10	0	0	0	0	40	40
Craig Murdock	7(6)	6(6)	2	2	0	0	0	0	8	8
Rob Nolan	15(5)	15(5)	5	5	0	0	0	0	20	20
Paul Parker	9(2)	9(2)	4	4	0	0	0	0	16	16
Ian Pickavance	4(2)	4(2)	2	2	0	0	0	0	8	8
Craig Poucher	17	17	2	2	0	0	0	0	8	8
Steve Prescott	19	18	7	5	43	40	2	2	116	102
Andrew Purcell	28	27	4	4	0	0	0	0	16	16
Robert Roberts	24(2)	24(2)	4	4	13	13	4	4	46	46
Matt Schultz	11(4)	11(4)	0	0	0	0	0	0	0	0
Fili Seru	16(1)	15(1)	2	2	0	0	0	0	8	8
Jamie Smith	16(2)	16(2)	3	3	0	0	0	0	12	12
Michael Smith	12(7)	12(6)	3	3	0	0	0	0	12	12
Richard Wilson	(3)	(3)	0	0	0	0	0	0	0	0
Johan Windley	2(2)	2(2)	1	1	0	0	0	0	4	4

LEAGUE RECORD
P30-W5-D0-L25
(13th, SL)
F422, A921, Diff-499
10 points.

CHALLENGE CUP
Round Four

ATTENDANCES
Best - v Bradford (SL - 6,577)
Worst - v Salford (SL - 3,100)
Total (SL only) - 65,194
Average (SL only) - 4,346
(Down by 1,395 on 1998)

MOST TACKLES
Karl Harrison 570

MOST CLEAN BREAKS
Gary Lester 25

MOST METRES GAINED
Steve Craven 3133

Barrie McDermott

SEASON'S HIGH POINT:
Got to be the victory at Wembley. Getting the Challenge Cup back to Leeds for the first time since 1978 made us all feel a part of history. What a great occasion.

SEASON'S LOW POINT:
Our performances at the end of the season in the semi-finals. We seemed to go stale for the last half-dozen games. It's the same for all teams but maybe we had played too much football by then.

MOST IMPRESSIVE TEAMMATE:
Has to be Iestyn. He works so hard at improving his game, he's just going to get better and better, and his leadership skills are amazing for a young bloke.

MOST IMPRESSIVE OPPONENT:
Jason Robinson, without a doubt. So fast and elusive. Big blokes don't mind tackling other big blokes but when you're faced with that sort of player it's frightening.

HOPES FOR 2000:
With two pieces of silverware up for grabs we have got to go for both. Retaining the Challenge Cup would be a real achievement.

LEEDS RHINOS

DATE	FIXTURE	RESULT	SCORERS	LGE	ATT
14/2/99	Wigan (h) (CCR4)	W28-18	t:Godden,Rivett,St Hilaire,Sheridan g:Harris(5) fg:Harris,Sheridan	N/A	15,500
27/2/99	St Helens (h) (CCR5)	W24-16	t:Sheridan,Newton g:Harris(8)	N/A	14,162
7/3/99	Gateshead (a)	W14-24	t:Glanville,Harris,Powell,Cummins g:Harris(4)	N/A	5,960
14/3/99	Widnes (a) (CCQF)	W10-46	t:Hay(3),Sinfield(2),Godden,Golden,McDermott,Rivett g:Harris(5)	N/A	6,375
19/3/99	Wigan (h)	L12-26	t:Sheridan,Golden g:Harris(2)	9th	15,160
28/3/99	Bradford (CCSF)	W10-23	t:Sheridan,St Hilaire,Harris g:Harris(5) fg:Sheridan	N/A	23,438
1/4/99	Bradford (a)	L18-14	t:Sheridan,Harris g:Harris(3)	9th	16,049
5/4/99	London (h)	W38-12	t:Lawford(2),Cummins,Farrell,Golden,Rivett,Harris g:Harris(5)	6th	12,665
11/4/99	Sheffield (a)	L22-16	t:Sterling,Morley g:Harris(4)	8th	5,101
16/4/99	Hull (h)	W22-18	t:Rivett(2),Jackson g:Harris(5)	6th	10,009
25/4/99	Huddersfield (a)	W20-42	t:Rivett(2),Cummins,Morley,Powell,St Hilaire,Godden,Sheridan g:Cummins(3),Harris(2)	6th	5,346
1/5/99	London (CCFN)	W52-16	t:Rivett(4),Godden,McDermott,St Hilaire,Harris,Cummins g:Harris(8)	N/A	73,242
4/5/99	St Helens (a)	L62-18	t:Fleary,Cummins,Hay g:Sinfield(3)	7th	11,314
7/5/99	Wakefield (h)	W22-8	t:Golden,Sheridan,Cummins g:Cummins(3),Lawford(2)	7th	11,109
12/5/99	Salford (a)	W30-38	t:St Hilaire(2),Cummins(2),Sheridan,Farrell,Fleary g:Harris(3),Cummins(2)	6th	3,455
16/5/99	Warrington (a)	W10-28	t:Cummins(3),Golden,Harris g:Harris(4)	6th	5,708
21/5/99	Halifax (h)	W70-22	t:Morley,Rivett(2),Godden,Newton,Powell,Farrell,Sheridan,Sterling,Harris,Cummins g:Harris(11)	3rd	12,649
30/5/99	Castleford (a)	D12-12	t:Jackson g:Harris(4)	3rd	10,462
4/6/99	Gateshead (h)	W32-14	t:Rivett(2),Cummins,Sheridan,Sterling,St Hilaire g:Harris(4)	4th	10,821
11/6/99	Wigan (a)	W4-13	t:Mathiou,Sterling g:Harris(2) fg:Harris	3rd	9,588
18/6/99	Bradford (h)	W45-16	t:Hay(3),Glanville,Morley,Rivett,Sterling g:Harris(8) fg:Powell	3rd	21,666
23/6/99	Castleford (h)	W50-22	t:Golden(3),Harris(2),Hay,St Hilaire,Rivett,Sterling g:Harris(5),Sinfield(2)	3rd	16,371
26/6/99	London (a)	W16-22	t:Cummins(2),McDermott g:Harris(5)	2nd	3,551
2/7/99	Sheffield (h)	W40-16	t:Sterling,Cummins,Sheridan,Newton,Powell,Harris,Godden g:Harris(6)	2nd	12,607
9/7/99	Hull (a)	W18-26	t:Sheridan(2),St Hilaire,Harris g:Harris(5)	2nd	3,522
16/7/99	Huddersfield (h)	W86-6	t:Harris(4),Sterling(3),St Hilaire(2),Speak,Farrell,Golden,Sheridan,Cummins,Masella g:Harris(13)	2nd	11,625
23/7/99	St Helens (h)	L12-28	t:Powell g:Harris(4)	4th	16,385
1/8/99	Wakefield (a)	W10-34	t:Blackmore(2),Godden,Harris,Sterling,Golden,Cummins g:Harris(3)	3rd	6,188
6/8/99	Warrington (h)	W34-30	t:Sterling(3),Hay(2),Glanville g:Harris(5)	3rd	10,670
13/8/99	Halifax (a)	L21-20	t:McDermott,Cummins,Sterling g:Harris(4)	4th	5,144
18/8/99	Salford (h)	W50-16	t:Cummins(2),Walker(2),Hay,Jackson,Godden,Sterling,Harris g:Sinfield(7)	3rd	10,117
22/8/99	Gateshead (a)	W18-30	t:Cummins,Farrell,Sheridan,Rivett g:Harris(5),Cummins(2)	3rd	5,498
27/8/99	Wigan (h)	W28-22	t:Cummins,Rivett,Harris,Godden,Sheridan g:Harris(4)	3rd	15,835
3/9/99	Bradford (h)	L19-18	t:Farrell,Walker g:Harris(5)	3rd	24,020
10/9/99	London (h)	W14-8	t:Cummins,Harris g:Harris(3)	3rd	14,643
17/9/99	St Helens (a) (QPO)	L38-14	t:Harris,Jackson g:Harris(3)	N/A	9,585
24/9/99	Castleford (h) (ESF)	L16-23	t:Cummins(2) g:Harris(4)	N/A	16,912

	APP		TRIES		GOALS		FG		PTS	
	ALL	SL	ALL	SL	ALL	SL	ALL	SL	ALL	SL
Richie Blackmore	6	2	2	2	0	0	0	0	8	8
Chris Chapman	(1)	(1)	0	0	0	0	0	0	0	0
Francis Cummins	35(2)	30(2)	26	25	10	10	0	0	124	120
Anthony Farrell	28(3)	24(3)	6	6	0	0	0	0	24	24
Darren Fleary	23(4)	18(4)	2	2	0	0	0	0	8	8
Marc Glanville	30(1)	25(1)	3	3	0	0	0	0	12	12
Brad Godden	29	24	9	6	0	0	0	0	36	24
Marvin Golden	24(3)	23(2)	10	9	0	0	0	0	40	36
Iestyn Harris	31(4)	26(4)	20	18	166	135	2	1	414	343
Andy Hay	21(10)	20(7)	11	8	0	0	0	0	44	32
Lee Jackson	5(23)	4(19)	4	4	0	0	0	0	16	16
Jamie Jones-Buchanan	(3)	(3)	0	0	0	0	0	0	0	0
Dean Lawford	3	3	2	2	2	2	0	0	12	12
Martin Masella	16(4)	15(3)	1	1	0	0	0	0	4	4
Jamie Mathiou	1(26)	1(21)	1	1	0	0	0	0	4	4
Barrie McDermott	29(3)	25(3)	4	2	0	0	0	0	16	8
Adrian Morley	27(4)	23(4)	5	5	0	0	0	0	20	20
Terry Newton	30	25	3	2	0	0	0	0	12	8
Daryl Powell	31(1)	26(1)	5	5	0	0	1	1	21	21
Karl Pratt	1(5)	1(5)	0	0	0	0	0	0	0	0
Leroy Rivett	29(4)	24(4)	19	13	0	0	0	0	76	52
Keith Senior	3	3	0	0	0	0	0	0	0	0
Ryan Sheridan	28(1)	23(1)	16	13	0	0	2	0	66	52
Kevin Sinfield	9(12)	9(11)	2	0	12	12	0	0	32	24
Andy Speak	4	4	1	1	0	0	0	0	4	4
Paul Sterling	25(7)	25(6)	16	16	0	0	0	0	64	64
Marcus St Hilaire	11(14)	11(10)	11	8	0	0	0	0	44	32
Chev Walker	1(3)	1(3)	3	3	0	0	0	0	12	12
Danny Ward	1(2)	1(2)	0	0	0	0	0	0	0	0
David Wrench	(2)	(2)	0	0	0	0	0	0	0	0

LEAGUE RECORD
P30-W22-D1-L7
(3rd, SL/Elimination Semi)
F910, A558, Diff+352
45 points.

CHALLENGE CUP
Winners

ATTENDANCES
Best - v Bradford (SL - 21,666)
Worst - v Hull (SL - 10,009)
Total (SL, inc play-offs) - 219,244
Average (SL, inc play-offs) - 13,703
(Up by 1,592 on 1998)

MOST TACKLES
Daryl Powell 537

MOST CLEAN BREAKS
Iestyn Harris 37

MOST METRES GAINED
Iestyn Harris 3498

Karle Hammond

SEASON'S HIGH POINT:
Getting to Wembley. It is every Rugby League player's ambition, even the Aussies, and it made it special being there for the last one.

SEASON'S LOW POINT:
The run of defeats in the first half of the season. We'd had the best pre-season preparation I have been involved with but we couldn't get the results. Losing both props Grant Young and Darren Bradstreet to injury was a big blow.

MOST IMPRESSIVE TEAMMATE:
The biggest strength of this team is the spirit in the side, every one of the players I regard as a close friend. It's one big family. If I had to mention any individuals it would be Steele Retchless and Shane Millard. They don't get much publicity but without them we wouldn't have won many games.

MOST IMPRESSIVE OPPONENT:
Sean Long. He's always been dangerous but Ellery seems to have brought the best out in him, and he is consistent every game, which a scrum-half needs to be.

HOPES FOR 2000:
To be consistent in a consistent side. We'll be aiming for top-five but with the mergers it is going to be even harder this year.

218

LONDON BRONCOS

DATE	FIXTURE	RESULT	SCORERS	LGE	ATT
14/2/99	Doncaster (h) (CCR4)	W64-0	t:Hammond(3),Bradstreet(2),Smyth,Timu,Young,Fleming,Toshack,Edwards g:Smyth(10)	N/A	2,164
28/2/99	Hull KR (a) (CCR5)	W0-6	t:Offiah g:Smyth	N/A	3,971
7/3/99	Huddersfield (h)	W24-18	t:Tollett,Fleming,Hammond,Offiah g:Warton(4)	N/A	2,278
14/3/99	Whitehaven (h) (CCQF)	W54-6	t:Offiah(5),Timu,Fleming,Beazley,Young,Edwards g:Warton(7)	N/A	1,598
20/3/99	Sheffield (a)	W20-26	t:Fleming(2),Offiah,Peters g:Warton(5)	4th	3,269
27/3/99	Castleford (CCSF)	W27-33	t:Hammond,Offiah,Beazley,Edwards,Gill,Retchless g:Warton(4) fg:Beazley	N/A	7,561
2/4/99	Hull (h)	W12-10	t:Seibold,Fleming g:Warton(2)	3rd	3,472
5/4/99	Leeds (a)	L38-12	t:Millard,Hammond g:Warton(2)	4th	12,665
9/4/99	St Helens (h)	L18-34	t:Warton,Gill,Fleming g:Warton(3)	7th	3,657
18/4/99	Wakefield (a)	L40-8	t:Tollett g:Tollett(2)	10th	3,097
24/4/99	Warrington (h)	L18-30	t:Toshack,Tollett,Offiah g:Smyth(2),Tollett	10th	2,378
1/5/99	Leeds (CCFN)	L52-16	t:Offiah,Simpson,Fleming g:Smyth(2)	N/A	73,242
5/5/99	Halifax (h)	L26-24	t:Beazley,Ryan,Fleming,Smyth g:Smyth(4)	10th	3,650
9/5/99	Castleford (h)	D12-12	t:Smyth,Callaway,Offiah	10th	2,347
16/5/99	Salford (a)	L31-14	t:Peters,Offiah,Fleming g:Hammond	10th	3,052
23/5/99	Gateshead (h)	D18-18	t:Wynyard,Fleming,Ryan g:Smyth(3)	11th	1,788
28/5/99	Wigan (a)	L12-30	t:Toshack,Callaway g:Smyth(2)	11th	3,373
6/6/99	Huddersfield (a)	W20-21	t:Fleming(2),Air,Hammond g:Tollett(2) fg:Air	11th	2,685
9/6/99	Bradford (a)	L74-12	t:Timu,Air g:Tollett,Fleming	11th	9,575
13/6/99	Sheffield (h)	W44-12	t:Ryan(2),Hammond(2),Tollett,Wynyard,Beazley,Timu g:Tollett(6)	10th	1,960
20/6/99	Hull (a)	W6-47	t:Peters(2),Ryan(2),Hammond(2),Air,Fleming g:Tollett(7) fg:Hammond	9th	3,833
26/6/99	Leeds (h)	L16-22	t:Hammond,Tollett,Seibold g:Tollett(2)	10th	3,551
4/7/99	St Helens (a)	W22-24	t:Toshack,Tollett,Fleming,Gill g:Tollett(3),Hammond	9th	6,860
7/7/99	Wigan (a)	L22-4	t:Tollett	9th	7,225
11/7/99	Wakefield (h)	W36-26	t:Fleming(2),Hammond,Tollett,Ryan,Callaway g:Warton(6)	8th	2,228
18/7/99	Warrington (a)	L28-14	t:Fleming,Peters g:Warton(2),Smyth	8th	4,419
23/7/99	Halifax (h)	W48-12	t:Hammond(4),Retchless,Timu,Fleming,Smyth,Wynyard,Toshack g:Warton(4)	8th	2,044
28/7/99	Bradford (h)	L16-19	t:Tollett,Callaway,Timu g:Warton(2)	8th	8,233
1/8/99	Castleford (a)	L52-16	t:Warton,Spencer,Edwards g:Warton,Millard	8th	5,693
7/8/99	Salford (h)	W28-14	t:Gill,Hammond,Toshack,Retchless,Fleming g:Warton(4)	8th	2,153
15/8/99	Gateshead (a)	W22-28	t:Callaway(2),Beazley,Fleming,Ryan g:Warton(4)	8th	2,631
22/8/99	Huddersfield (h)	W40-4	t:Fleming(3),Hammond(2),Smyth,Callaway,Millard g:Smyth(3),Warton	8th	2,011
28/8/99	Sheffield (h)	L20-16	t:Gill,Tollett,Warton g:Warton(2)	8th	2,024
5/9/99	Hull (h)	W28-12	t:Fleming(2),Edwards,Toshack,Seibold g:Warton(4)	8th	2,538
10/9/99	Leeds (a)	L14-8	t:Callaway g:Warton(2)	8th	14,643

	APP		TRIES		GOALS		FG		PTS	
	ALL	SL	ALL	SL	ALL	SL	ALL	SL	ALL	SL
Glen Air	21(2)	21(1)	3	3	0	0	1	1	13	13
Robbie Beazley	20(9)	15(9)	5	3	0	0	1	0	21	12
Darren Bradstreet	4	1	2	0	0	0	0	0	8	0
Dean Callaway	17(14)	17(9)	8	8	0	0	0	0	32	32
Scott Cram	15	15	0	0	0	0	0	0	0	0
Shaun Edwards	11(5)	6(5)	5	2	0	0	0	0	20	8
Greg Fleming	35	30	26	23	1	1	0	0	106	94
Peter Gill	24(5)	20(5)	5	4	0	0	0	0	20	16
Karle Hammond	33	28	20	16	2	2	1	1	85	69
Stefan Hughes	(5)	(5)	0	0	0	0	0	0	0	0
Ed Jennings	1(1)	1(1)	0	0	0	0	0	0	0	0
Dave Long	(1)	(1)	0	0	0	0	0	0	0	0
Shane Millard	25(2)	23(2)	2	2	1	1	0	0	10	10
Martin Offiah	14(3)	9(3)	13	5	0	0	0	0	52	20
Dominic Peters	18(7)	17(4)	5	5	0	0	0	0	20	20
Steele Retchless	29	24	3	2	0	0	0	0	12	8
Chris Ryan	23(5)	23(3)	8	8	0	0	0	0	32	32
Matt Salter	7(11)	6(10)	0	0	0	0	0	0	0	0
Anthony Seibold	22(3)	22(3)	3	3	0	0	0	0	12	12
Robbie Simpson	9(9)	6(7)	1	0	0	0	0	0	4	0
Rob Smyth	16(1)	13(1)	5	4	28	15	0	0	76	46
Ady Spencer	(15)	(15)	1	1	0	0	0	0	4	4
Wayne Sykes	(2)	(2)	0	0	0	0	0	0	0	0
Giles Thomas	1	1	0	0	0	0	0	0	0	0
John Timu	31	26	6	4	0	0	0	0	24	16
Tulsen Tollett	23(3)	18(3)	10	10	24	24	0	0	88	88
Matt Toshack	17(14)	14(12)	7	6	0	0	0	0	28	24
Brett Warton	18(1)	16	3	3	59	48	0	0	130	108
Andrew Wynyard	16(4)	16(4)	3	3	0	0	0	0	12	12
Grant Young	5	2	2	0	0	0	0	0	8	0

LEAGUE RECORD
P30-W13-D2-L15
(8th, SL)
F644, A708, Diff-64
28 points.

CHALLENGE CUP
Runners Up

ATTENDANCES
Best - v Bradford (SL - 8,233)
Worst - v Whitehaven (CC - 1,598)
Total (SL only) - 44,011
Average (SL only) - 2,935
(Down by 690 on 1998)

MOST TACKLES
Shane Millard 825

MOST CLEAN BREAKS
Greg Fleming 50

MOST METRES GAINED
Greg Fleming 3896

David Bradbury

SEASON'S HIGH POINT:

Just staying in Super League was an achievement last year with the run of injuries we had. It was pretty tough all season and the wins against Sheffield and Warrington kept us safe.

SEASON'S LOW POINT:

When Andy Gregory left the club. I hope he can get back into the game. He is a great of the game and a great bloke, but it just didn't work out for him.

MOST IMPRESSIVE TEAMMATE:

David Hulme for his sheer determination and total professionalism. He's been a great professional all year, all his career, and it is sad to see him leaving the club.

MOST IMPRESSIVE OPPONENT:

Jason Robinson amongst a lot of very good players in Super League. When Wigan beat us at the Willows he was unstoppable with his sheer pace.

HOPES FOR 2000:

For the club just to improve on last year and have a bit more luck on the injury front.

SALFORD CITY REDS

DATE	FIXTURE	RESULT	SCORERS	LGE	ATT
13/2/99	Sheffield (h) (CCR4)	W16-6	t:Smith,Martin g:Blakeley(4)	N/A	2,359
28/2/99	Huddersfield (a) (CCR5)	W14-22	t:Casey(2),Crompton,Martin g:Blakeley(3)	N/A	4,992
7/3/99	St Helens (h)	L12-30	t:Hayes,Crompton g:Blakeley(2)	N/A	6,378
13/3/99	Castleford (a) (CCQF)	L30-10	t:Broadbent g:Blakeley(3)	N/A	5,236
21/3/99	Wakefield (a)	L22-10	t:Carige,Casey g:Casey	13th	4,004
2/4/99	Warrington (h)	L22-26	t:Alker(2),Briggs,Hulme g:Blakeley(3)	13th	6,249
6/4/99	Halifax (a)	L30-14	t:Highton,Casey,Crompton g:Casey	13th	3,724
11/4/99	Castleford (h)	L17-29	t:Littler,Baynes,J Faimalo g:Blakeley(2) fg:Briggs	13th	3,663
18/4/99	Huddersfield (h)	L14-15	t:Blakeley,Carige g:Blakeley(3)	13th	4,125
25/4/99	Gateshead (a)	L38-14	t:Hayes,Martin,Svabic g:Blakeley	13th	1,780
3/5/99	Wigan (h)	L6-46	t:Briggs g:Blakeley	14th	4,418
9/5/99	Bradford (a)	L46-6	t:Thompson g:Blakeley	14th	11,863
12/5/99	Leeds (h)	L30-38	t:Johnson(2),Blakeley,Makin,Smith g:Blakeley(5)	14th	3,455
16/5/99	London (h)	W31-14	t:Blakeley(3),Johnson,Thompson g:Blakeley(5) fg:Blakeley	14th	3,052
22/5/99	Sheffield (a)	D26-26	t:Carige(2),Hulme,Johnson g:Blakeley(3),Casey(2)	13th	3,100
30/5/99	Hull (h)	W38-18	t:Brown(3),Broadbent,J Faimalo,Alker,Johnson g:Blakeley(3),Casey(2)	12th	3,699
6/6/99	St Helens (a)	L48-0	No Scorers	12th	7,402
13/6/99	Wakefield (h)	W28-14	t:Smith,Highton,Johnson,Crompton,Thompson g:Southern(4)	12th	4,632
20/6/99	Warrington (a)	L28-14	t:Carige,Crompton,J Faimalo g:Casey	12th	4,869
23/6/99	Hull (a)	L18-12	t:Highton,Casey g:Casey(2)	12th	3,100
27/6/99	Halifax (h)	L20-22	t:Smith,Brown,Briggs g:Casey(4)	12th	3,536
4/7/99	Castleford (a)	L38-10	t:Johnson,Highton g:Casey	13th	5,786
11/7/99	Huddersfield (a)	W10-24	t:Johnson(2),Littler,Baynes g:Southern(2),Casey(2)	12th	3,191
18/7/99	Gateshead (h)	L18-31	t:Broadbent,Carige,Smith g:Casey(3)	12th	5,611
25/7/99	Wigan (a)	L64-2	g:Casey	12th	7,144
1/8/99	Bradford (h)	L20-58	t:Highton,Blakeley,Ayres,Southern g:Casey(2)	12th	6,680
7/8/99	London (a)	L28-14	t:Littler,J Faimalo,Blakeley,Casey	12th	2,153
15/8/99	Sheffield (h)	W26-12	t:Johnson(2),Broadbent,Thompson g:Blakeley(4),Southern	12th	3,307
18/8/99	Leeds (a)	L50-16	t:Waring,Carige,Johnson g:Ayres(2)	12th	10,117
22/8/99	St Helens (a)	L10-23	t:Crompton g:Blakeley(3)	12th	5,149
29/8/99	Wakefield (a)	L36-10	t:Johnson,J Faimalo g:Southern	12th	2,736
5/9/99	Warrington (h)	W42-26	t:Brown(2),Smith,Broadbent,Crompton,Johnson,J Faimalo g:Blakeley(7)	12th	3,627
10/9/99	Halifax (a)	L32-20	t:Johnson,Thompson,Littler,Bradbury g:Thompson(2)	12th	5,764

	APP		TRIES		GOALS		FG		PTS	
	ALL	SL	ALL	SL	ALL	SL	ALL	SL	ALL	SL
Malcolm Alker	27	24	3	3	0	0	0	0	12	12
Warren Ayres	2(9)	2(9)	1	1	2	2	0	0	8	8
Neil Baynes	20(6)	17(6)	2	2	0	0	0	0	8	8
Steve Blakeley	23	20	7	7	53	43	1	1	135	115
David Bradbury	12(7)	12(7)	1	1	0	0	0	0	4	4
Carl Briggs	8(7)	8(5)	3	3	0	0	1	1	13	13
Gary Broadbent	26	23	5	4	0	0	0	0	20	16
Darren Brown	21(1)	19(1)	6	6	0	0	0	0	24	24
Paul Carige	27(1)	24(1)	7	7	0	0	0	0	28	28
Garen Casey	16(5)	13(5)	5	3	23	23	0	0	66	58
Martin Crompton	19(4)	16(4)	7	6	0	0	0	0	28	24
Esene Faimalo	(6)	(6)	0	0	0	0	0	0	0	0
Joe Faimalo	4(29)	4(26)	6	6	0	0	0	0	24	24
Jim Forshaw	(1)	(1)	0	0	0	0	0	0	0	0
Joey Hayes	11	9	2	2	0	0	0	0	8	8
Ricky Helliwell	(1)	(1)	0	0	0	0	0	0	0	0
Gareth Hewitt	2(1)	2(1)	0	0	0	0	0	0	0	0
Paul Highton	12(20)	12(17)	5	5	0	0	0	0	20	20
David Hulme	23	20	2	2	0	0	0	0	8	8
Mark Johnson	21(1)	21(1)	15	15	0	0	0	0	60	60
Mark Lee	5(2)	5(2)	0	0	0	0	0	0	0	0
Stuart Littler	23(1)	23(1)	4	4	0	0	0	0	16	16
Craig Makin	20(3)	20(3)	1	1	0	0	0	0	4	4
Scott Martin	10(3)	8(2)	3	1	0	0	0	0	12	4
Chris Morley	3(5)	3(5)	0	0	0	0	0	0	0	0
Julian Penni	1	1	0	0	0	0	0	0	0	0
Robert Russell	(1)	(1)	0	0	0	0	0	0	0	0
Hudson Smith	26(2)	23(2)	6	5	0	0	0	0	24	20
Paul Southern	28(3)	25(3)	1	1	8	8	0	0	20	20
Simon Svabic	3(6)	3(4)	1	1	0	0	0	0	4	4
Bobby Thompson	31	28	5	5	2	2	0	0	24	24
Phil Waring	5(2)	5(2)	1	1	0	0	0	0	4	4

LEAGUE RECORD
P30-W6-D1-L23
(12th, SL)
F526, A916, Diff-390
13 points.

CHALLENGE CUP
Quarter Finalists

ATTENDANCES
Best - v Bradford (SL - 6,680)
Worst - v Sheffield (CC - 2,359)
Total (SL only) - 67,581
Average (SL only) - 4,505
(Down by 170 on 1998)

MOST TACKLES
Malcolm Alker 914

MOST CLEAN BREAKS
Bobby Thompson 21

MOST METRES GAINED
Bobby Thompson 3151

Dale Laughton

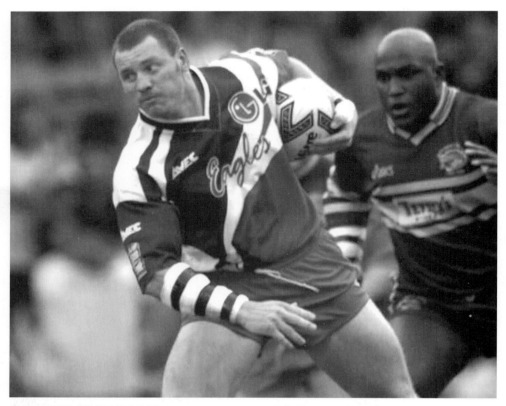

SEASON'S HIGH POINT:
I'd have to go back to the win against
Leeds at home when we had to come
from behind to beat a good team.
Apart from that it wasn't a great
season.

SEASON'S LOW POINT:
When we lost to Bradford at Saltergate
in Chesterfield by 52-2. There was a lot
of soul-searching among the players
after that.

MOST IMPRESSIVE TEAMMATE:
Steve Molloy. He outplayed me all year
and was unlucky not to get in the Great
Britain team. When I was suspended or
injured he kept things going.

MOST IMPRESSIVE OPPONENT:
Adrian Vowles. His aggression and
never-say-die game makes him a
difficult player to play against.

HOPES FOR 2000:
That as a side we should show
consistency. And that we have no
financial worries like the ones we had
hanging over us for most of last
season.

SHEFFIELD EAGLES

DATE	FIXTURE	RESULT	SCORERS	LGE	ATT
13/2/99	Salford (a) (CCR4)	L16-6	t:Senior g:Aston	N/A	2,359
7/3/99	Bradford (a)	L18-6	t:Watson g:Aston	N/A	12,044
20/3/99	London (h)	L20-26	t:Pearson(2),Shaw g:Aston(4)	11th	3,269
2/4/99	Huddersfield (h)	W32-28	t:Sodje,Laughton,Aston,Pearson,Turner g:Aston(5) fg:Pearson,Shaw	11th	3,621
5/4/99	Hull (a)	W21-23	t:Sodje(2),Lovell(2) g:Aston(3) fg:Aston	8th	3,995
11/4/99	Leeds (h)	W22-16	t:Doyle(2),Baldwin,Hardy g:Aston(3)	6th	5,101
18/4/99	St Helens (a)	L39-30	t:Powell,Sodje,Hardy,Turner g:Aston(7)	9th	9,010
25/4/99	Wakefield (h)	W22-12	t:Hardy,Watson,Sodje g:Aston(3),Pearson(2)	8th	4,387
3/5/99	Warrington (a)	L40-4	t:Crowther	8th	5,524
8/5/99	Halifax (h)	W27-8	t:Cardoza(2),Jackson,Senior,Hardy g:Pearson(3) fg:Pearson	8th	3,901
16/5/99	Castleford (a)	L10-6	t:Doyle g:Pearson	9th	5,748
22/5/99	Salford (h)	D26-26	t:Pearson,Lovell,Senior,Anderson g:Pearson(5)	8th	3,100
30/5/99	Gateshead (a)	L26-18	t:Senior,Molloy,Lovell g:Pearson(3)	8th	1,880
2/6/99	Wigan (a)	L28-0	No Scorers	8th	6,005
5/6/99	Bradford (h)	L2-52	g:Thorman	9th	4,801
13/6/99	London (a)	L44-12	t:Watson,Pearson g:Pearson(2)	11th	1,960
20/6/99	Huddersfield (a)	L37-18	t:Pearson(2),Crowther g:Pearson(3)	11th	2,363
26/6/99	Hull (h)	W18-8	t:Lawless,Powell g:Pearson(5)	11th	3,449
29/6/99	Gateshead (h)	L6-23	t:Doyle g:Pearson	11th	2,319
2/7/99	Leeds (a)	L40-16	t:Sodje(3) g:Pearson(2)	11th	12,607
10/7/99	St Helens (h)	L16-21	t:Stephens,Lovell g:Pearson(3),Thorman	11th	4,487
18/7/99	Wakefield (a)	W6-24	t:Sodje(2),Pearson,Doyle g:Pearson(4)	10th	3,107
21/7/99	Wigan (h)	L12-36	t:Baldwin,Crowther g:Pearson(2)	10th	3,526
24/7/99	Warrington (a)	L16-48	t:Sodje,Crowther,Thorman g:Crowther,Thorman	10th	2,614
1/8/99	Halifax (a)	W24-43	t:Doyle(2),Senior(2),Shaw,Crowther,Hardy,Sodje g:Thorman(5) fg:Thorman	9th	3,441
7/8/99	Castleford (h)	L0-22	No Scorers	9th	3,750
15/8/99	Salford (a)	L26-12	t:Sodje,Hardy g:Aston(2)	11th	3,307
22/8/99	Bradford (a)	L52-4	t:Slicker	11th	11,029
28/8/99	London (h)	W20-16	t:Sovatabua(2),Lovell g:Aston(4)	11th	2,024
4/9/99	Huddersfield (h)	W47-32	t:Lovell(2),Turner,Senior,Crowther,Sovatabua,Sodje,Pearson g:Aston(7) fg:Aston	9th	3,500
12/9/99	Hull (a)	L33-16	t:Hardy,Sodje,Thorman g:Aston(2)	10th	5,447

	APP		TRIES		GOALS		FG		PTS	
	ALL	SL	ALL	SL	ALL	SL	ALL	SL	ALL	SL
Paul Anderson	3(7)	3(7)	1	1	0	0	0	0	4	4
Mark Aston	14(2)	13(2)	1	1	42	41	2	2	90	88
Simon Baldwin	7(16)	7(15)	2	2	0	0	0	0	8	8
Dale Cardoza	11(4)	11(4)	2	2	0	0	0	0	8	8
Matt Crowther	18(1)	18(1)	6	6	1	1	0	0	26	26
Rod Doyle	19(5)	18(5)	7	7	0	0	0	0	28	28
Lee Greenwood	1(1)	1(1)	0	0	0	0	0	0	0	0
Jeff Hardy	23(4)	22(4)	7	7	0	0	0	0	28	28
Michael Jackson	14(12)	14(12)	1	1	0	0	0	0	4	4
Dale Laughton	20(3)	19(3)	1	1	0	0	0	0	4	4
Johnny Lawless	31	30	1	1	0	0	0	0	4	4
Karl Lovell	23(4)	22(4)	8	8	0	0	0	0	32	32
Steve Molloy	26(2)	26(2)	1	1	0	0	0	0	4	4
Chris Molyneux	1(3)	1(2)	0	0	0	0	0	0	0	0
Martin Pearson	18(6)	17(6)	9	9	36	36	2	2	110	110
Daio Powell	14(1)	13(1)	2	2	0	0	0	0	8	8
Keith Senior	30	29	7	6	0	0	0	0	28	24
Darren Shaw	29(1)	28(1)	2	2	0	0	1	1	9	9
Michael Slicker	(3)	(3)	1	1	0	0	0	0	4	4
Bright Sodje	27	26	15	15	0	0	0	0	60	60
Waisale Sovatabua	12(10)	11(10)	3	3	0	0	0	0	12	12
Gareth Stephens	14(2)	14(1)	1	1	0	0	0	0	4	4
Frederic Teixido	(4)	(4)	0	0	0	0	0	0	0	0
Chris Thorman	5(13)	5(13)	2	2	8	8	1	1	25	25
Darren Turner	22(3)	21(3)	3	3	0	0	0	0	12	12
Marcus Vassilakopoulos	(2)	(2)	0	0	0	0	0	0	0	0
Dave Watson	21(3)	21(2)	3	3	0	0	0	0	12	12
Ricky Wright	(8)	(8)	0	0	0	0	0	0	0	0

LEAGUE RECORD
P30-W10-D1-L19
(10th, SL)
F518, A818, Diff-300
21 points.

CHALLENGE CUP
Round Four

ATTENDANCES
Best - v Leeds (SL - 5,101)
Worst - v London (SL - 2,024)
Total (SL only) - 53,849
Average (SL only) - 3,590
(Down by 1,005 on 1998)

MOST TACKLES
Darren Shaw 710

MOST CLEAN BREAKS
Keith Senior 22

MOST METRES GAINED
Steve Molloy 3481

Tommy Martyn

SEASON'S HIGH POINT:

Bit of a daft question. The Grand Final couldn't have been better. Most people had been writing us off after the trouble mid-season but we just kept niggling away in the background and it paid off.

SEASON'S LOW POINT:

Probably the period when Ellery was suspended. After 13 wins from the first 14 games we were going well and then four losses just seemed to create turmoil. When Ellery returned it was all positive from then on in.

MOST IMPRESSIVE TEAMMATE:

Apollo Perelini for sheer guts and determination to play through the pain barrier. At times he didn't need a shower after a match because he couldn't get dirty, he was wearing that much strapping!

MOST IMPRESSIVE OPPONENT:

Henry Paul. He can turn a game on his own. When he scored at Old Trafford there was nothing on and then in a flash we were 70 metres back down the field, under the posts, having a teamtalk.

HOPES FOR 2000:

It will be hard to follow up this season, we are aware of that. A repeat of this year wouldn't be bad, although it's about time for another trip to Wembley too.

DATE	FIXTURE	RESULT	SCORERS	LGE	ATT
14/2/99	Hunslet (a) (CCR4)	W10-40	t:Stewart(2),Sculthorpe(2),Long,Davidson,Cunningham,Barrow g:Long(4)	N/A	2,201
27/2/99	Leeds (a) (CCR5)	L24-16	t:Newlove,Atcheson g:Long(4)	N/A	14,162
7/3/99	Salford (a)	W12-30	t:Long(3),Newlove(2),Sculthorpe g:Long(3)	N/A	6,378
21/3/99	Gateshead (h)	W34-22	t:Iro(2),Cunningham,Newlove,Perelini,Long g:Long(5)	2nd	5,910
2/4/99	Wigan (a)	W12-14	t:Sullivan,Atcheson,Iro g:Martyn	1st	16,283
5/4/99	Bradford (h)	W58-14	t:Sullivan(3),Stewart(2),Tuilagi,Jonkers,Martyn,Sculthorpe g:Martyn(11)	1st	15,042
9/4/99	London (a)	W18-34	t:Atcheson(3),Sullivan(2),Martyn,Jonkers g:Martyn(3)	1st	3,657
18/4/99	Sheffield (h)	W39-30	t:Iro,Wellens,Cunningham,Nickle,Stewart,Perelini g:Long(7) fg:Wellens	1st	9,010
25/4/99	Hull (a)	W10-30	t:Sullivan(2),Perelini,Cunningham,Long g:Long(5)	1st	5,879
4/5/99	Leeds (h)	W62-18	t:Sullivan(2),Long(2),Stewart(2),Newlove,Joynt,Sculthorpe,Atcheson,Nickle,Smith g:Long(7)	1st	11,314
7/5/99	Huddersfield (a)	W0-11	t:Tuilagi,Joynt g:Long fg:Long	1st	4,060
14/5/99	Wakefield (a)	L23-22	t:Cunningham,Sculthorpe,Wellens,Long g:Long(3)	1st	4,556
19/5/99	Castleford (a)	W14-33	t:Smith(3),Newlove(2),Long g:Long(4) fg:Martyn	1st	6,633
23/5/99	Warrington (h)	W57-20	t:Long(2),O'Neill(2),Joynt,Stewart,Newlove,Cunningham,Smith,Martyn g:Long(8) fg:Martyn	1st	10,042
30/5/99	Halifax (a)	W22-28	t:Newlove,Stewart,Nickle,Martyn,Tuilagi,Perelini g:Long(2)	1st	4,857
6/6/99	Salford (h)	W48-0	t:Smith(3),Nickle,Iro,Davidson,Tuilagi,Newlove,Cunningham g:Long(6)	1st	7,402
13/6/99	Gateshead (a)	L32-20	t:Smith,Long,Martyn,Tuilagi g:Long(2)	2nd	6,220
20/6/99	Wigan (h)	L18-24	t:Martyn,Newlove,Cunningham g:Long(3)	2nd	12,243
25/6/99	Bradford (a)	L46-22	t:Joynt(2),Sullivan,Davidson g:Long(3)	3rd	15,107
30/6/99	Halifax (h)	W46-10	t:Joynt(2),Atcheson,Sullivan,Stewart,Long,Wellens,Tuilagi,Cunningham g:Long(4),Wellens	2nd	5,788
4/7/99	London (h)	L22-24	t:Sculthorpe,Stewart,Nickle g:Long(3)	3rd	6,860
10/7/99	Sheffield (a)	W16-21	t:Sullivan,Wellens,Martyn g:Long(4) fg:Martyn	3rd	4,487
18/7/99	Hull (h)	W74-16	t:Sullivan(4),Atcheson(2),Long(2),Martyn,Cunningham,Joynt,Newlove,Tuilagi g:Martyn(11)	3rd	5,972
23/7/99	Leeds (a)	W12-28	t:Smith(3),Sullivan,Nickle g:Long(4)	2nd	16,385
30/7/99	Huddersfield (h)	W64-16	t:Long(2),Hall(2),Joynt,Tuilagi,Price,Smith,Sullivan,Cunningham,Atcheson g:Long(10)	2nd	5,213
8/8/99	Wakefield (h)	W42-34	t:Smith(2),Atcheson,Sullivan,Perelini,Tuilagi,Newlove,Price g:Martyn(4),Wellens	2nd	5,763
15/8/99	Warrington (a)	W12-35	t:Hall,Joynt,Cunningham,Wellens,Sullivan,Long g:Long(5) fg:Long	2nd	7,171
22/8/99	Salford (a)	W10-23	t:Wellens,Hall,Long g:Long(5) fg:Martyn	2nd	5,149
25/8/99	Castleford (h)	W42-14	t:Joynt(2),Newlove,Martyn,Sculthorpe,Tuilagi,Long g:Long(7)	2nd	7,976
30/8/99	Gateshead (h)	L32-36	t:Joynt(2),Newlove(2),Sculthorpe,Martyn g:Martyn(4)	2nd	5,993
5/9/99	Wigan (a)	L28-20	t:Sculthorpe,Sullivan,Iro,Martyn g:Martyn(2)	2nd	18,179
10/9/99	Bradford (h)	W25-16	t:Sculthorpe,Iro,Martyn,Sullivan g:Martyn(4) fg:Martyn	2nd	8,490
17/9/99	Leeds (h) (QPO)	W38-14	t:Newlove(2),Sullivan(2),Smith(2),Joynt,Tuilagi g:Wellens(2),Martyn	N/A	9,585
26/9/99	Bradford (a) (QSF)	L40-4	t:Newlove	N/A	16,126
3/10/99	Castleford (h) (FE)	W36-6	t:Martyn(2),Long(2),Sullivan,Joynt g:Long(5),Wellens	N/A	11,212
9/10/99	Bradford (GFN)	W6-8	t:Iro g:Long(2)	N/A	50,717

	APP		TRIES		GOALS		FG		PTS	
	ALL	SL	ALL	SL	ALL	SL	ALL	SL	ALL	SL
Phil Adamson	(3)	(1)	0	0	0	0	0	0	0	0
Paul Atcheson	31(1)	29(1)	11	10	0	0	0	0	44	40
Scott Barrow	4(8)	4(7)	1	0	0	0	0	0	4	0
Des Clark	4	4	0	0	0	0	0	0	0	0
Keiron Cunningham	34	32	12	11	0	0	0	0	48	44
Paul Davidson	15(6)	14(5)	3	2	0	0	0	0	12	8
Mark Edmondson	1(14)	1(14)	0	0	0	0	0	0	0	0
Steve Hall	1(6)	1(6)	4	4	0	0	0	0	16	16
Sean Hoppe	(5)	(5)	0	0	0	0	0	0	0	0
Kevin Iro	23(1)	23	8	8	0	0	0	0	32	32
Jason Johnson	1	1	0	0	0	0	0	0	0	0
Tim Jonkers	2(13)	2(13)	2	2	0	0	0	0	8	8
Chris Joynt	30(1)	29(1)	16	16	0	0	0	0	64	64
Sean Long	29(2)	27(2)	23	22	116	108	2	2	326	306
Tommy Martyn	26(3)	24(3)	14	14	41	41	5	5	143	143
Vila Matautia	3(18)	3(17)	0	0	0	0	0	0	0	0
Paul Newlove	29	28	19	18	0	0	0	0	76	72
Sonny Nickle	30(1)	28(1)	6	6	0	0	0	0	24	24
Julian O'Neill	30(3)	28(3)	2	2	0	0	0	0	8	8
Apollo Perelini	34	32	5	5	0	0	0	0	20	20
Gareth Price	(11)	(11)	2	2	0	0	0	0	8	8
Paul Sculthorpe	31	29	11	9	0	0	0	0	44	36
Chris Smith	27(7)	25(7)	17	17	0	0	0	0	68	68
Anthony Stewart	20(3)	18(3)	11	9	0	0	0	0	44	36
Anthony Sullivan	25(2)	24(2)	27	27	0	0	0	0	108	108
Fereti Tuilagi	23(12)	22(11)	11	11	0	0	0	0	44	44
Paul Wellens	15(16)	14(15)	6	6	5	5	1	1	35	35

LEAGUE RECORD
P30-W23-D0-L7
(2nd, SL/Grand Final Winners, Champions)
F1034, A561, Diff+473
46 points.

CHALLENGE CUP
Round Five

ATTENDANCES
Best - v Bradford (SL - 15,042)
Worst - v Huddersfield (SL - 5,213)
Total (SL, inc play-offs) - 143,815
Average (SL, inc play-offs) - 8,460
(Up by 1,222 on 1998)

MOST TACKLES
Keiron Cunningham 735

MOST CLEAN BREAKS
Sean Long 46

MOST METRES GAINED
Fereti Tuilagi 3028

Francis Stephenson

SEASON'S HIGH POINT:

The night we beat St Helens at Barnsley. Staying up was a great achievement but there was no other match that came anywhere near that one.

SEASON'S LOW POINT:

Probably when we played at Gateshead two games from the end of the season. We copped a flogging because we weren't really tuned in. It was a shame for the fans.

MOST IMPRESSIVE TEAMMATE:

Gary Price. When I used to play against him in the first division, I didn't realise what kind of a bloke he was. He's just a professional in every sense of the word.

MOST IMPRESSIVE OPPONENT:

Keiron Cunningham. It was the first time I had played against him this season and he is deceptively strong as well as having all the other attributes of a good dummy-half. Sean Long's been impressive too.

HOPES FOR 2000:

The way we have been team-building, if we didn't go all out for the top-five we'd be doing ourselves an injustice. It's not going to be easy because most other teams have strengthened too. For me personally, I want to go all out and win a place in the England team for the World Cup.

WAKEFIELD T WILDCATS

DATE	FIXTURE	RESULT	SCORERS	LGE	ATT
12/2/99	Batley (h) (CCR4)	W12-2	t:Stott,N Law g:Poching,N Law	N/A	2,322
28/2/99	Bradford (h) (CCR5)	L8-26	t:Kenward g:Hodgson(2)	N/A	7,385
7/3/99	Castleford (a)	L12-10	t:Poching,Crouthers g:Hodgson	N/A	7,233
21/3/99	Salford (h)	W22-10	t:D March(2),Stott,Poching g:G Law(3)	6th	4,004
2/4/99	Gateshead (a)	L24-6	t:G Law g:G Law	10th	3,460
5/4/99	Wigan (h)	L22-52	t:Hodgson(2),Talbot,N Law g:Talbot(3)	11th	6,104
11/4/99	Bradford (a)	L26-16	t:Kenward(2),N Law g:Hughes(2)	12th	11,802
18/4/99	London (h)	W40-8	t:Hughes(3),Poching,Kenward,McDonald,Stott g:Hughes(6)	11th	3,097
25/4/99	Sheffield (a)	L22-12	t:Hughes(2),N Law	11th	4,387
3/5/99	Hull (h)	L22-29	t:P March(2),F Watene,Brunker g:Hughes(3)	11th	4,546
7/5/99	Leeds (a)	L22-8	t:Fawcett g:Hughes(2)	11th	11,109
14/5/99	St Helens (h)	W23-22	t:Brunker,N Law,P March g:Hughes(5) fg:Stott	11th	4,556
23/5/99	Huddersfield (a)	W22-38	t:P March,Brunker,N Law,Kenward,McDonald,F Watene,Hughes g:Stott(3),Hughes(2)	10th	4,149
30/5/99	Warrington (a)	W22-36	t:N Law(2),Tomlinson,Brunker,Hughes,Price,D March g:Stott(3),Hughes	9th	4,467
6/6/99	Castleford (h)	W11-10	t:D March(2) g:Hughes fg:Kemp	8th	6,596
9/6/99	Halifax (a)	W16-36	t:Fisher,Poching,D March,F Watene,N Law,Hughes g:Hughes(6)	8th	3,466
13/6/99	Salford (a)	L28-14	t:Hughes,Tomlinson,N Law g:Hughes	8th	4,632
20/6/99	Gateshead (h)	L18-22	t:Tomlinson,Hughes,McDonald g:Hughes(3)	8th	3,400
27/6/99	Wigan (a)	L40-14	t:Songoro,P March g:P March(3)	8th	6,990
2/7/99	Bradford (h)	L8-36	t:Brunker,Songoro	10th	5,321
7/7/99	Warrington (h)	L8-15	t:D March g:Hughes(2)	10th	3,295
11/7/99	London (a)	L36-26	t:Poching(2),N Law,Songoro,Brunker g:P March(3)	10th	2,228
18/7/99	Sheffield (h)	L6-24	t:McDonald g:P March	11th	3,107
25/7/99	Hull (a)	L23-18	t:Poching,N Law,Hughes g:Talbot(3)	11th	3,602
28/7/99	Halifax (h)	W26-20	t:Fisher(2),Hughes,Stott,Poching g:Talbot(3)	9th	3,082
1/8/99	Leeds (h)	L10-34	t:Hughes,McDonald g:Talbot	10th	6,188
8/8/99	St Helens (a)	L42-34	t:N Law,McDonald,Songoro,Kemp,Poching,Kenward g:Talbot(5)	10th	5,763
15/8/99	Huddersfield (h)	W40-12	t:Poching(2),McDonald(2),Hughes(2),Fawcett g:Talbot(6)	9th	3,200
20/8/99	Castleford (a)	L30-18	t:N Law,Tomlinson,P March g:Talbot(3)	10th	6,322
29/8/99	Salford (h)	W36-10	t:Poching,Stephenson,N Law,P March,D March,Price g:Talbot(3),P March(3)	9th	2,736
5/9/99	Gateshead (a)	L66-6	t:Kenward g:G Law	10th	3,286
12/9/99	Wigan (h)	L24-60	t:Stott,Talbot,Stephenson,Kemp g:Talbot(4)	11th	4,279

	APP		TRIES		GOALS		FG		PTS	
	ALL	SL	ALL	SL	ALL	SL	ALL	SL	ALL	SL
Adrian Brunker	19	17	6	6	0	0	0	0	24	24
Kevin Crouthers	6(4)	4(4)	1	1	0	0	0	0	4	4
Gareth Ellis	(1)	(1)	0	0	0	0	0	0	0	0
Vince Fawcett	13(1)	13(1)	2	2	0	0	0	0	8	8
Jamie Field	9(15)	9(15)	0	0	0	0	0	0	0	0
Andy Fisher	23	21	3	3	0	0	0	0	12	12
Paul Hicks	(1)	(1)	0	0	0	0	0	0	0	0
Andy Hodgson	16(2)	14(2)	2	2	3	1	0	0	14	10
Adam Hughes	24(3)	24(3)	15	15	34	34	0	0	128	128
Paul Jackson	6(21)	6(21)	0	0	0	0	0	0	0	0
Tony Kemp	16(4)	15(4)	2	2	0	0	1	1	9	9
Shane Kenward	30	28	7	6	0	0	0	0	28	24
Graham Law	7(7)	7(5)	1	1	5	5	0	0	14	14
Neil Law	32	30	15	14	1	0	0	0	62	56
David March	21(4)	21(3)	8	8	0	0	0	0	32	32
Paul March	15(8)	15(8)	7	7	10	10	0	0	48	48
Wayne McDonald	9(19)	9(17)	8	8	0	0	0	0	32	32
Willie Poching	25(1)	23(1)	12	12	1	0	0	0	50	48
Gary Price	26	24	2	2	0	0	0	0	8	8
Sean Richardson	5(1)	5(1)	0	0	0	0	0	0	0	0
Alfred Songoro	8(5)	8(5)	4	4	0	0	0	0	16	16
Roy Southernwood	2(1)	1	0	0	0	0	0	0	0	0
Francis Stephenson	32	30	2	2	0	0	0	0	8	8
Lynton Stott	23	21	5	4	6	6	1	1	33	29
Ian Talbot	10(5)	9(5)	2	2	31	31	0	0	70	70
Glen Tomlinson	27(3)	25(3)	4	4	0	0	0	0	16	16
Frank Watene	12(14)	11(13)	3	3	0	0	0	0	12	12
Steve Watene	(1)	0	0	0	0	0	0	0	0	0
Ben Westwood	(1)	(1)	0	0	0	0	0	0	0	0

LEAGUE RECORD
P30-W10-D0-L20
(11th, SL)
F608, A795, Diff-187
20 points.

CHALLENGE CUP
Round Five

ATTENDANCES
Best - v Bradford (CC - 7,385)
Worst - v Batley (CC - 2,322)
Total (SL only) - 63,511
Average (SL only) - 4,235
(Up by 2,217 on 1998, D1)

MOST TACKLES
David March 623

MOST CLEAN BREAKS
Willie Poching 32

MOST METRES GAINED
Shane Kenward 3163

Toa Kohe-Love

SEASON'S HIGH POINT:

It was a rollercoaster year but the game that sticks in my mind was the 17-all draw with Wigan at Wilderspool. We took them all the way and should have won it.

SEASON'S LOW POINT:

The run of defeats in the last five games. When we lost at Halifax our chances of the top five had gone and the whole attitude of the players changed. We just nodded off.

MOST IMPRESSIVE TEAMMATE:

Simon Gillies. Just having him on the field, his experience was felt. He's the best player I have ever played with in the way he communicates and organises the rest of the team.

MOST IMPRESSIVE OPPONENT:

Paul Newlove, again. He did me a couple of times, I find him really difficult to play against.

HOPES FOR 2000:

Same as this year, to make the top-five and then we will take it from there. We'll miss Simon Gillies but we have signed some great players so it is looking pretty good.

WARRINGTON WOLVES

DATE	FIXTURE	RESULT	SCORERS	LGE	ATT
14/2/99	Featherstone (h) (CCR4)	W50-6	t:Forster(3),Hunte(3),Wilson,Kohe-Love,Roach g:Briers(7)	N/A	4,335
28/2/99	Halifax (h) (CCR5)	W34-4	t:Forster,Roper,Hunte,Kohe-Love,Penny g:Briers(7)	N/A	5,102
7/3/99	Halifax (a)	W14-16	t:McCurrie,Kohe-Love,Penny g:Briers(2)	N/A	4,687
14/3/99	Bradford (a) (CCQF)	L52-16	t:Wilson,Kohe-Love,Forster g:Briers(2)	N/A	10,430
21/3/99	Castleford (h)	W19-14	t:Kohe-Love(2),Knott,Briers g:Briers fg:Briers	5th	4,738
2/4/99	Salford (a)	W22-26	t:Roach(2),Penny,Kohe-Love,Forster g:Briers(3)	4th	6,249
5/4/99	Gateshead (h)	W23-18	t:Roach(2),Wainwright,Hunte,Forster g:Briers fg:Briers	2nd	4,919
11/4/99	Wigan (a)	L24-10	t:Hunte,Roach g:Briers	4th	9,845
18/4/99	Bradford (h)	L14-22	t:Penny,Forster g:Briers(3)	5th	7,591
24/4/99	London (a)	W18-30	t:Roach,Hunte,Penny,Forster,Kohe-Love g:Briers(3)	4th	2,378
3/5/99	Sheffield (h)	W40-4	t:Roper(2),Wilson(2),Hunte,Knott g:Briers(8)	3rd	5,524
9/5/99	Hull (a)	W22-33	t:Forster(2),Roach(2),Kohe-Love,Wilson g:Briers(4) fg:Briers	3rd	4,679
16/5/99	Leeds (h)	L10-28	t:Kohe-Love(2) g:Briers	5th	5,708
23/5/99	St Helens (a)	L57-20	t:Hunte,Gillies,Chambers,Roach g:Briers,Knott	6th	10,042
30/5/99	Wakefield (h)	L22-36	t:Nutley,Hanger,Kohe-Love g:Roper(5)	7th	4,467
4/6/99	Halifax (h)	W31-18	t:Roper,Kohe-Love(2),Hanger,Knott g:Briers(3) fg:Briers	6th	3,298
9/6/99	Huddersfield (h)	W48-16	t:Briers(2),Kohe-Love(2),Hanger,Penny,Hunte,Forster,Knott g:Briers(6)	5th	3,941
13/6/99	Castleford (a)	L39-6	t:Kohe-Love g:Briers	6th	5,551
20/6/99	Salford (h)	W28-14	t:Kohe-Love(2),Penny,Roper,Nutley g:Briers(4)	6th	4,869
25/6/99	Gateshead (a)	L26-20	t:Gillies,Penny,Kohe-Love,Hunte g:Briers(2)	7th	3,457
4/7/99	Wigan (h)	D17-17	t:Kohe-Love,Briers g:Briers(4) fg:Briers	7th	6,273
7/7/99	Wakefield (a)	W8-15	t:Hunte,Wilson g:Roper(3) fg:Briers	7th	3,295
11/7/99	Bradford (a)	L56-6	t:Hunte g:Roper	7th	13,063
18/7/99	London (a)	W28-14	t:Gillies(3),Kohe-Love,Briers g:Roper(4)	7th	4,419
24/7/99	Sheffield (a)	W16-48	t:Kohe-Love(3),Hunte(2),Briers,Chambers,Forster,Penny g:Roper(4),Briers(2)	7th	2,614
1/8/99	Hull (h)	W32-12	t:Kohe-Love,Wainwright,Penny,Hunte g:Briers(8)	7th	4,028
6/8/99	Leeds (a)	L34-30	t:McCurrie(2),Forster,Farrar,Hunte g:Briers(5)	7th	10,670
11/8/99	Huddersfield (a)	W12-40	t:Hunte(3),Penny(2),Forster,Wilson,Roper g:Briers(4)	7th	2,183
15/8/99	St Helens (h)	L12-35	t:Causey,Wainwright g:Roper(2)	7th	7,171
20/8/99	Halifax (a)	L23-22	t:Farrar,Kohe-Love,Knott,Hunte g:Roper(3)	7th	4,106
29/8/99	Castleford (h)	L6-8	t:Wilson g:Roper	7th	4,864
5/9/99	Salford (h)	L42-26	t:McCurrie,Farrar,Gillies,Highton,Roper g:Roper(3)	7th	3,627
12/9/99	Gateshead (h)	L22-48	t:Farrar(2),Kohe-Love,Forster g:Roper(3)	7th	4,834

	APP		TRIES		GOALS		FG		PTS	
	ALL	SL	ALL	SL	ALL	SL	ALL	SL	ALL	SL
Lee Briers	32(1)	29(1)	6	6	83	67	6	6	196	164
Dean Busby	9(14)	9(12)	0	0	0	0	0	0	0	0
Chris Causey	(6)	(6)	1	1	0	0	0	0	4	4
Gary Chambers	20(10)	20(7)	2	2	0	0	0	0	8	8
Will Cowell	(2)	(2)	0	0	0	0	0	0	0	0
John Duffy	3(8)	3(8)	0	0	0	0	0	0	0	0
Danny Farrar	31	28	5	5	0	0	0	0	20	20
Mark Forster	31(1)	28(1)	16	11	0	0	0	0	64	44
Simon Gillies	31	28	6	6	0	0	0	0	24	24
Dean Hanger	7(13)	7(11)	3	3	0	0	0	0	12	12
David Highton	3(5)	3(5)	1	1	0	0	0	0	4	4
Mark Hilton	15(1)	12(1)	0	0	0	0	0	0	0	0
Alan Hunte	32	29	21	17	0	0	0	0	84	68
Ian Knott	22(10)	21(8)	5	5	1	1	0	0	22	22
Toa Kohe-Love	33	30	28	25	0	0	0	0	112	100
Andy Leathem	2(8)	2(8)	0	0	0	0	0	0	0	0
Steve McCurrie	7(17)	5(16)	4	4	0	0	0	0	16	16
Danny Nutley	28	25	2	2	0	0	0	0	8	8
Lee Penny	30(1)	27(1)	12	11	0	0	0	0	48	44
Jason Roach	16(7)	13(7)	11	10	0	0	0	0	44	40
Jonathan Roper	24(4)	22(3)	8	7	29	29	0	0	90	86
Ian Sibbit	(5)	(5)	0	0	0	0	0	0	0	0
Warren Stevens	1(4)	1(4)	0	0	0	0	0	0	0	0
Mike Wainwright	26(5)	25(4)	3	3	0	0	0	0	12	12
Scott Wilson	26(1)	23(1)	8	6	0	0	0	0	32	24

LEAGUE RECORD
P30-W15-D1-L14
(7th, SL)
F700, A717, Diff-17
31 points.

CHALLENGE CUP
Quarter Finalists

ATTENDANCES
Best - v Bradford (SL - 7,591)
Worst - v Halifax (SL - 3,298)
Total (SL only) - 76,644
Average (SL only) - 5,110
(Up by 213 on 1998)

MOST TACKLES
Danny Farrar 933

MOST CLEAN BREAKS
Toa Kohe-Love 46

MOST METRES GAINED
Lee Penny 3219

Kris Radlinski

SEASON'S HIGH POINT:
Beating Saints in the last game at Central Park. It was such an emotional night for everyone involved with Wigan, we just had to win that one.

SEASON'S LOW POINT:
Losing in the play-off against Castleford. I've never been into a Wigan dressing room that was so down as after that game. We were up for it, with it being the first game at the JJB Stadium, but it just didn't happen.

MOST IMPRESSIVE TEAMMATE:
Mick Cassidy has been outstanding all season. He played in every game and has had his best year in my opinion.

MOST IMPRESSIVE OPPONENT:
Sean Long has been fantastic. He's just such an exciting player and as he is a mate it is good to see him doing so well.

HOPES FOR 2000:
We've got to do better in the Challenge Cup - getting knocked out at the first stage at Leeds wasn't the best of starts. We're out to get some silverware back.

DATE	FIXTURE	RESULT	SCORERS	LGE	ATT
14/2/99	Leeds (a) (CCR4)	L28-18	t:Haughton,Radlinski,Robinson g:Farrell(2),Florimo	N/A	15,500
5/3/99	Hull (h)	W58-6	t:Gilmour(3),Radlinski(2),Connolly,Cassidy,A Johnson,P Johnson, Cowie,Robinson g:Farrell(7)	N/A	9,186
19/3/99	Leeds (a)	W12-26	t:P Johnson(2),Cassidy(2),Gilmour g:Farrell(3)	1st	15,160
2/4/99	St Helens (h)	L12-14	t:Florimo,Moore g:Farrell(2)	5th	16,283
5/4/99	Wakefield (a)	W22-52	t:P Johnson(3),Betts,Robinson,Gilmour,Connolly,Davies,Cassidy g:Farrell(8)	3rd	6,104
11/4/99	Warrington (h)	W24-10	t:Reber,Connolly,Farrell,Moore g:Farrell(4)	2nd	9,845
16/4/99	Halifax (a)	L19-8	t:Cassidy g:Farrell(2)	3rd	5,107
25/4/99	Castleford (h)	L8-24	t:Reber g:Farrell(2)	5th	8,856
3/5/99	Salford (a)	W6-46	t:Robinson(3),T Smith(2),Bretherton,Davies,Florimo g:Farrell(7)	5th	4,418
9/5/99	Gateshead (h)	W16-13	t:Davies(2),Robinson g:Farrell(2)	4th	7,717
16/5/99	Huddersfield (h)	W36-2	t:Reber,Haughton,Cassidy,O'Connor,Radlinski,Betts,Bretherton, Davies g:Farrell,Radlinski	3rd	6,634
22/5/99	Bradford (a)	L19-2	g:Farrell	5th	13,476
28/5/99	London (a)	W12-30	t:Moore,Davies,Reber,T Smith,Clarke g:Jones(4),Florimo	5th	3,373
2/6/99	Sheffield (h)	W28-0	t:Davies(2),Radlinski,Reber,Cassidy,Moore g:Connolly,Jones	3rd	6,005
6/6/99	Hull (a)	W12-18	t:Florimo,Robinson,Connolly g:Jones(3)	3rd	4,117
11/6/99	Leeds (h)	L4-13	t:Cassidy	4th	9,588
20/6/99	St Helens (a)	W18-24	t:Radlinski,Robinson,Haughton,Connolly g:Jones(4)	4th	12,243
27/6/99	Wakefield (h)	W40-14	t:Connolly(2),Jones,Farrell,Robinson,Gilmour,T Smith g:Jones(6)	4th	6,990
4/7/99	Warrington (a)	D17-17	t:Farrell,Connolly g:Jones(4) fg:Farrell	4th	6,273
7/7/99	London (h)	W22-4	t:T Smith(2),Radlinski,Robinson g:Farrell(3)	4th	7,225
11/7/99	Halifax (h)	W30-4	t:Radlinski(3),Gilmour,Cassidy,P Johnson g:Farrell(3)	4th	6,836
16/7/99	Castleford (a)	L33-18	t:Clarke,Goldspink,Robinson g:Farrell(3)	4th	7,089
21/7/99	Sheffield (a)	W12-36	t:Betts(3),Farrell,Florimo,Radlinski g:Farrell(6)	4th	3,526
25/7/99	Salford (h)	W64-2	t:Florimo(2),T Smith(2),Robinson(2),Radlinski(2),Moore,Clarke, Cowie g:Clinch(10)	3rd	7,144
1/8/99	Gateshead (a)	L20-16	t:Betts(2),Farrell g:Farrell(2)	4th	4,978
8/8/99	Huddersfield (a)	W10-60	t:T Smith(2),Cowie,P Johnson,Radlinski,Florimo,Robinson,Connolly, Moore,Clinch g:Farrell(10)	4th	3,137
13/8/99	Bradford (h)	W14-0	t:Connolly g:Farrell(5)	3rd	10,734
20/8/99	Hull (h)	W58-0	t:Betts(4),P Johnson(2),M Smith,Clinch,Radlinski,Robinson g:Farrell(9)	4th	6,866
27/8/99	Leeds (a)	L28-22	t:P Johnson,Robinson,Clinch,Moore g:Farrell(3)	4th	15,835
5/9/99	St Helens (h)	W28-20	t:Robinson(2),Betts,Connolly,P Johnson g:Farrell(4)	4th	18,179
12/9/99	Wakefield (a)	W24-60	t:Radlinski(3),Moore(3),Robinson,Chester,O'Connor,Clinch, Mestrov g:Farrell(6),Clinch(2)	4th	4,279
19/9/99	Castleford (h) (EPO)	L10-14	t:Betts g:Farrell(3)	N/A	13,374

	APP		TRIES		GOALS		FG		PTS	
	ALL	SL	ALL	SL	ALL	SL	ALL	SL	ALL	SL
Rob Ball	3(2)	3(2)	0	0	0	0	0	0	0	0
Denis Betts	26(1)	26(1)	13	13	0	0	0	0	52	52
Liam Bretherton	(5)	(5)	2	2	0	0	0	0	8	8
Mick Cassidy	31(1)	30(1)	9	9	0	0	0	0	36	36
Chris Chester	4(7)	4(7)	1	1	0	0	0	0	4	4
Jon Clarke	10	10	3	3	0	0	0	0	12	12
Gavin Clinch	10(2)	10(2)	4	4	12	12	0	0	40	40
Gary Connolly	30	29	11	11	1	1	0	0	46	46
Neil Cowie	25(5)	25(4)	3	3	0	0	0	0	12	12
Wes Davies	13(7)	13(6)	8	8	0	0	0	0	32	32
Andy Farrell	27	26	5	5	98	96	1	1	217	213
Greg Florimo	19(2)	18(2)	7	7	2	1	0	0	32	30
Lee Gilmour	18(11)	17(11)	7	7	0	0	0	0	28	28
Brett Goldspink	6(17)	6(16)	1	1	0	0	0	0	4	4
Simon Haughton	7(14)	6(14)	3	2	0	0	0	0	12	8
Andrew Isherwood	(2)	(2)	0	0	0	0	0	0	0	0
Andy Johnson	1(6)	1(5)	1	1	0	0	0	0	4	4
Paul Johnson	16(1)	15(1)	12	12	0	0	0	0	48	48
Phil Jones	9(2)	9(2)	1	1	22	22	0	0	48	48
Tony Mestrov	15(14)	14(14)	1	1	0	0	0	0	4	4
Danny Moore	30(1)	29(1)	10	10	0	0	0	0	40	40
Terry O'Connor	18(11)	17(11)	2	2	0	0	0	0	8	8
Kris Radlinski	26	25	18	17	1	1	0	0	74	70
Mark Reber	10(6)	9(6)	5	5	0	0	0	0	20	20
Jason Robinson	31	30	20	19	0	0	0	0	80	76
Mark Smith	9(8)	9(8)	1	1	0	0	0	0	4	4
Tony Smith	21	21	10	10	0	0	0	0	40	40
Dwayne West	1(1)	1(1)	0	0	0	0	0	0	0	0

LEAGUE RECORD
P30-W21-D1-L8
(4th, SL/Elimination Play-Off)
F877, A390, Diff+487
43 points.

CHALLENGE CUP
Round Four

ATTENDANCES
Best - v St Helens (SL - 18,179)
Worst - v Sheffield (SL - 6,005)
Total (SL, inc play-offs) - 151,462
Average (SL, inc play-offs) - 9,466
(Down by 1,337 on 1998)

MOST TACKLES
Mick Cassidy 915

MOST CLEAN BREAKS
Jason Robinson 49

MOST METRES GAINED
Jason Robinson 4039

NORTHERN FORD PREMIERSHIP STATISTICS

BARROW BORDER RAIDERS

DATE	FIXTURE	RESULT	SCORERS	LGE	ATT
31/1/99	Dudley Hill (h) (CCR3)	W44-16	t:Thomas(2),Salmon(2),Hughes(2),Atkinson,Rhodes,Whitter g:Atkinson(3),Holt	N/A	1,157
7/2/99	Whitehaven (h)	W18-12	t:Manihera(2),Whiteley g:Holt(3)	N/A	1,556
14/2/99	Leigh (h) (CCR4)	L16-33	t:Manihera,Atkinson,Magorian g:Holt(2)	N/A	1,485
7/3/99	Featherstone (h)	W30-10	t:Rhodes(2),Luxon,Manihera,Whitter g:Holt(5)	2nd	1,139
12/3/99	Oldham (a)	L24-20	t:Manihera,Clark,Salmon g:Holt(4)	6th	1,123
21/3/99	Widnes (a)	L34-16	t:Luxon,Whitehead g:Holt(4)	13th	2,224
28/3/99	Leigh (h)	L26-44	t:Massey,Marshall,Luxon,Warwick g:Holt(5)	14th	1,261
2/4/99	Lancashire (a)	W16-58	t:Atkinson(3),Clark(3),Magorian,Manihera,Salmon g:Holt(11)	10th	350
5/4/99	Keighley (h)	L21-22	t:Holt(2),Manihera g:Holt(4) fg:Holt	10th	1,378
11/4/99	Swinton (a)	W24-31	t:Atkinson(2),Manihera,Holt,Wilson,Rhodes g:Holt(3) fg:Holt	8th	820
14/4/99	Rochdale (a)	L36-16	t:Atkinson,Warwick g:Holt(4)	8th	690
18/4/99	Workington (h)	W25-12	t:Atkinson,Holt,Barchard,Rhodes g:Holt(4) fg:Holt	8th	1,566
25/4/99	Batley (a)	L32-19	t:Manihera,McAllister,Holt g:Holt(3) fg:Holt	8th	468
9/5/99	Hull KR (h)	W43-20	t:Warwick(2),Atkinson(2),Barchard,Whitehead,Manihera g:Holt(7)	8th	1,326
16/5/99	Hunslet (a)	L46-14	t:Clark,Warwick,Whitehead g:Holt	11th	1,008
23/5/99	Doncaster (h)	W36-24	t:Atkinson(3),Manihera,Warwick,McDermott,Barchard g:Holt(3),Atkinson	10th	961
30/5/99	Bramley (a)	L24-16	t:Clark,Atkinson g:Holt(3),Atkinson	11th	315
6/6/99	York (h)	L18-25	t:Hutton,Manihera,Atkinson g:Atkinson(3)	11th	932
13/6/99	Dewsbury (a)	L46-7	t:Clark g:Atkinson fg:Manihera	12th	766
20/6/99	Whitehaven (a)	L32-26	t:Clark,Slater,McDermott,Luxon g:Atkinson(5)	12th	942
27/6/99	Rochdale (a)	W25-16	t:Clark(2),Hughes,Magorian g:Holt(2),Atkinson fg:Holt(2),Manihera	12th	964
4/7/99	Featherstone (a)	L46-6	t:Clark g:Holt	12th	1,469
11/7/99	Oldham (h)	W55-16	t:Atkinson(3),Holt(2),Manihera(2),Barchard,Hutton,Clark g:Holt(7) fg:Holt	11th	843
18/7/99	Widnes (h)	L4-27	g:Holt(2)	12th	1,387
25/7/99	Leigh (a)	L32-26	t:Magorian,Hughes,Holt,Salmon,Atkinson g:Holt(3)	13th	1,720
1/8/99	Lancashire (h)	W25-19	t:Rhodes,Barchard,Hutton,Magorian g:Holt(4) fg:Holt	12th	734
8/8/99	Keighley (a)	L22-20	t:Hutton(3) g:Holt(4)	12th	1,441
15/8/99	Swinton (h)	L14-33	t:Atkinson,Massey g:Holt(3)	13th	904
22/8/99	Workington (a)	W8-19	t:Manihera,Hutton g:Holt(4) fg:Marwood(2),Holt	11th	628
29/8/99	Batley (h)	W26-16	t:Hutton(3),Salmon,Rawlinson g:Holt(3)	10th	889

	APP		TRIES		GOALS		FG		PTS	
	ALL	NFP	ALL	NFP	ALL	NFP	ALL	NFP	ALL	NFP
Phil Atkinson	30	28	21	19	15	12	0	0	114	100
Ray Barchard	21(4)	21(4)	5	5	0	0	0	0	20	20
Gavin Chelton	(2)	(2)	0	0	0	0	0	0	0	0
Dave Clark	26(1)	25	12	12	0	0	0	0	48	48
Paul Gardner	(8)	(8)	0	0	0	0	0	0	0	0
Darren Holt	27	25	8	8	100	97	10	10	242	236
Jonathan Hughes	29	27	4	2	0	0	0	0	16	8
Glen Hutton	14	14	10	10	0	0	0	0	40	40
Steve Jackson	9(13)	9(13)	0	0	0	0	0	0	0	0
Mike Kavanagh	7(8)	5(8)	0	0	0	0	0	0	0	0
Neil Kilshaw	(1)	(1)	0	0	0	0	0	0	0	0
Sean Little	1(1)	1(1)	0	0	0	0	0	0	0	0
Geoff Luxon	29(1)	27(1)	4	4	0	0	0	0	16	16
Stuart Magorian	22(1)	20(1)	5	4	0	0	0	0	20	16
Tane Manihera	25(2)	24(1)	15	14	0	0	2	2	62	58
Jamie Marshall	9(8)	8(8)	1	1	0	0	0	0	4	4
Dean Marwood	(2)	(2)	0	0	0	0	2	2	2	2
Chris Massey	4(2)	4(2)	2	2	0	0	0	0	8	8
Ian McAllister	6	5	1	1	0	0	0	0	4	4
Brett McDermott	9	9	2	2	0	0	0	0	8	8
Paul McMillan	(2)	0	0	0	0	0	0	0	0	0
Ian Rawlinson	5(16)	5(15)	1	1	0	0	0	0	4	4
Stuart Rhodes	20(1)	18(1)	6	5	0	0	0	0	24	20
Gary Ruddy	2(1)	2(1)	0	0	0	0	0	0	0	0
Paul Salmon	28	26	6	4	0	0	0	0	24	16
Ben Slater	1(3)	1(3)	1	1	0	0	0	0	4	4
Gary Spenceley	(4)	(4)	0	0	0	0	0	0	0	0
Dean Thomas	6	4	2	0	0	0	0	0	8	0
Dave Warwick	17(1)	17(1)	6	6	0	0	0	0	24	24
Mike Whitehead	11(14)	11(12)	3	3	0	0	0	0	12	12
Chris Whiteley	19(2)	17(2)	1	1	0	0	0	0	4	4
Damien Whitter	7(1)	5(1)	2	1	0	0	0	0	8	4
Darren Wilson	5	5	1	1	0	0	0	0	4	4

Darren Holt

LEAGUE RECORD
P28-W12-D0-L16
(10th, NFP)
F660, A718, Diff-58
24 points.

CHALLENGE CUP
Round Four

ATTENDANCES
Best - v Workington (NFP - 1,566)
Worst - v Lancashire (NFP - 734)
Total (NFP only) - 15,840
Average (NFP only) - 1,131
(Up by 52 on 1998)

BATLEY BULLDOGS

DATE	FIXTURE	RESULT	SCORERS	LGE	ATT
31/1/99	Lock Lane (h) (CCR3)	W40-10	t:Harrison(2),Gleadhill(2),R Simpson,Walker,Flynn,Jackson g:Price(4)	N/A	713
7/2/99	Oldham (h)	W30-0	t:Miers,R Simpson,Harrison,Clarke,Lingard,Jackson g:Price(3)	N/A	1,018
12/2/99	Wakefield (a) (CCR4)	L12-2	g:Price	N/A	2,322
21/2/99	Hull KR (a)	L8-6	t:R Simpson g:Price	3rd	2,467
7/3/99	Hunslet (h)	L8-14	t:Price(2)	10th	847
14/3/99	Doncaster (a)	W20-29	t:Price(2),Wray(2),Flynn g:Price(4) fg:Jackson	5th	741
21/3/99	Bramley (h)	W14-12	t:Bargate,Price g:Price(3)	4th	566
28/3/99	York (a)	D20-20	t:Middleton,Price,R Simpson g:Price(4)	6th	804
2/4/99	Dewsbury (h)	L24-28	t:Middleton(2),Cass,Barnett g:Price(4)	7th	1,933
5/4/99	Whitehaven (a)	L21-8	t:Bargate,Clarke	8th	606
11/4/99	Rochdale (h)	L14-19	t:Harrison,Lingard,McWilliam g:Price	11th	478
18/4/99	Featherstone (a)	L16-15	t:Bargate,Barnett g:Price(3) fg:Dyson	11th	1,852
25/4/99	Barrow (h)	W32-19	t:R Simpson(2),Lingard(2),Miers,McWilliam g:Price(4)	10th	468
9/5/99	Widnes (a)	W16-17	t:R Simpson,Barnett,Lingard g:Price(2) fg:Barnett	10th	2,501
16/5/99	Leigh (h)	W25-16	t:Miers,Price,Bargate,Barnett g:Price(4) fg:Cass	9th	1,023
23/5/99	Lancashire (a)	W28-47	t:Middleton(2),Price,Gleadhill,Lingard,Harrison,Miers,Cass, R Simpson g:Price(5) fg:Cass	7th	232
30/5/99	Keighley (h)	L20-25	t:Gleadhill(2),Middleton,Flynn g:Price(2)	10th	708
13/6/99	Workington (h)	W42-8	t:Gleadhill(2),Barnett,Price,Harrison,Lingard,Flynn,Dyson g:Price(5)	8th	548
18/6/99	Oldham (a)	D20-20	t:Harrison(2),Flynn,Lingard g:Price(2)	8th	1,013
27/6/99	Hull KR (h)	L0-18	No Scorers	9th	1,113
4/7/99	Hunslet (a)	L32-15	t:Dyson,N Simpson g:Dyson(3) fg:Dyson	10th	1,652
7/7/99	Swinton (a)	L23-14	t:Dyson,Gleadhill g:Dyson(3)	10th	703
11/7/99	Doncaster (h)	W44-12	t:Harrison(4),Price,Dyson,Jackson,N Simpson g:Dyson(6)	10th	528
18/7/99	Bramley (a)	D16-16	t:Middleton,Lingard g:Dyson(3),Jackson	10th	500
25/7/99	York (h)	L22-35	t:Harrison,McWilliam,Flynn,Walker g:Price(3)	10th	491
1/8/99	Dewsbury (a)	L14-8	t:Jackson g:Price(2)	10th	1,312
8/8/99	Whitehaven (h)	L12-22	t:McDonald,Gleadhill g:Price(2)	10th	368
15/8/99	Rochdale (a)	L42-24	t:R Simpson(2),Clarke,Lingard g:Price(3),Stevens	11th	778
22/8/99	Featherstone (h)	L4-23	g:Price(2)	12th	910
29/8/99	Barrow (a)	L26-16	t:Price,R Simpson,Walker g:Price(2)	12th	889

	APP		TRIES		GOALS		FG		PTS	
	ALL	NFP	ALL	NFP	ALL	NFP	ALL	NFP	ALL	NFP
Lee Bardauskas	1(5)	1(5)	0	0	0	0	0	0	0	0
Lee Bargate	20	20	4	4	0	0	0	0	16	16
Gary Barnett	26(1)	26(1)	5	5	0	0	1	1	21	21
Neil Bradbrook	1(4)	1(2)	0	0	0	0	0	0	0	0
Richard Brook	3(2)	3(2)	0	0	0	0	0	0	0	0
Mark Cass	15(2)	14(1)	2	2	0	0	2	2	10	10
John Clarke	13(11)	12(10)	3	3	0	0	0	0	12	12
Jeremy Dyson	14	12	4	4	15	15	2	2	48	48
Wayne Flynn	26(2)	24(2)	6	5	0	0	0	0	24	20
Paul Gleadhill	28	26	9	7	0	0	0	0	36	28
Phil Hardwick	(5)	(5)	0	0	0	0	0	0	0	0
Paul Harrison	27(1)	26	13	11	0	0	0	0	52	44
Neil Hartley	3(1)	3(1)	0	0	0	0	0	0	0	0
Simon Jackson	15(5)	13(5)	4	3	1	1	1	1	19	15
Craig Lingard	7(17)	7(15)	10	10	0	0	0	0	40	40
Andrew Lippiatt	6(3)	6(3)	0	0	0	0	0	0	0	0
Gary Lord	21(2)	19(2)	0	0	0	0	0	0	0	0
Brock McDonald	8(1)	8(1)	1	1	0	0	0	0	4	4
Chris McWilliam	27	25	3	3	0	0	0	0	12	12
Graham Middleton	21(4)	20(3)	7	7	0	0	0	0	28	28
Grant Miers	22(1)	20(1)	4	4	0	0	0	0	16	16
Darren Moxon	4(9)	4(9)	0	0	0	0	0	0	0	0
Rob Padgett	(1)	(1)	0	0	0	0	0	0	0	0
Brett Patterson	4	3	0	0	0	0	0	0	0	0
Richard Price	30	28	11	11	66	61	0	0	176	166
Nick Simpson	3(10)	3(10)	2	2	0	0	0	0	8	8
Roger Simpson	26	24	11	10	0	0	0	0	44	40
Craig Stevens	(2)	(2)	0	0	1	1	0	0	2	2
Steve Walker	10(11)	8(11)	3	2	0	0	0	0	12	8
Tony Walton	7(6)	6(6)	0	0	0	0	0	0	0	0
Andy Wray	2(6)	2(6)	2	2	0	0	0	0	8	8

Richard Price

LEAGUE RECORD
P28-W9-D3-L16
(12th, NFP)
F546, A553, Diff-7
21 points.

CHALLENGE CUP
Round Four

ATTENDANCES
Best - v Dewsbury (NFP - 1,933)
Worst - v Whitehaven (NFP - 368)
Total (NFP only) - 10,999
Average (NFP only) - 786
(Up by 164 on 1998)

BRAMLEY

DATE	FIXTURE	RESULT	SCORERS	LGE	ATT
31/1/99	Leigh MR (h) (CCR3)	L12-18	t:Horner,Ford g:Smith(2)	N/A	500
7/2/99	Lancashire (a)	L13-12	t:Potter,D Gibbons g:Kite fg:Ford(2)	N/A	298
21/2/99	Keighley (h)	W14-12	t:Poynter(2),Potter g:D Gibbons	9th	1,000
7/3/99	Swinton (a)	L23-8	t:A Gibbons g:A Gibbons(2)	16th	887
14/3/99	Workington (a)	L22-16	t:Potter(2),G Freeman g:A Gibbons(2)	16th	852
21/3/99	Batley (a)	L14-12	t:Horner,Gibson g:A Gibbons(2)	17th	566
26/3/99	Hull KR (a)	L12-0	No Scorers	18th	1,902
2/4/99	Hunslet (a)	W11-16	t:A Gibbons,Poynter,Potter g:A Gibbons(2)	16th	1,522
6/4/99	Doncaster (h)	W28-10	t:W Freeman,O'Reilly,D Gibbons,Wray,Potter g:A Gibbons(4)	13th	500
11/4/99	Oldham (h)	W24-18	t:A Gibbons(2),Wray,Potter,W Freeman g:A Gibbons(2)	10th	500
18/4/99	York (a)	L22-12	t:Render(2),Wray	10th	984
26/4/99	Dewsbury (h)	L16-17	t:MacDonald,A Gibbons,D Gibbons g:Sibson(2)	12th	974
9/5/99	Whitehaven (a)	L40-16	t:A Gibbons,Potter g:Sibson(4)	15th	546
17/5/99	Rochdale (h)	W36-16	t:Potter(2),Ford,A Gibbons,McAllister,O'Reilly g:Sibson(6)	12th	371
23/5/99	Featherstone (a)	W12-20	t:D Gibbons(2),Sibson,Potter g:Sibson(2)	12th	1,309
30/5/99	Barrow (h)	W24-16	t:D Gibbons(2),Proctor,Potter,Gibson g:Sibson(2)	12th	315
6/6/99	Widnes (a)	L36-18	t:A Gibbons(2),W Freeman g:Sibson(3)	13th	2,820
11/6/99	Leigh (h)	L8-39	t:A Gibbons,David	13th	679
20/6/99	Lancashire (h)	L32-45	t:A Gibbons,D Gibbons,Potter,W Freeman,Currie,Munton g:Sibson(4)	13th	423
27/6/99	Keighley (a)	L36-10	t:Ford,Wray g:Sibson	13th	1,466
4/7/99	Swinton (h)	W20-14	t:Wray(2),Sibson(2) g:Sibson(2)	13th	354
11/7/99	Workington (h)	W28-12	t:Sibson(2),David,Poynter,Schofield g:Sibson(4)	12th	300
18/7/99	Batley (h)	D16-16	t:Poynter,Sibson g:Sibson(4)	11th	500
25/7/99	Hull KR (h)	W23-14	t:Sibson(3),A Gibbons,Poynter g:Sibson fg:Schofield	11th	676
1/8/99	Hunslet (h)	L22-29	t:Sibson(3),D Gibbons g:Sibson(3)	11th	853
8/8/99	Doncaster (a)	L38-14	t:Barnett,Sibson,MacDonald g:Sibson	11th	416
13/8/99	Oldham (a)	W8-22	t:A Gibbons(2),Potter,Sibson g:Sibson(3)	10th	621
22/8/99	York (h)	L10-23	t:O'Reilly g:Sibson(3)	10th	300
29/8/99	Dewsbury (a)	L28-12	t:Poynter(2) g:Russell(2)	11th	1,274

	APP		TRIES		GOALS		FG		PTS	
	ALL	NFP	ALL	NFP	ALL	NFP	ALL	NFP	ALL	NFP
Steve Barnett	5	5	1	1	0	0	0	0	4	4
Andrew Brent	9	9	0	0	0	0	0	0	0	0
Eugene Currie	4(7)	3(7)	1	1	0	0	0	0	4	4
Maea David	24(2)	24(2)	2	2	0	0	0	0	8	8
Joe Davis	(2)	(2)	0	0	0	0	0	0	0	0
Lee Denham	1(4)	1(4)	0	0	0	0	0	0	0	0
Steve Embleton	2(3)	2(3)	0	0	0	0	0	0	0	0
Tony Fella	1(4)	1(4)	0	0	0	0	0	0	0	0
Mike Ford	23(6)	22(6)	3	2	0	0	2	2	14	10
Glen Freeman	15(12)	14(12)	1	1	0	0	0	0	4	4
Wayne Freeman	28	27	4	4	0	0	0	0	16	16
Anthony Gibbons	25	24	14	14	14	14	0	0	84	84
David Gibbons	28	27	9	9	1	1	0	0	38	38
Mark Gibson	8(17)	8(16)	2	2	0	0	0	0	8	8
Mick Horner	8(9)	8(8)	2	1	0	0	0	0	8	4
Neil Kite	4(1)	3(1)	0	0	1	1	0	0	2	2
Ryan MacDonald	15(9)	14(9)	2	2	0	0	0	0	8	8
Danny McAllister	7(2)	7(2)	1	1	0	0	0	0	4	4
Hamish Munton	6(1)	6(1)	1	1	0	0	0	0	4	4
Tom O'Reilly	15(3)	15(3)	3	3	0	0	0	0	12	12
Dan Potter	29	28	14	14	0	0	0	0	56	56
Andy Poynter	17	16	8	8	0	0	0	0	32	32
Andy Proctor	23	22	1	1	0	0	0	0	4	4
Nick Render	3(4)	3(4)	2	2	0	0	0	0	8	8
Richard Russell	23(3)	22(3)	0	0	2	2	0	0	4	4
Garry Schofield	12(7)	12(7)	1	1	0	0	1	1	5	5
Andy Senior	1(3)	1(3)	0	0	0	0	0	0	0	0
Mark Sibson	17	17	14	14	45	45	0	0	146	146
Kris Smith	(2)	(1)	0	0	2	0	0	0	4	0
Richard Stead	1(1)	1(1)	0	0	0	0	0	0	0	0
Giles Thomas	(1)	(1)	0	0	0	0	0	0	0	0
Mark Webster	1(7)	1(6)	0	0	0	0	0	0	0	0
Simon Wray	22	21	6	6	0	0	0	0	24	24

Tom O'Reilly

LEAGUE RECORD
P28-W11-D1-L16
(11th, NFP)
F489, A596, Diff-107
23 points.

CHALLENGE CUP
Round Three

ATTENDANCES
Best - v Keighley (NFP - 1,000)
Worst - v Workington & York
(NFP - 300)
Total (NFP only) - 7,745
Average (NFP only) - 553
(Down by 7 on 1998)

DEWSBURY RAMS

DATE	FIXTURE	RESULT	SCORERS	LGE	ATT
31/1/99	Siddal (h) (CCR3)	W38-10	t:Williams(2),Kershaw,Spink,Godfrey,Agar,Graham g:Eaton(5)	N/A	1,447
7/2/99	Widnes (a)	L30-12	t:Godfrey,Kershaw g:Eaton(2)	N/A	2,782
15/2/99	Oldham (a) (CCR4)	L18-10	t:Kershaw,Williams g:Eaton	N/A	1,620
21/2/99	Leigh (h)	W31-16	t:Graham(2),Evans,Flynn,Medley g:Eaton(5) fg:Agar	10th	1,314
7/3/99	Lancashire (a)	L22-12	t:Godfrey g:Eaton(4)	15th	360
14/3/99	Keighley (h)	W35-8	t:Flynn(3),Godfrey(2),Graham,Hicks g:Eaton(3) fg:Eaton	7th	1,010
21/3/99	Swinton (a)	W19-29	t:Evans(2),Graham,Williams,Ball g:Eaton(4) fg:Eaton	5th	1,040
28/3/99	Workington (h)	W58-24	t:Godfrey(3),Williams(2),Flynn(2),Eaton,Evans,Graham,Long g:Eaton(7)	4th	849
2/4/99	Batley (a)	W24-28	t:Flynn(3),Evans,Eaton g:Eaton(4)	3rd	1,933
5/4/99	Hull KR (h)	W25-14	t:Flynn,Pearce,Evans,Agar g:Eaton(4) fg:Agar	2nd	1,732
11/4/99	Hunslet (a)	W20-21	t:Williams(2),Flynn,Eaton g:Eaton(2) fg:Ball	2nd	1,621
18/4/99	Doncaster (h)	W42-3	t:Flynn(2),Spink,O'Meara,Long,Eaton,Ball,Godfrey g:Eaton(5)	2nd	1,038
26/4/99	Bramley (a)	W16-17	t:Ball(2),Eaton g:Eaton(2) fg:Agar	2nd	974
7/5/99	York (h)	W30-4	t:Graham(2),Kershaw,Delaney,Agar g:Eaton(5)	1st	1,007
23/5/99	Whitehaven (h)	W18-20	t:Graham,D Wood,Williams,Ball g:Eaton(2)	1st	607
30/5/99	Rochdale (h)	L12-19	t:Pearce g:Eaton(3),Pearce	2nd	820
6/6/99	Featherstone (a)	D24-24	t:Godfrey(2),Medley(2),Williamson g:Pearce(2)	3rd	1,790
13/6/99	Barrow (h)	W46-7	t:Godfrey(4),Eaton(2),Hicks,Flynn g:Pearce(7)	3rd	766
20/6/99	Widnes (h)	L16-26	t:Haigh,Williams g:Pearce(4)	4th	1,407
27/6/99	Leigh (a)	L24-10	t:Godfrey g:Eaton(3)	5th	2,049
4/7/99	Lancashire (h)	W34-27	t:Eaton(2),Flynn,O'Meara,Haigh,Spink g:Eaton(4),Pearce	5th	621
7/7/99	Oldham (a)	W12-28	t:Godfrey(2),Williams(2),Delaney,Graham g:Eaton(2)	4th	859
11/7/99	Keighley (a)	D24-24	t:Williams,Richardson,Flynn,Medley g:Eaton(4)	4th	1,584
18/7/99	Swinton (h)	W27-26	t:Flynn(2),Spink,Delaney g:Eaton(5) fg:Pearce	4th	841
25/7/99	Workington (a)	W6-25	t:Ball,Flynn,O'Meara,Eaton g:Eaton(4) fg:Agar	4th	570
1/8/99	Batley (h)	W14-8	t:Godfrey,Flynn g:Eaton(3)	4th	1,312
8/8/99	Hull KR (a)	W0-20	t:Ball(2),Spink g:Eaton(4)	3rd	2,218
15/8/99	Hunslet (h)	W10-6	t:Graham,Richardson g:Eaton	2nd	1,642
22/8/99	Doncaster (a)	W10-32	t:Eaton,Flynn,D Wood,Hicks g:Eaton(8)	1st	911
29/8/99	Bramley (h)	W28-12	t:Haigh,O'Meara,Eaton,Flynn,Medley g:Eaton(3) fg:Eaton,Agar	1st	1,274
12/9/99	Widnes (h) (QSF)	W28-6	t:Ball(2),Graham,O'Meara,Spink g:Eaton(2) fg:Agar(3),Eaton	N/A	3,210
25/9/99	Hunslet (GFN)	L11-12	t:Flynn,Ball g:Eaton fg:Agar	N/A	5,783

	APP		TRIES		GOALS		FG		PTS	
	ALL	NFP	ALL	NFP	ALL	NFP	ALL	NFP	ALL	NFP
Richard Agar	30(1)	28(1)	3	2	0	0	9	9	21	17
Richard Arrowsmith	(1)	(1)	0	0	0	0	0	0	0	0
Damian Ball	24(6)	23(6)	11	11	0	0	1	1	45	45
Darren Ballantyne	5(1)	5(1)	0	0	0	0	0	0	0	0
Alan Boothroyd	21(2)	20(1)	0	0	0	0	0	0	0	0
Gareth Cochrane	5(8)	5(8)	0	0	0	0	0	0	0	0
Paul Delaney	32	30	3	3	0	0	0	0	12	12
Barry Eaton	32	30	12	12	102	96	4	4	256	244
Paul Evans	15	14	6	6	0	0	0	0	24	24
Jason Firth	(3)	(1)	0	0	0	0	0	0	0	0
Adrian Flynn	32	30	23	23	0	0	0	0	92	92
Alex Godfrey	32	30	19	18	0	0	0	0	76	72
Nathan Graham	31	29	12	11	0	0	0	0	48	44
Mark Haigh	16(4)	16(3)	3	3	0	0	0	0	12	12
Simon Hicks	15(17)	15(15)	3	3	0	0	0	0	12	12
Robin Jowitt	10(5)	10(5)	0	0	0	0	0	0	0	0
Billy Kershaw	11(1)	9(1)	4	2	0	0	0	0	16	8
Matthew Long	8(16)	7(15)	2	2	0	0	0	0	8	8
George Mack	(1)	(1)	0	0	0	0	0	0	0	0
Paul Medley	3(24)	1(24)	5	5	0	0	0	0	20	20
Brendan O'Meara	19(3)	19(3)	5	5	0	0	0	0	20	20
Greg Pearce	7(16)	7(16)	2	2	15	15	1	1	39	39
Sean Richardson	2(7)	2(7)	2	2	0	0	0	0	8	8
Gary Rose	5	3	0	0	0	0	0	0	0	0
Andrew Spink	24	23	6	5	0	0	0	0	24	20
Brendan Williams	25(3)	24(2)	13	10	0	0	0	0	52	40
Leon Williamson	7(1)	6(1)	1	1	0	0	0	0	4	4
Danny Wood	3(5)	3(5)	2	2	0	0	0	0	8	8
Gavin Wood	2(2)	1(2)	0	0	0	0	0	0	0	0

Nathan Graham

LEAGUE RECORD
P28-W21-D2-L5
(1st, NFP/Grand Final Runners Up)
F710, A449, Diff+261
44 points.

CHALLENGE CUP
Round Four

ATTENDANCES
Best - v Widnes (QSF - 3,210)
Worst - v Lancashire (NFP - 621)
Total (NFP, inc play-offs) - 18,843
Average (NFP, inc play-offs) - 1,256
(Up by 68 on 1998)

DONCASTER DRAGONS

DATE	FIXTURE	RESULT	SCORERS	LGE	ATT
31/1/99	Oldham SA (h) (CCR3)	W35-21	t:Creasser,Maher,Bell,Bruce,Schofield,Adams,Moore g:Creasser(3) fg:Southernwood	N/A	1,614
7/2/99	Keighley (a)	L42-16	t:Morgan(2),Miller g:Edwards(2)	N/A	2,472
14/2/99	London (a) (CCR4)	L64-0	No Scorers	N/A	2,164
21/2/99	Swinton (h)	W22-18	t:Alfie Goulbourne(3),Alex Goulbourne g:Creasser(3)	13th	762
28/2/99	Rochdale (a)	L26-10	t:Moore,C Watson g:Creasser	15th	740
7/3/99	Workington (a)	D22-22	t:Alfie Goulbourne(2),Okul,Summerill g:Creasser(3)	8th	1,002
14/3/99	Batley (h)	L20-29	t:Alfie Goulbourne,Kerr,Southernwood,Summerill g:Creasser(2)	11th	741
21/3/99	Hull KR (a)	L12-2	g:Creasser	14th	2,056
28/3/99	Hunslet (a)	L30-18	t:Ellis,Okul,Moore g:Ellis(3)	15th	1,257
2/4/99	Oldham (h)	L12-27	t:Kerr,Adams g:Creasser(2)	17th	878
6/4/99	Bramley (a)	L28-10	t:Moore,Kerr g:Creasser	17th	500
11/4/99	York (h)	L18-28	t:Maher,Southernwood g:Creasser(5)	18th	550
18/4/99	Dewsbury (a)	L42-3	g:Creasser fg:Maher	18th	1,038
25/4/99	Whitehaven (h)	L30-40	t:Miller(2),Moore,Carter,Watene g:Maher(3),Summerill(2)	18th	450
16/5/99	Featherstone (h)	W33-24	t:Maher(2),Carter,Alex Goulbourne,Watene g:Maher(6) fg:Maher	18th	787
23/5/99	Barrow (a)	L36-24	t:Southernwood(2),Miller,Watene g:Maher(4)	18th	961
30/5/99	Widnes (h)	L18-38	t:Southernwood,Draine,Naidole,Morgan g:Allen	18th	750
6/6/99	Leigh (a)	L72-6	t:Moore g:Maher	18th	1,372
13/6/99	Lancashire (h)	L18-45	t:Miller,Hewitt,Bruce,Walker g:Allen	18th	449
20/6/99	Keighley (h)	L18-23	t:Walker(2),Bartle,Okul g:Allen	18th	521
27/6/99	Swinton (a)	L48-2	g:Conway	18th	779
4/7/99	Workington (h)	W44-4	t:Allen(2),Morgan(2),Okul,Carter,Moore,Conway,Lister g:Summerill(3),Allen	18th	396
11/7/99	Batley (a)	L44-12	t:Okul(2) g:Mycoe(2)	18th	528
18/7/99	Hull KR (h)	L16-42	t:Okul(2),Adams g:Mycoe(2)	18th	1,293
25/7/99	Hunslet (a)	L16-50	t:Southernwood,Morgan,Maher g:Mycoe(2)	18th	610
30/7/99	Oldham (a)	L22-17	t:Okul,Maher,Southernwood g:Mycoe(2) fg:Southernwood	18th	676
8/8/99	Bramley (h)	W38-14	t:Okul(3),Morgan(2),Mycoe g:Mycoe(7)	18th	416
15/8/99	York (a)	L35-8	t:Morgan,Miller	18th	764
22/8/99	Dewsbury (h)	L10-32	t:Moore(2) g:Mycoe	18th	911
29/8/99	Whitehaven (a)	L38-10	t:Carter,Moore g:Hewitt	18th	930

	APP		TRIES		GOALS		FG		PTS	
	ALL	NFP	ALL	NFP	ALL	NFP	ALL	NFP	ALL	NFP
Guy Adams	24(2)	22(2)	3	2	0	0	0	0	12	8
Kieran Allen	11	11	2	2	4	4	0	0	16	16
Dean Andrews	(5)	(5)	0	0	0	0	0	0	0	0
Jamie Bartle	4	4	1	1	0	0	0	0	4	4
Glen Bell	1	0	1	0	0	0	0	0	4	0
Joe Bonasera	2	2	0	0	0	0	0	0	0	0
Sebastian Bouche	1(3)	1(2)	0	0	0	0	0	0	0	0
John Bruce	21(1)	19(1)	2	1	0	0	0	0	8	4
Aaron Campbell	7	7	0	0	0	0	0	0	0	0
Colin Carter	13	13	4	4	0	0	0	0	16	16
Billy Conway	11(2)	11(2)	1	1	1	1	0	0	6	6
Dean Creasser	12(1)	11	1	0	22	19	0	0	48	38
Darryl Derose	22(1)	22(1)	0	0	0	0	0	0	0	0
Dean Draine	2	2	1	1	0	0	0	0	4	4
John Edwards	1(1)	(1)	0	0	2	2	0	0	4	4
St John Ellis	5(2)	5(2)	1	1	3	3	0	0	10	10
Stuart Flowers	(2)	(2)	0	0	0	0	0	0	0	0
Alex Goulbourne	5(2)	5(2)	2	2	0	0	0	0	8	8
Alfie Goulbourne	10(1)	10(1)	6	6	0	0	0	0	24	24
Richard Hewitt	8(4)	8(4)	1	1	1	1	0	0	6	6
Ken Kerr	10(2)	10(2)	3	3	0	0	0	0	12	12
Paul Lister	8(1)	8(1)	1	1	0	0	0	0	4	4
Gareth Lloyd	(5)	(5)	0	0	0	0	0	0	0	0
Lee Maher	25	23	6	5	14	14	2	2	54	50
Colin Maskill	3(1)	2	0	0	0	0	0	0	0	0
Tony Miller	25	23	6	6	0	0	0	0	24	24
Craig Moore	22(4)	20(4)	10	9	0	0	0	0	40	36
Gavin Morgan	9(21)	8(20)	9	9	0	0	0	0	36	36
James Mosley	6	6	0	0	0	0	0	0	0	0
David Mycoe	7	7	1	1	16	16	0	0	36	36
Joe Naidole	4(2)	4(2)	1	1	0	0	0	0	4	4
John Okul	19(2)	17(2)	12	12	0	0	0	0	48	48
Chris Parr	(1)	(1)	0	0	0	0	0	0	0	0
Gareth Pratt	8(7)	8(7)	0	0	0	0	0	0	0	0
Martin Rowse	6(1)	5	0	0	0	0	0	0	0	0
Garry Schofield	7	5	1	0	0	0	0	0	4	0
Lee Senior	1(2)	(1)	0	0	0	0	0	0	0	0
Graham Southernwood	13(5)	12(5)	7	7	0	0	2	1	30	29
Darren Summerill	11(5)	9(5)	2	2	5	5	0	0	18	18
Jamie Thackray	4	4	0	0	0	0	0	0	0	0
Darren Towart	1(1)	1(1)	0	0	0	0	0	0	0	0
Dominic Turner	1	1	0	0	0	0	0	0	0	0
Chris Verity	12(2)	12(2)	0	0	0	0	0	0	0	0
James Walker	6(1)	6(1)	3	3	0	0	0	0	12	12
Steve Watene	8(2)	8(2)	3	3	0	0	0	0	12	12
Chris Watson	8(15)	8(14)	1	1	0	0	0	0	4	4
Ian Watson	5(3)	3(3)	0	0	0	0	0	0	0	0
Mark Webster	1	1	0	0	0	0	0	0	0	0

Lee Maher

LEAGUE RECORD
P28-W4-D1-L23
(18th, NFP)
F473, A911, Diff-438
9 points.

CHALLENGE CUP
Round Four

ATTENDANCES
Best - v Oldham St A (CC - 1,614)
Worst - v Workington (NFP - 396)
Total (NFP only) - 9,514
Average (NFP only) - 680
(Up by 175 on 1998)

238

FEATHERSTONE ROVERS

DATE	FIXTURE	RESULT	SCORERS	LGE	ATT
31/1/99	Thornhill (h) (CCR3)	W70-6	t:Stokes(3),Handley(2),Chapman,Hall,Law,Okesene,Clarkson, Horsley,Dooler,Slater g:Chapman(8),Dickens	N/A	1,187
7/2/99	Rochdale (h)	W32-12	t:Stokes(2),Clarkson,Hall,Law,Dooler g:Chapman(4)	N/A	1,762
14/2/99	Warrington (a) (CCR4)	L50-6	t:Thompson g:Chapman	N/A	4,335
7/3/99	Barrow (a)	L30-10	t:Simonds,Bramald g:Chapman	13th	1,139
17/3/99	Widnes (h)	W28-12	t:Dooler,Hall,Slater,Lowe,Bramald g:Chapman(2),Dickens(2)	8th	1,774
21/3/99	Leigh (a)	L16-12	t:Simonds,Stokes g:Chapman(2)	10th	1,603
28/3/99	Lancashire (h)	W32-18	t:Handley(2),Hall,Chapman,Bramald,Horsley g:Chapman(4)	8th	1,589
2/4/99	Keighley (a)	W18-32	t:Simonds(4),Handley,Chapman g:Dickens(4)	6th	2,242
5/4/99	Swinton (h)	W50-20	t:Simonds(2),Law(2),Amone(2),Newlove(2),Evans g:Dickens(7)	6th	1,885
11/4/99	Workington (a)	W10-15	t:Bramald,Chapman g:Dickens(3) fg:Dickens	4th	1,007
18/4/99	Batley (h)	W16-15	t:Tuuta,Stokes,Newlove g:Dickens(2)	4th	1,852
25/4/99	Hull KR (a)	L23-12	t:Simonds,Chapman g:Dickens(2)	6th	2,503
9/5/99	Hunslet (h)	L15-26	t:Stokes,Handley,Lowe g:Dickens fg:Horsley	7th	1,914
16/5/99	Doncaster (a)	L33-24	t:Chapman,Rooney,Simonds,Evans g:Dickens(4)	7th	787
23/5/99	Bramley (h)	L12-20	t:Bramald,Lowe g:Dickens(2)	9th	1,309
30/5/99	York (a)	W18-21	t:Bramald,Heptinstall,Evans g:Rooney(4) fg:Rooney	8th	987
6/6/99	Dewsbury (h)	D24-24	t:Rooney,Amone,Simonds,Stokes g:Rooney(4)	7th	1,790
9/6/99	Oldham (a)	W18-25	t:Okesene,Stokes,Simonds g:Dickens(6) fg:Dickens	7th	901
13/6/99	Whitehaven (a)	L19-14	t:Chapman,Law g:Dickens(2),Rooney	7th	701
20/6/99	Rochdale (a)	W14-29	t:Newlove,Stokes,Handley,Chapman,Law g:Rooney(3),Dickens fg:Rooney	6th	837
27/6/99	Oldham (h)	W61-6	t:Handley(3),Rooney,Newlove,Stokes,Coventry,Amone,Bramald, Tuuta g:Rooney(10) fg:Rooney	6th	1,437
4/7/99	Barrow (h)	W46-6	t:Stokes(2),Okesene,Simonds,Slater,Rooney,Chapman,Handley g:Rooney(7)	6th	1,469
11/7/99	Widnes (a)	W14-20	t:Handley,Stokes,Bramald g:Rooney(3) fg:Rooney(2)	6th	3,885
18/7/99	Leigh (h)	L18-24	t:Rooney(2),Heptinstall g:Rooney(3)	6th	2,145
23/7/99	Lancashire (a)	W8-16	t:Bramald(2),Simonds g:Rooney(2)	6th	305
1/8/99	Keighley (h)	W40-20	t:Simonds(2),Thompson,Law,Bramald,Rooney,Chapman g:Rooney(6)	6th	1,473
8/8/99	Swinton (h)	W22-24	t:Simonds(2),Stokes(2),Rooney g:Rooney(2)	6th	943
15/8/99	Workington (h)	W40-6	t:Law,Handley,Evans,Dooler,Newlove,Clarkson g:Rooney(8)	6th	1,386
22/8/99	Batley (h)	W4-23	t:Handley g:Rooney(6),Heptinstall fg:Rooney	6th	910
29/8/99	Hull KR (h)	W23-10	t:Bramald(2),Coventry,Simonds,Stokes g:Rooney fg:Chapman	5th	3,103
5/9/99	Leigh (a) (EPO)	W4-17	t:Newlove,Tuuta,Chapman g:Rooney(2) fg:Rooney	N/A	3,032
12/9/99	Hunslet (a) (ESF)	L17-9	t:Law g:Rooney(2) fg:Rooney	N/A	1,620

	APP		TRIES		GOALS		FG		PTS	
	ALL	NFP	ALL	NFP	ALL	NFP	ALL	NFP	ALL	NFP
Asa Amone	18(12)	17(11)	4	4	0	0	0	0	16	16
Matthew Bramald	32	30	13	13	0	0	0	0	52	52
Richard Chapman	20(9)	18(9)	11	10	22	13	1	1	89	67
Micky Clarkson	10(13)	10(12)	3	2	0	0	0	0	12	8
Jamie Coventry	16(5)	16(3)	2	2	0	0	0	0	8	8
Stuart Dickens	19(9)	18(9)	0	0	37	36	2	2	76	74
Steve Dooler	10(9)	8(9)	4	3	0	0	0	0	16	12
Danny Evans	16(14)	15(13)	4	4	0	0	0	0	16	16
Carl Hall	12(1)	10(1)	4	3	0	0	0	0	16	12
Paddy Handley	31(1)	29(1)	14	12	0	0	0	0	56	48
Andy Heptinstall	11(3)	11(3)	2	2	1	1	0	0	10	10
Ryan Horsley	13(5)	11(5)	2	1	0	0	1	1	9	5
Martin Law	31(1)	29(1)	9	8	0	0	0	0	36	32
Neil Lowe	15(14)	14(14)	3	3	0	0	0	0	12	12
Dale Morgan	(1)	0	0	0	0	0	0	0	0	0
Richard Newlove	10(5)	10(5)	7	7	0	0	0	0	28	28
Hitro Okesene	30(2)	28(2)	3	2	0	0	0	0	12	8
Rob Padgett	1(3)	1(2)	0	0	0	0	0	0	0	0
Jamie Rooney	17(1)	17(1)	9	9	64	64	8	8	172	172
Wayne Simonds	27	27	19	19	0	0	0	0	76	76
Richard Slater	24(3)	22(3)	3	2	0	0	0	0	12	8
Jamie Stokes	27(4)	25(4)	18	15	0	0	0	0	72	60
Gavin Swinson	(1)	0	0	0	0	0	0	0	0	0
Ian Thompson	6	4	2	1	0	0	0	0	8	4
Brendon Tuuta	20(4)	20(4)	3	3	0	0	0	0	12	12

Danny Evans

LEAGUE RECORD
P28-W19-D1-L8
(5th, NFP/Elimination Semi)
F714, A466, Diff+248
39 points.

CHALLENGE CUP
Round Four

ATTENDANCES
Best - v Hull KR (NFP - 3,103)
Worst - v Thornhill (CC - 1,187)
Total (NFP only) - 24,888
Average (NFP only) - 1,778
(Down by by 64 on 1998)

HULL KINGSTON ROVERS

DATE	FIXTURE	RESULT	SCORERS	LGE	ATT
31/1/99	Wath Brow (h) (CCR3)	W56-4	t:R Smith(2),Kitching(2),Thompson,Dixon,Danby,Gray,Chamberlain, Bibby g:Gray(5),Charles(3)	N/A	1,908
7/2/99	Workington (a)	W14-21	t:Wray(2),Danby,Kitching g:Gray(2) fg:Gray	N/A	1,444
13/2/99	Leigh MR (a) (CCR4)	W0-52	t:Wray(3),Fletcher(3),R Smith,Gray,Gene,Hughes g:Gray(3),Kitching(3)	N/A	1,317
21/2/99	Batley (h)	W8-6	t:Dixon g:Charles(2)	2nd	2,467
28/2/99	London (h) (CCR5)	L0-6	No Scorers	N/A	3,971
14/3/99	Hunslet (a)	W14-26	t:Gene,Kitching,Rouse,Taewa g:Charles(5)	3rd	2,054
17/3/99	Oldham (h)	D8-8	t:Hughes,Kitching	1st	2,080
21/3/99	Doncaster (a)	W12-2	t:Danby,Bibby g:Charles(2)	1st	2,056
26/3/99	Bramley (h)	W12-0	t:Gene(2) g:Charles(2)	1st	1,902
2/4/99	York (h)	W22-16	t:Taewa,R Smith,Gene g:Charles(5)	1st	2,401
5/4/99	Dewsbury (a)	L25-14	t:Fletcher,R Smith,Kitching g:Charles	1st	1,732
11/4/99	Whitehaven (h)	W44-18	t:Hughes,Fletcher,Kitching,R Smith,Rouse,Dixon,Gray g:Charles(8)	1st	1,817
18/4/99	Rochdale (a)	W14-20	t:Dixon,Rouse,Gene,A Smith g:Charles,Gray	1st	1,179
25/4/99	Featherstone (h)	W23-12	t:Kitching(2),Gene g:Gray(5) fg:Donohue	1st	2,503
9/5/99	Barrow (a)	L43-20	t:Gene,Taewa,R Smith,Bibby g:Gray(2)	3rd	1,326
16/5/99	Widnes (h)	W14-2	t:Fletcher,Gray g:Gray(3)	1st	2,125
23/5/99	Leigh (a)	L27-20	t:Taewa(2),R Smith,Fletcher g:Gray(2)	3rd	2,419
30/5/99	Lancashire (h)	W48-12	t:Chamberlain(3),Gene(2),A Smith,Wray,Taewa g:Kitching(8)	1st	1,809
6/6/99	Keighley (a)	W2-17	t:Taewa,Chamberlain,R Smith g:Sibary,Kitching fg:Donohue	1st	2,183
13/6/99	Swinton (h)	W30-10	t:Chamberlain(2),A Smith,Taewa,R Smith g:Charles(5)	1st	2,005
20/6/99	Workington (h)	W18-10	t:Gene,Fletcher,Wray g:Charles(3)	1st	2,007
27/6/99	Batley (a)	W0-18	t:Gene,R Smith,Taewa g:Charles(3)	1st	1,113
4/7/99	Oldham (a)	W22-44	t:Danby(2),Thompson(2),Fletcher,Charles,Dixon,Blanchard g:Charles(6)	1st	1,190
11/7/99	Hunslet (h)	W16-13	t:Hughes,Charles g:Charles(4)	1st	3,004
18/7/99	Doncaster (a)	W16-42	t:Wray(3),Gray(2),Danby,Kitching,Fletcher g:Gray(5)	1st	1,293
25/7/99	Bramley (a)	L23-14	t:Wray,Fletcher,Dixon g:Kitching	1st	676
1/8/99	York (a)	L29-12	t:Chambers,Fletcher g:Charles,Sibary	1st	1,740
8/8/99	Dewsbury (h)	L0-20	No Scorers	4th	2,218
15/8/99	Whitehaven (a)	L32-10	t:Hughes,Taewa g:A Smith	5th	1,174
22/8/99	Rochdale (h)	W30-12	t:Molloy(2),Fletcher,Taewa,R Smith,Bovill g:Yeaman(3)	5th	1,703
29/8/99	Featherstone (a)	L23-10	t:Yeaman,Fletcher g:Yeaman	6th	3,103

	APP		TRIES		GOALS		FG		PTS	
	ALL	NFP	ALL	NFP	ALL	NFP	ALL	NFP	ALL	NFP
Mike Bibby	4(6)	3(5)	3	2	0	0	0	0	12	8
Mark Blanchard	1	1	1	1	0	0	0	0	4	4
Jamie Bovill	(2)	(2)	1	1	0	0	0	0	4	4
Richard Chamberlain	12(9)	10(8)	7	6	0	0	0	0	28	24
Anthony Chambers	4(2)	4(2)	1	1	0	0	0	0	4	4
Chris Charles	19(3)	16(3)	3	3	51	48	0	0	114	108
Rob Danby	16(1)	13(1)	6	5	0	0	0	0	24	20
Andy Dannatt	9(2)	9(2)	0	0	0	0	0	0	0	0
Mike Dixon	21(4)	20(3)	6	5	0	0	0	0	24	20
Jason Donohue	9(2)	9(2)	0	0	0	0	2	2	2	2
Allan Dunham	1(1)	1(1)	0	0	0	0	0	0	0	0
Paul Fletcher	28(3)	26(2)	14	11	0	0	0	0	56	44
Stanley Gene	18(1)	15(1)	11	10	0	0	0	0	44	40
Kevin Gray	11(6)	10(5)	6	4	28	20	1	1	81	57
Craig Hardy	2(20)	2(19)	0	0	0	0	0	0	0	0
Des Harrison	4(23)	2(22)	0	0	0	0	0	0	0	0
Ian Hughes	23(6)	22(4)	5	4	0	0	0	0	20	16
Chris Kitching	27	24	10	8	13	10	0	0	66	52
David Luckwell	18(7)	17(5)	0	0	0	0	0	0	0	0
Gavin Molloy	2(1)	2(1)	2	2	0	0	0	0	8	8
Wayne Parker	5(6)	5(6)	0	0	0	0	0	0	0	0
Paul Rouse	13(2)	12(2)	3	3	0	0	0	0	12	12
Paul Scott	(5)	(5)	0	0	0	0	0	0	0	0
Lee Sibary	5(6)	5(6)	0	0	2	2	0	0	4	4
Andy Smith	31	28	3	3	1	1	0	0	14	14
Richard Smith	25	22	12	9	0	0	0	0	48	36
Whetu Taewa	28	25	11	11	0	0	0	0	44	44
Alex Thompson	31	28	3	2	0	0	0	0	12	8
Marcus Vassilakopoulos	4	4	0	0	0	0	0	0	0	0
Colin Wilson	(1)	(1)	0	0	0	0	0	0	0	0
Jon Wray	30	27	11	8	0	0	0	0	44	32
Scott Yeaman	2	2	1	1	4	4	0	0	12	12

Paul Fletcher

LEAGUE RECORD
P28-W19-D1-L8
(6th, NFP)
F573, A425, Diff+148
39 points.

CHALLENGE CUP
Round Five

ATTENDANCES
Best - v London (CC - 3,971)
Worst - v Rochdale (NFP - 1,703)
Total (NFP only) - 30,097
Average (NFP only) - 2,150
(Down by 269 on 1998)

HUNSLET HAWKS

DATE	FIXTURE	RESULT	SCORERS	LGE	ATT
31/1/99	Townville (h) (CCR3)	W66-6	t:Baker(3),Wilson(2),Walker,Mycoe,Ross,Pachniuk,St Hilaire,Irwin,Plange g:Ross(9)	N/A	749
7/2/99	Swinton (a)	W10-21	t:Wilson,Pachniuk,Fletcher g:Fletcher(4) fg:Fletcher	N/A	1,500
14/2/99	St Helens (h) (CCR4)	L10-40	t:Fatnowna g:Fletcher(3)	N/A	2,201
21/2/99	Workington (h)	W48-6	t:Pachniuk(3),Tawhai,D'Arcy,Thackray,Walker,Fatnowna g:Fletcher(8)	1st	1,325
7/3/99	Batley (a)	W8-14	t:Fletcher,Fatnowna g:Fletcher(3)	1st	847
14/3/99	Hull KR (h)	L14-26	t:Irwin,Walker g:Fletcher(3)	1st	2,054
21/3/99	Oldham (h)	W44-2	t:Plange(4),Wilson(2),Fatnowna,Tawhai g:Fletcher(6)	2nd	1,533
28/3/99	Doncaster (h)	W30-18	t:Tawhai(2),Fatnowna,D'Arcy,Baker g:Fletcher(5)	2nd	1,257
2/4/99	Bramley (h)	L11-16	t:Fatnowna,Wilson g:Fletcher fg:Fletcher	2nd	1,522
5/4/99	York (a)	L16-6	t:Tawhai g:Fletcher	5th	1,204
11/4/99	Dewsbury (h)	L20-21	t:Tawhai,Higgins,Walker g:Fletcher(4)	7th	1,621
18/4/99	Whitehaven (h)	W36-16	t:Walker(2),Plange,Fatnowna,Baker g:Fletcher(8)	7th	1,004
25/4/99	Rochdale (h)	W33-12	t:Filipo(2),Higgins,Ross,Tawhai g:Fletcher(6) fg:Fletcher	5th	1,181
9/5/99	Featherstone (a)	W15-26	t:Ross,Walker,Irwin,Pachniuk g:Fletcher(5)	4th	1,914
16/5/99	Barrow (h)	W46-14	t:Tawhai,Pachniuk(3),D'Arcy g:Fletcher(9)	4th	1,008
23/5/99	Widnes (a)	L32-24	t:Irwin,D'Arcy,Ross,Tawhai g:Fletcher(3),Ross	4th	2,561
30/5/99	Leigh (h)	W35-12	t:Baker,North,Walker,Pryce,D'Arcy,Irwin g:Fletcher(5) fg:Fletcher	4th	1,867
6/6/99	Lancashire (a)	W12-53	t:Walker(2),Fatnowna(2),Tawhai,D'Arcy,St Hilaire,North,Pachniuk g:Fletcher(8) fg:Wilson	4th	321
13/6/99	Keighley (h)	W48-8	t:Pryce(2),North(2),Baker,Tawhai,Fatnowna,Pachniuk,Bowes g:Fletcher(5),Mycoe	4th	1,672
20/6/99	Swinton (h)	W22-8	t:Irwin,Fatnowna g:Fletcher(7)	3rd	1,402
27/6/99	Workington (a)	W12-44	t:Fatnowna(2),Pachniuk(2),North,Baker g:Fletcher(8)	3rd	870
4/7/99	Batley (h)	W32-15	t:North,Filipo,D'Arcy,Higgins g:Fletcher(8)	2nd	1,652
11/7/99	Hull KR (a)	L16-13	t:Fatnowna,Pachniuk g:Fletcher(2) fg:Tawhai	3rd	3,004
18/7/99	Oldham (h)	W12-56	t:Pachniuk(2),Kennedy(2),St Hilaire,Wilson,Fletcher,Tawhai,Cook,Higgins g:Fletcher(8)	3rd	896
25/7/99	Doncaster (a)	W16-50	t:Higgins(3),Fatnowna(2),Baker,Pachniuk,Tawhai,Leighton g:Cook(4),Fletcher(3)	3rd	610
1/8/99	Bramley (a)	W22-29	t:Pachniuk(2),Cook,Fatnowna,Leighton g:Cook(4) fg:Leighton	2nd	853
8/8/99	York (h)	W15-14	t:Pachniuk,Ross g:Cook(2) fg:Tawhai(3)	1st	1,632
15/8/99	Dewsbury (a)	L10-6	t:Pachniuk g:Fletcher	3rd	1,642
22/8/99	Whitehaven (a)	W22-31	t:Pachniuk(2),Cook,Vassilakopoulos,Irwin g:Cook(5) fg:Vassilakopoulos	2nd	925
29/8/99	Rochdale (a)	W10-38	t:Fatnowna,St Hilaire,Tawhai,Higgins,Pachniuk,Walker g:Cook(7)	2nd	1,005
5/9/99	Widnes (h) (QPO)	L21-24	t:Irwin(2),Fatnowna,Ross g:Cook(2) fg:Tawhai	N/A	2,245
12/9/99	Featherstone (h) (ESF)	W17-9	t:Pachniuk(2),Baker g:Ross(2) fg:Tawhai	N/A	1,620
19/9/99	Widnes (h) (FE)	W10-8	t:Baker g:Ross(3)	N/A	1,824
25/9/99	Dewsbury (GFN)	W11-12	t:Cook,Higgins g:Ross fg:Tawhai,Leighton	N/A	5,783

	APP		TRIES		GOALS		FG		PTS	
	ALL	NFP	ALL	NFP	ALL	NFP	ALL	NFP	ALL	NFP
Richard Allwood	1(3)	1(3)	0	0	0	0	0	0	0	0
Richard Baker	23(5)	21(5)	11	8	0	0	0	0	44	32
Tony Bowes	3(3)	3(3)	1	1	0	0	0	0	4	4
Aaron Campbell	(2)	(2)	0	0	0	0	0	0	0	0
Paul Cook	10(1)	10(1)	4	4	24	24	0	0	64	64
Mick Coyle	23(4)	22(4)	0	0	0	0	0	0	0	0
Rob D'Arcy	19(7)	18(6)	7	7	0	0	0	0	28	28
Nicky Dobson	(4)	(4)	0	0	0	0	0	0	0	0
Steve Embling	(1)	(1)	0	0	0	0	0	0	0	0
Abraham Fatnowna	33(1)	31(1)	20	19	0	0	0	0	80	76
Lafaele Filipo	1(3)	1(3)	3	3	0	0	0	0	12	12
Mike Fletcher	23(3)	22(2)	3	3	124	121	4	4	264	258
Matthew Green	1	1	0	0	0	0	0	0	0	0
Richard Hayes	22(2)	21(2)	0	0	0	0	0	0	0	0
Anthony Henderson	(1)	(1)	0	0	0	0	0	0	0	0
Iain Higgins	23(2)	21(2)	9	9	0	0	0	0	36	36
Shaun Irwin	31	29	9	8	0	0	0	0	36	32
Phil Kennedy	2(13)	2(13)	2	2	0	0	0	0	8	8
Gareth King	(7)	(7)	0	0	0	0	0	0	0	0
Jamie Leighton	2(9)	2(9)	2	2	0	0	2	2	10	10
Adam Moore	(2)	(2)	0	0	0	0	0	0	0	0
David Mycoe	13(3)	11(3)	1	0	1	1	0	0	6	2
Joe Naidole	1(3)	1(3)	0	0	0	0	0	0	0	0
Chris North	10(6)	10(6)	6	6	0	0	0	0	24	24
Richard Pachniuk	25(2)	23(2)	26	25	0	0	0	0	104	100
Steve Parnell	(1)	(1)	0	0	0	0	0	0	0	0
David Plange	6(4)	6(3)	6	5	0	0	0	0	24	20
Steve Pryce	21(4)	21(2)	3	3	0	0	0	0	12	12
Craig Richards	11(6)	9(6)	0	0	0	0	0	0	0	0
Chris Ross	16(2)	14(2)	6	5	16	7	0	0	56	34
Lee St Hilaire	29(3)	27(3)	4	3	0	0	0	0	16	12
Latham Tawhai	30(1)	30	16	16	0	0	7	7	71	71
Jamie Thackray	12(6)	12(5)	1	1	0	0	0	0	4	4
Marcus Vassilakopoulos	12(1)	12(1)	1	1	0	0	1	1	5	5
James Walker	17(9)	15(9)	11	10	0	0	0	0	44	40
Rob Wilson	22(3)	20(3)	7	5	0	0	1	1	29	21

Richard Pachniuk

LEAGUE RECORD
P28-W21-D0-L7
(2nd, NFP/Grand Final Winners,
Champions)
F845, A401, Diff+444
42 points.

CHALLENGE CUP
Round Four

ATTENDANCES
Best - v Widnes (QPO - 2,245)
Worst - v Townville (CC - 749)
Total (NFP, inc play-offs) - 26,419
Average (NFP, inc play-offs) - 1,554
(Down by 188 on 1998)

KEIGHLEY COUGARS

DATE	FIXTURE	RESULT	SCORERS	LGE	ATT
31/1/99	Rochdale M (h) (CCR3)	W48-2	t:Ramshaw(3),Laurence,Foster,Antonik,Rich,Lee,Robinson g:Antonik(6)	N/A	2,219
7/2/99	Doncaster (h)	W42-16	t:Smith(2),Wood(2),Lee,Foster,Laurence,Rich g:Rich(4),Antonik	N/A	2,472
14/2/99	Widnes (a) (CCR4)	L28-20	t:Smits,Ramshaw,Smith g:Wood(4)	N/A	3,003
21/2/99	Bramley (a)	L14-12	t:Ramshaw,Lee g:Wood(2)	4th	1,000
7/3/99	York (h)	L8-10	t:Calvert,Larder	9th	1,878
14/3/99	Dewsbury (a)	L35-8	t:Ramshaw g:Wood(2)	15th	1,010
21/3/99	Whitehaven (h)	W30-16	t:Wood(2),Ramshaw,Foster,Lee g:Wood(5)	12th	1,616
2/4/99	Featherstone (h)	L18-32	t:Antonik,Wood,M Campbell g:Wood(3)	14th	2,242
5/4/99	Barrow (a)	W21-22	t:Schick,Foster,Ramshaw,Antonik g:Wood(3)	12th	1,378
11/4/99	Widnes (h)	W24-22	t:Lee(2),Antonik,Tyrer,Foster g:Wood(2)	9th	2,103
18/4/99	Leigh (a)	L28-16	t:Lee,Ramshaw g:Wood(3),Tyrer	9th	1,856
25/4/99	Lancashire (h)	W40-14	t:Foster(5),Antonik,M Campbell g:Dixon(4),Tyrer,Larder	9th	1,680
9/5/99	Oldham (h)	W32-28	t:Foster(2),Ramshaw,Dixon,Lee,M Campbell g:Wood(4)	9th	1,842
16/5/99	Swinton (a)	W14-15	t:Lee(2),Tomlinson g:Wood fg:Ramshaw	8th	1,035
23/5/99	Workington (h)	L18-22	t:Lee,Foster,Stephenson g:Wood(3)	11th	1,650
30/5/99	Batley (a)	W20-25	t:Lee(2),M Campbell,Rich g:Wood(4) fg:Tyrer	9th	708
6/6/99	Hull KR (h)	L2-17	g:Wood	9th	2,183
13/6/99	Hunslet (a)	L48-8	t:Tyrer,Dixon	11th	1,672
20/6/99	Doncaster (a)	W18-23	t:Lee(2),Robinson,Tomlinson g:Wood(3) fg:Ramshaw	10th	521
23/6/99	Rochdale (a)	W18-26	t:Lee,Laurence,Foster,Antonik g:Lee(3),Rich(2)	7th	833
27/6/99	Bramley (h)	W36-10	t:Foster(4),Laurence,Wood,Ramshaw g:Wood(4)	7th	1,466
4/7/99	York (a)	L24-14	t:Wood(2),Smits g:Rich	8th	1,084
11/7/99	Dewsbury (h)	D24-24	t:Lee,Schick,Owen,Larder g:Rich(4)	8th	1,584
18/7/99	Whitehaven (a)	L22-20	t:Ramshaw,Schick,Foster g:Tyrer(3),Wood	9th	803
25/7/99	Rochdale (h)	W30-20	t:Antonik,Foster,Rich,Ramshaw g:Tyrer(7)	8th	1,503
1/8/99	Featherstone (a)	L40-20	t:Lee(2),Antonik,Laurence g:Tyrer(2)	9th	1,473
8/8/99	Barrow (h)	W22-20	t:Laurence,Schick,Ramshaw g:Rich(5)	9th	1,441
15/8/99	Widnes (a)	L24-16	t:Lee(2),Kirk g:Rich(2)	9th	3,649
22/8/99	Leigh (h)	W29-14	t:Lee(2),Rich,S Campbell,Stephenson g:Rich(2),Tyrer(2) fg:Tyrer	9th	2,498
29/8/99	Lancashire (a)	L21-4	t:Antonik	9th	528

Jason Lee

	APP		TRIES		GOALS		FG		PTS	
	ALL	NFP	ALL	NFP	ALL	NFP	ALL	NFP	ALL	NFP
Nathan Antonik	29	27	9	8	7	1	0	0	50	34
Rob Bailey	(1)	(1)	0	0	0	0	0	0	0	0
Lee Baines	1	1	0	0	0	0	0	0	0	0
Tareq Bilel	(1)	(1)	0	0	0	0	0	0	0	0
Craig Brown	(1)	(1)	0	0	0	0	0	0	0	0
Stuart Calvert	4(3)	4(2)	1	1	0	0	0	0	4	4
Mark Campbell	15(8)	13(8)	4	4	0	0	0	0	16	16
Steve Campbell	16(8)	15(8)	1	1	0	0	0	0	4	4
David Chapman	2	1	0	0	0	0	0	0	0	0
Keith Dixon	5(2)	5(2)	2	2	4	4	0	0	16	16
Matthew Foster	24	23	20	19	0	0	0	0	80	76
Steve Hall	28(2)	26(2)	0	0	0	0	0	0	0	0
Chris Hannah	1(2)	1(2)	0	0	0	0	0	0	0	0
Chris Hartley	1(5)	1(5)	0	0	0	0	0	0	0	0
Kris Kirk	3(1)	3(1)	1	1	0	0	0	0	4	4
David Larder	20(2)	19(2)	2	2	1	1	0	0	10	10
Jason Laurence	19(1)	17(1)	6	5	0	0	0	0	24	20
Jason Lee	28	26	23	22	3	3	0	0	98	94
Davide Longo	3	1	0	0	0	0	0	0	0	0
Steve McManus	(1)	(1)	0	0	0	0	0	0	0	0
Paul Owen	9(9)	9(8)	1	1	0	0	0	0	4	4
Jason Ramshaw	26(1)	24(1)	14	10	0	0	2	2	58	42
Pat Rich	15(7)	14(7)	5	4	20	20	0	0	60	56
Chris Robinson	9(12)	9(10)	2	1	0	0	0	0	8	4
Andrew Schick	24	23	4	4	0	0	0	0	16	16
Karl Smith	21(2)	20(1)	3	2	0	0	0	0	12	8
Alex Smits	8(20)	7(19)	2	1	0	0	0	0	8	4
Phil Stephenson	14(10)	14(9)	2	2	0	0	0	0	8	8
Max Tomlinson	14(3)	14(3)	2	2	0	0	0	0	8	8
Christian Tyrer	16(2)	14(2)	2	2	16	16	2	2	42	42
Chris Wainwright	13(6)	13(6)	0	0	0	0	0	0	0	0
Martin Wood	22	20	8	8	45	41	0	0	122	114

LEAGUE RECORD
P28-W14-D1-L13
(9th, NFP)
F584, A612, Diff-28
29 points.

CHALLENGE CUP
Round Four

ATTENDANCES
Best - v Leigh (NFP - 2,498)
Worst - v Barrow (NFP - 1,441)
Total (NFP only) - 26,158
Average (NFP only) - 1,868
(Down by 249 on 1998)

LANCASHIRE LYNX

DATE	FIXTURE	RESULT	SCORERS	LGE	ATT
31/1/99	Askam (h) (CCR3)	W50-3	t:Parsley(4),Murray(2),Donno,Walsh,Norton g:P Jones(7)	N/A	408
7/2/99	Bramley (h)	W13-12	t:Abram(2) g:P Jones(2) fg:Hodgkinson	N/A	298
14/2/99	Whitehaven (a) (CCR4)	L24-6	g:P Jones(3)	N/A	827
21/2/99	York (a)	L32-6	t:P Jones g:P Jones	14th	792
7/3/99	Dewsbury (h)	W22-12	t:P Jones(2),Walsh g:P Jones(4) fg:Flanagan(2)	7th	360
17/3/99	Whitehaven (a)	L24-12	t:Gee,P Jones g:P Jones(2)	11th	604
21/3/99	Rochdale (a)	W22-27	t:Abram,P Jones,Gildart,Parsley g:P Jones(5) fg:P Jones	8th	714
28/3/99	Featherstone (a)	L32-18	t:Murray,Hodgkinson,Parsley g:Murray(2),James	9th	1,589
2/4/99	Barrow (h)	L16-58	t:Solomon(2),Murray g:Murray(2)	12th	350
5/4/99	Widnes (a)	L40-4	t:Parsley	14th	3,064
11/4/99	Leigh (h)	L24-44	t:Murray(2),S Geritas,S Smith g:Campbell(4)	15th	777
25/4/99	Keighley (a)	L40-14	t:S Geritas,Parsley,Solomon g:Danny Jones	16th	1,680
3/5/99	Workington (h)	L24-38	t:Parsley(2),S Geritas,Gildart g:Danny Jones(2)	16th	326
9/5/99	Swinton (h)	L10-56	t:Solomon,Flanagan g:Danny Jones	16th	344
16/5/99	Workington (a)	L36-8	t:Alexander g:Danny Jones(2)	16th	799
23/5/99	Batley (h)	L28-47	t:Alexander(4),S Geritas g:Danny Jones(4)	16th	232
30/5/99	Hull KR (a)	L48-12	t:Alexander g:Danny Jones(2)	16th	1,809
6/6/99	Hunslet (h)	L12-53	t:Walsh g:Roberts(4)	17th	321
13/6/99	Doncaster (a)	W18-45	t:Alexander(4),Parsley(2),Flanagan,Abram g:Danny Jones(4),Murray(2) fg:Flanagan	17th	449
20/6/99	Bramley (a)	W32-45	t:Flanagan(2),Abram,Ratcliffe,Parsley,Norton,Solomon,Walsh g:Danny Jones(6) fg:Abram	16th	423
27/6/99	York (h)	L22-29	t:Flanagan(2),Guest,Solomon g:Roberts(3)	17th	212
4/7/99	Dewsbury (a)	L34-27	t:Ratcliffe,Gee,Alexander,Solomon,Hodgkinson g:Murray(3) fg:Flanagan	17th	621
9/7/99	Whitehaven (h)	L8-21	t:Solomon g:Rose(2)	17th	232
18/7/99	Rochdale (h)	L13-34	t:Abram,Gee g:Alexander(2) fg:Flanagan	16th	281
23/7/99	Featherstone (h)	L8-16	t:Prest g:Roberts(2)	16th	305
1/8/99	Barrow (a)	L25-19	t:Ratcliffe,Parsley,Abram g:Roberts(2),Flanagan fg:Flanagan	17th	734
8/8/99	Widnes (a)	L14-24	t:Abram,Murray,Hodgkinson g:Alexander	17th	939
15/8/99	Leigh (a)	L32-20	t:Alexander,Murray,David Jones g:Alexander(4)	17th	1,806
22/8/99	Oldham (a)	W26-52	t:Alexander(3),Parsley(3),Murray,Roberts,Gee g:Roberts(8)	16th	677
29/8/99	Keighley (h)	W21-4	t:Bennett,Murray,Roberts,Gee g:Alexander(2) fg:Roberts	16th	528

	APP		TRIES		GOALS		FG		PTS	
	ALL	NFP	ALL	NFP	ALL	NFP	ALL	NFP	ALL	NFP
Darren Abram	28	26	8	8	0	0	1	1	33	33
Neil Alexander	15	15	16	16	9	9	0	0	82	82
Andy Bennett	10	10	1	1	0	0	0	0	4	4
Konrad Bisping	(4)	(3)	0	0	0	0	0	0	0	0
Craig Campbell	6(1)	5(1)	0	0	4	4	0	0	8	8
John Donno	9	7	1	0	0	0	0	0	4	0
Andy Fisher	1(9)	1(9)	0	0	0	0	0	0	0	0
Steve Fisher	(1)	(1)	0	0	0	0	0	0	0	0
Neil Flanagan	26	24	6	6	1	1	6	6	32	32
Steve Gee	7(8)	5(8)	5	5	0	0	0	0	20	20
Danny Geritas	1(6)	1(6)	0	0	0	0	0	0	0	0
Shaun Geritas	11(11)	11(11)	4	4	0	0	0	0	16	16
Ian Gildart	11(2)	11(2)	2	2	0	0	0	0	8	8
Danny Guest	3(14)	3(12)	1	1	0	0	0	0	4	4
Tommy Hodgkinson	27	25	3	3	0	0	1	1	13	13
Martin Horton	9(2)	9(2)	0	0	0	0	0	0	0	0
Andy James	4(3)	4(3)	0	0	1	1	0	0	2	2
Danny Jones	8(1)	8(1)	0	0	24	24	0	0	48	48
David Jones	20	18	1	1	0	0	0	0	4	4
Phil Jones	7	5	5	5	24	14	1	1	69	49
Neil Mawdsley	(1)	0	0	0	0	0	0	0	0	0
Doc Murray	28	26	10	8	9	9	0	0	58	50
Paul Norton	19	17	2	1	0	0	0	0	8	4
Jason O'Loughlin	7	7	0	0	0	0	0	0	0	0
Neil Parsley	30	28	17	13	0	0	0	0	68	52
Neil Prescott	(1)	(1)	0	0	0	0	0	0	0	0
Lee Prest	19(8)	17(8)	1	1	0	0	0	0	4	4
Dave Ratcliffe	10	10	3	3	0	0	0	0	12	12
Paul Roberts	6(4)	6(4)	2	2	19	19	1	1	47	47
Robert Rose	1	1	0	0	2	2	0	0	4	4
Paul Rostance	(1)	(1)	0	0	0	0	0	0	0	0
Lee Rushton	4(3)	4(3)	0	0	0	0	0	0	0	0
Dave Smith	7(2)	7(2)	0	0	0	0	0	0	0	0
Simon Smith	2(10)	2(8)	1	1	0	0	0	0	4	4
PJ Solomon	28(1)	26(1)	8	8	0	0	0	0	32	32
Ian Speed	2(1)	2(1)	0	0	0	0	0	0	0	0
Joe Walsh	15(15)	14(14)	4	3	0	0	0	0	16	12
John Welsh	5(2)	5(2)	0	0	0	0	0	0	0	0
Kyle White	4(4)	4(3)	0	0	0	0	0	0	0	0

PJ Solomon

LEAGUE RECORD
P28-W7-D0-L21
(16th, NFP)
F544, A889, Diff-345
14 points.

CHALLENGE CUP
Round Four

ATTENDANCES
Best - v Widnes (NFP - 939)
Worst - v York (NFP - 212)
Total (NFP only) - 5,505
Average (NFP only) - 393
(Down by 350 on 1998)

DATE	FIXTURE	RESULT	SCORERS	LGE	ATT
31/1/99	Norland (h) (CCR3)	W42-6	t:Arkwright(3),Liku,Patel,Street,Cruckshank,Ingram g:Dean(5)	N/A	1,400
7/2/99	York (h)	W16-12	t:Kendrick,Fairclough g:Kendrick(4)	N/A	1,546
14/2/99	Barrow (a) (CCR4)	W16-33	t:Ingram(2),Liku,Hadcroft,Donlan,Fairclough g:Kendrick(4) fg:Kendrick	N/A	1,485
21/2/99	Dewsbury (a)	L31-16	t:Hadcroft,Hilton,Fairclough g:Kendrick(2)	12th	1,314
28/2/99	Widnes (a) (CCR5)	L20-17	t:Burrows,Murray,Lewis g:Kendrick(2) fg:Kendrick	N/A	4,054
7/3/99	Whitehaven (h)	W24-20	t:K Purtill(2),Hilton,Murray,Hadcroft g:D Purtill(2)	6th	1,124
14/3/99	Rochdale (a)	W22-40	t:Ingram(3),Fairclough(2),Dean,Kendrick,Murray g:D Purtill(4)	4th	1,203
21/3/99	Featherstone (h)	W16-12	t:Ingram,Hadcroft,Fairclough g:D Purtill(2)	3rd	1,603
28/3/99	Barrow (a)	W26-44	t:Dean(2),Murray(2),Donlan,Liku,Kennedy,Fairclough g:D Purtill(6)	3rd	1,261
2/4/99	Widnes (h)	L22-23	t:Fairclough(2),Street,Ingram g:P Wingfield(3)	4th	2,750
5/4/99	Oldham (a)	W20-26	t:Street(2),Bowker,Ingram,Murray g:P Wingfield(3)	4th	2,163
11/4/99	Lancashire (a)	W24-44	t:P Wingfield(2),Murray(2),Bowker,Fairclough,Hilton,Kennedy g:P Wingfield(6)	3rd	777
18/4/99	Keighley (h)	W28-16	t:Cruckshank,Ingram,Murray,Arkwright,Street,Fairclough g:P Wingfield(2)	3rd	1,856
25/4/99	Swinton (a)	W22-34	t:Norman(2),Cruckshank,Bowker,K Purtill g:P Wingfield(7)	2nd	1,300
9/5/99	Workington (h)	W42-10	t:Ingram(2),Donlan(2),Murray(2),Hadcroft g:P Wingfield(7)	2nd	1,484
16/5/99	Batley (a)	L25-16	t:Fairclough,Parr,Murray g:P Wingfield(2)	3rd	1,023
23/5/99	Hull KR (h)	W27-20	t:Hadcroft,Ingram,Cruckshank,Fairclough g:P Wingfield(5) fg:P Wingfield	2nd	2,419
30/5/99	Hunslet (h)	L35-12	t:Kendrick(2) g:P Wingfield,Kendrick	3rd	1,867
6/6/99	Doncaster (h)	W72-6	t:Patel(2),Arkwright(2),Murray(2),Ingram(2),Hadcroft,Jenkins,Kerr, Kendrick,Fairclough g:Kendrick(7),Ingram(3)	2nd	1,372
11/6/99	Bramley (a)	W8-39	t:Hadcroft(2),Fairclough,Kerr,Kennedy,Whittle,Pucill g:Kendrick(5) fg:K Purtill	2nd	679
20/6/99	York (a)	W12-14	t:Cruckshank,Hadcroft g:Kendrick(3)	2nd	1,147
27/6/99	Dewsbury (h)	W24-10	t:Arkwright,Murray,Kendrick g:P Wingfield(6)	2nd	2,049
4/7/99	Whitehaven (a)	L22-16	t:Patel,K Purtill,Ingram g:P Wingfield(2)	3rd	953
11/7/99	Rochdale (h)	W34-20	t:Whittle,Kendrick,Higham,Anderson,Bowker,Kennedy g:Kendrick(5)	2nd	1,568
18/7/99	Featherstone (a)	W18-24	t:Bowker(2),Donlan,P Wingfield g:P Wingfield(4)	2nd	2,145
25/7/99	Barrow (h)	W32-26	t:Anderson,Street,Ingram,Donlan,Cruckshank g:P Wingfield(6)	2nd	1,720
1/8/99	Widnes (a)	L9-6	t:Patel g:P Wingfield	3rd	5,230
8/8/99	Oldham (h)	W66-6	t:Murray(3),Fairclough(2),Kendrick(2),Kennedy,P Wingfield,Kerr,Donlan, Higham g:P Wingfield(9)	2nd	1,619
15/8/99	Lancashire (h)	W32-20	t:K Purtill(2),Murray,Kerr,Cruckshank g:P Wingfield(6)	1st	1,806
22/8/99	Keighley (a)	L29-14	t:Murray,Kerr,K Purtill g:P Wingfield	4th	2,498
29/8/99	Swinton (h)	W22-20	t:Halliwell,Bowker,Kerr,Donlan g:P Wingfield(3)	4th	2,174
5/9/99	Featherstone (h) (EPO)	L4-17	t:P Wingfield	N/A	3,032

	APP		TRIES		GOALS		FG		PTS	
	ALL	NFP	ALL	NFP	ALL	NFP	ALL	NFP	ALL	NFP
Paul Anderson	5	5	2	2	0	0	0	0	8	8
James Arkwright	22(4)	20(4)	7	4	0	0	0	0	28	16
Radney Bowker	7(12)	7(10)	7	7	0	0	0	0	28	28
Mark Burrows	2(2)	1(2)	1	0	0	0	0	0	4	0
Graeme Close	2(2)	2(2)	0	0	0	0	0	0	0	0
John Costello	1(5)	(4)	0	0	0	0	0	0	0	0
Heath Cruckshank	21(4)	20(4)	7	6	0	0	0	0	28	24
Craig Dean	8	7	3	3	5	0	0	0	22	12
Stuart Donlan	30	27	8	7	0	0	0	0	32	28
Andy Fairclough	25	22	17	16	0	0	0	0	68	64
Alan Hadcroft	23(1)	20(1)	10	9	0	0	0	0	40	36
Darren Hall	(1)	(1)	0	0	0	0	0	0	0	0
Chris Halliwell	2(3)	2(3)	1	1	0	0	0	0	4	4
Mick Higham	4(6)	4(5)	2	2	0	0	0	0	8	8
Scott Hilton	6(2)	5(2)	3	3	0	0	0	0	12	12
David Ingram	26(4)	24(4)	17	14	3	3	0	0	74	62
Nick Jenkins	5(4)	4(3)	1	1	0	0	0	0	4	4
Phil Kendrick	21(2)	19(1)	9	9	33	27	2	0	104	90
Jamie Kennedy	24	24	5	5	0	0	0	0	20	20
Ken Kerr	12	12	6	6	0	0	0	0	24	24
Ian Lewis	(4)	(3)	1	0	0	0	0	0	4	0
Tau Liku	15(3)	12(3)	3	1	0	0	0	0	12	4
Anthony Murray	22(6)	19(6)	20	19	0	0	0	0	80	76
Paul Norman	4(10)	4(10)	2	2	0	0	0	0	8	8
Chris Parr	2(4)	2(3)	1	1	0	0	0	0	4	4
Safraz Patel	15(11)	12(11)	5	4	0	0	0	0	20	16
Chris Platt	(1)	0	0	0	0	0	0	0	0	0
Andy Pucill	2(18)	2(18)	1	1	0	0	0	0	4	4
Dean Purtill	4	4	0	0	14	14	0	0	28	28
Keiron Purtill	25(1)	22(1)	7	7	0	0	1	1	29	29
Tim Street	32	29	6	5	0	0	0	0	24	20
David Whittle	29(3)	26(3)	2	2	0	0	0	0	8	8
Craig Wingfield	1(5)	1(4)	0	0	0	0	0	0	0	0
Paul Wingfield	19	19	5	5	74	74	1	1	169	169

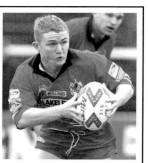

Paul Wingfield

LEAGUE RECORD
P28-W21-D0-L7
(4th, NFP/Elimination Play-Off)
F802, A524, Diff+278
42 points.

CHALLENGE CUP
Round Five

ATTENDANCES
Best - v Featherstone (EPO - 3,032)
Worst - v Whitehaven (NFP - 1,124)
Total (NFP, inc play-offs) - 28,122
Average (NFP, inc play-offs) - 1,875
(Up by 692 on 1998)

OLDHAM

DATE	FIXTURE	RESULT	SCORERS	LGE	ATT
1/2/99	Eccles (h) (CCR3)	W26-7	t:Meade(2),Brown,Prescott,Clegg g:Minut(3)	N/A	1,764
7/2/99	Batley (a)	L30-0	No Scorers	N/A	1,018
15/2/99	Dewsbury (h) (CCR4)	W18-10	t:Meade,Clegg,Brown g:Minut(2),Brown	N/A	1,620
28/2/99	Whitehaven (a) (CCR5)	L18-2	g:Brown	N/A	1,438
12/3/99	Barrow (h)	W24-20	t:Brown(2),Bostock(2) g:Minut(2),Quinlan(2)	18th	1,123
17/3/99	Hull KR (a)	D8-8	t:Bostock g:Quinlan,Brown	12th	2,080
21/3/99	Hunslet (a)	L44-2	g:Martindale	15th	1,533
28/3/99	Widnes (h)	L18-33	t:McNicholas(2),Jackman g:Wood(3)	16th	1,515
2/4/99	Doncaster (a)	W12-27	t:McNicholas,Hough,Meade,Brown,Wood g:Wood(3) fg:Wood	13th	878
5/4/99	Leigh (h)	L20-26	t:Meade(2),Farrell g:Wood(4)	15th	2,163
11/4/99	Bramley (a)	L24-18	t:McNicholas,Farrell,Martindale g:Minut(3)	16th	500
25/4/99	York (h)	L14-43	t:Brown,Meade,Farrell g:Wood	17th	1,125
3/5/99	Rochdale (a)	L29-18	t:Clegg,Martindale g:Brown(5)	17th	1,568
9/5/99	Keighley (a)	L32-28	t:McNicholas(2),Brown,Hough,Farrell g:Brown(3),Wood	17th	1,842
23/5/99	Swinton (a)	L31-24	t:Brown,Clegg,Round,Quinlan g:Brown(4)	17th	1,478
30/5/99	Whitehaven (h)	L24-32	t:Clegg,Sinfield,Varley,Round g:Brown(4)	17th	775
6/6/99	Workington (a)	W17-22	t:Crook(2),Shaw,Minut,Leuila g:Brown	16th	1,148
9/6/99	Featherstone (h)	L18-25	t:Crook,Jackman,Hough g:Brown(3)	16th	901
13/6/99	Rochdale (h)	W26-18	t:Minut,Darkes,Hough,Jackman g:Brown(5)	16th	3,023
18/6/99	Batley (h)	D20-20	t:Round,Brown,McNicholas,Shaw g:Brown,Coates	16th	1,013
27/6/99	Featherstone (a)	L61-6	t:Farrell g:Farrell	16th	1,437
4/7/99	Hull KR (h)	L22-44	t:Shaw,Brennan,Farrell,Hough g:Brown(3)	16th	1,190
7/7/99	Dewsbury (h)	L12-28	t:Leuila,Brown g:Brown(2)	16th	859
11/7/99	Barrow (a)	L55-16	t:McNicholas,Jackman,Brown g:Brown(2)	16th	843
18/7/99	Hunslet (h)	L12-56	t:Leuila,Brassington g:Brown(2)	16th	896
25/7/99	Widnes (a)	L84-0	No Scorers	17th	3,136
30/7/99	Doncaster (h)	W22-17	t:Casey,Brown,Round,Hough g:Brown(3)	16th	676
8/8/99	Leigh (a)	L66-6	t:Meade g:Brown	16th	1,619
13/8/99	Bramley (h)	L8-22	t:Hough g:Salisbury(2)	16th	621
22/8/99	Lancashire (h)	L26-52	t:Brennan(2),Brown(2),Darkes g:Salisbury(3)	17th	677
29/8/99	York (a)	L70-8	t:Perrett g:Salisbury(2)	17th	728

	APP		TRIES		GOALS		FG		PTS	
	ALL	NFP	ALL	NFP	ALL	NFP	ALL	NFP	ALL	NFP
Craig Barker	1(7)	1(7)	0	0	0	0	0	0	0	0
Josh Bostock	7	4	3	3	0	0	0	0	12	12
Paul Brassington	6	6	1	1	0	0	0	0	4	4
Keith Brennan	5(2)	5(2)	3	3	0	0	0	0	12	12
Daniel Brown	30(1)	27(1)	14	12	42	40	0	0	140	128
Leo Casey	28	25	1	1	0	0	0	0	4	4
Jason Clegg	30	27	5	3	0	0	0	0	20	12
Michael Coates	2(4)	2(4)	0	0	1	1	0	0	2	2
Gary Coulter	1(5)	(3)	0	0	0	0	0	0	0	0
Jimmy Cowan	1	1	0	0	0	0	0	0	0	0
Paul Crook	16(6)	15(5)	3	3	0	0	0	0	12	12
Richard Darkes	9(2)	9(2)	2	2	0	0	0	0	8	8
Mick Farrell	13(2)	13(2)	6	6	1	1	0	0	26	26
Stuart Fraser	(2)	(2)	0	0	0	0	0	0	0	0
Danny Guest	1(4)	1(4)	0	0	0	0	0	0	0	0
John Hough	30	27	7	7	0	0	0	0	28	28
Emerson Jackman	20(9)	17(9)	4	4	0	0	0	0	16	16
Afi Leuila	19	16	3	3	0	0	0	0	12	12
Dave Lewis	(1)	(1)	0	0	0	0	0	0	0	0
Martin Maders	1(2)	1(2)	0	0	0	0	0	0	0	0
Mick Martindale	10	9	2	2	1	1	0	0	10	10
Joe McNicholas	31	28	8	8	0	0	0	0	32	32
Adrian Meade	31	28	8	5	0	0	0	0	32	20
Laurent Minut	19	16	2	2	10	5	0	0	28	18
Joe Naidole	4(3)	4(3)	0	0	0	0	0	0	0	0
Emmanuel Peralta	8(18)	7(16)	0	0	0	0	0	0	0	0
Mark Perrett	7(7)	5(6)	1	1	0	0	0	0	4	4
Mike Prescott	6(17)	6(14)	1	0	0	0	0	0	4	0
Paul Round	16(4)	16(3)	4	4	0	0	0	0	16	16
Brian Quinlan	4(7)	4(5)	1	1	3	3	0	0	10	10
Jim Salisbury	3	3	0	0	7	7	0	0	14	14
Graeme Shaw	20(2)	17(2)	3	3	0	0	0	0	12	12
Ian Sinfield	5(3)	5(3)	1	1	0	0	0	0	4	4
Nathan Varley	6(5)	6(5)	1	1	0	0	0	0	4	4
Danny Webster	7	7	0	0	0	0	0	0	0	0
Danny Wood	6	6	1	1	12	12	1	1	29	29

Leo Casey

LEAGUE RECORD
P28-W5-D2-L21
(17th, NFP)
F449, A999, Diff-550
12 points.

CHALLENGE CUP
Round Five

ATTENDANCES
Best - v Rochdale (NFP - 3,023)
Worst - v Bramley (NFP - 621)
Total (NFP only) - 16,557
Average (NFP only) - 1,183
(Down by 645 on 1998)

ROCHDALE HORNETS

DATE	FIXTURE	RESULT	SCORERS	LGE	ATT
31/1/99	Wigan SJ (h) (CCR3)	W52-12	t:Coussons(3),Coult(2),Hough,Fox,Hilton,Eyres,Stephenson g:Fox(6)	N/A	883
7/2/99	Featherstone (a)	L32-12	t:Eyres,Swann g:Fox(2)	N/A	1,762
14/2/99	York (h) (CCR4)	L19-22	t:Coult,Hudson,Hall g:Fox(3) fg:Fox	N/A	609
28/2/99	Doncaster (h)	W26-10	t:Swann,Hudson,Hall,Knowles g:Fox(4),Fitzgerald	11th	740
7/3/99	Widnes (a)	L6-2	g:Fitzgerald	14th	2,684
14/3/99	Leigh (h)	L22-40	t:Burgess,Fitzgerald,Hilton,Knowles g:Fox(3)	17th	1,203
21/3/99	Lancashire (h)	L22-27	t:Coult,Hilton,Fitzgerald,Cameron g:Fox(3)	18th	714
2/4/99	Swinton (a)	L28-24	t:Coussons,Knowles,Fitzgerald,Marsh g:Fox(4)	18th	1,048
11/4/99	Batley (a)	W14-19	t:Hepi(2),Coussons,Hudson g:Fox fg:Fox	17th	478
14/4/99	Barrow (h)	W36-16	t:Fitzgerald(2),Wilde,Cooper,Fox,Hepi,Bunce g:Fox(4)	13th	690
18/4/99	Hull KR (h)	L14-20	t:Bunce,Marsh,Hepi g:Fox	13th	1,179
25/4/99	Hunslet (a)	L33-12	t:Aston,Cooper g:Fox(2)	14th	1,181
28/4/99	York (h)	W18-10	t:Fitzgerald,Cooper,Cameron g:Fitzgerald(3)	13th	743
3/5/99	Oldham (h)	W29-18	t:Fitzgerald,Kelly,Swann,Wilde g:Fitzgerald(6) fg:Fitzgerald	11th	1,568
17/5/99	Bramley (a)	L36-16	t:Coussons,Hudson,Stephenson g:Fitzgerald(2)	13th	371
30/5/99	Dewsbury (a)	W12-19	t:Knowles,Cooper,Kelly g:Fitzgerald(3) fg:Fitzgerald	13th	820
6/6/99	Whitehaven (h)	L6-44	t:Swann g:Fitzgerald	14th	780
13/6/99	Oldham (a)	L26-18	t:Fitzgerald,Bunce,Eyres g:Fitzgerald(3)	14th	3,023
20/6/99	Featherstone (h)	L14-29	t:Cooper,Rose g:Rose(3)	14th	837
23/6/99	Keighley (h)	L18-26	t:Newall,Hudson,Eyres g:Fox(3)	14th	833
27/6/99	Barrow (a)	L25-16	t:Bradbury,Bunce,Swann g:Fox(2)	15th	964
2/7/99	Widnes (h)	L16-38	t:Shaw,Eyres,Hudson g:Swann(2)	15th	1,429
11/7/99	Leigh (a)	L34-20	t:Aston,Hudson,Kelly g:Winroe(4)	15th	1,568
18/7/99	Lancashire (a)	W13-34	t:Fitzgerald(2),Swann(2),Hudson,Knowles g:Fitzgerald(5)	15th	281
25/7/99	Keighley (h)	L30-20	t:Fitzgerald(2),Coussons,Bunce g:Fitzgerald(2)	15th	1,503
1/8/99	Swinton (h)	W32-29	t:Cooper(3),Robinson,Coussons,Knowles g:Fitzgerald(4)	15th	917
8/8/99	Workington (a)	L36-10	t:Cooper,Stephenson g:Fitzgerald	15th	452
15/8/99	Batley (h)	W42-24	t:Fitzgerald(2),Wilde,Knowles,Bunce,Eyres,Coult g:Fitzgerald(7)	15th	778
22/8/99	Hull KR (a)	L30-12	t:Aston,Cooper g:Fitzgerald(2)	15th	1,703
29/8/99	Hunslet (h)	L10-38	t:Swann,Eyres g:Fitzgerald	15th	1,005

	APP		TRIES		GOALS		FG		PTS	
	ALL	NFP	ALL	NFP	ALL	NFP	ALL	NFP	ALL	NFP
Jon Aston	28	26	3	3	0	0	0	0	12	12
David Best	1(1)	1(1)	0	0	0	0	0	0	0	0
Jason Best	3(1)	3(1)	0	0	0	0	0	0	0	0
Gary Bradbury	3(2)	3(2)	1	1	0	0	0	0	4	4
Martin Bunce	18(10)	18(8)	6	6	0	0	0	0	24	24
Andy Burgess	6(8)	4(8)	1	1	0	0	0	0	4	4
Steve Cameron	5(6)	5(6)	2	2	0	0	0	0	8	8
Sean Cooper	22	22	10	10	0	0	0	0	40	40
Mick Coult	16(14)	14(14)	5	2	0	0	0	0	20	8
Phil Coussons	25	23	8	5	0	0	0	0	32	20
Andy Eyres	21	19	7	6	0	0	0	0	28	24
Peter Fitzgerald	23(1)	23(1)	14	14	42	42	2	2	142	142
Deryck Fox	15(2)	13(2)	2	1	38	29	2	1	86	63
Michael Francis	2(5)	2(5)	0	0	0	0	0	0	0	0
Rob Hall	1(7)	1(5)	2	1	0	0	0	0	8	4
Ian Hayes	1	1	0	0	0	0	0	0	0	0
Brad Hepi	7	7	4	4	0	0	0	0	16	16
Chris Hilton	7(2)	5(2)	3	2	0	0	0	0	12	8
Chris Holland	3(3)	3(3)	0	0	0	0	0	0	0	0
Chris Hough	3(2)	2(2)	1	0	0	0	0	0	4	0
Lee Hudson	20(6)	20(4)	8	7	0	0	0	0	32	28
Chris Kelly	12(4)	12(4)	3	3	0	0	0	0	12	12
Matt Knowles	28	26	7	7	0	0	0	0	28	28
Steve Marsh	1(8)	1(8)	2	2	0	0	0	0	8	8
Chris McKinney	18(7)	16(7)	0	0	0	0	0	0	0	0
Marlon Miller	1	1	0	0	0	0	0	0	0	0
Chris Newall	13	13	1	1	0	0	0	0	4	4
Mark Powell	1	1	0	0	0	0	0	0	0	0
Darren Robinson	4(3)	4(3)	1	1	0	0	0	0	4	4
Robert Rose	2(1)	2(1)	1	1	3	3	0	0	10	10
Danny Sculthorpe	6(17)	6(15)	0	0	0	0	0	0	0	0
Mick Shaw	10(1)	9(1)	1	1	0	0	0	0	4	4
Ian Sherratt	(1)	(1)	0	0	0	0	0	0	0	0
David Stephenson	23(1)	21(1)	3	2	0	0	0	0	12	8
Willie Swann	19(5)	17(5)	8	8	2	2	0	0	36	36
Steve Wilde	21	19	3	3	0	0	0	0	12	12
Jamie Winroe	1	1	0	0	4	4	0	0	8	8

David Stephenson

LEAGUE RECORD
P28-W9-D0-L19
(15th, NFP)
F539, A724, Diff-185
18 points.

CHALLENGE CUP
Round Four

ATTENDANCES
Best - v Oldham (NFP - 1,568)
Worst - v York (CC - 609)
Total (NFP only) - 13,416
Average (NFP only) - 958
(Up by 83 on 1998)

SWINTON LIONS

DATE	FIXTURE	RESULT	SCORERS	LGE	ATT
31/1/99	Moldgreen (h) (CCR3)	W38-4	t:Ashcroft(3),Stazicker,Taylor,McCabe,Watson g:S Gartland(5)	N/A	951
7/2/99	Hunslet (h)	L10-21	t:Ashcroft,Welsby g:S Gartland	N/A	1,500
14/2/99	Huddersfield (a) (CCR4)	L78-4	t:Stazicker	N/A	2,277
21/2/99	Doncaster (a)	L22-18	t:P Barrow,Blease,Evans g:Watson(2),S Gartland	15th	762
7/3/99	Bramley (h)	W23-8	t:Cleary,McCabe,Eccles g:Watson(4),S Gartland fg:S Gartland	12th	887
14/3/99	York (a)	L16-15	t:Billy,Evans,S Gartland g:S Gartland fg:Watson	14th	831
21/3/99	Dewsbury (a)	L19-29	t:Cleary,Hill,Henare g:Watson(3) fg:Watson	16th	1,040
28/3/99	Whitehaven (a)	W4-12	t:Watson,S Gartland g:Watson(2)	13th	625
2/4/99	Rochdale (h)	W28-24	t:Price-Jones,Rogers,McCabe,Henare,Stevens g:Watson(4)	11th	1,048
5/4/99	Featherstone (a)	L50-20	t:Henare,Eccles,Casey g:Watson(4)	13th	1,885
11/4/99	Barrow (h)	L24-31	t:Price-Jones,Henare,P Barrow,Cushion g:S Gartland(4)	14th	820
18/4/99	Widnes (a)	L25-10	t:Welsby,Casey g:S Gartland	15th	2,650
25/4/99	Leigh (h)	L22-34	t:Welsby,Ashcroft,Taylor g:S Gartland(5)	15th	1,300
9/5/99	Lancashire (a)	W10-56	t:Casey(2),S Gartland(2),Henare,Ashcroft,Hill,Welsby,P Barrow, Cushion g:S Gartland(5),Watson(3)	14th	344
16/5/99	Keighley (h)	L14-15	t:P Barrow,Casey g:S Gartland(3)	14th	1,035
23/5/99	Oldham (h)	W31-24	t:Rogers(2),Billy(2),Bateman g:S Gartland(5) fg:Casey	13th	1,478
30/5/99	Workington (a)	L37-20	t:Smith,S Gartland,Casey g:S Gartland(4)	15th	806
13/6/99	Hull KR (a)	L30-10	t:Welsby,Casey g:S Gartland	15th	2,005
20/6/99	Hunslet (a)	L22-8	t:P Gartland,Welsby	15th	1,402
27/6/99	Doncaster (h)	W48-2	t:Welsby(3),Hunter,Billy,Eyres,Bateman,Ashcroft,Evans g:S Gartland(6)	14th	779
4/7/99	Bramley (a)	L20-14	t:Billy,P Barrow g:S Gartland(3)	14th	354
7/7/99	Batley (h)	W23-14	t:Hill,Eyres,Welsby,Henare g:Watson(2) fg:Watson(2),Casey	14th	703
11/7/99	York (h)	W23-12	t:Henare,Casey,P Gartland g:Watson(5) fg:Casey	14th	736
18/7/99	Dewsbury (a)	L27-26	t:Welsby,P Barrow,Cleary,Hill g:Watson(5)	14th	841
25/7/99	Whitehaven (h)	W51-28	t:Henare(3),Welsby(2),Watson,S Gartland,Smith,Hill g:Watson(7) fg:Watson	12th	705
1/8/99	Rochdale (a)	L32-29	t:Eccles,Welsby,Smith,Eyres,Cleary g:Watson(4) fg:Watson	13th	917
8/8/99	Featherstone (h)	L22-24	t:Bateman,Hill,Evans g:Watson(5)	14th	943
15/8/99	Barrow (a)	W14-33	t:Watson(2),Nanyn(2),Evans,Cleary g:Watson(4) fg:Watson	12th	904
22/8/99	Widnes (h)	L16-44	t:Eccles,Watson,Henare g:Watson(2)	13th	1,664
29/8/99	Leigh (a)	L22-20	t:Johnson(2),Welsby,Bateman g:Watson(2)	13th	2,174

	APP		TRIES		GOALS		FG		PTS	
	ALL	NFP	ALL	NFP	ALL	NFP	ALL	NFP	ALL	NFP
Steve Allison	(1)	(1)	0	0	0	0	0	0	0	0
Simon Ashcroft	13(3)	12(3)	7	4	0	0	0	0	28	16
Paul Barrow	21(1)	20(1)	6	6	0	0	0	0	24	24
Tony Barrow	14(5)	13(5)	0	0	0	0	0	0	0	0
Matt Bateman	12(1)	12(1)	4	4	0	0	0	0	16	16
Marlon Billy	21(2)	19(2)	5	5	0	0	0	0	20	20
Ian Blease	17(9)	15(9)	1	1	0	0	0	0	4	4
Sean Casey	24	23	8	8	0	0	3	3	35	35
Damien Cleary	12(3)	12(2)	5	5	0	0	0	0	20	20
Andy Coley	2	1	0	0	0	0	0	0	0	0
Phil Cushion	17(10)	16(9)	2	2	0	0	0	0	8	8
Cliff Eccles	23(2)	21(2)	4	4	0	0	0	0	16	16
Jim Evans	20(5)	20(4)	5	5	0	0	0	0	20	20
Richie Eyres	7(4)	7(4)	3	3	0	0	0	0	12	12
Paul Gartland	6	6	2	2	0	0	0	0	8	8
Steve Gartland	16(11)	15(10)	6	6	46	41	1	1	117	107
Martin Gleeson	(1)	(1)	0	0	0	0	0	0	0	0
Richard Henare	17(1)	17(1)	11	11	0	0	0	0	44	44
Howard Hill	22(4)	22(4)	6	6	0	0	0	0	24	24
Jason Hunter	6	6	1	1	0	0	0	0	4	4
Jake Johnson	(1)	(1)	2	2	0	0	0	0	8	8
Gerrard Killeen	1	1	0	0	0	0	0	0	0	0
Carl McCabe	18(1)	16(1)	3	2	0	0	0	0	12	8
Dave McComas	1(1)	1	0	0	0	0	0	0	0	0
Mick Nanyn	3(1)	3(1)	2	2	0	0	0	0	8	8
Gareth Norman	(1)	(1)	0	0	0	0	0	0	0	0
Gavin Price-Jones	13(3)	11(3)	2	2	0	0	0	0	8	8
Wes Rogers	9(10)	9(9)	3	3	0	0	0	0	12	12
Paul Smith	2(12)	2(12)	3	3	0	0	0	0	12	12
Ryan Stazicker	3(6)	1(6)	2	0	0	0	0	0	8	0
Paul Stevens	6	4	1	1	0	0	0	0	4	4
Steve Taylor	4(7)	3(6)	2	1	0	0	0	0	8	4
Ian Watson	30	28	6	5	58	58	7	7	147	143
Mark Welsby	30	28	15	15	0	0	0	0	60	60
Darren Williams	(1)	0	0	0	0	0	0	0	0	0

Mark Welsby

LEAGUE RECORD
P28-W10-D0-L18
(13th, NFP)
F645, A641, Diff+4
20 points.

CHALLENGE CUP
Round Four

ATTENDANCES
Best - v Widnes (NFP - 1,664)
Worst - v Batley (NFP - 703)
Total (NFP only) - 14,638
Average (NFP only) - 1,046
(Down by 196 on 1998)

WHITEHAVEN WARRIORS

DATE	FIXTURE	RESULT	SCORERS	LGE	ATT
31/1/99	Saddleworth (h) (CCR3)	W22-6	t:Lewthwaite(2),Joe,Chambers g:K Hetherington(2),Kitchin	N/A	779
7/2/99	Barrow (a)	L18-12	t:K Hetherington,Wilson g:K Hetherington(2)	N/A	1,556
14/2/99	Lancashire (h) (CCR4)	W24-6	t:Charlton,Chambers,K Hetherington,Lewthwaite g:K Hetherington(4)	N/A	827
21/2/99	Widnes (h)	W28-6	t:Kitchin,Walsh,Joe,Morton,Kiddie g:K Hetherington(4)	7th	1,005
28/2/99	Oldham (h) (CCR5)	W18-2	t:Seeds(2),Lewthwaite g:K Hetherington(2),Kitchin	N/A	1,438
7/3/99	Leigh (a)	L24-20	t:Seeds(2),Kitchin g:Kitchin(4)	11th	1,124
14/3/99	London (a) (CCQF)	L54-6	t:Chambers g:K Hetherington	N/A	1,598
17/3/99	Lancashire (h)	W24-12	t:Fatialofa(2),Walsh,Dymtrowski g:K Hetherington(4)	6th	604
21/3/99	Keighley (a)	L30-16	t:Walsh(2),Lewthwaite g:K Hetherington(2)	11th	1,616
28/3/99	Swinton (h)	L4-12	g:K Hetherington(2)	12th	625
2/4/99	Workington (a)	L30-16	t:Seeds,Kitchin g:K Hetherington(3),Kitchin	15th	3,124
5/4/99	Batley (h)	W21-8	t:Morton,Kitchin,Chambers g:Kitchin(4) fg:Joe	11th	606
11/4/99	Hull KR (a)	L44-18	t:Seeds(2),Kiddie(2) g:Charlton	13th	1,817
18/4/99	Hunslet (a)	L36-16	t:Wilson,Seeds,Frazer g:Kitchin(2)	14th	1,004
25/4/99	Doncaster (a)	W30-40	t:Kitchin(2),Charlton(2),Wilson,Lester,Frazer g:Kitchin(6)	13th	450
9/5/99	Bramley (h)	W40-16	t:K Hetherington(2),Frazer,Kiddie,Chambers,Wilson,Lewthwaite,Lester g:Kitchin(4)	12th	546
16/5/99	York (a)	L46-0	No Scorers	13th	514
23/5/99	Dewsbury (a)	L18-20	t:Chambers(2),Seeds g:Kitchin(3)	15th	607
30/5/99	Oldham (a)	W24-32	t:K Hetherington(2),Lewthwaite,Lester,R Purdham,Wilson g:R Purdham(2),Kitchin,K Hetherington	14th	775
6/6/99	Rochdale (a)	W6-44	t:Frazer(3),Lewthwaite(2),Walsh,Wilson,K Hetherington g:K Hetherington(5) fg:R Purdham,Kiddie	12th	780
13/6/99	Featherstone (h)	W19-14	t:R Purdham,Walsh,Seeds g:R Purdham(3) fg:Kiddie	10th	701
20/6/99	Barrow (h)	W32-26	t:Walsh(3),Seeds(2) g:K Hetherington(6)	9th	942
27/6/99	Widnes (a)	L52-12	t:Frazer,Lewthwaite g:K Hetherington(2)	10th	3,152
4/7/99	Leigh (h)	W22-16	t:Kiddie,Kitchin,Wilson,Lewthwaite g:K Hetherington(3)	9th	953
9/7/99	Lancashire (a)	W8-21	t:Cox,Lewthwaite,Walsh g:K Hetherington(4) fg:Kiddie	9th	232
18/7/99	Keighley (h)	W22-20	t:Kitchin,Chambers,Walsh,K Hetherington g:K Hetherington(3)	8th	803
25/7/99	Swinton (a)	L51-28	t:Kiddie(3),Morton,Lewthwaite g:K Hetherington(4)	9th	705
30/7/99	Workington (h)	W32-8	t:K Hetherington(2),Seeds,Kiddie,Walsh g:K Hetherington(6)	8th	1,544
8/8/99	Batley (a)	W12-22	t:Kiddie,Wilson,Kitchin g:K Hetherington(5)	8th	368
15/8/99	Hull KR (h)	W32-10	t:Lester(2),Joe,K Hetherington,Walsh,Seeds g:K Hetherington(2),Kitchin(2)	8th	1,174
22/8/99	Hunslet (h)	L22-31	t:Lester,Walsh,Frazer,Kiddie g:Kitchin(3)	8th	925
29/8/99	Doncaster (h)	W38-10	t:Seeds(2),Wignall(2),Kitchin,Kiddie,R Purdham g:Kitchin(3),Joe,K Hetherington	8th	930

	APP		TRIES		GOALS		FG		PTS	
	ALL	NFP	ALL	NFP	ALL	NFP	ALL	NFP	ALL	NFP
Alan Bone	14(16)	14(12)	0	0	0	0	0	0	0	0
Craig Chambers	32	28	8	5	0	0	0	0	32	20
Gary Charlton	15(4)	11(4)	3	2	1	1	0	0	14	10
Mark Cox	18(1)	15(1)	1	1	0	0	0	0	4	4
Tony Dymtrowski	2(6)	2(4)	1	1	0	0	0	0	4	4
David Fatialofa	32	28	2	2	0	0	0	0	8	8
Neil Frazer	24(3)	23(2)	8	8	0	0	0	0	32	32
Gary Hetherington	5(9)	4(9)	0	0	0	0	0	0	0	0
Kevin Hetherington	28(2)	25(1)	11	10	68	59	0	0	180	158
Leroy Joe	24(1)	20(1)	3	2	1	1	1	1	15	11
Lee Kiddie	25(2)	22(2)	12	12	0	0	3	3	51	51
Wayne Kitchin	23(6)	19(6)	10	10	35	33	0	0	110	106
Aaron Lester	28(3)	25(2)	6	6	0	0	0	0	24	24
Graeme Lewthwaite	23(5)	19(5)	13	9	0	0	0	0	52	36
Matt Lynch	20(11)	17(10)	0	0	0	0	0	0	0	0
Steve McCourt	(1)	(1)	0	0	0	0	0	0	0	0
Graeme Morton	23(5)	21(4)	3	3	0	0	0	0	12	12
Gary Purdham	(6)	(6)	0	0	0	0	0	0	0	0
Robert Purdham	3(5)	3(5)	3	3	5	5	1	1	23	23
Barry Quayle	2(3)	2(2)	0	0	0	0	0	0	0	0
Warren Rudd	5	5	0	0	0	0	0	0	0	0
David Seeds	23(2)	19(2)	16	14	0	0	0	0	64	56
Daniel Sowerby	(1)	(1)	0	0	0	0	0	0	0	0
George Suafoa	(13)	(13)	0	0	0	0	0	0	0	0
Dean Vaughan	3(12)	3(8)	0	0	0	0	0	0	0	0
Craig Walsh	21(4)	18(4)	14	14	0	0	0	0	56	56
Jonathan Wignall	1(1)	1(1)	2	2	0	0	0	0	8	8
Wesley Wilson	20	18	8	8	0	0	0	0	32	32

David Fatialofa

LEAGUE RECORD
P28-W16-D0-L12
(8th, NFP)
F651, A620, Diff+31
32 points.

CHALLENGE CUP
Quarter Finalists

ATTENDANCES
Best - v Workington (NFP - 1,544)
Worst - v Bramley (NFP - 546)
Total (NFP only) - 11,965
Average (NFP only) - 855
(Down by 181 on 1998)

WIDNES VIKINGS

DATE	FIXTURE	RESULT	SCORERS	LGE	ATT
31/1/99	West Hull (h) (CCR3)	W34-4	t:Percival(2),Mansson,Cassidy,Munro,Mann,Devecchi g:Salisbury(3)	N/A	2,412
7/2/99	Dewsbury (h)	W30-12	t:Savelio,Devecchi,Briers,Mansson g:Salisbury(7)	N/A	2,782
14/2/99	Keighley (h) (CCR4)	W28-20	t:Briers,Percival,Savelio,Myler,Harris g:Salisbury(4)	N/A	3,003
21/2/99	Whitehaven (a)	L28-6	t:Briers g:Salisbury	11th	1,005
28/2/99	Leigh (h) (CCR5)	W20-17	t:Argent,Cassidy,Cantillon,Briers g:Salisbury,Hewitt	N/A	4,054
7/3/99	Rochdale (h)	W6-2	g:Hewitt(3)	5th	2,684
14/3/99	Leeds (h) (CCQF)	L10-46	t:Munro g:Hewitt(3)	N/A	6,375
17/3/99	Featherstone (a)	L28-12	t:Devecchi,Critchley g:Hewitt(2)	10th	1,774
21/3/99	Barrow (h)	W34-16	t:Cassidy(2),Salisbury,Devecchi,Mansson,Munro g:Salisbury(5)	7th	2,224
28/3/99	Oldham (a)	W18-33	t:Cantillon(2),Devecchi(2),Adams g:Salisbury(5),Hewitt fg:Hewitt	5th	1,515
2/4/99	Leigh (h)	W22-23	t:Critchley,Cantillon,Salisbury g:Hewitt(3) fg:Hewitt	5th	2,750
5/4/99	Lancashire (h)	W40-4	t:Munro(2),Myler(2),Cassidy,Harris,Percival g:Hewitt(6)	3rd	3,064
11/4/99	Keighley (a)	L24-22	t:Adams(2),Munro g:Hewitt(5)	5th	2,103
18/4/99	Swinton (h)	W25-10	t:Cantillon(2),Devecchi,Percival g:Hewitt(4) fg:Hewitt	5th	2,650
25/4/99	Workington (a)	L30-24	t:Hewitt(2),Myler,Garcia g:Hewitt(4)	7th	1,105
9/5/99	Batley (h)	L16-17	t:Munro,Cassidy,Mansson g:Hewitt(2)	6th	2,501
16/5/99	Hull KR (a)	L14-2	g:Hewitt	6th	2,125
23/5/99	Hunslet (h)	W32-24	t:Hulme(2),Munro(2),Mansson,Percival,Adams g:Verbickas(2)	6th	2,561
30/5/99	Doncaster (a)	W18-38	t:D Smith(2),Munro(2),Devecchi,Hulme,Briers g:Verbickas(5)	5th	750
6/6/99	Bramley (h)	W36-18	t:Verbickas(2),Munro,Hansen,Percival g:Hewitt(7),Verbickas	5th	2,820
13/6/99	York (a)	W10-25	t:Munro,P Smith,Hewitt,Cross g:Hewitt(4) fg:Hewitt	5th	1,214
20/6/99	Dewsbury (a)	W16-26	t:Percival,Mansson,Hewitt,Munro,P Smith g:Hewitt(3)	5th	1,407
27/6/99	Whitehaven (h)	W52-12	t:Verbickas(3),Cantillon(2),Munro,Percival,P Smith g:Hewitt(10)	4th	3,152
2/7/99	Rochdale (a)	W16-38	t:Mansson(2),Munro,Verbickas,Cantillon g:Hewitt(8),Myler	4th	1,429
11/7/99	Featherstone (h)	L14-20	t:Verbickas,Briers g:Hewitt(3)	5th	3,885
18/7/99	Barrow (a)	W4-27	t:Percival,Mann,Munro,Myler,Hewitt g:Hewitt(3) fg:Hewitt	5th	1,387
25/7/99	Oldham (h)	W84-0	t:Cantillon(5),Munro(2),Verbickas(2),Mansson,P Smith,Briers,Mann,Myler g:Hewitt(14)	5th	3,136
1/8/99	Leigh (h)	W9-6	t:Mansson g:Hewitt(2) fg:Hewitt	5th	5,230
8/8/99	Lancashire (a)	W14-24	t:Mann,Adams,Hewitt,Hill g:Hewitt(4)	5th	939
15/8/99	Keighley (h)	W24-16	t:Verbickas(2),P Smith,Munro g:Hewitt(4)	4th	3,649
22/8/99	Swinton (a)	W16-44	t:P Smith(2),Mansson(2),Munro(2),Verbickas,Savelio g:Hewitt(6)	3rd	1,664
29/8/99	Workington (h)	W46-0	t:Verbickas(2),Hewitt,Mansson,Munro,Percival,Devecchi g:Hewitt(9)	3rd	4,011
5/9/99	Hunslet (a) (QPO)	W21-24	t:Hewitt(2),Munro g:Hewitt(6)	N/A	2,245
12/9/99	Dewsbury (a) (QSF)	L28-6	t:Mansson g:Hewitt	N/A	3,210
19/9/99	Hunslet (a) (FE)	L10-8	t:Briers,Hewitt	N/A	1,824

	APP		TRIES		GOALS		FG		PTS	
	ALL	NFP	ALL	NFP	ALL	NFP	ALL	NFP	ALL	NFP
Gareth Adams	23(4)	21(4)	5	5	0	0	0	0	20	20
Steve Argent	3(6)	2(5)	1	0	0	0	0	0	4	0
Lee Birdseye	(3)	(3)	0	0	0	0	0	0	0	0
James Briers	24(3)	20(3)	8	6	0	0	0	0	32	24
Phil Cantillon	35	31	14	13	0	0	0	0	56	52
Jim Cassidy	13(14)	12(11)	6	4	0	0	0	0	24	16
Jason Critchley	9(2)	9(2)	3	3	0	0	0	0	12	12
Dean Cross	7(5)	5(4)	1	1	0	0	0	0	4	4
Fabien Devecchi	18(3)	15(2)	9	8	0	0	0	0	36	32
John-Paul Doherty	(3)	(3)	0	0	0	0	0	0	0	0
Richie Eyres	(2)	(2)	0	0	0	0	0	0	0	0
Anton Garcia	1	1	1	1	0	0	0	0	4	4
Lee Hansen	35	31	1	1	0	0	0	0	4	4
Paul Harris	14	10	2	1	0	0	0	0	8	4
Phil Hassan	5(2)	5(2)	0	0	0	0	0	0	0	0
Mark Hewitt	25(6)	24(3)	10	10	119	115	6	6	284	276
Mike Hill	4(9)	4(9)	1	1	0	0	0	0	4	4
Paul Hulme	19(1)	19(1)	3	3	0	0	0	0	12	12
Jason Hunter	(3)	(2)	0	0	0	0	0	0	0	0
Eddie Kilgannon	(2)	(2)	0	0	0	0	0	0	0	0
George Mann	28(6)	24(6)	4	3	0	0	0	0	16	12
Paul Mansson	30(1)	26(1)	14	13	0	0	0	0	56	52
Damian Munro	35	31	24	22	0	0	0	0	96	88
Chris Murphy	(2)	(2)	0	0	0	0	0	0	0	0
Danny Myler	10(12)	7(12)	6	5	1	1	0	0	26	22
Kevin O'Loughlin	(5)	(3)	0	0	0	0	0	0	0	0
Andrew O'Neill	(3)	(3)	0	0	0	0	0	0	0	0
Chris Percival	30(1)	27(1)	11	8	0	0	0	0	44	32
Terry Reid	4(4)	4(2)	0	0	0	0	0	0	0	0
Jim Salisbury	12	8	2	2	26	18	0	0	60	44
Lokeni Savelio	26(4)	22(4)	3	2	0	0	0	0	12	8
Dave Smith	5(6)	5(6)	2	2	0	0	0	0	8	8
Peter Smith	22(1)	22(1)	7	7	0	0	0	0	28	28
Simon Verbickas	18	18	14	14	8	8	0	0	72	72
John Waterworth	(1)	(1)	0	0	0	0	0	0	0	0

Damian Munro

LEAGUE RECORD
P28-W21-D0-L7
(3rd, NFP/Final Eliminator)
F792, A415, Diff+377
42 points.

CHALLENGE CUP
Quarter Finalists

ATTENDANCES
Best - v Leeds (CC - 6,375)
Worst - v Barrow (NFP - 2,224)
Total (NFP only) - 44,349
Average (NFP only) - 3,168
(Up by 1,022 on 1998)

WORKINGTON TOWN

DATE	FIXTURE	RESULT	SCORERS	LGE	ATT
31/1/99	Skirlaugh (h) (CCR3)	W30-4	t:Tubman(2),Williams(2),Dempsey g:Fisher(5)	N/A	1,316
7/2/99	Hull KR (h)	L14-21	t:Williams,Knox,Wallace g:Branthwaite	N/A	1,444
14/2/99	Bradford (a) (CCR4)	L92-0	No Scorers	N/A	7,593
21/2/99	Hunslet (a)	L48-6	t:Arnold g:Branthwaite	18th	1,325
7/3/99	Doncaster (h)	D22-22	t:Forber(2),Close g:Close(5)	17th	1,002
14/3/99	Bramley (h)	W22-16	t:Close(3),Jenkins,Woodcock g:Williams	10th	852
21/3/99	York (h)	W26-14	t:Woodcock,Arnold,Jenkins,Forber,Colin Armstrong g:Close(3)	9th	904
28/3/99	Dewsbury (a)	L58-24	t:Close,Riley,Keenan,Fisher g:Close(4)	10th	849
2/4/99	Whitehaven (h)	W30-16	t:Dempsey(2),Samuel,Stalker g:Close(7)	9th	3,124
11/4/99	Featherstone (h)	L10-15	t:Jenkins,Cochrane g:Fisher	12th	1,007
18/4/99	Barrow (a)	L25-12	t:Fisher,Close g:Close(2)	12th	1,566
25/4/99	Widnes (h)	W30-24	t:Roden(2),Wallace,Jenkins g:Close(7)	11th	1,105
3/5/99	Lancashire (a)	W24-38	t:Close(3),J Allen,Cochrane,Knox g:Close(7)	8th	326
9/5/99	Leigh (a)	L42-10	t:Close,Riley g:Close	11th	1,484
16/5/99	Lancashire (h)	W36-8	t:Jenkins(2),Wallace,Cochrane,Close,Dempsey g:Close(3),Cochrane(3)	10th	799
23/5/99	Keighley (a)	W18-22	t:Dempsey,Stalker,Jenkins,J Allen g:Cochrane(2),Dempsey	8th	1,650
30/5/99	Swinton (h)	W37-20	t:J Allen(2),Stalker(2),Dempsey,Woodcock,Knox g:Dempsey(2),Fisher(2) fg:Fisher	7th	806
6/6/99	Oldham (h)	L17-22	t:Stalker,Keenan,Heaton g:Huddart(2) fg:Fisher	8th	1,148
13/6/99	Batley (a)	L42-8	t:Knox g:Close,Huddart	9th	548
20/6/99	Hull KR (a)	L18-10	t:Dempsey,J Allen g:Huddart	11th	2,007
27/6/99	Hunslet (h)	L12-44	t:Lambert(2),Roden	11th	870
4/7/99	Doncaster (a)	L44-4	t:Huddart	11th	396
11/7/99	Bramley (a)	L28-12	t:Stalker,Forber g:Fisher(2)	13th	300
18/7/99	York (a)	L72-2	g:Fisher	13th	641
25/7/99	Dewsbury (h)	L6-25	g:McGee(3)	14th	570
30/7/99	Whitehaven (a)	L32-8	t:Dempsey,Samuel	14th	1,544
8/8/99	Rochdale (h)	W36-10	t:L Allen,Bethwaite,Quayle,McGee,Fisher g:McGee(8)	13th	452
15/8/99	Featherstone (a)	L40-6	t:L Allen g:McGee	14th	1,386
22/8/99	Barrow (h)	L8-19	t:J Allen g:McGee(2)	14th	628
29/8/99	Widnes (a)	L46-0	No Scorers	14th	4,011

	APP		TRIES		GOALS		FG		PTS	
	ALL	NFP	ALL	NFP	ALL	NFP	ALL	NFP	ALL	NFP
John Allen	22(4)	21(3)	6	6	0	0	0	0	24	24
Lee Allen	6(1)	6(1)	2	2	0	0	0	0	8	8
Colin Armstrong	29(1)	27(1)	1	1	0	0	0	0	4	4
Craig Armstrong	2(1)	2(1)	0	0	0	0	0	0	0	0
Steve Arnold	7	6	2	2	0	0	0	0	8	8
Craig Barker	4(9)	4(9)	0	0	0	0	0	0	0	0
Jamie Beaumont	(3)	(3)	0	0	0	0	0	0	0	0
Mike Bethwaite	7(1)	7(1)	1	1	0	0	0	0	4	4
Paul Branthwaite	4	3	0	0	2	2	0	0	4	4
Graeme Close	13(1)	12(1)	11	11	40	40	0	0	124	124
Evan Cochrane	12(1)	12(1)	3	3	5	5	0	0	22	22
Michael Dempsey	22(3)	21(3)	8	7	3	3	0	0	38	34
Craig Fisher	6(18)	5(17)	3	3	11	6	2	2	36	26
Andrew Fleming	(1)	(1)	0	0	0	0	0	0	0	0
Paul Forber	22	20	4	4	0	0	0	0	16	16
Steve Heaton	13(6)	13(6)	1	1	0	0	0	0	4	4
Richard Holliday	(1)	(1)	0	0	0	0	0	0	0	0
Chris Houston	(2)	(2)	0	0	0	0	0	0	0	0
Anthony Huddart	10(1)	10(1)	1	1	4	4	0	0	12	12
Mick Jenkins	12	12	7	7	0	0	0	0	28	28
Mark Kear	(3)	(3)	0	0	0	0	0	0	0	0
Mark Keenan	18(1)	17	2	2	0	0	0	0	8	8
Simon Knox	20(2)	18(2)	4	4	0	0	0	0	16	16
Andrew Lambert	10	10	2	2	0	0	0	0	8	8
Paul McGee	5(1)	5(1)	1	1	14	14	0	0	32	32
Gary Murdock	1	1	0	0	0	0	0	0	0	0
Jamie Nixon	(1)	(1)	0	0	0	0	0	0	0	0
Andy Platt	16(4)	15(4)	0	0	0	0	0	0	0	0
Stewart Quayle	7(8)	7(8)	1	1	0	0	0	0	4	4
Peter Riley	4(20)	3(19)	2	2	0	0	0	0	8	8
Carl Roden	16(7)	14(7)	3	3	0	0	0	0	12	12
Anthony Samuel	26	24	2	2	0	0	0	0	8	8
Carl Sice	2(1)	2(1)	0	0	0	0	0	0	0	0
Craig Stalker	20(1)	18(1)	6	6	0	0	0	0	24	24
Chris Sullivan	1(1)	1(1)	0	0	0	0	0	0	0	0
Mark Tubman	1(2)	(1)	2	0	0	0	0	0	8	0
Craig Tunstall	(1)	0	0	0	0	0	0	0	0	0
Mark Wallace	22(1)	20(1)	3	3	0	0	0	0	12	12
Barry Williams	6(2)	4(2)	3	1	1	1	0	0	14	6
Matthew Woodcock	24(1)	24(1)	3	3	0	0	0	0	12	12

Carl Roden

LEAGUE RECORD
P28-W9-D1-L18
(14th, NFP)
F468, A813, Diff-345
19 points.

CHALLENGE CUP
Round Four

ATTENDANCES
Best - v Whitehaven (NFP - 3,124)
Worst - v Rochdale (NFP - 452)
Total (NFP only) - 14,711
Average (NFP only) - 1,051
(Up by 250 on 1998)

YORK WASPS

DATE	FIXTURE	RESULT	SCORERS	LGE	ATT
31/1/99	Egremont (h) (CCR3)	W57-2	t:Deakin(3),Cain(2),Goddard(2),Austerfield,Judge,Hopcutt g:Benn(8) fg:Strange	N/A	768
7/2/99	Leigh (a)	L16-12	t:Strange,Deakin,Judge	N/A	1,546
14/2/99	Rochdale (a) (CCR4)	W19-22	t:Cain,Sini,Lambert g:Benn(3)	N/A	609
21/2/99	Lancashire (h)	W32-6	t:Strange(2),Cain,Hopcutt,Booth,Lambert g:Benn(4)	5th	792
26/2/99	Castleford (a) (CCR5)	L28-2	g:Benn	N/A	5,411
7/3/99	Keighley (a)	W8-10	t:Lambert,Benn g:Benn	3rd	1,878
14/3/99	Swinton (h)	W16-15	t:Benn(2),Callaghan,Hill	2nd	831
21/3/99	Workington (a)	L26-14	t:Sini,Edwards,Benn g:Benn	6th	904
28/3/99	Batley (h)	D20-20	t:Cain,Callaghan g:Benn(6)	7th	804
2/4/99	Hull KR (a)	L22-16	t:Lambert,Pallister,Goddard g:Benn(2)	8th	2,401
5/4/99	Hunslet (h)	W16-6	t:Edwards,Cain g:Benn(4)	7th	1,204
11/4/99	Doncaster (a)	W18-28	t:Cain(2),Goddard,Lambert,Callaghan g:Precious(3),Callaghan	6th	550
18/4/99	Bramley (h)	W22-12	t:Goddard,Deakin,Pallister g:Benn(4) fg:Precious,Callaghan	6th	984
25/4/99	Oldham (a)	W14-43	t:Goddard(2),Benn(2),McKenzie,Strange,Ramsden g:Benn(7) fg:Precious	4th	1,125
28/4/99	Rochdale (a)	L18-10	t:Lambert g:Benn(2),Precious	4th	743
7/5/99	Dewsbury (a)	L30-4	t:McKenzie	5th	1,007
16/5/99	Whitehaven (h)	W46-0	t:Callaghan(2),Cain(2),Benn,Darley,Strange,Tichener g:Benn(7)	5th	514
30/5/99	Featherstone (h)	L18-21	t:Deakin(2),Booth g:Benn(2) fg:Precious,Callaghan	6th	987
6/6/99	Barrow (a)	W18-25	t:Austerfield,Strange,Callaghan,Sini g:Booth(3),Precious fg:Strange	6th	932
13/6/99	Widnes (h)	L10-25	t:Sini,Austerfield g:Goddard	6th	1,214
20/6/99	Leigh (h)	L12-14	t:Darley g:Benn(4)	7th	1,147
27/6/99	Lancashire (a)	W22-29	t:Darley(2),Lambert,Goddard g:Benn(5) fg:Benn(2),Precious	8th	212
4/7/99	Keighley (h)	W24-14	t:Cain(2),Sini,Preston g:Benn(4)	7th	1,084
11/7/99	Swinton (a)	L23-12	t:Sini(2) g:Benn(2)	7th	736
18/7/99	Workington (h)	W72-2	t:Goddard(2),Cain(2),Callaghan(2),Deakin(2),Hagan,Sini,Judge, Preston,Austerfield g:Benn(9),Precious	7th	641
25/7/99	Batley (a)	W22-35	t:Atkins,Goddard,Benn,Lambert,Deakin,Judge g:Benn(5) fg:Benn	7th	491
1/8/99	Hull KR (h)	W29-12	t:Deakin(2),Atkins,Precious,Strange g:Benn(3),Precious fg:Benn	7th	1,740
8/8/99	Hunslet (a)	L15-14	t:Deakin,Benn,Preston g:Benn	7th	1,632
15/8/99	Doncaster (h)	W35-8	t:Sini(2),Darley,Tichener,Callaghan,Edwards g:Benn(5) fg:Precious	7th	764
22/8/99	Bramley (a)	W10-23	t:Preston,Goddard,Austerfield,Judge g:Benn(2),Precious fg:Precious	7th	300
29/8/99	Oldham (h)	W70-8	t:Sini(4),Callaghan(2),Pallister,Precious,Benn,Judge,Atkins g:Benn(13)	7th	728

	APP		TRIES		GOALS		FG		PTS	
	ALL	NFP	ALL	NFP	ALL	NFP	ALL	NFP	ALL	NFP
Gary Atkins	2(6)	2(6)	3	3	0	0	0	0	12	12
Shaun Austerfield	23(2)	20(2)	5	4	0	0	0	0	20	16
Jamie Benn	27	24	10	10	105	93	4	4	254	230
Craig Booth	9(5)	6(5)	2	2	3	3	0	0	14	14
Mark Cain	27	24	14	11	0	0	0	0	56	44
Darren Callaghan	21(10)	21(7)	11	11	1	1	2	2	48	48
Mick Crane	2(1)	2(1)	0	0	0	0	0	0	0	0
Paul Darley	19(5)	19(5)	5	5	0	0	0	0	20	20
Leigh Deakin	23	20	14	10	0	0	0	0	56	40
Peter Edwards	30(1)	27(1)	3	3	0	0	0	0	12	12
Lee Franks	(1)	(1)	0	0	0	0	0	0	0	0
Richard Goddard	24(3)	21(3)	12	10	1	1	0	0	50	42
Mick Hagan	10(10)	10(8)	1	1	0	0	0	0	4	4
Steve Hill	18(2)	15(2)	1	1	0	0	0	0	4	4
Chris Hopcutt	3(3)	3(1)	2	1	0	0	0	0	8	4
Chris Judge	25(5)	22(5)	6	5	0	0	0	0	24	20
Matt Lambert	25(5)	22(5)	8	7	0	0	0	0	32	28
Phil Lawrence	(1)	(1)	0	0	0	0	0	0	0	0
Leroy McKenzie	7(2)	7(2)	2	2	0	0	0	0	8	8
Alan Pallister	25(5)	22(5)	3	3	0	0	0	0	12	12
Andy Precious	11(15)	11(13)	2	2	8	8	6	6	30	30
Andy Preston	12(8)	11(8)	4	4	0	0	0	0	16	16
Mick Ramsden	3(12)	3(11)	1	1	0	0	0	0	4	4
Fata Sini	22(4)	20(4)	14	13	0	0	0	0	56	52
John Strange	21(3)	18(3)	7	7	0	0	2	1	30	29
Lee Tichener	14(11)	14(9)	2	2	0	0	0	0	8	8
Peter Walsh	(1)	(1)	0	0	0	0	0	0	0	0

Jamie Benn

LEAGUE RECORD
P28-W17-D1-L10
(7th, NFP)
F697, A425, Diff+272
35 points.

CHALLENGE CUP
Round Five

ATTENDANCES
Best - v Hull KR (NFP - 1,740)
Worst - v Whitehaven (NFP - 514)
Total (NFP only) - 13,434
Average (NFP only) - 960
(Up by 169 on 1998)

SUPER LEAGUE

(Play-offs in brackets, inc. in totals)

TRIES

1. Anthony Sullivan
   St Helens 27 (3)
2. Matt Daylight
   Gateshead . . . . .25 (-)
   Francis Cummins
   Leeds 25 (2)
   Toa Kohe-Love
   Warrington . . . . .25 (-)
5. Greg Fleming
   London . . . . .23 (-)
6. Sean Long
   St Helens 22 (2)
7. Darren Rogers
   Castleford 19 (0)
   Jason Robinson
   Wigan 19 (0)
9. Iestyn Harris
   Leeds 18 (1)
   Paul Newlove
   St Helens 18 (3)

GOALS

1. Iestyn Harris
   Leeds 135 (7)
2. Sean Long
   St Helens 108 (7)
3. Ian Herron
   Gateshead . . . . .105 (-)
4. Andy Farrell
   Wigan 96 (3)
5. Steve McNamara
   Bradford 95 (7)
6. Danny Orr
   Castleford 83 (9)
7. Graham Holroyd
   Halifax . . . . .74 (-)
8. Lee Briers
   Warrington . . . . .67 (-)
9. Bobbie Goulding
   Huddersfield . . . . .54 (-)
10. Brett Warton
    London . . . . .48 (-)

POINTS

1. Iestyn Harris
   Leeds 343 (18)
2. Sean Long
   St Helens 306 (22)
3. Ian Herron
   Gateshead . . . . .226 (-)
4. Andy Farrell
   Wigan 213 (6)
5. Steve McNamara
   Bradford 211 (14)
   Danny Orr
   Castleford 211 (18)
7. Graham Holroyd
   Halifax . . . . .165 (-)
8. Lee Briers
   Warrington . . . . .164 (-)
9. Tommy Martyn
   St Helens 143 (10)
10. Adam Hughes
    Wakefield . . . . .128 (-)

Anthony Sullivan

PREMIERSHIP

(Play-offs in brackets, inc. in totals)

TRIES

1. Richard Pachniuk
   Hunslet 25 (2)
2. Adrian Flynn
   Dewsbury 23 (1)
3. Jason Lee
   Keighley . . . . .22 (-)
   Damian Munro
   Widnes 22 (1)
5. Phil Atkinson
   Barrow . . . . .19 (-)
   Wayne Simonds
   Featherstone 19 (0)
   Abraham Fatnowna
   Hunslet 19 (1)
   Matthew Foster
   Keighley . . . . .19 (-)
   Anthony Murray
   Leigh 19 (0)
10. Alex Godfrey
    Dewsbury 18 (0)

GOALS

1. Mike Fletcher
   Hunslet 121 (0)
2. Mark Hewitt
   Widnes 115 (7)
3. Darren Holt
   Barrow . . . . .97 (-)
4. Barry Eaton
   Dewsbury 96 (3)
5. Jamie Benn
   York . . . . .93 (-)
6. Paul Wingfield
   Leigh 74 (0)
7. Jamie Rooney
   Featherstone 64 (4)
8. Richard Price
   Batley . . . . .61 (-)
9. Kevin Hetherington
   Whitehaven . . . . .59 (-)
10. Ian Watson
    Swinton . . . . .58 (-)

POINTS

1. Mark Hewitt
   Widnes 276 (26)
2. Mike Fletcher
   Hunslet 258 (0)
3. Barry Eaton
   Dewsbury 244 (7)
4. Darren Holt
   Barrow . . . . .236 (-)
5. Jamie Benn
   York . . . . .230 (-)
6. Jamie Rooney
   Featherstone 172 (10)
7. Paul Wingfield
   Leigh 169 (4)
8. Richard Price
   Batley . . . . .166 (-)
9. Kevin Hetherington
   Whitehaven . . . . .158 (-)
10. Mark Sibson
    Bramley . . . . .146 (-)

Richard Pachniuk

CHALLENGE CUP

TRIES

1. Martin Offiah
   London 8
2. Leroy Rivett
   Leeds 6
3. Tevita Vaikona
   Bradford 5
   Michael Withers
   Bradford 5
   Mark Forster
   Warrington 5
6. James Lowes
   Bradford 4
   Nathan McAvoy
   Bradford 4
   Brad Davis
   Castleford 4
   Darren Rogers
   Castleford 4
   Jason Ramshaw
   Keighley 4
   Neil Parsley
   Lancashire 4
   Karle Hammond
   London 4
   Alan Hunte
   Warrington 4
   Graeme Lewthwaite
   Whitehaven 4
   Leigh Deakin
   York 4

GOALS

1. Iestyn Harris
   Leeds 31
2. Lee Briers
   Warrington 16
3. Paul Deacon
   Bradford 15
4. Danny Orr
   Castleford 14
5. Graham Holroyd
   Halifax 13
   Bobbie Goulding
   Huddersfield 13
   Rob Smyth
   London 13
8. Jamie Benn
   York 12
9. Brett Warton
   London 11
10. Phil Jones
    Lancashire 10
    Steve Blakeley
    Salford 10

POINTS

1. Iestyn Harris
   Leeds 71
2. Paul Deacon
   Bradford 34
   Graham Holroyd
   Halifax 34
4. Danny Orr
   Castleford 33
5. Martin Offiah
   London 32
   Lee Briers
   Warrington 32
7. Bobbie Goulding
   Huddersfield 30
   Rob Smyth
   London 30
9. Kevin Gray
   Hull Kingston Rovers 24
   Leroy Rivett
   Leeds 24
   Jamie Benn
   York 24

Martin Offiah

ALL COMPETITIONS

TRIES

1	Toa Kohe-Love *Warrington*	28
2	Anthony Sullivan *St Helens*	27
3	Richard Pachniuk *Hunslet*	26
	Francis Cummins *Leeds*	26
	Greg Fleming *London*	26
6	Matt Daylight *Gateshead*	25
7	Damian Munro *Widnes*	24
8	Darren Rogers *Castleford*	23
	Adrian Flynn *Dewsbury*	23
	Jason Lee *Keighley*	23
	Sean Long *St Helens*	23

GOALS

1	Iestyn Harris *Leeds*	166
2	Mike Fletcher *Hunslet*	124
3	Mark Hewitt *Widnes*	119
4	Sean Long *St Helens*	116
5	Ian Herron *Gateshead*	105
	Jamie Benn *York*	105
7	Barry Eaton *Dewsbury*	102
8	Darren Holt *Barrow*	100
9	Andy Farrell *Wigan*	98
10	Steve McNamara *Bradford*	97
	Danny Orr *Castleford*	97

POINTS

1	Iestyn Harris *Leeds*	414
2	Sean Long *St Helens*	326
3	Mark Hewitt *Widnes*	284
4	Mike Fletcher *Hunslet*	264
5	Barry Eaton *Dewsbury*	256
6	Jamie Benn *York*	254
7	Danny Orr *Castleford*	244
8	Darren Holt *Barrow*	242
9	Ian Herron *Gateshead*	226
10	Steve McNamara *Bradford*	219

Toa Kohe-Love

TABLES & ATTENDANCES

SUPER LEAGUE

	P	W	D	L	F	A	D	PTS
Bradford	30	25	1	4	897	445	452	51
St Helens	30	23	0	7	1034	561	473	46
Leeds	30	22	1	7	910	558	352	45
Wigan	30	21	1	8	877	390	487	43
Castleford	30	19	3	8	712	451	261	41
Gateshead	30	19	1	10	775	576	199	39
Warrington	30	15	1	14	700	717	-17	31
London	30	13	2	15	644	708	-64	28
Halifax	30	11	0	19	573	792	-219	22
Sheffield	30	10	1	19	518	818	-300	21
Wakefield	30	10	0	20	608	795	-187	20
Salford	30	6	1	23	526	916	-390	13
Hull	30	5	0	25	422	921	-499	10
H'dersfield	30	5	0	25	463	1011	-548	10

	1999 Avg	1998 Avg	Diff
Leeds	13,703	12,111	+1,592
Bradford	13,398	13,026	+372
Wigan	9,466	10,803	-1,337
St Helens	8,460	7,238	+1,222
Castleford	6,877	6,395	+482
Warrington	5,110	4,897	+213
Salford	4,505	4,675	-170
Halifax	4,483	5,651	-1,168
Hull	4,346	5,741	-1,395
Wakefield	4,235	2,018	+2,217
Gateshead	3,895	N/A	N/A
Huddersfield	3,727	5,142	-1,415
Sheffield	3,590	4,595	-1,005
London	2,935	3,625	-690

'99 Avg 6,409 / **'98 Avg** 7,087 / **Diff** -678

BEST CROWDS

50,717 Bradford v St Helens *(GFN)* 9/10/99
24,020 Bradford v Leeds *(R26)* 3/9/99
21,666 Leeds v Bradford *(R15)* 18/6/99
18,179 Wigan v St Helens *(R20)* 5/9/99
16,912 Leeds v Castleford *(ESF)* 24/9/99
16,385 Leeds v St Helens *(R20)* 23/7/99
16,371 Leeds v Castleford *(R15)* 23/6/99
16,283 Wigan v St Helens *(R3)* 2/4/99
16,126 Bradford v St Helens *(QSF)* 26/9/99
16,049 Bradford v Leeds *(R3)* 1/4/99

WORST CROWDS

1,580 Gateshead v Hull *(R10)* 19/5/99
1,780 Gateshead v Salford *(R7)* 25/4/99
1,788 London v Gateshead *(R11)* 23/5/99
1,880 Gateshead v Sheffield *(R12)* 30/5/99
1,960 London v Sheffield *(R14)* 13/6/99
2,011 London v Huddersfield *(R24)* 22/8/99
2,024 Sheffield v London *(R25)* 28/8/99
2,044 London v Halifax *(R20)* 23/7/99
2,153 London v Salford *(R22)* 7/8/99
2,183 Huddersfield v Warrington *(R22)* ..11/8/99

CHALLENGE CUP

BEST CROWDS

73,242 Leeds v London *(FN)* 1/5/99
23,438 Bradford v Leeds *(SF)* 28/3/99
15,500 Leeds v Wigan *(R4)* 14/2/99
14,162 Leeds v St Helens *(R5)* 27/2/99
10,430 Bradford v Warrington *(QF)* 14/3/99
7,593 Bradford v Workington *(R4)* 14/2/99
7,561 Castleford v London *(SF)* 27/3/99
7,385 Wakefield v Bradford *(R5)* 28/2/99
6,375 Widnes v Leeds *(QF)* 14/3/99
6,107 Castleford v Hull *(R4)* 14/2/99

WORST CROWDS

408 Lancashire v Askam *(R3)* 31/1/99
500 Bramley v Leigh M Rangers *(R3)* ..31/1/99
609 Rochdale v York *(R4)* 14/2/99
713 Batley v Cas' Lock Lane *(R3)* 31/1/99
749 Hunslet v Townville *(R3)* 31/1/99
768 York v Egremont *(R3)* 31/1/99
779 Whitehaven v Saddleworth *(R3)* ...31/1/99
827 Whitehaven v Lancashire *(R4)* ...14/2/99
883 Rochdale v Wigan St Judes *(R3)* ..31/1/99
951 Swinton v Moldgreen *(R3)* 31/1/99

PREMIERSHIP

	P	W	D	L	F	A	D	PTS
Dewsbury	28	21	2	5	710	449	261	44
Hunslet	28	21	0	7	845	401	444	42
Widnes	28	21	0	7	792	415	377	42
Leigh	28	21	0	7	802	524	278	42
F'therstone	28	19	1	8	714	466	248	39
Hull KR	28	19	1	8	573	425	148	39
York	28	17	1	10	697	425	272	35
Whitehaven	28	16	0	12	651	620	31	32
Keighley	28	14	1	13	584	612	-28	29
Barrow	28	12	0	16	660	718	-58	24
Bramley	28	11	1	16	489	596	-107	23
Batley	28	9	3	16	546	553	-7	21
Swinton	28	10	0	18	645	641	4	20
Workington	28	9	1	18	468	813	-345	19
Rochdale	28	9	0	19	539	724	-185	18
Lancashire	28	7	0	21	544	889	-345	14
Oldham	28	5	2	21	449	999	-550	12
Doncaster	28	4	1	23	473	911	-438	9

	1999 Avg	1998 Avg	Diff
Widnes	3,168	2,146	+1,022
Hull KR	2,150	2,419	-269
Leigh	1,875	1,183	+692
Keighley	1,868	2,117	-249
Featherstone	1,778	1,842	-64
Hunslet	1,554	1,742	-188
Dewsbury	1,256	1,188	+68
Oldham	1,183	1,828	-645
Barrow	1,131	1,079	+52
Workington	1,051	801	+250
Swinton	1,046	1,242	-196
York	960	791	+169
Rochdale	958	875	+83
Whitehaven	855	1,036	-181
Batley	786	622	+164
Doncaster	680	505	+175
Bramley	553	560	-7
Lancashire	393	743	-350

'99 Avg 1,291 / **'98 Avg** 1,467 ● / **Diff** -176
● *Combined Division One & Two*

BEST CROWDS

5,783 Dewsbury v Hunslet *(GFN)* 25/9/99
5,230 Widnes v Leigh *(R24)* 1/8/99
4,011 Widnes v Workington *(R28)* 29/8/99
3,885 Widnes v Featherstone *(R21)* 11/7/99
3,649 Widnes v Keighley *(R26)* 15/8/99
3,210 Dewsbury v Widnes *(QSF)* 12/9/99
3,152 Widnes v Whitehaven *(R19)* 27/6/99
3,136 Widnes v Oldham *(R23)* 25/7/99
3,124 Workington v Whitehaven *(R7)* 2/4/99
3,103 Featherstone v Hull KR *(R28)* 29/8/99

WORST CROWDS

212 Lancashire v York *(R19)* 27/6/99
232 Lancashire v Batley *(R14)* 23/5/99
232 Lancashire v Whitehaven *(R21)* 9/7/99
281 Lancashire v Rochdale *(R22)* 18/7/99
298 Lancashire v Bramley *(R1)* 7/2/99
300 Bramley v Workington *(R21)* 11/7/99
300 Bramley v York *(R27)* 22/8/99
305 Lancashire v Featherstone *(R23)* ..23/7/99
315 Bramley v Barrow *(R15)* 30/5/99
321 Lancashire v Hunslet *(R16)* 6/6/99

Iestyn Harris

Super League 2000 - The Fixtures

Round 1

Weekend of March 5

Castleford v Wigan
Warrington v London
Halifax v Hull
Hudd-Sheff v Salford
Leeds v Wakefield
St Helens v Bradford

Round 2

Weekend of March 19

Bradford v Warrington
London v Hudd-Sheff
Salford v Castleford
Wakefield v Halifax
Hull v St Helens
Wigan v Leeds

Round 3

Weekend of April 2

Castleford v London
Warrington v Hull
Halifax v Leeds
Hudd-Sheff v Bradford
Salford v Wigan
St Helens v Wakefield

Round 4

Weekend of April 9

Bradford v Castleford
Wigan v Halifax
Leeds v St Helens
London v Salford
Wakefield v Warrington
Hull v Hudd-Sheff

Round 5

Weekend of April 16

Castleford v Hull
Warrington v Leeds
Hudd-Sheff v Wakefield
Salford v Bradford
St Helens v Halifax
Wigan v London

Round 6

Good Friday, April 21

Bradford v London
Halifax v Warrington
Leeds v Hudd-Sheff
Wakefield v Castleford
St Helens v Wigan
Hull v Salford

Round 7

Easter Monday, April 24

Castleford v Leeds
Warrington v St Helens
Hudd-Sheff v Halifax
London v Hull v
Salford v Wakefield
Wigan v Bradford

Round 8

Monday, May 1

Warrington v Wigan
Halifax v Castleford
Leeds v Salford
St Helens v Hudd-Sheff
Wakefield v London
Hull v Bradford

Round 9

Weekend of May 7

Bradford v Wakefield
Castleford v St Helens
Hudd-Sheff v Warrington
London v Leeds
Salford v Halifax
Wigan v Hull

Round 10

Weekend of May 14

Bradford v Halifax
Castleford v Hudd-Sheff
London v St Helens
Salford v Warrington
Wigan v Wakefield
Hull v Leeds

Round 11

Weekend of May 21

Warrington v Castleford
Halifax v London
Hudd-Sheff v Wigan
Leeds v Bradford
St Helens v Salford
Wakefield v Hull

Round 12

Weekend of May 28

Castleford v Salford
Warrington v Bradford
Halifax v Wakefield
Hudd-Sheff v London
St Helens v Hull
Leeds v Wigan

Round 13

Weekend of June 4

Bradford v St Helens
London v Warrington
Salford v Hudd-Sheff
Wakefield v Leeds
Hull v Halifax
Wigan v Castleford

Round 14

Weekend of June 11

Bradford v Hudd-Sheff
Leeds v Halifax
London v Castleford
Wakefield v St Helens
Hull v Warrington
Wigan v Salford

Round 15

Weekend of June 18
Castleford v Bradford
Warrington v Wakefield
Hudd-Sheff v Hull
Salford v London
St Helens v Leeds
Halifax v Wigan

Round 16

Weekend of June 25
Bradford v Salford
Halifax v St Helens
Leeds v Warrington
London v Wigan
Wakefield v Hudd-Sheff
Hull v Castleford

Round 17

Weekend of July 2
Bradford v Wigan
Halifax v Hudd-Sheff
Leeds v Castleford
St Helens v Warrington
Wakefield v Salford
Hull v London

Round 18

Weekend of July 9
Castleford v Wakefield
Warrington v Halifax
Hudd-Sheff v Leeds
London v Bradford
Salford v Hull
Wigan v St Helens

Round 19

Weekend of July 16
Bradford v Hull
Castleford v Halifax
Hudd-Sheff v St Helens
London v Wakefield
Salford v Leeds
Wigan v Warrington

Round 20

Weekend of July 23
Warrington v Hudd-Sheff
Halifax v Salford
Leeds v London
St Helens v Castleford
Wakefield v Bradford
Hull v Wigan

Round 21

Weekend of July 30
Bradford v Leeds
Castleford v Warrington
London v Halifax
Salford v St Helens
Hull v Wakefield
Wigan v Hudd-Sheff

Round 22

Weekend of August 6
Warrington v Salford
Halifax v Bradford
Hudd-Sheff v Castleford
Leeds v Hull
St Helens v London
Wakefield v Wigan

Round 23

Weekend of August 13
Bradford v Castleford
Hudd-Sheff v Leeds
London v Salford
Wakefield v St Helens
Warrington v Hull
Wigan v Halifax

Round 24

Weekend of August 20
Bradford v Hudd-Sheff
Castleford v Leeds
Hull v Halifax
St Helens v Warrington
Salford v Wigan
Wakefield v London

Round 25

Weekend of August 27
Hull v Hudd-Sheff
Halifax v Castleford
Leeds v Wakefield
London v Warrington
St Helens v Salford
Wigan v Bradford

Round 26

Weekend of September 3
Castleford v London
Halifax v Bradford
Hudd-Sheff v Wakefield
Leeds v St Helens
Salford v Hull
Warrington v Wigan

Round 27

Weekend of September 10
Bradford v Leeds
Hudd-Sheff v Castleford
London v St Helens
Salford v Halifax
Wakefield v Warrington
Wigan v Hull

Round 28

Weekend of September 17
Castleford v Wakefield
Hull v Bradford
Halifax v Hudd-Sheff
Leeds v London
St Helens v Wigan
Warrington v Salford